THE COMPENDIUM

A Critical Analysis of the Arab-Israeli Conflict July 2000 - July 2002

Compiled By George D. Hanus

Essays and Articles by:

Mitchell Bard
William J. Bennett
Yehezkel Bin-Nun
Yaron Brook
David Brooks
George W. Bush
Daniel Doron
Thomas L. Friedman
Marc Ginsberg
Jamie Glazov
Mayer Gniwisch
Dore Gold
Patrick Goodenough
Hirsh Goodman
Jordan B. Gorfinkel
Yossi Klein Halevi
Victor Davis Hanson
Amos Harel
Eric Hoffer
David Horowitz
Steve Huntley
James M. Inhofe
Raphael Israeli
Jeff Jacoby
Paul Johnson
Efraim Karsh
Michael Kelly
Jack Kemp

Alan Keyes
Jeanne Kirkpatrick
Charles Krauthammer
Bernard Lewis
John Lewis
John McCain
Larry Miller
Binyamin Netanyahu
Ehud Olmert
Daniel Pipes
Dennis Prager
Naomi Ragen
Dennis B. Ross
Michael Rubin
William Safire
Peter Schwartz
Natan Sharansky
George M. Stanislavski
Bret Stephens
David Tell
Cal Thomas
Bruce S. Thornton
Jonathan Tobin
Charlotte West
Diana West
Elie Wiesel
George F. Will
Ehud Ya'ari

For information address Gravitas Media L.L.C., 333 West Wacker Drive, Suite 2750, Chicago, IL 60606, 312-332-4172, FAX: 312-332-2119 GRAVITASMEDIA@AOL.COM

ISBN: 0-9722913-9-3

ACKNOWLEDGEMENTS

I would like to acknowledge the most important personal elements in my life; my family and friends. My wife, Barbara, the central love of my life for close to three decades, and my children, Edy, Jonny, Becky and Julie, my precious jewels, are my true love and joy. They embody all that is good in this world. The combination of their intellectual integrity, kindness, compassion for humanity and striving for personal excellence, is my inspiration and delight.

My mother, Magda Hanus; all of my siblings and their spouses, as well as all of my special nieces and nephews, are an integral part of my extended family. I love them all and I continue to be very proud of each of them, both in their own accomplishments and individualistic approaches to life.

I am only saddened that my father, John Hanus, is not alive to see the vibrant continuity of the next generation of his family that was almost exterminated by the Holocast and urban crime.

I would also like to thank Jodie Engel, Scott Lapin, Rachel Slovin, Dorothy Kubiak, Tom Page and David Nadoff for their assistance in helping prepare this publication for printing.

TABLE OF CONTENTS

PROLOGUE

The Immortal Jews

If the statistics are right, the Jews constitute but one percent of the human race. It suggests a nebulous dim puff of star dust lost in the blaze of the Milky Way. Properly the Jew ought hardly to be heard of; but he is heard of, has always been heard of.

He is as prominent on the planet as any other people, and his commercial importance is extravagantly out of proportion to the smallness of his bulk. His contributions to the world's list of great names in literature, science, art, music, finance, medicine, and abstruse learning are also away out of proportion to the weakness of his numbers. He has made a marvelous fight in this world, in all the ages; and has done it with his hands tied behind him. He could be vain of himself, and be excused for it. The Egyptian, the Babylonian, and the Persian rose, filled the planet with sound and splendor, then faded to dream-stuff and passed away; the Greek and the Roman followed, and made a vast noise, and they are gone; other peoples have sprung up and held their torch high for a time, but it burned out, and they sit in twilight now, or have vanished. The Jew saw them all, beat them all, and is now what he always was, exhibiting no decadence, no infirmities of age, no weakening of his parts, no slowing of his energies, no dulling of his alert and aggressive mind. All things are mortal but the Jew; all other forces pass, but he remains. What is the secret of his immortality?

Mark Twain

Introduction

" Intensive Jewish education, taught by each generation to the next, is the guarantor of the continuity and survival of the Jewish people."   George D. Hanus

I guess I shouldn't be surprised. Four thousand years of world history have documented that the Jews have rarely been masters of their own destiny. The Jewish people have only been able to settle where the Gentile rulers gave permission. They only engaged in occupations consented to by the Gentile dominion and had to subject themselves to discrimination, oppression, and continuous contemptuous treatment. The Jews have been the victims of attacks, atrocities, pogroms and massacres and forced on pain of death to convert to the religion of the ruling majority. The Jews have been expelled from nearly every country in which they have been allowed to live. Sixty years ago, during the Holocaust ,the Jews were singled out to be the focus of a diabolical and systematic genocide. The civilized world watched as six million Jews were murdered in the most horrific and monstrous methods devised by man. Many more millions of survivors and their children have been physically and emotionally scarred forever.

In 1948, three years after the conclusion of World War II, the Jews were told by the guilt ridden world community to reunite and given permission, to start a new country, in the land called Israel. Now another movement, which fosters a culture of hatred, has resurrected itself to throw the Jews out of this land and drive them into the Mediterranean Sea. When you think about these events in terms of equity and justice, or the lack thereof, emotions rise and boil into extraordinary anger.

Many individuals share a common experience, after hearing a dynamic speaker, "She expressed exactly what I was thinking. I wish I could do that." The ability to articulate our emotions and innermost thoughts is a rare talent that few of us possess. There are gifted writers and commentators that have that uncanny capacity to express their views and feelings with remarkable clarity and eloquence.

My own ability to channel emotions into thoughtful dialogue has been severely tested by the current Arab-Israeli conflict. Although my frustration has been simmering for several months, early in 2002 it reached a crescendo. I began to see the world around me as an eerily insensitive community that too readily accepts human suffering and death. The slaughter of innocent civilians has once again become a world spectator sport that appeals to an indifferent voyeurism exemplified in the cold daily tally of casualties that has resurfaced as an accepted norm of societal response. The nightly news began to resemble cars slowing down on the highway to gape at an accident.

This preposterous epiphany erupted for me one night when casualty counts from a bombing in Jerusalem appeared along with the baseball scores streaming across the bottom of my screen. There it was, on my TV -- White Sox 3, Red Sox 1; Yankees 8, Indians 2; Israelis killed 3, Palestinians killed 1. My viewing experience was all the more surreal because the program featured back-to-back interviews with the terror victims' families and the terrorists' families, fostering the contemporary myth of moral equivalency. In the face of such callousness and ethical confusion, one is scarcely surprised at the latest lunacy reported in the media - a gambling ring that takes bets on where the next homicide bombing will take place and gives odds on how many will

11

be killed and wounded (Can combat between gladiators and lions in public arenas be far behind?). As I witness these incredible developments, I become very disturbed, yet I find myself unable to clearly express my sense that all meaningful standards of good and evil are out of play and some bizarre circus morality has taken over.

Seemingly rational and responsible commentators, the politically correct talking heads so desperately sought after by all the networks purport to justify the brutal murder of innocent Jews. There is no mention of the insanity and evil of a culture that conditions and educates its men, women and children to hate, and then trains and sends them to blow up innocent civilians. Newspapers and television are full of commentators, reporters, apologists and revisionists striving to create the appearance of journalistic balance by means of an aloof and artificial impartiality. There is not the slightest suggestion of disapprobation, let alone outrage.

On one night alone, I watched several of these TV pundits each present a different banal rationale for the suicide bombers' drive to kill innocents. One suggested that they are motivated by theological considerations, while another proclaimed that Israel forces them to kill by depriving them of hope. Then came the deniers and revisionists, promoters of the "big lie" so essential to Palestinian propaganda, who fabricate "facts" and confidently declare falsehoods (e.g., the Jews were responsible for 9/11). The common theme is blaming and reviling the victims while rationalizing and apologizing for the murderers in a way that would be unthinkable if the subject were the September 11th attacks or even a school bus bombing on Main Street, U.S.A. Yet the cycle of apologetic and mendacious justifications continues, without the intervention of truth or ethical standards. Many of us feel an intense sense of frustration over this. We know instinctively that their logic and approach are intellectually dishonest and morally wrong. Our frustration is compounded by our inability to effectively express our outrage and give voice to the truth.

The impetus for compiling this volume is to bring journalistic integrity to bear on the evaluation of these events and give articulate expression to the reactions that many of us share. "The Compendium: A Critical Analysis of the Arab-Israeli Conflict - July 2000 - July 2002" is an anthology of editorials and essays written about these times. The authors and writers included are among the best in their fields. The pieces appear in chronological order and are preceded by a section entitled "The Human Timeline," which enables the reader to relate each article to events in proximity to the date of its composition. Some of the essays are acerbic and others are philosophical and contemplative, but they all encapsulate important insights and emotions in precise language.

The mission of this publication is to help readers understand the rightfulness of the Israeli position in the conflict and subsequently articulate their own views of the crisis. "The Compendium: A Critical Analysis of the Arab-Israeli Conflict - July 2000 - July 2002" is designed to be convenient and easily used. The Essays reflect a variety of writing styles and lengths and the compositions are short and easily digestible -- written with panache and elegance. I am confident that the impact of these masterfully crafted essays is enhanced by bringing them together to form a central reservoir of reliable information and insight.

It is a true shame and disgrace that after 4,000 years, the Jewish people still have to justify to the world the legitimacy of their survival.

Human Timeline: Arab-Israeli Conflict July 2000-July 2002

Before we analyze the political impact of the current intifada, with a cool objectivity and an emotionless prism, it is important to understand the human toll that the past two years have taken on families and communities. Behind every statistic is the name of a human being. That human being is an individual just like you and me, somebody who had a family, friends and acquaintances. They all lived in a neighborhood and shopped at someone's store. Each person had loved ones, who will never see that casualty again. Every wounded person, who somehow gets treated flippantly and dismissingly by the news media, is impacted for life. Each death or injury dramatically alters hundreds and thousands of friends and family members forever. The ripple effect is exponential and boundless.

Before a discussion of the political events can begin, it is mandatory that we understand this human toll. This human timeline of the events between July 2000 and July 2002 is an arbitrary parameter and no disrespect is intended to the memory of the many who died before, and I am sorry to say, those who will die after.

This human timeline attempts to name individuals who were murdered, their ages and where they were killed. They are more than statistics. They are us. Between September 29, 2000 and June 30, 2002, 563 people were killed and 4,122 injured. [Information provided by Israel Ministry of Foreign Affairs- www.israel.org/MFA]

July 11, 2000 - The peace summit opens at Camp David, where the Middle East peace process began 22 years ago. The new talks address the most intractable of the outstanding issues between the Israelis and the Palestinians: final borders of the Palestinian state, a right of return for Palestinian refugees, and the future status of Jerusalem.

July 19, 2000 - Ehud Barak announces that he's had enough and is going home. Ninety minutes later President Clinton announces that the two visiting delegations will in fact stay in Camp David and talk on.

July 25, 2000 - The marathon negotiation at Camp David finally breaks down without agreement.

July 31, 2000 - Moshe Katsav, a relatively unknown member of the opposition Likud bloc, is elected to the largely ceremonial presidency of Israel. The election is another blow to Ehud Barak, who had backed veteran statesman, former prime minister and Nobel peace laureate, Shimon Peres. Barak also narrowly survives a motion of no confidence in the Knesset - the second of the month.

August 16, 2000 - Israel's new foreign minister, Shlomo Ben Ami, holds his first talks with Palestinian officials amid signals that both sides are reaching towards a peace deal.

September 7, 2000 - President Bill Clinton admits he made no progress in talks with Ehud Barak and Yasser Arafat at the UN Millennium summit in New York. Arafat now has less than a week to decide whether he will declare an independent Palestinian state on September 13, as he has long threatened.

September 10, 2000 - Yasser Arafat and the central committee of the Palestine Liberation Organization postpone, yet again, the planned declaration of statehood.

September 19, 2000 - Israel suspends talks with the Palestinians, indefinitely, on the grounds that Yasser Arafat is hardening his line on outstanding issues, particularly Jerusalem.

Sept 27, 2000 - Sgt. David Biri, 19, of Jerusalem, was fatally wounded in a bombing near Netzarim in the Gaza Strip.

Sept 29, 2000 - Border Police Supt. Yossi Tabaja, 27, of Ramle was shot to death by his Palestinian counterpart on a joint patrol near Kalkilya.

September 29, 2000 - Violent rioting breaks out in Jerusalem allegedly after Ariel Sharon visits holy Muslim shrine in the city. It is the start of the alleged al-Aqsa intifada (uprising).

Oct 1, 2000 - Border Police Cpl. Yosef Madhat, 19, of Beit Jann, died of gunshot wounds sustained in a gun battle with Palestinians at Joseph's Tomb in Nablus.

Oct 2, 2000 - Wichlav Zalsevsky, 24, of Ashdod, was shot in the head in the village of Masha on the trans-Samaria highway. Sgt. Max Hazan, 20, of Dimona, died of gunshot injuries sustained near Beit Sahur.

October 7, 2000 - Hizbullah, the Iranian-backed militant Islamist group active in south Lebanon, captures three Israeli soldiers, and demands the release of 19 prisoners in Israel in return for the trio's return.

Oct 8, 2000 - The bullet-riddled body of Hillel Lieberman, 36, of Elon Moreh was found at the southern entrance to Nablus.

Oct 12, 2000 - First Cpl. Yosef Avrahami and First Sgt. Vadim Novesche, 33, two reserve IDF soldiers, were lynched by a Palestinian mob at the police building in Ramallah.

October 12, 2000 - The director of the CIA, George Tenet, flies to the Middle East to try to set up high-level security talks between the Israelis and the Palestinians.

October 12, 2000 - At least four US servicemen are killed and 12 more are missing, feared dead, after the destroyer USS Cole is rammed by suicide bombers on a rubber dinghy in the Yemeni port of Aden.

October 12, 2000 - Fears of war in the Middle East send world stock markets tumbling and oil prices rocketing to 10-year highs.

October 16, 2000 - President Clinton flies to Egypt for a crisis summit meeting in the Red Sea resort of Sharm el-Sheikh. It is a deeply acrimonious meeting, but Clinton persuades Israeli Prime Minister Ehud Barak and Palestinian president Yasser Arafat to issue calls for an end to the violence.

Oct 19, 2000 - Rabbi Binyamin Herling, 64, of Kedumim, was killed when Fatah members and Palestinian security forces opened fire on a group of Israeli men, women, and

14

children on a trip at Mount Ebal near Nablus.

October 22, 2000 - Ehud Barak announces that he is suspending the peace process. He is also negotiating to form an emergency grand coalition, including Israel's most hawkish politician, Ariel Sharon of the Likud faction.

Oct 28, 2000 - The body of Marik Gavrilov, 25, of Bnei Aysh was found inside his burned-out car, between the village of Bitunia and Ramallah.

Oct 30, 2000 - Eish-Kodesh Gilmor, 25, of Mevo Modi'in, was shot and killed while on duty as a security guard at the National Insurance Institute's East Jerusalem branch. Another guard was injured. Amos Machlouf, 30, of the Gilo neighborhood in Jerusalem, was found murdered in a ravine near Beit Jala.

Nov 1, 2000 - Lt. David-Hen Cohen, 21, of Karmiel and Sgt. Shlomo Adshina, 20, of Kibbutz Ze'elim were killed in a shooting incident in the Al-Hader area, near Bethlehem.

Nov 1, 2000 - Maj. (res.) Amir Zohar, 34, of Jerusalem was killed in the Nahal Elisha settlement in the Jordan Valley while on active reserve duty.

Nov 2, 2000 - Ayelet Shahar Levy, 28, and Hanan Levy, 33, were killed in a car bomb explosion near the Mahane Yehuda market in Jerusalem. 10 people were injured in the blast. The Islamic Jihad claimed responsibility for the attack.

Nov 8, 2000 - Noa Dahan, 25, of Moshav Mivtahim in the south, was shot to death while driving to her job at the Rafah border crossing in Gaza.

Nov 10, 2000 - Sgt. Shahar Vekret, 20, of Lod was fatally shot by a Palestinian sniper near Rachel's Tomb at the entrance to Bethlehem.

Nov 11, 2000 - Sgt. 1st Class Avner Shalom, 28, of Eilat, was killed in a shooting attack at the Gush Katif junction in the Gaza Strip.

Nov 13, 2000 - Sarah Leisha, 42, of Neveh Tzuf was killed by gunfire from a passing car while travelling near Ofra, north of Ramallah. Cpl. Elad Wallenstein, 18, of Ashkelon, and Cpl. Amit Zanna, 19, of Netanya were killed by gunfire from a car passing the military bus carrying them near Ofra.

Nov 13, 2000 - Gabi Zaghouri, 36, of Netivot was killed by gunfire directed at the truck he was driving near the Kissufim junction in the southern part of the Gaza Strip.

Nov 18, 2000 - St.-Sgt. Baruch (Snir) Flum, 21, of Tel-Aviv was shot and killed by a senior Palestinian Preventive Security Service officer who infiltrated the Kfar Darom greenhouses in the Gaza Strip. St.-Sgt. Sharon Shitoubi, 21, of Ramle, wounded in the Palestinan shooting attack in Kfar Darom, died of his wounds on Nov 20.

Nov 20, 2000 - Miriam Amitai, 35, and Gavriel Biton, 34, both of Kfar Darom, were killed when a roadside bomb exploded alongside a bus carrying children from Kfar Darom to school in Gush Katif. Nine others, including 5 children, were injured.

Nov 21, 2000 - Itamar Yefet, 18, of Netzer Hazani died from a gunshot wound to the head by Palestinian sniper fire at the Gush Katif junction.

Nov 22, 2000 - Shoshana Reis, 21, of Hadera, and Meir Bahrame, 35, of Givat Olga, were killed, and 60 wounded when a powerful car bomb was detonated alongside a passing bus on Hadera's main street, when the area was packed with shoppers and people driving home from work. Sixty were wounded in the blast.

Nov 23, 2000 - Lt. Edward Matchnik, 21, of Beersheba, was killed in an explosion at the District Coordination Office near Gush Katif in the Gaza Strip. (The joint DCOs were established at the borders of Palestinian-ruled areas under the interim peace accords and were responsible for coordinating security and humanitarian cooperation.)

Nov 23, 2000 - Sgt. Samar Hussein, 19, of Hurfeish, was killed when Palestinian snipers opened fire at soldiers patrolling the border fence near the Erez crossing.

Nov 24, 2000 - Maj. Sharon Arameh, 25, of Ashkelon was killed by Palestinian sniper fire in fighting near Neve Dekalim in the Gaza Strip.

Nov 24, 2000 - Ariel Jeraffi, 40, of Petah Tikva, a civilian employed by the IDF, was killed by Palestinian fire as he travelled near Otzarin in the West Bank.

Nov 28, 2000 - Israel's prime minister, Ehud Barak, calls early elections.

Dec 8, 2000 - Rina Didovsky, 39, a Beit Hagai school teacher on her way to work, and Eliyahu Ben-Ami, 41, of Otniel, the driver of the van, were killed when a car full of gunmen opened fire on the van near Kiryat Arba.

Dec 8, 2000 - Sgt. Tal Gordon, 19, was killed when gunmen in a passing car opened fire on an Egged bus traveling south from Tiberias to Jerusalem on the Jericho bypass road.

Dec 9, 2000 - Ehud Barak announces his resignation as prime minister and says there will be a new election for the post. He will stay on as caretaker in the meantime.

Dec 18, 2000 - Israeli and Palestinian negotiators leave for Washington, in a last bid to secure a peace agreement before President Clinton leaves office.

Dec 21, 2000 - Eliahu Cohen, 29, of Modi'in was shot and killed by Palestinian terrorists waiting in ambush on the road between Givat Ze'ev and Beit Horon.

Dec 28, 2000 - Capt. Gad Marasha, 30, of Kiryat Arba and Border Police Sgt.-Maj. Yonatan Vermullen, 29, of Ben-Shemen, were killed when called to dismantle a roadside bomb near the Sufa crossing in the Gaza Strip. The bomb was dismantled, but another bomb exploded, killing both and injuring two other soldiers. The Islamic Jihad claimed responsibility for the attack.

Dec 31, 2000 - Binyamin Zeev Kahane, the son of the late right-wing leader Meir Kahane, and his wife, Talia, were killed when Palestinian snipers opened fire while they were driving on the Ramallah bypass road. Five of their children, aged two months to 10 years, were injured.

Jan 8, 2001 - Bill Clinton's last ditch formula for a permanent settlement is rejected by the Palestinians.

Jan 14, 2001 - The bullet-ridden body of Ron Tzalah, 32, of Kfar Yam in Gush Katif, apparently killed on Sunday night (Jan 14), was found the following morning near the Kfar Yam hothouses.

Jan 17, 2001 - Ofir Rahum, 16, of Ashkelon, traveled to Jerusalem to meet a young woman with whom he had conducted a relationship over the Internet. She then drove him toward Ramallah. At a prearranged location, another vehicle drove up and three Palestinian gunmen inside shot Rahum more than 15 times. One terrorist drove off with Rahum's body and dumped it, while the others fled in the second vehicle.

Jan 23, 2001 - Motti Dayan, 27, and Etgar Zeituny, 34, cousins from Tel Aviv, were abducted from a restaurant in Tulkarem by masked Palestinian gunmen and executed.

Jan 25, 2001 - Akiva Pashkos, 45, of Jerusalem, was shot dead in a terror attack near the Atarot industrial zone north of Jerusalem.

Jan 28, 2001 - Ehud Barak breaks off peace talks with the Palestinians until after the prime ministerial election on February 6, after offering Arafat 98% of everything he demanded. Peace talks are held at Egyptian town of Taba, but break up after Arafat gives a vitriolic speech to an international forum accusing Israel of being "fascist": January 21-27.

Jan 29, 2001 - Arye Hershkowitz, 55, of Ofra, was killed by shots fired from a passing car near the Rama junction north of Jerusalem.

Feb 1, 2001 - Dr. Shmuel Gillis, 42, of Carmei Tzur, was killed by Palestinian gunmen who fired at his car near the Aroub refugee camp on the Jerusalem-Hebron highway.

Feb 1, 2001 - Lior Attiah, 23, of Afula was shot to death by terrorists while traveling near Jenin.

Feb 5, 2001 - St.-Sgt. Rujayah Salameh, 23, was killed by sniper fire near Rafah.

Feb 6, 2001 - Election of Ariel Sharon as Prime Minister of Israel.

Feb 11, 2001 - Tzachi Sasson, 35, of Kibbutz Rosh Tzurim in Gush Etzion, was shot and killed by Palestinian gunmen as he drove home from Jerusalem.

Feb 14, 2001 - Simcha Shitrit, 30, of Rishon Lezion; Staff-Sgt. Ofir Magidish, 20, of Kiryat Malachi; Sgt. David Iluz, 21, of Kiryat Malachi; Sgt. Julie Weiner, 21, of Jerusalem; Sgt. Rachel Levi, 19, of Ashkelon; Sgt. Kochava Polanski, 19, of Ashkelon; Cpl. Alexander Manevich, 18, of Ashkelon; and Cpl. Yasmin Karisi, 18, of Ashkelon were killed when a bus driven by a Palestinian terrorist plowed into a group of soldiers and civilians waiting at a bus stop near Holon, south of Tel-Aviv. In addition, 25 people were injured in the attack.

Feb 26, 2001 - The body of Mordechai Shefer, 55, of Kfar Sava, was found in an olive grove near Moshav Hagor. An autopsy revealed that he was murdered. Investigators suspect terrorist motives.

Mar 1, 2001 - Claude Knap, 29, of Tiberias was killed and 9 people injured when a terrorist detonated a bomb in a Tel Aviv to Tiberias service taxi at the Mei Ami junction in Wadi Ara.

Mar 4, 2001 - Naftali Dean, 85, of Tel Mond; his niece, Shlomit Ziv, 58, of Netanya; and Yevgenya Malchin, 70, of Netanya were killed in a suicide bombing in downtown Netanya; 60 people were injured. The Hamas claimed responsibility for the attack.

Mar 7, 2001 - Ariel Sharon formally takes office as Israeli prime minister.

Mar 19, 2001 - Baruch Cohen, 59, of Efrat, was killed by shots fired at his car while driving to work in Jerusalem from his home in the Gush Etzion area. After being hit by bullets, he lost control of the car and collided with an oncoming truck.

Mar 26, 2001 - Shalhevet Pass, age 10 months, was killed by sniper fire at the entrance to the Avraham Avinu neighborhood in Hebron.

Mar 28, 2001 - Eliran Rosenberg-Zayat, 15, of Givat Shmuel and Naftali Lanzkorn, 13, of Petah Tikva were killed in a suicide bombing at the Mifgash Hashalom ("peace stop") gas station several hundred meters from an IDF roadblock near the entrance to Kalkilya, east of Kfar Saba. Four people were injured. Hamas claimed responsibility for the attack.

Apr 1, 2001 - Staff Sgt. Ya'akov Krenschel, 23, of Nahariya, an IDF reserve soldier, was killed in a firefight between army and Palestinian forces southeast of Nablus.

Apr 1, 2001 - Dina Guetta, 42, of Haifa, was stabbed to death on Ha'atzmaut Street. Her murder was the initiation rite into a terrorist cell apprehended in July.

Apr 2, 2001 - Sgt. Danny Darai, 20, of Arad, was killed by a Palestinian sniper after completing guard duty at Rachel's Tomb at the entrance to Bethlehem.

Apr 21, 2001 - The mutilated body of Stanislav Sandomirsky, 38, of Beit Shemesh, was found in the trunk of his car near a village north of Ramallah. Terrorist motives are suspected.

Apr 22, 2001 - Dr. Mario Goldin, 53, of Kfar Sava, was killed when a terrorist detonated a powerful bomb he was carrying near a group of people waiting at a bus stop on the corner of Weizman and Tchernichovsky streets. About 60 people were injured in the blast. Hamas claimed responsibility.

Apr 28, 2001 - Sgt. Shlomo Elmakias, 20, of Netanya, was killed and four women passengers wounded in a drive-by terrorist shooting attack on the Wadi Ara highway in the Galilee.

Apr 28, 2001 - Simcha Ron, 60, of Nahariya, was found stabbed to death in Kfar Ba'aneh, near Carmiel in the Galilee. The terrorists responsible for the attack were apprehended in July.

May 1, 2001 - Assaf Hershkowitz, 30, of Ofra, was killed when his vehicle was fired upon and overturned at a junction between Ofra and Beit El.

May 8, 2001 - Arnaldo Agranionic, 48, was murdered by terrorists as he guarded the Binyamin Farm, a lonely outpost where he lived, on an isolated hilltop east of Itamar in Samaria.

May 9, 2001 - Yossi Ish-Ran, 14, and Kobi Mandell, 14, both of Tekoa, were found stoned to death in a cave about 200 meters from the small community south of Jerusalem where they lived.

May 10, 2001 - Constantin Straturula, 52, and Virgil Martinesc, 29, two Romanian citizens employed by an Israeli contractor, were killed in a bomb attack while repairing a vandalized fence at the Kissufim Crossing into the Gaza District.

May 15, 2001 - Idit Mizrahi, 20, of Rimonim, was fatally shot in a terrorist ambush as she drove with her father and brother on the Alon Highway to attend a family wedding. Terrorists fired 30 bullets, 19 of which hit the family's car.

May 18, 2001 - Tirza Polonsky, 66, of Moshav Kfar Haim; Miriam Waxman, 51, of Hadera; David Yarkoni, 53, of Netanya; Yulia Tratiakova, 21, of Netanya; and Vladislav Sorokin, 34, of Netanya were killed in a suicide bombing at Hasharon Mall in the seaside city of Netanya, in which more than 100 were wounded. Hamas claimed responsibility for the attack.

May 18, 2001 - Lt. Yair Nebenzahl, 22, of Neve Tzuf (Halamish), was killed and his mother seriously wounded, in a Palestinian roadside ambush north of Jerusalem.

May 21, 2001 - In his long awaited report on the Middle East conflict, former US senator George Mitchell calls for an immediate ceasefire, to be followed by confidence building measures and ultimately by renewed peace negotiations.

May 23, 2001 - Asher Iluz, 33, of Modi'in was killed outside Ariel en route to supervise a road paving in the area, when Palestinian gunmen opened fire in an ambush.

May 25, 2001 - The burnt body of Yosef Alfasi, 50, of Rishon Letzion, was discovered near the West Bank city of Tulkarem.

May 29, 2001 - Gilad Zar, 41, of Itamar, was shot dead in a terrorist ambush while driving in the West Bank between Kedumim and Yizhar. The Fatah Tanzim claimed responsibility for the attack.

May 29, 2001 - Sarah Blaustein, 53, and Esther Alvan, 20, of Efrat, were killed in a drive-by shooting near Neve Daniel in the Gush Etzion block south of Jerusalem. The Fatah Tanzim claimed responsibility for the attack.

May 31, 2001 - Zvi Shelef, 63, of Mevo Dotan, was killed in a drive-by shooting attack in northern Samaria north of Tulkarem. He was shot in the head and died en route to the hospital.

June 1, 2001 - Marina Berkovizki, 17, of Tel Aviv; Roman Dezanshvili, 21, of Bat Yam; Ilya Gutman, 19, of Bat Yam; Anya Kazachkov, 16, of Holon; Katherine Kastaniyada-Talkir, 15, of Ramat Gan; Aleksei Lupalu, 16, of the Ukraine; Mariana Medvedenko, 16, of Tel Aviv; Irina Nepomneschi, 16, of Bat Yam; Yelena Nelimov, 18, of Tel Aviv; Yulia Nelimov, 16, of Tel Aviv; Raisa Nimrovsky, 15, of Netanya; Pvt. Diez (Dani) Normanov, 21, of Tel Aviv; Simona Rodin, 18, of Holon; Ori Shahar, 32, of Ramat Gan; Liana Sakiyan, 16, of Tel Aviv;

Maria Tagilchev, 14, of Netanya; and Irena Usdachi, 18, of Holon were killed when a suicide bomber blew himself up outside a disco near Tel Aviv's Dolphinarium along the seafront promenade just before midnight. Sergei Pancheskov, 20, of the Ukraine; Yael-Yulia Sklianik, 15, of Holon; Jan Bloom, 25, of Ramat Gan; and Yevgenia Dorfman, 15, of Bat Yam died subsequently from their injuries. 120 people were wounded in the bombing.

June 11, 2001 - Yehuda Shoham, aged 5 months, of Shilo, died of injuries incurred in a fatal stoning on June 5. He was critically injured by a rock thrown at the family's car near Shilo in Samaria.

June 12, 2001 - U.S. CIA Director George Tenet negotiates a cease-fire, but Palestinians break it within a few hours of its announcement.

June 12, 2001 - Father Georgios Tsibouktzakis, 34, a Greek Orthodox monk from the St. George Monastery in Wadi Kelt in the Judean desert, was shot and killed while driving on the Jerusalem-Ma'ale Adumim road.

June 14, 2001 - Lt.Col. Yehuda Edri, 45, of Ma'ale Adumim was killed by a Palestinian informant for Israeli intelligence in a shooting attack on the Bethlehem bypass tunnel road connecting the Gush Etzion block with Jerusalem. One of his security guards was seriously injured.

June 18, 2001 - Dan Yehuda, 35, of Homesh was killed in a drive-by shooting attack between Homesh and Shavei Shomron, near Nablus. Alex Briskin, 17, was moderately injured.

June 18, 2001 - Doron Zisserman, 38, of Einav, was shot and killed in his car by sniper fire near the entrance to Einav, east of Tulkarem. Fatah claimed responsibility for the attack.

June 20, 2001 - Ilya Krivitz, 62, of Homesh in Samaria was shot and killed at close range in an ambush in the nearby Palestinian town of Silat a-Dahar.

June 22, 2001 - Sgt. Aviv Iszak, 19, of Kfar Saba, and Sgt. Ofir Kit, 19, of Jerusalem, were killed in a suicide bombing near Dugit in the Gaza Strip as a jeep with yellow Israeli license plates, supposedly stuck in the sand, blew up as they approached.

June 28, 2001 - Ekaterina (Katya) Weintraub, 27, of Ganim in northern Samaria was killed and another woman injured by shots fired at the two-car convoy on the Jenin bypass road.

July 2, 2001 - Aharon Obadyan, 41, of Zichron Ya'akov was shot and killed near Baka a-Sharkia, north of the West Bank city of Tulkarem and close to the 1967 Green Line border, after shopping at the local market.

July 2, 2001 - The body of Yair Har Sinai, 51, of Susiya in the Hebron hills, missing since July 2 was found early July 3, shot in the head and chest.

July 4, 2001 - Eliahu Na'aman, 32, of Petah Tikva, was shot at point-blank range just inside the Green Line at Sueika, near Tulkarem.

July 9, 2001 - Capt. Shai Shalom Cohen, 22, of Pardes Hanna, was killed and another soldier was wounded when an explosive charge detonated beneath their jeep after leaving the Adoraim IDF base south of Hebron.

July 13, 2001 - Yehezkel (Hezi) Mualem, 49, father of four from Kiryat Arba, was shot and killed between Kiryat Arba and Hebron while protesting a shooting attack in the area the previous day.

July 14, 2001 - David Cohen, 28, of Betar Illit, died of injuries sustained in a drive-by shooting in Kiryat Arba on July 12.

July 15, 2001 - Israel insists on seven days of calm before it will resume peace talks with Palestinians but violence continues to escalate.

July 16, 2001 - Cpl. Hanit Arami, 19, and St.Sgt. Avi Ben Harush, 20, both of Zichron Yaakov, were killed and 11 wounded - 3 seriously - when a bomb exploded in a suicide terrorist attack at a bus stop near the train station in Binyamina, halfway between Netanya and Haifa. The Islamic Jihad claimed responsibility for the attack.

July 24, 2001 - The body of Yuri Gushchin, 18, of Jerusalem, brutally murdered, bearing stab and gunfire wounds, was found in Ramallah.

July 26, 2001 - Ronen Landau, 17, of Givat Ze'ev, was shot and killed by Palestinian terrorists while returning home from Jerusalem with his father.

Aug 5, 2001 - Tehiya Bloomberg, 40, of Karnei Shomron, mother of five and 5 months pregnant, was killed when Palestinian gunmen opened fire on the family vehicle between Alfei Menashe and Karnei Shomron. Three people were seriously wounded, including her husband, Shimon, and daughter, Tzippi, 14.

Aug 6, 2001 - Yitzhak Snir, 51, of Ra'anana, an Israeli diamond merchant, was shot dead in Amman, in the yard of the building where he kept a flat. His body was found the following morning.

Aug 7, 2001 - Wael Ghanem, 32, an Arab Israeli resident of Taibeh, was shot and killed by Palestinian assailants on the road near Kalkilya. Police believe he was murdered because of suspected collaboration with Israeli authorities.
Zohar Shurgi, 40, of Moshav Yafit in the Jordan Valley, was shot and killed by terrorists while driving home at night on the Trans-Samaria Highway.

Aug 9, 2001 - Giora Balash, 60, of Brazil; Zvika Golombek, 26, of Carmiel; Shoshana Yehudit Greenbaum, 31, of the U.S.; Tehila Maoz, 18, of Jerusalem; Frieda Mendelsohn, 62, of Jerusalem; Michal Raziel, 16, of Jerusalem; Malka Roth, 15, of Jerusalem; Mordechai Schijveschuurder, 43, of Neria; Tzira Schijveschuurder, 41, of Neria; Ra'aya Schijveschuurder, 14, of Neria; Avraham Yitzhak Schijveschuurder, 4, of Neria; Hemda Schijveschuurder, 2, of Neria; Lily Shimashvili, 33, of Jerusalem; Tamara Shimashvili, 8, of Jerusalem; and Yocheved Shoshan, 10, of Jerusalem were killed and about 130 injured in a suicide bombing at the Sbarro pizzeria on the corner of King George Street and Jaffa Road in the center of Jerusalem. Hamas and the Islamic Jihad claimed responsibility for the attack.

Aug 9, 2001 - Aliza Malka, 17, a boarding student at Kibbutz Merav, was killed by terrorists in a drive-by shooting at the entrance to the kibbutz in the Gilboa region, west of Beit

She'an. Three teenage girls who were with her in the car were injured, one seriously.

Aug 25, 2001 - Maj. Gil Oz, 30, of Kfar Sava; St.-Sgt. Kobi Nir, 21, of Kfar Sava; and Sgt. Tzahi Grabli, 19 of Holon were killed and seven soldiers wounded when two Palestinian terrorists infiltrated an IDF base in Gush Katif in the Gaza Strip at about 3:00 am. The attackers, members of the PLO Fatah faction and of the Palestinian security forces, were killed by IDF soldiers. The Democratic Front claimed responsibility for the attack.

Aug 25, 2001 - Sharon, 26, and Yaniv Ben-Shalom, 27, of Ofarim, were killed when Palestinian gunmen opened fire on their car as they were returning home on the Jerusalem-Modi'in road Saturday night. Their children, aged one and two, were lightly wounded. Sharon's brother, Doron Sviri, 20, of Jerusalem was fatally wounded and died the following day.

Aug 26, 2001 - Dov Rosman, 58, of Netanya was killed in a shooting attack near the entrance to the village of Zaita, opposite Kibbutz Magal. Fatah claimed responsibility for the attack.

Aug 27, 2001 - Meir Lixenberg, 38, of Itamar, father of five, was shot and killed by Palestinian terrorists from a roadside ambush while traveling between the communities of Har Bracha and Itamar, south of Nablus.

Aug 29, 2001 - Oleg Sotnikov, 35, of Ashdod, a truck driver employed by Dor Energy, was killed in a terrorist shooting attack outside the Palestinian village of Kutchin, west of Nablus.

Aug 30, 2001 - Amos Tajouri, 60, of Modi'in, was shot in the head at point-blank range by a masked gunman in the Arab village of Na'alin, while dining at a restaurant owned by close friends.

Sept 6, 2001 - Lt. Erez Merhavi, 23, of Moshav Tarum was killed in an ambush shooting near Kibbutz Bahan, east of Hadera, while driving to a wedding. A female officer with him in the car was seriously injured. Fatah-Tanzim claimed responsibility for the attack.

Sept 9, 2001 - Ya'akov Hatzav, 42, of Hamra in the Jordan Valley, the driver, and Sima Franko, 24, of Beit She'an, a kindergarten teacher, were killed in a shooting attack 300 meters south of the Adam Junction in the Jordan Valley. A minibus transporting teachers to the regional school was attacked by Palestinian terrorists.

Sept 9, 2001 - Dr. Yigal Goldstein, 47, of Jerusalem; Morel Derfler, 45, of Mevasseret Zion; and Sgt. Daniel Yifrah, 19, of Jerusalem were killed and some 90 injured, most lightly, in a suicide bombing near the Nahariya train station in northern Israel.

Sept 11, 2001 - Border Policemen Sgt. Tzachi David, 19, of Tel-Aviv, and St.-Sgt. Andrei Zledkin, 26, of Carmiel, were killed just after midnight when Palestinian gunmen opened fire on the Ivtan Border Police base near Kibbutz Bachan in central Israel. A Fatah group claimed responsibility for the attack.

Sept 11, 2001 - Suicide bombers in hijacked airliners attacked the eastern seaboard of the United States, destroying the World Trade Center and part of the Pentagon.

Sept 12, 2001 - Ruth Shua'i, 46, of Alfei Menashe, was traveling home around 7:30 pm when shots were fired from a passing vehicle near the village of Habla near Kalkilya. She sustained injuries to her head and stomach and died en route to Meir Hospital in Kfar Saba.

Sept 15, 2001 - Meir Weisshaus, 23, of Jerusalem, was fatally shot late Saturday night in a drive-by shooting on the Ramot-French Hill road in northern Jerusalem.

Sept 16, 2001 - Sgt. David Gordukal, 23, of Upper Nazareth, was killed in the exchange of fire on Saturday night in the south of Ramallah, during which five senior Palestinian terrorists were arrested and a number of Palestinian positions and a Force 17 camp were attacked.

Sept 20, 2001 - Sarit Amrani, 26, of Nokdim, was killed Thursday morning and her husband Shai was seriously wounded in a shooting attack near Tekoa, south of Bethlehem. The couple's three children who were traveling in the vehicle were not injured. Fatah claimed responsibility for the attack.

Sept 24, 2001 - Salit Sheetrit, 28, of Kibbutz Sde Eliyahu was killed by gunfire shortly after 6:30 near Shadmot Mehola on the Jordan Valley road. The Islamic Jihad claimed responsibility for the attack.

Oct 2, 2001 - Cpl. Liron Harpaz, 19, of Alei Sinai, and Assaf Yitzhaki, 20, of Lod, were killed when a Palestinian terrorist cell infiltrated the northern Gaza District community of Alei Sinai, opening fire on residents and hurling grenades into homes. Fifteen others were wounded in the attack.

Oct 4, 2001 - Sgt. Tali Ben-Armon, 19, an off-duty woman soldier from Pardesia, Haim Ben-Ezra, 76, of Givat Hamoreh, and Sergei Freidin, 20, of Afula were killed when a Palestinian terrorist, dressed as an Israeli paratrooper, opened fire on Israeli civilians waiting at the central bus station in Afula. Thirteen other Israelis were wounded in the attack. Fatah claimed responsibility for the attack.

October 5, 2001 - American relations with Israel plunge to their lowest point in a decade, as the White House denounces as "unacceptable" statements by the Israeli prime minister comparing the US coalition-building in the Arab world with British appeasement of the Nazis in the 1930s.

Oct 5, 2001 - Hananya Ben-Avraham, 46, of Elad was killed by Palestinian terrorists in a machine gun ambush near Avnei Hefetz in central Israel.

Oct 7, 2001 - Yair Mordechai, 43, of Kibbutz Sheluhot was killed when a Palestinian suicide terrorist detonated a large bomb strapped to his body near the entrance of the kibbutz in the Beit She'an Valley.

Oct 17, 2001 - Tourism Minister Rechavam Ze'evy, 75, was assassinated by two shots to the head outside his room at the Jerusalem Hyatt Hotel. The Popular Front for the Liberation of Palestine claimed responsibility for the attack.

Oct 18, 2001 - Lior Kaufman, 30, of Ramat Sharon was killed and two injured, one seriously, by shots fired by terrorists at their jeep in the Judean desert, near the Mar Saba monastery.

Oct 28, 2001 - St.-Sgt. Yaniv Levy, 22, of Zichron Yaakov was killed by Palestinian terrorists in a drive-by machine-gun ambush near Kibbutz Metzer in northern Israel. The Tanzim wing of Arafat's Fatah faction claimed responsibility for the murder.

Oct 28, 2001 - Ayala Levy, 39, of Elyachin; Smadar Levy, 23, of Hadera; Lydia Marko, 63, of Givat Ada; and Sima Menachem, 30, of Zichron Yaakov were killed when two Palestinian terrorists, members of the Palestinian police, armed with assault rifles and expanding bullets, opened fire from a vehicle on Israeli pedestrians at a crowded bus-stop in downtown Hadera. About 40 were wounded, three critically. The Islamic Jihad claimed responsiblity for the attack.

Nov 2, 2001 - St.-Sgt. Raz Mintz, 19, of Kiryat Motzkin was killed by Palestinian gun-men at 5:45 pm at an IDF roadblock near Ofra, north of Ramallah. The Fatah-affiliated Al-Aksa Brigade claimed responsibility for the attack.

Nov 4, 2001 - Shoshana Ben Ishai, 16, of Betar Illit and Menashe (Meni) Regev, 14, of Jerusalem were killed when a Palestinian terrorist opened fire with a sub-machine gun shortly before 16:00 at a No. 25 Egged bus at the French Hill junction in northern Jerusalem. Forty-five people were injured in the attack.

Nov 6, 2001 - Capt. (Res.) Eyal Sela, 39, of Moshav Nir Banim, was shot dead in an ambush by three Palestinian terrorists on the southern Nablus bypass road.

Nov 9, 2001 - Hadas Abutbul, 39, of Mevo Dotan in northern Samaria was shot and killed by Palestinian terrorists as she drove from work in nearby Shaked.

Nov 11, 2001 - Aharon Ussishkin, 50, head of security at Moshav Kfar Hess, east of Netanya, was shot and killed at the entrance to the Moshav on Sunday evening, after being summoned to investigate a suspicious person.

Nov 24, 2001 - St.-Sgt. Barak Madmon, 26, of Holon, an IDF reservist, was killed by a mortar shell that landed in the soccer field of Kfar Darom in Gush Katif, while on his way to take up guard duty. Hamas claimed responsibility for the attack.

Nov 27, 2001 - Noam Gozovsky, 23, of Moshav Ramat Zvi, and Michal Mor, 25, of Afula were killed when two Palestinian terrorists from the Jenin area opened fire with Kalashnikov assault rifles on a crowd of people near the central bus station in Afula. Police officers and a reserve soldier confronted them, killing the terrorists in the ensu-ing firefight. Another 50 people were injured, 10 of them moderately to seriously. Fatah and the Islamic Jihad claimed joint responsibility.

Nov 27, 2001 - Etty Fahima, 45, of Netzer Hazani was killed and three others were injured when a Palestinian terrorist threw grenades and opened fire at a convoy on the road between the Kissufim crossing and Gush Katif in the Gaza Strip on Tuesday evening. Hamas claimed responsibility for the attack.

Nov 29, 2001 - 1st Sgt. Yaron Pikholtz, 20, of Ramat Gan, was killed and a second sol-dier was injured in a drive-by shooting incident on the Green Line, near the West Bank village of Baka el-Sharkiya.

Nov 29, 2001 - Inbal Weiss, 22, of Zichron Ya'akov; Yehiav Elshad, 28, of Tel-Aviv; and Samuel Milshevsky, 45, of Kfar Sava were killed and nine wounded in a suicide bombing on an Egged 823 bus en route from Nazereth to Tel Aviv near the city of Hadera. The Islamic Jihad and Fatah claimed responsibility for the attack.

Dec 1, 2001 - Assaf Avitan, 15, of Jerusalem; Michael Moshe Dahan, 21, of Jerusalem; Israel Ya'akov Danino, 17, of Jerusalem; Yosef El-Ezra, 18, of Jerusalem; Sgt. Nir Haftzadi, 19, of Jerusalem; Yuri (Yoni) Korganov, 20, of Ma'alei Adumim; Golan Turgeman, 15, of Jerusalem; Guy Vaknin, 19, of Jerusalem; Adam Weinstein, 14, of Givon Hahadasha, and Moshe Yedid-Levy, 19, of Jerusalem were killed and about 180 injured - 17 seriously - when explosive devices were detonated by two suicide bombers close to 11:30 pm on Ben Yehuda Street, the pedestrian mall in the center of Jerusalem. A car bomb exploded nearby 20 minutes later. Hamas claimed responsibility for the attack.
Ido Cohen, 17, of Jerusalem, fatally injured in the attack, died of his wounds on December 8.

Dec 2, 2001 - Prof. Baruch Singer, 51, of Gedera was killed when Palestinian gunmen opened fire on his car near the northern Gaza settlement of Elei Sinai. Hamas claimed responsibility for the attack.

Dec 2, 2001 - Tatiana Borovik, 23, of Haifa; Mara Fishman, 51, of Haifa; Ina Frenkel, 60, of Haifa; Riki Hadad, 30, of Yokne'am; Ronen Kahalon, 30, of Haifa; Samion Kalik, 64, of Haifa; Mark Khotimliansky, 75, of Haifa; Cecilia Kozamin, 76, of Haifa; Yelena Lomakin, 62, of Haifa; Rosaria Reyes, 42, of the Philippines; Yitzhak Ringel, 41, of Haifa; Rassim Safulin, 78, of Haifa; Leah Strick, 73, of Haifa; Faina Zabiogailu, 64, of Haifa; Mikhail Zaraisky, 71, of Haifa were killed and 40 injured in a suicide bombing on an Egged bus No. 16 in Haifa. Hamas claimed responsibility for the attack.

Dec 12, 2001 - Yair Amar, 13, of Emmanuel; Esther Avraham, 42, of Emmanuel; Border Police Chief Warrant Officer Yoel Bienenfeld, 35, of Moshav Tel Shahar; Moshe Gutman, 40, of Emmanuel; Avraham Nahman Nitzani, 17, of Betar Illit; Yirmiyahu Salem, 48, of Emmanuel; Israel Sternberg, 46, of Emmanuel; David Tzarfati, 38, of Ginot Shomron; Hananya Tzarfati, 32, of Kfar Saba; Ya'akov Tzarfati, 64, of Kfar Saba were killed when three terrorists attacked a No. 189 Dan bus and several passenger cars with a roadside bomb, anti-tank grenades, and light arms fire near the entrance to Emmanuel in Samaria. About 30 others were injured. Both Fatah and Hamas claimed responsibility for the attack. Haim Chiprot, 52, of Emmanuel, injured in the attack, died of his wounds on March 25, 2002.

Dec 25, 2001 - Sgt. Michael Sitbon, 23, of Beit Shemesh, an IDF reserve soldier, was killed, and four other soldiers were injured, in a shooting attack near the Jordanian border north of Beit She'an.

Jan 3, 2002 - Israel captures Karine-A, a ship laden with 50 tons of weapons from Iran bound for the Palestinian Authority.

Jan 9, 2002 - Maj. Ashraf Hawash, 28, of Beit Zarzir; Sgt.-Maj. Ibrahim Hamadieh, 23, of Rehaniya; Sgt.-Maj. Hana (Eli) Abu-Ghanem, 25, of Haifa; and St.-Sgt. Mofid Sawaid, 25, of Abu Snan, four IDF soldiers of the Bedouin desert patrol unit, were killed and two injured when two armed Palestinian terrorists from the southern Gaza Strip, carrying explosive belts, assault rifles, grenades, and dressed in Palestinian Authority police uniforms, infiltrated into Israel at 04:30 this morning and attacked an IDF post near Kerem Shalom. The terrorists, one a member of the Palestinian Authority's naval force, and the second a Hamas operative, were killed. Hamas claimed responsibility for the attack.

Jan 14, 2002 - Sgt. Elad Abu-Gani, 19, of Tiberias, was killed and an officer sustained gunshot wounds in a terrorist ambush near Kuchin, between Nablus and Tulkarm. Fatah claimed responsibility for the attack.

Jan 15, 2002 - Avraham (Avi) Boaz, 71, of Ma'aleh Adumim, an American citizen, was kidnapped at a PA security checkpoint in Beit Jala. His bullet-riddled body was found in a car in Beit Sahur, in the Bethlehem area. The Fatah's Al-Aksa Brigade claimed responsibility for the murder.

Jan 15, 2002 - Yoela Chen, 45, of Givat Ze'ev, was shot and killed by Palestinian terrorists near the gas station at the entrance to Givat Ze'ev. Her aunt, who was with her in the car, was injured. The Fatah's Al-Aqsa Brigade claimed responsibility for the murder.

Jan 16, 2002 - Shahada Dadis, 30, an Arab resident of Beit Hanina in East Jerusalem, was killed in a drive-by terrorist shooting. He was found dead in a car bearing Israeli license plates south of Jenin in the West Bank.

Jan 17, 2002 - Edward Bakshayev, 48, of Or Akiva; Anatoly Bakshayev, 63, of Or Akiva; Aharon Ben Yisrael-Ellis, 32, of Ra'anana; Dina Binayev, 48, of Ashkelon; Boris Melikhov, 56, of Sderot; and Avi Yazdi, 25, of Hadera were killed and 35 injured, several seriously, when a terrorist burst into a bat mitzva reception in a banquet hall in Hadera shortly before 11:00 pm, opening fire with an M-16 assault rifle. The Fatah Al-Aqsa Brigades claimed responsibility for the attack.

Jan 22, 2002 - Sarah Hamburger, 79, and Svetlana Sandler, 56, both of Jerusalem, were killed and 40 were injured when a Palestinian terrorist opened fire with an M-16 assault rifle near a bus stop in downtown Jerusalem. The Fatah Al-Aqsa Brigades claimed responsibility for the attack.

Jan 27, 2002 - Pinhas Tokatli, 81, of Jerusalem was killed and over 150 people were wounded, four seriously, in a suicide bombing on Jaffa Road, in the center of Jerusalem, shortly before 12:30. The female terrorist, identified as a Fatah member, was armed with more than 10 kilos of explosives.

Feb 6, 2002 - Miri Ohana, 45, and her daughter Yael, 11, were murdered in their home when an armed terrorist infiltrated Moshav Hamra, halfway between Jericho and Beit She'an in the Jordan Valley on Wednesday evening, opening fire. IDF reserve soldier, St.-Sgt. Maj.(res.) Moshe Majos Meconen, 33, of Beit She'an, was also killed in the attack. The terrorist, who entered the Ohana home disguised in IDF uniform, was killed by IDF forces. Both Fatah and Hamas claimed responsibility.

Feb 8, 2002 - Moranne Amit, 25, of Kibbutz Kfar Hanasi was stabbed to death by four Palestinians, aged 14 to 16, while strolling on the Sherover Promenade in Jerusalem's Armon Hanatziv neighborhood Friday afternoon.

Feb 9, 2002 - Atala Lipobsky, 78, of Ma'ale Ephraim was shot dead while driving on the Trans-Samaria Highway with her son. Palestinian gunmen opened fire on the car, apparently from an ambush, between Ariel and the Tapuah Junction.

Feb 10, 2002 - Lt. Keren Rothstein, 20, of Ashkelon and Cpl. Aya Malachi, 18, of Moshav

Ein Habesor were killed in a drive-by terrorist shooting at the entrance to the IDF Southern Command base in Be'er Sheva. Four others were wounded, one critically. One of the terrorists was killed at the scene; the second, wearing an explosives belt, fled in the direction of a nearby school when he was shot and killed by a soldier and police officer. Hamas claimed responsibility for the attack.

Feb 14, 2002 - St.-Sgt. Ron Lavie, 20, of Katzrin, St.-Sgt. Moshe Peled, 20, of Rehovot, and St.-Sgt. Asher Zaguri, 21, of Shlomi were killed and four soldiers injured when a powerful mine exploded under an IDF tank on the Karni-Netzarim road in the Gaza Strip Thursday night, following the detonation of a roadside bomb at a civilian convoy of cars and a bus.

Feb 15, 2002 - St.-Sgt. Lee Nahman Akunis, 20, of Holon, was shot and killed by gunmen on Friday night at a roadblock north of Ramallah. The Fatah's Al-Aksa Brigade claimed responsibility for the attack.

Feb 16, 2002 - Nehemia Amar, 15, and Keren Shatsky, 15, both of Ginot Shomron were killed and about 30 people were wounded, six seriously, when a suicide bomber blew himself up on Saturday night at a pizzeria in the shopping mall in Karnei Shomron in Samaria. Rachel Thaler, 16, of Ginot Shomron died of her wounds on February 27. The Popular Front for the Liberation of Palestine claimed responsibility for the attack.

Feb 18, 2002 - Policeman Ahmed Mazarib, 32, of the Bedouin village Beit Zarzir in the Galilee, was killed by a suicide bomber whom he had stopped for questioning on the Ma'ale Adumim-Jerusalem road. The terrorist succeeded in detonating the bomb in his car. The Fatah al-Aqsa Martyrs Brigades claimed responsibility for the attack.

Feb 18, 2002 - Ahuva Amergi, 30, of Ganei Tal in Gush Katif was killed and a 60-year-old man was injured when a Palestinian terrorist opened fire on her car. Maj. Mor Elraz, 25, of Kiryat Ata and St.-Sgt. Amir Mansouri, 21, of Kiryat Arba, who came to their assistance, were killed while trying to intercept the terrorist. The terrorist was killed when the explosives he was carrying were detonated. The Fatah al-Aqsa Martyrs Brigades claimed responsibility for the attack.

Feb 19, 2002 - Lt. Moshe Eini, 21, of Petah Tikva; St.-Sgt. Benny Kikis, 20, of Carmiel; St.-Sgt. Mark Podolsky, 20, of Tel Aviv; St.-Sgt. Erez Turgeman, 20, of Jerusalem; St.-Sgt. Tamir Atsmi, 21, of Kiryat Ono; and St.-Sgt. Michael Oxsman, 21, of Haifa were killed and one wounded in an attack near a roadblock west of Ramallah. Several terrorists opened fire at soldiers at the roadblock, including three off-duty soldiers inside a structure at the roadblock, killing them at point-blank range. The Fatah al-Aqsa Martyrs Brigades claimed responsibility for the attack.

Feb 22, 2002 - Valery Ahmir, 59, of Beit Shemesh was killed by terrorists in a drive-by shooting on the Atarot-Givat Ze'ev road north of Jerusalem as he returned home from work. Fatah claimed responsibility for the attack.

Feb 25, 2002 - Avraham Fish, 65, and Aharon Gorov, 46, both of Nokdim, were killed in a terrorist shooting attack between Tekoa and Nokdim, south of Bethlehem. Fish's daughter, 9 months pregnant, was seriously injured but delivered a baby girl. The Fatah al-Aksa Brigades claimed responsibility for the attack.

Feb 25, 2002 - Police officer 1st Sgt. Galit Arbiv, 21, of Nesher, died after being fatally shot, when a terrorist opened fire at a bus stop in the Neve Ya'akov residential neighborhood in northern Jerusalem. Eight others were injured, two seriously. The Fatah al-Aksa Brigades claimed responsibility for the attack.

Feb 27, 2002 - Gad Rejwan, 34, of Jerusalem, was shot and killed early Wednesday morning by one of his Palestinian employees in a factory in the Atarot industrial area, north of Jerusalem. Two Fatah groups issued a joint statement taking responsibility for the murder.

Feb 28, 2002 - IDF soldier St.-Sgt. Haim Bachar, 20, of Tel Aviv was killed during clashes with Palestinians in the Balata refugee camp near Nablus. IDF forces entered the camp to search for wanted terrorists.

Mar 1, 2002 - IDF soldier Sgt. Ya'acov Avni, 20, of Kiryat Ata was killed by Palestinian sniper fire in the Jenin refugee camp.

Mar 2, 2002 - The bullet-ridden body of Jerusalem police detective Chief-Supt. Moshe Dayan, 46, of Ma'aleh Adumim, was discovered next to his trail motorcycle, near the Mar Saba Monastery in the Judean Desert. Tanzim claimed responsibility for the attack.

Mar 2, 2002 - Eleven people were killed and over 50 were injured, 4 critically, in a suicide bombing at 7:15 pm near a yeshiva in the ultra-Orthodox Beit Yisrael neighborhood in the center of Jerusalem where people had gathered for a bar-mitzva celebration. The terrorist detonated the bomb next to a group of women waiting with their baby carriages for their husbands to leave the nearby synagogue. The victims: Shlomo Nehmad, 40, his wife Gafnit, 32, and their daughters Shiraz, 7, and Liran, 3, of Rishon Lezion; Shaul Nehmad, 15, of Rishon Lezion; Lidor Ilan, 12, and his sister Oriah, 18 months, of Rishon Lezion; Tzofia Ya'arit Eliyahu, 23, and her son Ya'akov Avraham, 7 months, of Jerusalem. Avi Hazan, 37, of Moshav Adora, died of his injuries on Monday morning (Mar 4). Avraham Eliahu Nehmad, 17, of Rishon Lezion, died of his injuries on June 20. The Fatah Al-Aqsa Martyrs Brigade took responsibility for the attack.

Mar 3, 2002 - Ten Israelis - 7 soldiers and 3 civilians - were killed and 6 injured when a terrorist opened fire at an IDF roadblock near Ofra in Samaria: Capt. Ariel Hovav, 25, of Eli; Lt.(res.) David Damelin, 29, of Kibbutz Metzar; 1st Sgt.(res.) Rafael Levy, 42, of Rishon Lezion; Sgt.-Maj.(res.) Avraham Ezra, 38, of Kiryat Bialik; Sgt.-Maj.(res.) Eran Gad, 24, of Rishon Letzion; Sgt.-Maj.(res.) Yochai Porat, 26, of Kfar Sava; Sgt.-Maj.(res.) Kfir Weiss, 24, of Beit Shemesh; Sergei Butarov, 33, of Ariel; Vadim Balagula, 32, of Ariel; and Didi Yitzhak, 66, of Eli. The Fatah Al-Aqsa Martyrs Brigade claimed responsibility for the attack.

Mar 3, 2002 - Sgt. Steven Kenigsberg, 19, of Hod Hasharon was killed and 4 soldiers injured when a Palestinian gunman opened fire near the Kissufim crossing in the Gaza Strip. The Islamic Jihad and Tanzim claimed responsibility for the attack.

Mar 5, 2002 - Police officer FSM Salim Barakat, 33, of Yarka; Yosef Habi, 52, of Herzliya; and Eli Dahan, 53, of Lod were killed and over 30 people were wounded in Tel-Aviv when a Palestinian terrorist opened fire on two adjacent restaurants shortly after 2:00 AM. The Fatah Al-Aqsa Martyrs Brigade claimed responsibility for the attack.

Mar 5, 2002 - Devorah Friedman, 45, of Efrat, was killed and her husband injured in shooting attack on the Bethlehem bypass "tunnel road", south of Jerusalem. The Fatah

Al-Aqsa Martyrs Brigade claimed responsibility for the attack.

Mar 5, 2002 - Maharatu Tagana, 85, of Upper Nazareth was killed and a large number of people injured, most lightly, when a suicide bomber exploded in an Egged No. 823 bus as it entered the Afula central bus station. The Islamic Jihad claimed responsibility for the attack.

Mar 6, 2002 - 1st Lt. Pinhas Cohen, 23, of Jerusalem, was killed overnight near the southern Gaza town of Khan Yunis, in the course of anti-terrorist activity. Cpl.(res.) Alexander Nastarenko, 37, of Netanya was killed when Palestinian gunmen crossed the border fence and ambushed an army jeep on the patrol road near Kibbutz Nir Oz.

Mar 7, 2002 - Arik Krogliak of Beit El, Tal Kurtzweil of Bnei Brak, Asher Marcus of Jerusalem, Eran Picard of Jerusalem, and Ariel Zana of Jerusalem, all aged 18, were killed and 23 people were injured, four seriously, when a Palestinian gunman penetrated the pre-military training academy in the Gush Katif settlement of Atzmona. Hamas claimed responsibility for the attack.

Mar 8, 2002 - St.-Sgt. Edward Korol, 20, of Ashdod, was killed by a Palestinian sniper in Tulkarem.

Mar 9, 2002 - Avia Malka, 9 months, of South Africa, and Israel Yihye, 27, of Bnei Brak were killed and about 50 people were injured, several seriously, when two Palestinians opened fire and threw grenades at cars and pedestrians in the coastal city of Netanya, close to the city's boardwalk and hotels. The terrorists were killed by Israeli border police. The Fatah Al Aqsa Brigades claimed responsibility for the attack.

Mar 9, 2002 - Limor Ben-Shoham, 27, of Jerusalem; Nir Borochov, 22, of Givat Ze'ev; Danit Dagan, 25, of Tel-Aviv; Livnat Dvash, 28, of Jerusalem; Tali Eliyahu, 26, of Jerusalem; Uri Felix, 25, of Givat Ze'ev; Dan Imani, 23, of Jerusalem; Natanel Kochavi, 31, of Kiryat Ata; Baruch Lerner, 29, of Eli; Orit Ozerov, 28, of Jerusalem; Avraham Haim Rahamim, 28, of Jerusalem were killed and 54 injured, 10 of them seriously, when a suicide bomber exploded at 10:30 pm in a crowded cafe at the corner of Aza and Ben-Maimon streets in the Rehavia neighborhood in the center of Jerusalem. Hamas claimed responsibility for the attack.

Mar 10, 2002 - St.-Sgt. Kobi Eichelboim, 21, of Givatayim died Sunday afternoon from wounds suffered in the morning when a Palestinian gunman disguised as a worker opened fire at the entrance to Netzarim in the Gaza Strip.

Mar 12, 2002 - Eyal Lieberman, 42, of Tzoran was killed and another person was wounded in a shooting attack at the Kiryat Sefer checkpoint, east of Modi'in.

Mar 12, 2002 - Yehudit Cohen, 33, of Shlomi; Ofer Kanarick, 44, of Moshav Betzet; Alexei Kotman, 29, of Kibbutz Beit Hashita; Lynne Livne, 49, and her daughter Atara, 15, of Kibbutz Hanita; and Lt. German Rozhkov, 25, of Kiryat Shmona were killed when two terrorists opened fire from an ambush on Israeli vehicles traveling between Shlomi and Kibbutz Metzuba near the northern border with Lebanon. Seven others were injured. Israeli forces killed the two gunmen, who were dressed in IDF uniforms, and carried out wide-scale searches for additional terrorists.

Mar 13, 2002 - Lt. Gil Badihi, 21, of Nataf died of injuries suffered Wednesday morning in Ramallah. He was shot in the head by a Palestinian gunman as he stood next to his tank.

Mar 14, 2002 - St.-Sgt. Matan Biderman, 21, of Carmiel, St.-Sgt. Ala Hubeishi, 21, of Julis, and Sgt. Rotem Shani, 19, of Hod Hasharon were killed and two soldiers were injured in the morning when a tank escorting a civilian convoy drove over a land mine and exploded on the Karni-Netzarim road in the Gaza Strip. Terrorists hiding in a nearby mosque detonated the remote-controlled explosive charge beneath the armored vehicle. The Democratic Front for the Liberation of Palestine and the Fatah's al-Aksa Martyrs Brigade both claimed responsibility.

Mar 17, 2002 - Noa Auerbach, 18, of Kfar Sava was killed and 16 people were injured when a terrorist opened fire on passersby in the center of Kfar Sava. The gunman was shot and killed by police.

Mar 19, 2002 - 1st Lt. Tal Zemach, 20, of Kibbutz Hulda, was killed and three soldiers were injured when Palestinian terrorists opened fire on them in the Jordan Valley. Hamas claimed responsibility for the attack.

Mar 20, 2002 - Sgt. Michael Altfiro, 19, of Pardes Hanna; St.-Sgt. Shimon Edri, 20, of Pardes Hanna; SWO Meir Fahima, 40, of Hadera; Cpl. Aharon Revivo, 19, of Afula; Alon Goldenberg, 28, of Tel Aviv; Mogus Mahento, 75, of Holon; and Bella Schneider, 53, of Hadera were killed and about 30 people were wounded, several seriously, in a suicide bombing of an Egged bus No. 823 traveling from Tel Aviv to Nazareth at the Musmus junction on Highway 65 (Wadi Ara) near Afula. The Islamic Jihad claimed responsibility for the attack.

Mar 21, 2002 - Gadi (34) and Tzipi (29) Shemesh, of Jerusalem and Yitzhak Cohen, 48, of Modi'in were killed and 86 people injured, 3 of them seriously, in a suicide bombing on King George Street in the center of Jerusalem. The terrorist detonated the bomb, packed with metal spikes and nails, in the center of a crowd of shoppers. The Fatah al-Aqsa Brigades claimed responsibility for the attack.

Mar 24, 2002 - Esther Kleiman, 23, of Neve Tzuf, was killed in a shooting attack northwest of Ramallah, while traveling to work in a reinforced Egged bus.

Mar 24, 2002 - Avi Sabag, 24, of Otniel was killed in a terrorist shooting south of Hebron.

Mar 26, 2002 - Major Cengiz Soytunc of Turkey and Catherine Berruex of Switzerland, members of the TIPH observer force in Hebron, were killed in an ambush shooting by a Palestinian gunman near Halhul.

Mar 27, 2002 - Twenty-nine people were killed and 140 injured - 20 seriously - in a suicide bombing in the Park Hotel in the coastal city of Netanya, in the midst of the Passover holiday seder with 250 guests. Hamas claimed responsibility for the attack. The victims: Shula Abramovitch, 63, of Holon; David Anichovitch, 70, of Netanya; Sgt.-Maj. Avraham Beckerman, 25, of Ashdod; Shimon Ben-Aroya, 42, of Netanya; Andre Fried, 47, of Netanya; Idit Fried, 47, of Netanya; Miriam Gutenzgan, 82, Ramat Gan; Ami Hamami, 44, of Netanya; Perla Hermele, 79, of Sweden; Dvora Karim, 73, of Netanya;

Michael Karim, 78, of Netanya; Yehudit Korman, 70, of Ramat Hasharon; Marianne Lehmann Zaoui, 77, of Netanya; Lola Levkovitch, 85, of Jerusalem; Furuk Na'imi, 62, of Netanya; Eliahu Nakash, 85, of Tel-Aviv; Irit Rashel, 45, of Moshav Herev La'et; Yulia Talmi, 87, of Tel-Aviv; St.-Sgt. Sivan Vider, 20, of Bekaot; Ernest Weiss, 79, of Petah Tikva; Eva Weiss, 75, of Petah Tikva; Meir (George) Yakobovitch, 76, of Holon. Chanah Rogan, 92, of Netanya; Zee'v Vider, 50, of Moshav Bekaot; Alter Britvich, 88, and his wife Frieda, 86, of Netanya died of their injuries on April 2 3. Sarah Levy-Hoffman, 89, of Tel-Aviv died of her injuries on April 7. Anna Yakobovitch, 78, of Holon died of her injuries on April 11. Eliezer Korman, 74, of Ramat Hasharon died of his wounds on May 5.

Mar 28, 2002 - Rachel and David Gavish, 50, their son Avraham Gavish, 20, and Rachel's father Yitzhak Kanner, 83, were killed when a terrorist infiltrated the community of Elon Moreh in Samaria, entered their home and opened fire on its inhabitants. Hamas claimed responsibility for the attack.

Mar 29, 2002 - Tuvia Wisner, 79, of Petah Tikva and Michael Orlansky, 70, of Tel-Aviv were killed Friday morning, when a Palestinian terrorist infiltrated the Neztarim settlement in the Gaza Strip.

Mar 29, 2002 - Lt. Boaz Pomerantz, 22, of Kiryat Shmona and St.-Sgt. Roman Shliapstein, 22, of Ma'ale Efraim were killed in the course of the IDF anti-terrorist action in Ramallah (Operation Defensive Shield).

Mar 29, 2002 - Rachel Levy, 17, and Haim Smadar, 55, the security guard, both of Jerusalem, were killed and 28 people were injured, two seriously, when a female suicide bomber blew herself up in the Kiryat Yovel supermarket in Jerusalem. The Fatah Al-Aqsa Martyrs Brigades claimed responsibility for the attack.

Mar 30, 2002 - Border Policeman Sgt.-Maj. Constantine Danilov, 23, of Or Akiva was shot and killed in Baka al-Garbiyeh, during an exchange of fire with two Palestinians trying to cross into Israel to carry out a suicide attack. The Fatah Al-Aqsa Martyrs Brigades claimed responsibility.

Mar 31, 2002 - Fifteen people were killed and over 40 injured in a suicide bombing in Haifa, in the Matza restaurant of the gas station near the Grand Canyon shopping mall. Hamas claimed responsibility for the attack. The victims: Suheil Adawi, 32, of Turan; Dov Chernevroda, 67, of Haifa; Shimon Koren, 55; his sons Ran, 18, and Gal, 15, of Haifa; Moshe Levin, 52, of Haifa; Danielle Manchell, 22, of Haifa; Orly Ofir, 16, of Haifa; Aviel Ron, 54; his son Ofer, 18, and daughter Anat, 21, of Haifa; Ya'akov Shani, 53, of Haifa; Adi Shiran, 17, of Haifa; Daniel Carlos Wegman, 50, of Haifa. Carlos Yerushalmi, 52, of Karkur, died on April 1 of wounds sustained in the attack.

Apr 1, 2002 - Sgt.-Maj. Ofir Roth, 22, of Gan Yoshiya, an IDF reserve soldier, was killed at a roadblock near Jerusalem's Har Homa neighborhood by a Palestinian sniper firing from Beit Sahur, near Bethlehem.

Apr 1, 2002 - Tomer Mordechai, 19, of Tel-Aviv, a policeman, was killed in Jerusalem, when a Palestinian suicide bomber driving toward the city center blew himself up after being stopped at a roadblock. The Fatah al-Aqsa Martyrs Brigades claimed responsibility for the attack.

Apr 3, 2002 - IDF reservist Maj. Moshe Gerstner, 29, of Rishon Lezion was killed in Jenin during anti-terrorist action (Operation Defensive Shield).

Apr 4, 2002 - Rachel Charhi, 36, of Bat-Yam, critically injured in a suicide bombing in a cafe on the corner of Allenby and Bialik streets in Tel-Aviv on March 30, died of her wounds. Some 30 others were injured in the attack. The Fatah Al-Aqsa Martyrs Brigades claimed responsibility.

Apr 4, 2002 - Border Police Supt. Patrick Pereg, 30, of Rosh Ha'ayin, head of operations in an undercover unit, was killed while attempting to arrest a wanted member of Fatah's al-Aqsa Martyrs Brigade.

Apr 4, 2002 - Sgt.-Maj.(res.) Einan Sharabi, 32, of Rehovot; Lt. Nissim Ben-David, 22, of Ashdod; and St.-Sgt. Gad Ezra, 23, of Bat-Yam were killed during the IDF anti-terrorist action in Jenin (Operation Defensive Shield).

Apr 5, 2002 - Sgt. Marom Moshe Fisher, 19, of Moshav Avigdor; Sgt. Ro'i Tal, 21, of Ma'alot; and Sgt. Oded Kornfein, 20, of Kibbutz Ha'on - were killed in exchanges of fire between IDF troops and Palestinian gunmen in Jenin (Operation Defensive Shield).

Apr 6, 2002 - St.-Sgt. Nisan Avraham, 26, of Lod was killed and five other soldiers were lightly injured when two Palestinian gunmen opened fire and threw grenades at the entrance to Rafiah Yam in the Gaza Strip. The Palestinians, members of the Islamic Jihad, were killed.

Apr 8, 2002 - St.-Sgt. Matanya Robinson, 21, of Kibbutz Tirat Zvi, and Sgt. Shmuel Weiss, 19, of Kiryat Arba were killed in an ambush by Palestinian gunfire in the Jenin refugee camp (Operation Defensive Shield).

Apr 9, 2002 - Thirteen IDF soldiers were killed and 7 injured in the Jenin refugee camp by Palestinian terrorists. An IDF patrol by reserve soldiers was ambushed during operations in the refugee camp. Explosive devices were detonated against them, as well as gunfire directed against the soldiers from the rooftops of the surrounding buildings. The soldiers killed: Maj.(res.) Oded Golomb, 22, of Kibbutz Nir David; Capt.(res.) Ya'akov Azoulai, 30, of Migdal Ha'emek; Lt.(res.) Dror Bar, 28, of Kibbutz Einat; Lt.(res.) Eyal Yoel, 28, of Kibbutz Ramat Rachel; 1st Sgt.(res.) Tiran Arazi, 33, of Hadera; 1st Sgt.(res.) Yoram Levy, 33, of Elad; 1st Sgt.(res.) Avner Yaskov, 34, of Be'er Sheva; Sgt. 1st Class (res.) Ronen Alshochat, 27, of Ramle; gt. 1st Class (res.) Eyal Eliyahu Azouri, 27, of Ramat Gan; Sgt. 1st Class (res.) Amit Busidan, 22, of Bat Yam; Sgt. 1st Class (res.) Menashe Hava, 23, of Kfar Sava; Sgt. 1st Class (res.) Shmuel Dani Mayzlish, 27, of Moshav Hemed; Sgt. 1st Class (res.) Eyal Zimmerman, 22, of Ra'anana.

Apr 9, 2002 - Maj. Assaf Assoulin, 30, of Tel Aviv was killed in an exchange of fire in Nablus.

Apr 9, 2002 - St.-Sgt. Gedalyahu Malik, 21, of Jerusalem was killed and 12 soldiers were injured in Jenin when an explosive charge was thrown at a patrol.

Apr 10, 2002 - Avinoam Alfia, 26, of Kiryat Ata; Sgt.-Maj.(res.) Shlomi Ben Haim, 27, of Kiryat Yam; Sgt.-Maj.(res.) Nir Danieli, 24, of Kiryat Ata; Border Police Lance Cpl. Keren

Franco, 18, of Kiryat Yam; Sgt.-Maj.(res.) Ze'ev Hanik, 24, of Karmiel; Border Police Lance Cpl. Noa Shlomo, 18, of Nahariya; Prison Warrant Officer Shimshon Stelkol, 33, of Kiryat Yam; and Sgt. Michael Weissman, 21, of Kiryat Yam were killed and 22 people injured in a suicide bombing on Egged bus #960, en route from Haifa to Jerusalem, which exploded near Kibbutz Yagur, east of Haifa. Hamas claimed responsibility for the attack.

Apr 12, 2002 - Lt. Dotan Nahtomi, 22, of Kibbutz Tzuba, died of wounds sustained earlier in the week during IDF operations in Dura (Operation Defensive Shield).

Apr 12, 2002 - Border policeman St.-Sgt. David Smirnoff, 22, of Ashdod was killed when a Palestinian gunman opened fire near the Erez crossing, in the Gaza Strip, killing one and injuring another four Israelis. The terrorist killed one and injured three Palestinian workers in the same shooting spree. The Islamic Jihad claimed responsibility for the attack.

Apr 12, 2002 - Nissan Cohen, 57; Rivka Fink, 75; Suheila Hushi, 48; and Yelena Konrab, 43, all of Jerusalem; and Ling Chang Mai, 34, and Chai Siang Yang, 32, both foreign workers from China, were killed and 104 people were wounded when a woman suicide bomber detonated a powerful charge at a bus stop on Jaffa road at the entrance to Jerusalem's Mahane Yehuda open-air market. The Al-Aqsa Martyrs' Brigades claimed responsibility for the attack.

Apr 20, 2002 - Border Policeman St.-Sgt. Uriel Bar-Maimon, 21 of Ashkelon was killed in an exchange of fire near the Erez industrial park in the northern Gaza Strip. Israeli forces pursued the Palestinian gunman and killed him. An explosive belt was found on his body. The Fatah Al-Aqsa Martyrs Brigades claimed responsibility.

Apr 22, 2002 - Sgt. Maj. Nir Krichman, 22 of Hadera, was killed in an exchange of gunfire, when IDF forces entered the village of Asira a-Shamaliya, north of Nablus, to arrest known Hamas terrorists.

Apr 27, 2002 - Danielle Shefi, 5; Arik Becker, 22; Katrina (Katya) Greenberg, 45; and Ya'acov Katz, 51, all of Adora, were killed when terrorists dressed in IDF uniforms and combat gear cut through the settlement's defensive perimeter fence and entered Adora, west of Hebron. Seven other people were injured, one seriously. The terrorists entered several homes, firing on people in their bedrooms. Both Hamas and the PFLP claimed responsibility for the attack.

May 3, 2002 - IDF officer Major Avihu Ya'akov, 24, of Kfar Hasidim, was killed and two other soldiers injured in Nablus in a raid against a terror cell that was planning a suicide attack in Israel.

May 7, 2002 - Fifteen people were killed and 55 wounded in a crowded game club in Rishon Lezion, southeast of Tel-Aviv, when a suicide bomber detonated a powerful charge in the 3rd floor club, causing part of the building to collapse. Hamas claimed responsibility for the attack. The victims: Esther Bablar, 54, of Bat Yam; Yitzhak Bablar, 57, of Bat Yam; Avi Bayaz, 26, of Nes Ziona; Regina Malka Boslan, 62, of Jaffa; Edna Cohen, 61, of Holon; Rafael Haim, 64, of Tel-Aviv; Pnina Hikri, 60, of Tel-Aviv; Nawa Hinawi, 51, of Tel-Aviv; Rahamim Kimhi, 58, of Rishon Lezion; Nir Lovatin, 31, of Rishon Lezion; Shoshana Magmari, 51, of Tel-Aviv; Dalia Masa, 56, of Nahalat Yehuda; Rassan Sharouk, 60, of Holon; Israel Shikar, 49, of Rishon Lezion; Anat Teremforush, 36, of Ashdod.

May 12, 2002 - Nisan Dolinger, 43, of Pe'at Sadeh in the southern Gaza Strip was shot and killed by a Palestinian laborer. The assailant was apprehended.

May 19, 2002 - Yosef Haviv, 70, Victor Tatrinov, 63, and Arkady Vieselman, 40, all of Netanya, were killed and 59 people were injured - 10 seriously - when a suicide bomber, disguised as a soldier, blew himself up in the market in Netanya. Both Hamas and the PFLP took responsibility for the attack.

May 22, 2002 - Elmar Dezhabrielov, 16, and Gary Tauzniaski, 65, both of Rishon Lezion, were killed and about 40 people were wounded when a suicide bomber detonated himself in the Rothschild Street downtown pedestrian mall of Rishon Lezion.

May 24, 2002 - Reserve IDF Sgt. 1st Class Oren Tzelnik, 23, of Bat Yam was killed and two soldiers wounded when terrorists opened fire on their APC during a counter-terrorist operation in Tulkarm.

May 27, 2002 - Ruth Peled, 56, of Herzliya and her infant granddaughter Sinai Keinan, aged 14 months, of Petah Tikva were killed and 37 people were injured, some seriously, when a suicide bomber detonated himself near an ice cream parlor outside a shopping mall in Petah Tikva. The Fatah Al-Aqsa Martyrs' Brigades claimed responsibility for the attack.

May 28, 2002 - Albert Maloul, 50, of Jerusalem, was killed when shots were fired at the car in which he was traveling south on the Ramallah bypass road. Maloul and his cousin, who was lightly injured, were returning home to Jerusalem from Eli, where they operate the swimming pool. The Fatah Al Aqsa Martyrs' Brigades claimed responsibility for the attack.

May 28, 2002 - Netanel Riachi, 17, of Kochav Ya'akov; Gilad Stiglitz, 14, of Yakir; and Avraham Siton, 17, of Shilo - three yeshiva high school students - were killed and two others wounded in Itamar, southeast of Nablus, when a Palestinian gunman infiltrated the community and opened fire on the teenagers playing basketball, before he was shot dead by a security guard. The Fatah Al Aqsa Martyrs' Brigades claimed responsibility for the attack.

June 5, 2002 - 17 people were killed and 38 injured when a car packed with a large quantity of explosives struck Egged bus No. 830 traveling from Tel-Aviv to Tiberias at the Megiddo junction near Afula. The bus, which burst into flames, was completely destroyed. The terrorist, who drove the car bomb, was killed in the blast. The Islamic Jihad claimed responsibility for the attack. The victims: Cpl. Liron Avitan, 19, of Hadera; Cpl. Avraham Barzilai, 19, of Netanya; Cpl. Dennis Bleuman, 20, of Hadera; St.-Sgt. Eliran Buskila, 21, of Hadera; St.-Sgt. Zvi Gelberd, 20 of Hadera; Sgt. Violetta Hizgayev, 20, of Hadera; St.-Sgt. Ganadi Issakov, 21, of Hadera; Sgt. Sariel Katz, 21, of Netanya; Cpl. Vladimir Morari, 19, of Hadera; Sgt. Yigal Nedipur, 21, of Netanya; Sgt. Dotan Reisel, 22, of Hadera; St.-Sgt. David Stanislavksy, 23, of Netanya; Sgt. Sivan Wiener, 19, of Holon; Zion Agmon, 50, of Hadera; Adi Dahan, 17, of Afula; Shimon Timsit, 35, of Tel-Aviv. The 17th victim, a man aged about 50-60, was not identified, and was laid to rest on June 20 in the Ashkelon cemetery.

June 6, 2002 - Erez Rund, 18, of Ofra died of gunshot wounds to the chest sustained in a shooting attack near Ofra, north of Ramallah, when Palestinian terrorists opened fire from an ambush.

June 8, 2002 - St.-Sgt. Eyal Sorek, 23, his wife Yael, 24 - 9 months pregnant - of Carmei Tzur, and St.-Sgt.-Maj.(res.) Shalom Mordechai, 35, of Nahariya were killed and five others injured when terrorists infiltrated the community of Carmei Tzur in the Gush Etzion bloc and opened fire at 2:30 am. The Hamas claimed responsibility for the attack.

June 11, 2002 - Hadar Hershkowitz, 14, of Herzliya was killed and 15 others were wounded when a Palestinian suicide bomber set off a relatively small pipe bomb at a shwarma restaurant in Herzliya.

June 15, 2002 - St.-Sgt. Haim Yehezkel (Hezki) Gutman, 22, of Beit El, and St.-Sgt. Alexei Gladkov, 20, of Be'er Sheva were killed and four soldiers were wounded in a confrontation with terrorists near Alei Sinai and Dugit in the northern Gaza Strip. Hamas claimed responsibility.
Lt. Anatoly Krasik, 22, of Petah Tikva died of his wounds on June 22.

June 18, 2002 - Nineteen people were killed and 74 were injured - six seriously - in a suicide bombing at the Patt junction in Egged bus no. 32A traveling from Gilo to the center of Jerusalem. The bus, which was completely destroyed, was carrying many students on their way to school. Hamas claimed responsibility for the attack. The names of 18 of the victims have been released: Boaz Aluf, 54, of Jerusalem; Shani Avi-Zedek, 15, of Jerusalem; Leah Baruch, 59, of Jerusalem; Mendel Bereson, 72, of Jerusalem; Rafael Berger, 28, of Jerusalem; Michal Biazi, 24, of Jerusalem; Tatiana Braslavsky, 41, of Jerusalem; Galila Bugala, 11, of Jerusalem; Raisa Dikstein, 67, of Jerusalem; Dr. Moshe Gottlieb, 70, of Jerusalem; Baruch Gruani, 60, of Jerusalem; Orit Hayla, 21, of Jerusalem; Helena Ivan, 63, of Jerusalem; Iman Kabha, 26, of Barta; Shiri Negari, 21, of Jerusalem; Gila Nakav, 55, of Jerusalem; Yelena Plagov, 42, of Jerusalem; Liat Yagen, 24 of Jerusalem; Rahamim Zidkiyahu, 51, of Jerusalem.

June 19, 2002 - Noa Alon, 60, of Ofra; Gal Eisenman, 5, of Ma'ale Adumim; Michal Franklin, 22, of Jerusalem; Tatiana Igelski, 43, of Moldova; Hadassah Jungreis, 20, of Migdal Haemek; Gila Sara Kessler, 19, of Eli; and Shmuel Yerushalmi, 17, of Shilo were killed and 50 people were injured - three of them in critical condition - when a suicide bomber blew himself up at a crowded bus stop and hitchhiking post at the French Hill intersection in northern Jerusalem shortly after 7:00 P.M., as people were returning home from work. The Fatah Al-Aqsa Martyrs Brigades claimed responsibility for the attack.

June 19, 2002 - Maj. Shlomi Cohen, 26, of Rehovot and St.-Sgt. Yosef Talbi, 20, of Yehud were killed and four soldiers were wounded Wednesday night in Kalkilya when Palestinian gunmen opened fire while the soldiers were in pursuit of two terrorists inside a building.

June 20, 2002 - Rachel Shabo, 40, and three of her sons - Neria, 16, Zvika, 12, and Avishai, 5, as well as a neighbor, Yosef Twito, 31, who came to their aid, were murdered when a terrorist entered their home in Itamar, south of Nablus, and opened fire. Two other children were injured, as well as two soldiers. The terrorist was killed by IDF forces. The PFLP and the Fatah Al Aqsa Brigades claimed responsibility for the attack.

Israel's Peculiar Position

Eric Hoffer
Los Angeles Times
May 26, 1968

The Jews are a peculiar people: things permitted to other nations are forbidden to the Jews.

Other nations drive out thousands, even millions of people and there is no refugee problem. Russia did it, Poland and Czechoslovakia did it, Turkey threw out a million Greeks, and Algeria a million Frenchman. Indonesia threw out heaven knows how many Chinese-and no one says a word about refugees.

But in the case of Israel the displaced Arabs have become eternal refugees. Everyone insists that Israel must take back every single Arab. Arnold Toynbee calls the displacement of the Arabs an atrocity greater than any committed by the Nazis.

Other nations when victorious on the battlefield dictate peace terms. But when Israel is victorious it must sue for peace. Everyone expects the Jews to be the only real Christians in this world.

Other nations when they are defeated survive and recover but should Israel be defeated it would be destroyed. Had Nasser triumphed last June he would have wiped Israel off the map, and no one would have lifted a finger to save the Jews.

No commitment to the Jews by any government, including our own, is worth the paper it is written on. There is a cry of outrage all over the world when people die in Vietnam or when two Negroes are executed in Rhodesia. But when Hitler slaughtered Jews no one remonstrated with him.

The Swedes, who are ready to break off diplomatic relations with America because of what we do in Vietnam, did not let out a peep when Hitler was slaughtering Jews. They sent Hitler choice iron ore, and ball bearings, and serviced his troop trains to Norway.

The Jews are alone in the world. If Israel survives, it will be solely because of Jewish efforts. And Jewish resources.

Yet at this moment Israel is our only reliable and unconditional ally. We can rely more on Israel than Israel can rely on us. And one has only to imagine what would have happened last summer had the Arabs and their Russian backers won the war to realize how vital the survival of Israel is to America and the West in general.

I have a premonition that will not leave me; as it goes with Israel so will it go with all of us. Should Israel perish the holocaust will be upon us.

Israel's Moment Of Truth

Daniel Pipes
Commentary Magazine
February, 2000

It might appear that things have never been going better for Israel, or worse for those who wish it ill.

Consider: the Jewish state has signed peace treaties with Egypt and Jordan, and five agreements with the Palestinian Authority (PA), its "partner for peace." With Syria, high-level negotiations now under way appear so promising that both sides have publicly predicted they could be wrapped up within a few months. Other diplomatic ties are stronger than ever: Israel has a powerful regional ally in Turkey, enjoys growing links to such giants as India and China, and is generally shedding the near-pariah status that hobbled it in the recent past. The connection to the United States is warm, deep, personal, and reciprocal.

Should diplomacy fail for any reason, moreover, Israel can fall back on its military strength. As the only country in the Middle East participating in the much-bruited "revolution in military affairs"--essentially, the application of high-tech to armaments--it has built so great a lead in conventional arms, including planes and tanks, that several Arab states have basically conceded they cannot compete with it on that level. Instead, they have directed their attention higher (to weapons of mass destruction) and lower (to terrorism). But even in those arenas, Israel is far from helpless: it has a missile-defense system, the Arrow, in the works and, for retaliatory purposes, weapons of mass destruction of its own, as well as formidable anti-terrorist capabilities.

Security matters hardly exhaust the list of Israel's advantages. Economically, it enjoys today a per-capita income of $18,000, placing it a bit ahead of Spain and a bit behind Canada--in other words, in the big leagues. Better yet, it has shown a very impressive annual growth rate since 1990. Thanks to its "Silicon Wadi," Israel is a high-tech giant, with a computer and Internet sector larger in absolute terms than that of any other country in the world outside the United States. Demographically, the birth rate of 2.6 children per woman among Israeli Jews is one of the highest in the West, and the country also remains a magnet for immigration; with 5 million Jews, it is quickly gaining on the United States as the place with the largest Jewish population in the world.

Finally, there is the political scene. Unlike its neighbors and rivals, Israel benefits from a lively and robust civic culture in which everyone has his say, party lines are (notoriously) fluid, and no one defers to politicians. And yet, however colorful and argumentative the public forum, when it comes to key security issues the major parties find much common ground. In last year's elections, for example, the two candidates for the post of prime minister differed on the tone and pace but hardly at all on the substance of the peace process: yes, they concurred, the Palestinians should do more to live up to their promises, but no, their failings in this area were not reason enough to cut off negotiations.

If Israelis appear to be faring well, Arabs--and Iran, too--seem to be faring less well. Arab countries are, in the words of a UN official, "particularly exceptional in being the highest spenders in the world on military purposes": they devote 8.8 percent of their GDP to the military, versus 2.4 percent for the world as a whole. Nevertheless, despite all this spending, Arab conventional forces are in decline. To be sure, a few states (like Egypt) have access to advanced American arms, but their lack of technical proficiency means that they are nearly always consumers of military hardware, paying for completed goods that others have to teach them how to operate.

Allies? The Soviet Union is gone, and no one has come close to replacing it. The Arab states darkly suspect the United States of engaging in conspiracies against them, and these suspicions—as, most recently, in the case of the EgyptAir crash off New York—impede closer relations with the world's only superpower. Arabs also lack an effective counterpunch to the pro-Israel lobby in Washington, and have failed to respond to the growing cooperation between Turkey and Israel in a way that would advance their own interests.

Outside Israel, the Middle East boasts--if that is the right word--the world's highest quotient of autocratic regimes, not to mention an inordinate number of rogue states, including Iran, Iraq, Syria, Sudan, and Libya. A culture of deference and intimidation remains dominant everywhere; movements for democracy and human rights are feeble. Arab states are particularly vulnerable to Islamism, a totalitarian ideology in the tradition of fascism and Marxism-Leninism. While Islamists have suffered reverses in recent years, they are still the major opposition force in countries like Algeria, Egypt, and Saudi Arabia, threatening the stability of government after government.

Nor are Arab economies doing well. The recent jump in oil prices, however welcome to producers, cannot obscure some dismal realities, principally a per-capita annual income among Arabic-speaking peoples that does not rise to one-tenth of Israel's. Yes, Kuwait weighs in (just like Israel) at $18,000; but in Yemen the annual per-capita income is $270; more to the point, Egypt, Jordan, and Syria all hover in the neighborhood of $1,000. A paltry one percent of world equity flowing to emerging markets these days ends up in Arabic-speaking countries. When it comes to high technology, the Middle East is a black hole, with few sales and even less innovation. As the historian R. Stephen Humphreys has noted, "with the partial exception of Turkey and of course Israel ... there is not one Middle Eastern manufactured item that can be sold competitively on world markets."

Demographically, the Arabs and Iran have too much of a good thing: a birth rate so high that schools cannot maintain standards, and economies cannot manufacture enough jobs. The demographer Onn Winckler has named population growth as the Middle East's "most critical socioeconomic problem."

Taken together, all these factors seem to suggest that Israel has at long last achieved a definitive edge over its historic enemies. Such, indeed, appears to be the view of Israeli leaders themselves. Thanks to Israel's position of strength, Prime Minister Ehud Barak now speaks confidently of an "end to wars" and of his country's being finally accepted as a permanent presence by its neighbors. These sentiments are widely echoed both in Israel and in Washington.

And yet--two trends suggest otherwise. The first has to do with Arab strengths, the second with Israeli weaknesses. In both cases, the phenomena I will be discussing are only partly material in nature, lying more in the realm of such elusive and intangible qualities as internal spirit and morale. But these are precisely the qualities that in the end can decide the fates of nations and peoples. Some improvements in the Arab position, whether actual or imminent, have long been recognized: greater control over a huge portion of the world's oil and gas reserves, steady acquisition of weapons of mass destruction, movement toward economic modernization (notably in Egypt). Progress in any or all of these areas can seriously threaten Israel's qualitative edge and its security in the medium term--unless Arab enmity toward the Jewish state has dissipated in the interim. But just here is where the greatest reason for concern resides.

Historically, Arab "rejectionism"--that is, the refusal to accept the permanent existence of a sovereign Jewish state in its historic homeland --has been based on one or another local variant (pan-Arab, pan-Syrian, Palestinian, or the like) of nationalism, a European import into the Middle East. It has suffered from two disabilities: limited reach and factionalism. But as, recent years, the rejection of Israel has taken on a less secular and more Islamic complexion, it has gained a deeper resonance among ordinary Arabs, with Israel's existence now cast as an affront to God's will, and has also benefited operationally from a somewhat greater degree of unity (Islamists are surprisingly good at working together). The net effect has been not to moderate but, on the contrary, to solidify and to sharpen Arab antagonism to Israel--vocal rejectionist elements now include pious Muslims and Islamists, Arab nationalists, despots, and intellectuals--and to give fresh impetus to the age-old dream of destroying it.

The point cannot be made often or strongly enough that, in their great majority, Arabic speakers do continue to repudiate the idea of peace with Israel. Despite having lost six rounds of war, they seem nothing loath to try again. In one of the most recent in-depth surveys of Arab opinion, conducted by the political scientist Hilal Khashan of the American University of Beirut, sixteen hundred respondents, divided equally among Jordanians, Lebanese, Palestinians, and Syrians, stated by a ratio of 69 to 28 percent that they personally did not want peace with Israel. By 79 to 18 percent, they rejected the idea of doing business with Israelis even after a total peace. By 80 to 19 percent, they rejected learning about Israel. By 87 to 13 percent, they supported attacks by Islamic groups against Israel.

This is the view of Israel that dominates political debate in the Arab world and that is conveyed to the public in every arena from scholarly discourse to the popular media to nursery-school jingles. True, some Arabs think otherwise. The late King Hussein of Jordan spoke eloquently of the need to put aside the conflict with Israel and to get on with things; his son and successor appears to be of like mind. Some Arab army officers would undoubtedly prefer not to confront Israel's military forces any time soon. Kuwaitis and Lebanese Christians, sobered by occupation, now mostly wish to leave Israel alone. And there are business leaders who believe, as one Arab banker succinctly put it, that "the whole purpose of peace is business." But these elements, overall, represent but a minority of the Arab population, and have not shifted the underlying hostility.

An incident from the sports pages makes the point. Only a few months ago, Israeli athletes ventured on a first-ever official match to an Arab capital--the capital not of a front-line "confrontation state" but of the tiny and moderate Persian Gulf sheikhdom of Qatar. The experience turned out to be, as Agence France-Presse aptly characterized it, "a bruising ordeal." Forced to live in nearly complete isolation from other athletes, the Israeli champions had to enter and leave their hotel via a side door. Among the flags of the competing nations, Israel's alone was not raised in public. Huge crowds turned up to jeer at the Jewish athletes, and the media touted their presence as "an occasion to express the Arabs' rejection of all that is Israeli."

Twenty years of relations between Egypt and Israel since the treaty of 1979 testify bitterly to the same state of affairs. Formally there is peace, but Cairo permits, even sponsors, a vicious propaganda campaign against Israel that includes the crudest forms of anti-Semitism, and it is rapidly building up offensive military forces that could be deployed against the Jewish state. In effect, Egyptian authorities are telling their people, for all sorts of reasons we have to be in contact with Israelis and sign certain pieces of paper, but we still hate them, and you should, too. In Jordan, where the government does not play this double game, things are in some ways worse: the best efforts of two kings have failed to induce in the Jordanian populace a more peaceable and friendly outlook toward Israel.

Fueling the dream of Arab rejectionists is the immensely important fact that within Israel itself (that is, within the 1967 borders), the Jewish proportion of the population has fallen from a one-time high of 87 percent to 79 percent today, and is inexorably trailing downward. In 1998, of Israel's total population growth of 133,000, only 80,000 were Jews, with Arabs making up the bulk of the remainder. From such statistics, some demographers predict a non-Jewish majority by the middle of the 21st century.

But the Jewish nature of the "Jewish state" will shift in the Arabs' favor long before they reach majority status there. At present, were Israeli Arabs to be represented in the Knesset in proportion to their numbers, they would already hold 24 out of its 120 seats. Even with the seven seats they now occupy, as the analyst Eric Rozenman has noted, the Arab electorate and Arab Knesset members ... have helped override Jewish majorities on such vital matters as the creation of Prime Minister Yitzhak Rabin's coalition in 1992 and approval of the Oslo and Oslo II accords in 1993 and 1995 respectively. All seven Israeli Arab members voted for both agreements; the former passed 61 to 50, with nine abstentions, the latter passed 61 to 59.

These trends will undoubtedly persist, Rozenman writes, especially as Israeli Arabs become "energized by a new Palestinian state next door (and perhaps also by an increasingly Palestinian Jordan)." By the time the numbers of Arabs approach or even exceed parity with the Jews, "the state might still be democratic, but the civic atmosphere, the public culture, would not likely be Jewish in the tacit, general sense it is today."

The growing power and enfranchisement of Muslims in the United States provide further grounds for Arab optimism. Not only is the American Muslim community approaching the Jewish community in absolute size, it is also making strides in education, economic well-being, and political savvy. If the old pro-Arab lobby was hampered by its dependence on oil money, retired American diplomats, and left-wing Christian Arabs, dynamic new organizations like the American Muslim Council and the Council on American-Islamic Relations are another matter altogether. Although foreign policy is hardly their only cause, "Palestine" remains the single most mobilizing issue for American Muslims, and the position articulated by Muslim organizations on this issue is almost uniformly extremist--against negotiations with Israel or almost any form of accommodation with it.

Not only are these extremist Muslim organizations intent on making themselves heard, but the Clinton administration, at least, has openly welcomed them at the highest levels. At a dinner she hosted to break the fast of Ramadan this past December, Secretary of State Madeleine K. Albright told her guests: "I want to be sure that the legitimate concerns of Muslim Americans are taken into account when shaping the programs, activities, and reports of this Department." Seated before her was a Who's Who of American Muslim radicals. Is it any wonder that many Arabs, knowing such facts, or hearing such heady words from the lips of the American Secretary of State, should become newly imbued with a sense of confidence about the future? And that sense can only be bolstered by what they see happening on the other side, within Israel itself.

Once renowned for its self-confidence, bravery, and purpose, Israel today is a changed society. Whatever the undoubted strength of its military machine, few in a position to know the heart and soul of the country try to hide the fact of a widespread demoralization, even within that military machine itself. As a retired colonel summed it up neatly, "the Israeli public is really tired of war."

Fatigue takes many forms in contemporary Israel. The pervasive feeling that they have fought long enough, and that the time has come to settle, leads many to express openly their annoyance with the need for military preparedness and the huge expense of maintaining a modern armed force. They are weary of the constant loss of life, they want escape from the fear that terrorism imparts, they yearn to close down an atavistic tribal war--and peace treaties promise a quick way out. (As one Israeli put it to me, "My grandfather, father, myself, and my son have all fought the Arabs; I want to make sure my grandson does not also have to.") Among young people, draft evasion, hitherto all but unknown, has become a serious problem, and within the army itself, morale is hardly what it once was, as the IDF's decidedly unheroic record in Lebanon has revealed to all, including the Hizbullah enemy.

At the same time, Israel's soaring economy has given many citizens a taste for the good life that cannot be easily reconciled with the need for patience and fortitude--and, especially, sacrifice--in confronting a seemingly unchanging enemy. Middle-aged Israeli men are increasingly unwilling to go off and "play soldier" on reserve duty for several weeks a year when they could be at the office increasing their net worth or enjoying what that net worth makes possible. For those with an active social conscience, a number of long-deferred domestic problems--persistent poverty, a faulty educational system, worsening relations between secular and religious--seem much worthier of attention, and of state expenditure, than does grappling endlessly with Israel's opponents.

Finally, Israelis are tired of the moral opprobrium their country has long suffered--at the United Nations, in Western academic circles, and in editorial boardrooms. Indeed, in an extreme reaction to this ongoing moral ostracism, some of the country's foremost intellectuals have, as it were, defected: they have accommodated sizable chunks of the Arab side's version of the Arab-Israeli conflict, promulgating them as important new truths. Thus, to cite an especially influential expression of this line of thinking, the school of "new historians" in Israel argues that the Jewish state is guilty of an "original sin"--the alleged dispossession of Palestine's native inhabitants--and can therefore be considered to some extent illegitimate. Others, known as "post-Zionists," have characterized Jewish nationalism--Zionism--as, if not racist, then at best an outdated and parochial ideology, and one which should no longer form the basis of Israel's public life.

Such ideas, first incubated on the far Left and in the prestige universities, then spread to students, artists, and journalists, and are now the stuff of television documentaries and educational textbooks. As of the current Israeli school year, ninth graders no longer learn that Israel's war of independence in 1948-49 was a battle of the few against the many but, to the contrary, that the Jews enjoyed military superiority over the Arabs. They also learn that many Palestinians fled the country in those war years not to clear the way for invading Arab armies thought to be on their march to victory, but out of well-founded fears of Jewish brutality and terror.

In a front-page report on the introduction of these books into the schools, the New York Times rightly characterized them as marking a "quiet revolution." That revolution has by now reached the cosnsciousness of politicians, business leaders, and even military officers; its impact can hardly be exaggerated. Thanks to the inroads of post-Zionism, as Meyrav Wurmser has observed in the Middle East Quarterly, Israeli society "is now facing a crisis of identity and values that strikes at the basic components and elements of [its] identity: Judaism and nationalism." Without those two components, clearly, little remains of the Zionist project.

What are the implications, for politics and diplomacy, of Israeli fatigue, and of the intense self-absorption that is its corollary? What strikes one above all is how little attention Israelis are paying these days to their Arab neighbors. Sick of fighting, bent on building an Internet economy, they seem to have decided that Arabs feel the same way, and want the same things they do. (In psychology, the term for this is projection.) According to a survey conducted by the Jaffee Center at Tel Aviv University, fully two-thirds of Israelis now agree with the following dubious assertions: that most Palestinians want peace; that signing agreements will end the Arab-Israeli conflict; and that if forced to choose between negotiations and increased military strength, Israel should opt for the former. Prime Minister Ehud Barak perfectly sums up this outlook in his repeated invocation of a peace that will "work for everyone," the unspoken assumption being that Arabs no less than Israelis seek to resolve their century-old conflict on harmonious terms.

Of course, at some level Israelis know full well about continued Arab rejectionism: the signs are too conspicuous for even the most ostrich-like to be truly ignorant. But they have clearly chosen to de-emphasize or even ignore the phenomenon. How else explain the absence of a single full-time Israeli journalist reporting from an Arab capital, or the fact that Hilal Khashan's meticulous survey of Arab opinion, with its thoroughly dismaying news, received no attention whatsoever in the Israeli press when it appeared last summer??? "These are only words. Let them talk," is how Shimon Peres, speaking for many of his countrymen, has airily dismissed the undeniable evidence of Arab feelings and attitudes.

Peres's disdainful remark encapsulates a delusional but widespread Israeli assumption: that peace in the Middle East is Israel's for the making, and that if Israelis want to end the long-drawn-out struggle, they can do so on their own. They can "solve" the Palestinian problem by acceding to the creation of a state in the West Bank and Gaza; they can eliminate anti-Zionism by helping to funnel money to the Arabs, who will use their new-found affluence to become good neighbors (and never to amass more powerful arsenals); or--in the post-Zionist scenario--they can win Arab hearts by dismantling the Jewish attributes of the Jewish state.

Whatever the preferred tactic, the underlying premise is the same: that the key decisions of war and peace in the Arab-Israeli conflict are made in Jerusalem and Tel Aviv rather than--what is in fact the case--in Cairo, Gaza, Amman, and Damascus. Under the spell of this fantasy, Israelis now seem prepared to execute what will amount to a unilateral transfer of hard-won territory--to Syria in the north, to the Palestinian Authority in the center of the country--in the hope that their troubles will thereby disappear. Indeed, they sometimes appear prepared to go to extreme lengths to induce their Arab interlocutors to accept the gifts they mean to confer on them.

Listening to the Israeli prime minister and the foreign minister of Syria as they inaugurated a new round of talks in December 1999, for example, one might have thought that Israel was the party that had instigated--and then lost--the Six-Day War of 1967, and was now desperately suing Damascus for terms. Barak spoke pleadingly of the need "to put behind us the horrors of war and to step forward toward peace," and of creating, "together with our Syrian partners, ... a different Middle East where nations are living side by side in peaceful relationships and in mutual respect and good-neigh-borliness." By contrast, the Syrian foreign minister blustered like a conqueror, insisting that Israel had "provoked" the 1967 clash and demanding the unconditional return of "all its occupied land." The very fact that a prime minister had agreed to meet with a mere foreign minister, breaching a cardinal protocol of diplomacy, was signal enough; that the foreign minister of Syria lacks any decision-making power whatsoever further confirmed who in this encounter was the wooer, who the wooed.

When it comes to Lebanon, Israelis appear to have convinced themselves that the unilateral withdrawal of troops from their "security zone" in the south will cause their main Lebanese opponent, Hizbullah, to leave them alone, despite repeated and overt statements by Hizbullah leadership that it intends to continue fighting until it reaches Jerusalem and that it "will never recognize the existence of a state called Israel even if all the Arabs do so." More, Israelis seem persuaded that prospect of their with-drawal from Lebanon is one of the things that has the Syrians worried, quite as if the best way to scare your enemy were to threaten a retreat.

On the Palestinian track, the ostensibly more muscular party--Israel--has pointed-ly refrained from requiring that the ostensibly more vulnerable party fulfill the many obli-gations it has undertaken since 1993, with the result that the PA has neither turned over criminals and terrorists, nor ceased its unrelenting incitements to violence, nor restricted the size of its armed forces. The PA's logo brazenly shows a map of a future Palestine stretching from the Jordan River to the Mediterranean Sea--a Palestine, that is, not along-side Israel but instead of it. To all this, the Israeli body politic appears to pay no heed.

The newspaper Ha'aretz reports that Israeli negotiators have already conceded in principle to the Palestinian Authority day-to-day control of parts of Jerusalem. At the very end of 1999, when Prime Minister Barak took the unprecedented step of releasing two Palestinian prisoners who had killed Israelis, his action was met, predictably, not with gratitude but with noisy demonstrations chanting aggressive slogans--"Barak, you coward. Our prisoners will not be humiliated"--and by the demand that Israel now let go all of the estimated 1,650 jailed Palestinians. No doubt, the demonstrators will eventually get their way. Israelis are on their own road to peace, and no "partners," however hostile, will deflect them from it.

Today's Israel, in sum, is hugely different from the Israel of old. For four decades and more, the country made steady progress vis-à-vis its enemies through the application of patience and will, backed when necessary by military courage and might. From a fledgling state in 1948 invaded by five Arab armies, it established itself as a pow-erful force, overcoming oil boycotts, terrorism, and the enmity of a superpower. But by the time of the Oslo accord of August 1993, the signs of exhaustion were becoming increasingly manifest; by now they are unmistakable.

As recently as the 1996 national elections, a lively debate took place in Israel over Palestinian non-compliance and over the wisdom of handing the Golan Heights back to Syria. By the time of the 1999 elections, with very little having changed on the ground, those issues had disappeared.Perhaps 10 to 15 percent of the population still adheres to the old Likud view that Israel should keep control of the territories until the Arabs have shown a true change of heart. Today, the debate is over timing and tone, not over substance. Symbolic of the new consensus is the fact that the Third Way, a party that was exclusively focused on retaining the Golan Heights under Israeli control and that took four Knesset seats in 1996, vaporized in 1999, winning not a single seat. Even former Prime Minister Benjamin Netanyahu, the reputed arch-hardliner, signed two empty agreements with Arafat and, on the Syrian track, was ready to concede virtually everything Asad demanded. As Ehud Barak has correctly noted, "there are only microscopic differences between the things Netanyahu was willing to discuss and those discussed by [Shimon] Peres and [Yitzhak] Rabin."

Many who bemoan the weakness of current Israeli policy are tempted to place the onus on Washington. But (to put it symbolically) how can one become exercised over Hillary Clinton's advocacy of a Palestinian state when, only weeks earlier, Simon Peres had already specified a date for such a state's inception? Israelis are perfectly capable of choosing leaders prepared to resist American pressure, and they have done so in the past. The collapse of a meaningful opposition party in 1999--the son and political heir of Menachem Begin, who won two elections as prime minister in 1997 and 1981, had to withdraw from the race because his support was so trivial--rebuts the notion that weak politicians are doing the bidding of Washington; rather, they are doing the bidding of their electorate. No, it is inward to the Israeli spirit that one must look for the roots of the present disposition to ignore repeated Palestinian flouting of solemnly signed agreements, to turn the Golan Heights over to a still-fanged Syria, to withdraw unilaterally from Lebanon, and to acquiesce in huge American sales of military equipment to an unfriendly and potentially quite ominously threatening Egypt.

Israel today has money and weapons, the Arabs have will. Israelis want a resolution to conflict, Arabs want victory. Israel has high capabilities and low morale, the Arabs have low capabilities and high morale. Again and again, the record of world history shows, victory goes not to the side with greater firepower, but to the side with greater determination.

Among democracies, few precedents exist for the malaise now on display in Israel. Imperfect analogies include the atmosphere of pacifism and appeasement that pervaded significant sectors of opinion in England and France in the 1930s, the United States during the Vietnam period, and Western Europe in the early 1980s. But none of these situations quite matches Israel's in the extent of the debilitation. Even more critically, none of those countries lived with so narrow a margin of safety. The United States lost a long, bloody war in Vietnam, but the nation as a whole was hardly at risk. In Israel the stakes are far higher, the room for error correspondingly minute.

This is not to say that the Jewish state is in immediate danger; it continues to have a strong military and a relatively healthy body politic, and democracies have demonstrated the capacity to right their mistakes at five minutes to midnight. But one shudders to think of what calamity Israel must experience before its people wake up and assume, once again, the grim but inescapable task of facing the implacable enemies around them.

A Letter To Mesora

Alan Keyes
www.mesora.com
April 26, 2000

"I write to express my solidarity with the people of Israel in this difficult time, and to assure you of what I know you cannot doubt, that millions of Americans stand with Israel as well. We will remember the truth of Israel's honorable record, insist that others treat Israel in light of that truth, and not succumb to the cowardly passions of the moment.

When the European Union asserts its moral authority to coerce Israel into a shameful surrender of its just claims, we will remember that many Europeans sat on their hands and did nothing while millions of Jews were slaughtered in the era that gave birth to the State of Israel.

When 'the international community' asserts its moral authority to dictate Israel's security policy, we will remember what the 'international community' did in 1967, when Arab forces were amassing to launch a death blow to Israel, when Egypt's President Nassar kicked out the U.N. troops from the Sinai, and the international community did precisely nothing.

We will remember how the 'international community' sat and waited for those hundreds of thousands of Arab troops to deliver a death blow to Israel, and we will remember that such a blow wasn't thwarted by international outrage, but by the unanticipated brilliance of the Israeli military.

We will remember that Israel acquired the Sinai, West Bank, and Gaza not in a war of conquest, but in a desperate and just defensive war of survival.

We will remember the 'international community,' that territory acquired in a defensive war of survival can, according to universal understanding, international law, and common sense, be retained until a negotiated peace is reached. And we will proclaim the truth that the Israeli people have again and again shown their willingness to put those territories on the table in the hope of achieving just such a negotiated settlement for just peace.

Israel's friends in America will insist that the world acknowledge that the Israelis have shown that they will negotiate in good faith, and keep agreements reached in good faith. We will remember the historic Camp David accords between Israel and Egypt in 1978, which resulted in Israel's peaceful return of the Sinai to the Egyptians. An agreement made, an agreement kept.

We remember that with Egypt, with Jordan, and even quietly with Syria, the Israelis have proved to be a people of their word, when faced with a negotiating partner willing to meet its solemn obligations.

And because we will remember all these things, we will continue to insist that America and international policy recognize the poisonous significance of the unbroken record of murderous deceit which is the history of the PLO, the Palestinian Authority, and Yasser Arafat. While the Israelis have made concession after concession, and followed through with real and dangerous steps, such as turning over to Yasser Arafat authority in the West Bank and Gaza, Arafat has consistently refused to honor those agreements, to make significant conclusions, and to do the one needful thing to stop killing Israelis. We remember, and see to this day, what the 'international community' of appeasement refuses to see that the Palestinian strategy remains the manipulation of all discussion through the intentional use of terrorist violence, and with the ultimate goal of destroying a demoralized, intimidated and isolated Israel.

We will remember these things, and speak the truth about them not only out of respect and solidarity with the decent and heroic people of Israel. We will do so as well because we know that peace for all people of the region cannot be built on a foundation of manipulation, deception, violence.

The first prerequisite for peace, and for self-government, is the restraint of one's own passions and violence out of respect for justice and fairness. Israel's noble restraint is unique in the history of the world. Israel has continued, to this day, to impose on herself the rational restraints of justice and truth, under circumstances of danger and assault far exceeding those normally sufficient to entice a people to submit entirely to rage and retribution. It is difficult to find words to express the contemptibility of the moral lectures such a noble people routinely receive from the self-appointed guardians of moral smugness in Europe and elsewhere.

The people in the Middle East deserve a better fate than tragic self-immolation. They will attain such a better fate only when they understand that the plea of victimization even if truth, which in this case it is not, cannot excuse the surrender to evil in one's own soul. The friends of Israel serve the cause of the people of the entire region when we insist that the path to peace requires dismantling the Palestinian terror machine.

The truth, and the truth alone, will set the Palestinian people free, for they are imprisoned not by Israel's just defense of its right to exist and defend its people, but by the self-imposed hatred that poisons the soul, and withers the future.

Israel is today, as Israel has always been, a sign of hope that G-d's children can seek to be pleasing in His sight. Israel is today, as Israel has always been, hateful in the eyes of those whose neck is stiff, and whose heart is filled with hate and falsehood. Until it shall please G-d to make the land of His special favor a pleasing sight to all the nations, may it please Him to continue to give to all Americans the eyes to see in Israel, as is truly the case, a beacon of justice, courage, and truth.

My prayers, my heart, are with the brave people of Israel."

We Affirm Our Solidarity With Israel

Elie Wiesel
Transcript From Rally In New York City
October 12, 2000

"We have gathered here to affirm our solidarity with Israel. We are outraged by the hypocritical vote in the Security Council, which did not condemn Palestinian excessive reactions but condemned Israel's response to them. We stand by Israel whose present struggle was imposed upon her by the intransigence of the Chairman of the Palestinian Authority.

Those of us who reject hatred and fanaticism as options and who consider peace as the noblest of efforts finally recognize Yasir Arafat for what he is: ignorant, devious and unworthy of trust.

We had hoped for a genuine peace between Israel and her Arab neighbors, including the Palestinians. We had dreams of Israeli and Palestinian children playing together, studying together, laughing together, and discovering each other's worlds. The pain, the agony, the death of any child, Palestinian or Jewish, is a torment to us. But why does Chairman Arafat not protect them but instead uses them as shields for adults throwing stones and worse?

Yes, it is with a heavy heart that we say that our dreams of peace have gone up in the smoke of ransacked synagogues, in the lynching of Israeli prisoners and of blood-thirsty mobs shouting their version of a Jerusalem without Jews and a Middle East without Israel. And I blame the supreme leader of the Palestinians, Yasir Arafat.

By rejecting Israel's unprecedented generous territorial concessions, he is burying the peace process; in so doing, he has betrayed the confidence not only of his negotiating partners but of President Clinton and other western leaders, just as he has betrayed the highest honor society can bestow upon a person. How can a leader, any leader in Israel renew discussions with him before all the kidnapped soldiers are returned to their families?

By unleashing mob violence and bloodshed in the streets rather than guiding his frustrated people toward coexistence and peace, he renounced their legitimate aspirations for a future free of suffering and hatred.

I hold him responsible for the murder of Rabbi Hillel Lieberman and the lynching of two young reservists. All his promises were lies; all his commitments were false. Indeed many peace activists here and in Israel are now reassessing the Oslo accords.

Under Israel sovereignty, Christians, Jews, and Muslims alike could pray without fear in Jerusalem, our capital, which is at the center of Jewish history. A Jew may be Jewish far from Jerusalem; but not without Jerusalem. Though a Jew may not live in Jerusalem, Jerusalem lives inside him.

No other nation's memory is as identified with its memory as ours. No people have been as faithful to its name, or have celebrated its past with as much fervor. None of our prayers are as passionate as those that speak of Jerusalem.

Jerusalem is the dream of our dreams, the light that illuminates our hopeless moments. Its legitimacy lies in its sovereignty. To oppose one is to deny the other. Israel will never give up either. I accuse him of being morally weak, politically shortsighted and an obstacle to peace.

I accuse him of murdering the hopes of an entire generation. His and ours."

Afraid Of The Truth

Natan Sharansky
Israel Report
October 12, 2000

Nearly 20 years ago, confined to an eight-by-ten cell in a prison on the border of Siberia, I was granted by my Soviet jailers the 'privilege' of reading the latest copy of Pravda, official mouthpiece of the Communist regime. Splashed across the front page was a condemnation of Ronald Reagan for having the temerity to call the Soviet Union an 'evil empire.'

Tapping on walls and talking through toilets, prisoners quickly spread the word of Reagan's 'provocation' throughout the prison. The dissidents were ecstatic. Finally, the leader of the free world had spoken the truth - a truth that burned inside the heart of each and everyone of us.

For decades, with few exceptions, the moral authority of the Soviet Union had rarely been challenged. Some, particularly those who saw in communism's egalitarian ideals the antidote to all the ills of capitalism and democracy, were simply duped by a totalitarian society that could so easily manipulate the picture it presented to the outside world.

But sadly, most were not blind to the truth - they were just frightened by it. They understood what the Soviet Union represented but, knowing the price of confrontation, preferred to close their eyes to it. Rationalizing their cowardice with morally comforting words such as 'peace' and 'co-existence,' they pursued the path of appeasement.

Today the nations of the free world also prefer to close their eyes to the truth in the Middle East in general and the Arab-Israeli conflict in particular. While in practice the Arab states do not pose the threat of a belligerent superpower, the West's attitude toward these authoritarian regimes is all too familiar. Some, who see Palestinian stone throwers as David to Israel's Goliath, are again duped by the manipulations of a brutal dictator who sends children to the front lines to achieve through tragedy what he cannot achieve through diplomacy.

But most people are not so easily duped. They simply choose to blindfold themselves rather than confront a discomforting truth. Instead of pressuring Arab tyrants to free their own peoples from the yoke of oppression, the West prefers to view them as a 'stabilizing' force.

When the peace process began, Israel and the West had a remarkable opportunity to use their influence to ensure that the emerging Palestinian society could evolve into a liberal, democratic state. Instead they spent the better part of 10 years subsidizing tyranny.

The goal was to strengthen Yasser Arafat and his PLO, supposedly a force for moderation and compromise. With his 40,000-man armed police force, Arafat was supposed to serve as Israel's proxy in the war of terror, and would do it, as the late prime minister Yitzhak Rabin said, "without a Supreme Court, without human rights organizations and without bleeding-heart liberals."

This policy, supported by the West, was not designed to solve a genuine Palestinian human rights problem but to export it. In the past two weeks we have seen the consequences of this folly. The man who promised at Oslo to renounce the violent struggle against the Jewish state once again uses violence as an instrument of negotiation. His police have turned their guns against the state that armed them, while his kangaroo courts have released dozens of Hamas terrorists drenched with the blood of his 'partner' in peace. Needing an external enemy to justify internal repression, he continues to incite against Israel. With new textbooks depicting a map of Palestine that stretches from the Mediterranean to the Dead Sea but does not include a Jewish state, he is educating the next generation of Palestinians that they will soon take up arms in a holy jihad.

In response to all this, the world can summon sufficient courage only to condemn a democratic Israel for defending itself against enemies within and without who seek its destruction. It is assailed for provoking the Palestinians by visiting our people's holiest site, when the real provocation is not our sovereignty over a Temple Mount that is the soul of the Jewish people but our sovereignty, period.

No doubt a government that is prepared to make far-reaching and dangerous concessions will soon be pressed to make more, so that the free states can remain safely behind their blindfolds. The only free state in this vast region of tyranny will be asked to concede more in the name of 'peace' and 'coexistence' to an Arab world that wants nothing of the sort.

Thirty years ago, Democratic Sen. Henry Jackson of Washington state courageously stood against the bipartisan forces of appeasement and issued a moral challenge to an immoral state. By speaking the same truth a decade later, Republican President Ronald Reagan helped free hundreds of millions of people around the world, and sparked a democratic flame that continues to engulf and threaten tyrannies. Who will speak the truth today and allow freedom to reach this region where only one nation carries its torch?

Radical Islam: The Enemy In Our Midst

Patrick Goodenough
www.cnsnews.com
October 18, 2000

On Monday morning, an orthodox Jewish student traveling in a bus in London was stabbed more than 20 times in an attack British police said could be linked to the situation in the Middle East. An Arab man has been charged with attempted murder.

That same day, leaders of Britain's 280,000-strong Jewish community called on the authorities to arrest militant Muslims in the UK who have been calling for Jews to be murdered. Leaflets had been distributed, said the UK Board of Jewish Deputies, in at least three major British cities during the recent violence in Israel and the Palestinian self-rule areas.

They included such slogans as: "The final hour will not come until the Muslims kill the Jews." Last Friday, outside London's main mosque, similar sentiments were expressed in public. "Kill the Jews," shouted several hundred demonstrating Muslims as leaders on a makeshift platform burned American and Israeli flags.

The demonstration was led by Sheikh Omar Bakri Mohammed, a Syrian-born cleric who issued a written statement calling for the murder of Jews. Describing President Clinton as a "murderer" and Ehud Barak and Tony Blair his "co-conspirators," it called U.S. "army, embassies, bases and planes" legitimate targets for Muslims worldwide.

"Down, down USA, USA, you will pay, Osama is on his way," the protestors chanted, invoking the anti-western terror chief Osama bin Laden. "Bomb, bomb Tel Aviv, bomb, bomb the White House, bomb, bomb Downing Street."

A line of British policemen stood impassively by, trying to prevent the blockading of a busy road in front of the mosque but otherwise taking no action as the waves of incitement washed over them.

"There are six million Muslims in the UK," one man shouted through a megaphone. "We must stand and fight against the Jews." Actually there are closer to two million Muslims in Britain, and the vast majority of them would repudiate what they would see as the misinterpretation of their religion.

But it is the vocal minority, stirred up by such leaders as Bakri, who are setting the agenda, and creating a climate in which 20-year David Meyers is stabbed repeatedly with a six-inch blade on a public bus. Britain's Jewish community is on its highest alert since the 1991 Gulf War because of threats linked to the Middle East violence. (In France 750,000 Jews, 3-4 million Muslims some 80 attacks have occurred on Jewish property over the past fortnight. Jewish leaders have asked the government to deploy troops to protect synagogues if the situation worsens, while mainstream Islamic leaders have said the perpetrators are not representatives of the Muslim faith.)

In response to Myers' stabbing, Bakri had this to say: "'I warn and advise the Jewish community in the UK to distance themselves from the state of Israel. Muslims are not after the Jewish nations and communities around the world [but] if you support Israel financially, verbally or physically you will become part of the conflict."

It's not clear how Myers was expressing such support for Israel. But he was wearing a Jewish kippa and reading from a book of psalms apparently sufficient association with the enemy as far as his assailant was concerned.

Bakri is a free man, free to disseminate his vitriolic literature and stir up his followers. There are several other UK-based militants with similar agendas, including the imam (religious leader) of a north London mosque, Abu Hamza al-Masri, whose activities have been the subject of concerned questions in the British parliament.

And it's not just happening in Britain.

As far back as 1994, a PBS documentary called Jihad in America presented video footage and documents which investigative reporter Steven Emerson said proved America has become fertile ground for militants looking for recruits and raising funds for Mideast terror.

Footage from several Islamic gatherings around the country shows leaders calling openly for jihad (holy war) against Jews, Christians, and America. One of them, named as Fayiz Azram, tells a meeting in Atlanta: "Blood must flow. There must be widows, there must be orphans. Hands and limbs must be cut, and the limbs and blood must be spread everywhere."

The rhetoric could come straight out of a gory description of the aftermath of a Hamas suicide-bombing on a public bus in Jerusalem. Indeed, Emerson argued that legitimate Muslim organizations operating in the U.S. serve as "fronts" for rejectionist groups like Hamas and Hizballah.

Emerson's documentary won favorable reviews. The Los Angeles Times in November 1994 called his reporting "dogged and more than slightly gutsy" but Muslim leaders slammed it.

The Council on American-Islamic Relations, which describes itself "a Washington based Islamic advocacy group," described Emerson in a mailing five months ago as someone with a "long history of defamatory and inaccurate attacks on the Islamic community in this country."

Emerson has stressed that he clearly differentiates between militant and mainstream Islam. But State Department figures show that 98.3 percent of Americans killed or wounded in terrorism between 1993 and 1999 were attacked either in the Middle East and South Asia, or by perpetrators associated with those two regions.

That reality, says Emerson, is "not an invention of Hollywood nor a stereotype but rather reflects an accurate and sober assessment of the truth."
Nationally syndicated columnist Cal Thomas wrote in the LA Times this week that the government's primary obligation was to protect and defend the U.S. and its constitution from all enemies, domestic and foreign.

Referring to radical Islam, he said: "It's time for a new approach to an enemy that, unlike communism, is unlikely to collapse under its own weight. Rather it is intent on making sure we collapse and is willing to die by the thousands to ensure that happens."

The freedoms enjoyed by westerners is what makes their societies so attractive to Islamic militants. But a situation in which rights and freedoms are exercised without accompanying responsibilities and duties creates a breeding ground for extremism.

In Britain, new terrorism legislation enacted last July widens the current definition of terrorism to include violence for religious and ideological ends, and creates a new criminal offence of inciting acts of terror outside the UK.

But the recent introduction of a wide ranging Human Rights Act is going to make it even more difficult than ever to enforce the law, deport troublemakers, or clamp down on militant organizations.

As Sheikh Bakri told me several months ago, "We will use your democracy to destroy your democracy."

It's time the West woke up.

Phony Truce

Michael Kelly
October 25, 2000

Oh, what a splendid truce that was. Actually, it is clear now, there never really was a truce; what the Israelis and the Palestinians agreed to under intense pressure from the Clinton administration last week in the Egyptian town of Sharm el-Sheikh was something much less than that.

Jibril Rajoub, the chief of security for Yasser Arafat's Palestinian Authority, made the front page of Tuesday's Boston Globe with a simple statement: "There was not an agreement at all in Sharm el-Sheikh, not public nor private, not security nor political." This was, as is typically the case with statements from Arafat's regime, a self-serving distortion. But there is some truth here; and a good starting point for contemplating what we have now in Israel--which is not peace, not even truce, but war and the promise of more war, because the Palestinians want more war--is to assess what really came out of Sharm el-Sheikh.

Rajoub is wrong to say that no agreement at all was reached there. In a very narrow sense, an agreement of sorts was reached: Israel and the Palestinian Authority agreed, separately, to take several individual steps that, it was very cautiously hoped, would end the fighting, or at least reduce it, and begin the process of returning to the status quo ante. Israel promised to reopen the Gaza airport, pull back its troops from the edges of the Palestinian territory and reopen the borders. The Palestinian Authority promised to take steps to stop attacks on Israeli positions and civilians, to curtail public incitement to further attacks and to re-arrest Islamic terrorists the authority had released from prison the week before.

But these commitments did not constitute an agreement between Israel and the Palestinian Authority, only between those entities and the United States. Neither side ever agreed with the other to anything close to a truce, nor did they agree to anything resembling a pact. Nobody signed anything at Sharm el-Sheikh.

"The important commitments" President Clinton announced were described only in the president's oral statement, and therefore meant only what the U.S. government interpreted them to mean. What Israeli Prime Minister Ehud Barak and, more important, Arafat thought they meant we do not know, because the White House did not allow Barak or Arafat to speak at the conclusion of the meeting. The reason is obvious in retrospect: Had Arafat opened his mouth it would have been instantly clear that he did not view the "important commitments" as either important or commitments.

The phony truce was exposed for what it was immediately. Although the Palestinian Authority did (or at least so it was claimed) re-arrest some of the released terrorists and issue a brief, tepid call for an end to violence, these steps were the merest pro forma nod, a sort of jest in the context of the overall Palestinian response.

Palestinian attacks on Israel and Israelis never stopped. The first new attacks came the day after the agreement, when a powerful bomb exploded on a Gaza road as a convoy of Israeli military and civilian vehicles passed. Numerous other attacks were counted that day. The next day, Palestinians opened fire on 37 Jewish settlers, including women and children, who were traveling to a hill overlooking the remains of Joseph's Tomb, a Jewish holy site near Nablus previously destroyed by the Palestinians. The resultant gun battle claimed two lives, an Israeli and a Palestinian. The violence, generally instigated by the Palestinians, has continued ever since.

The Palestinian Authority has not acted in any serious way to stop the continual incitement to violence against Jews that spews from its radio and television stations--stations owned and entirely controlled by the authority. The Israelis are referred to as "war criminals," and the Palestinian victims of the violence are portrayed as holy martyrs; shootings of Palestinians are played on television over and over, while the exceptionally brutal murder of two Israeli soldiers never has been shown. The authority did allow, however, one response to that double murder to be aired--a sermon the next day by Sheik Ahmad Abu Halabaya defending the killings. The sermon's title: "Whether Likud or Labor, Jews are Jews."

As for Arafat himself? He wants peace so sincerely that he took the conciliatory step, on the very day that a reluctant Barak called for a "timeout" in the peace process, of telling Barak that the Palestinians would "continue on their road to Jerusalem, the capital of our independent state." And if Barak did not accept that, the great peace-processor added, "Let him go to hell."

At least now we all know where we stand.

A Crash Course In The Real Facts.

Mayer Gniwisch
www.netanyahu.com
April 2, 2001

1. Nationhood and Jerusalem Israel became a nation in 1312 B.C.E., two thousand years before the rise of Islam.

2. Arab refugees in Israel began identifying themselves as part of a Palestinian people in 1967, two decades after the establishment of the Modern State of Israel.

3. Since the Jewish conquest in 1272 B.C.E. the Jews have had dominion over the land for one thousand years with a continuous presence in the land for the past 3,300 years.

4. The only Arab dominion since the conquest in 635 C.E. lasted no more than 22 years.

5. For over 3,300 years, Jerusalem has been the Jewish capital. Jerusalem has never been the capital of any Arab or Muslim entity. Even when the Jordanians occupied Jerusalem, they never sought to make it their capital, and Arab leaders did not come to visit.

6. Jerusalem is mentioned over 700 times in Tanach, the Jewish Holy Scriptures. Jerusalem is not mentioned once in the Koran.

7. King David founded the city of Jerusalem. Mohammed never came to Jerusalem.

8. Jews pray facing Jerusalem. Muslims pray with their backs toward Jerusalem.

9. Arab and Jewish Refugees: In 1948 the Arab refugees were encouraged to leave Israel by Arab leaders promising to purge the land of Jews. Sixty-eight percent left without ever seeing an Israeli soldier.

10. The Jewish refugees were forced to flee from Arab lands due to Arab brutality, persecution and pogroms.

11. The number of Arab refugees who left Israel in 1948 is estimated to be around 630,000. The number of Jewish refugees from Arab lands is estimated to be the same.

12. Arab refugees were INTENTIONALLY not absorbed or integrated into the Arab lands to which they fled, despite the vast Arab territory. Out of the 100,000,000 refugees since World War II, theirs is the only refugee group in the world that has never been absorbed or integrated into their own peoples' lands. Jewish refugees were completely absorbed into Israel, a country no larger than the state of New Jersey.

13. The Arab - Israeli Conflict; The Arabs are represented by eight separate nations, not including the Palestinians. There is only one Jewish nation. The Arab nations initiated all five wars and lost. Israel defended itself each time and won.

14. The P.L.O.'s Charter still calls for the destruction of the State of Israel. Israel has

given the Palestinians most of the West Bank land, autonomy under the Palestinian Authority, and has supplied them with weapons.

15. Under Jordanian rule, Jewish holy sites were desecrated and the Jews were denied access to places of worship. Under Israeli rule, all Muslim and Christian sites have been preserved and made accessible to people of all faiths.

16. The U.N. Record on Israel and the Arabs of the 175 Security Council resolutions passed before 1990, 97 were directed against Israel.

17. Of the 690 General Assembly resolutions voted on before 1990, 429 were directed against Israel.

18. The U.N was silent while 58 Jerusalem Synagogues were destroyed by the Jordanians.

19. The U.N. was silent while the Jordanians systematically desecrated the ancient Jewish cemetery on the Mount of Olives.

20. The U.N. was silent while the Jordanians enforced an apartheid-like policy of preventing Jews from visiting the Temple Mount and the Western Wall.

These are incredible times. We have to ask what our role should be. What will we tell our grandchildren we did when there was a turning point in Jewish destiny, an opportunity to make a difference?

Untenable Linkages:
Tying A Cessation Of Palestinian Violence To An Israeli Settlement Freeze

Dore Gold
Jerusalem Center For Public Affairs
May 15, 2001

New Diplomatic Initiatives

Israel has been increasingly facing new diplomatic initiatives that, in effect, call for a freeze in Israeli settlement activity in exchange for a cessation of the eight-month-old, low-scale warfare on the part of the PLO, which the Palestinians call the Al-Aqsa Intifada. This new linkage has arisen in two distinct forms. First, according to early versions of the Egyptian-Jordanian Initiative of April 2001, the Palestinians are called upon to end incitement to violence and guarantee security cooperation, but Israel is expected, inter alia, to freeze new settlement activity.[1]

Second, the Sharm el-Sheikh Fact-Finding Committee, headed by former Senator George J. Mitchell, adopted a similar approach in its initial report dated April 30, 2001. The Mitchell Committee accepted the PLO argument that the continuing growth of settlements served as a source of genuine popular anger that provided one of the roots of the current violence. Therefore, besides calling for an end to violence, the Mitchell Committee Report specifically includes in its recommendations that "The Government of Israel should freeze all settlement activity, including the 'natural growth' of existing settlements."[2] Palestinians understood that a direct trade-off is being suggested here: "Now the Mitchell Committee has presented a new equation for the restart of negotiations: Total freeze of settlement activity and the total cessation of Palestinian resistance."[3]

This implicit linkage between a cessation of Palestinian violence and a freeze on settlement growth raises serious questions. The employment of violence in any manner as a negotiating tool for settling Israeli-Palestinian differences is a violation of the Oslo Agreements. In contrast, settlement activity is specifically defined as an issue with which the parties are to deal in permanent status negotiations; in the interim, the Oslo Agreements do not prohibit the growth of settlements which remain under Israeli jurisdiction any more than they prohibit the growth of Palestinian towns and villages under PLO jurisdiction. Thus, the proposed linkage requires that Israel make a new concession to the PLO, beyond its Oslo responsibilities, in exchange for PLO compliance with the Palestinians' Oslo responsibilities. Advocates of linkage, in short, seek to re-write the Oslo Accords.

Moreover, this proposed Israeli concession is being sought in the aftermath of more than half a year of Palestinian-incited violence against Israel. Clearly, under such circumstances, any new Israeli acceptance of a settlement freeze could easily be interpreted as a reward for violence, thereby undermining any future cease-fire between the parties over time; after all, violence will have demonstrably led to a tangible Israeli concession and thus have proven its utility. In order to better elucidate these points, the respective obligations of Israel and the PLO regarding violence in the Oslo Agreements are discussed in the analysis below. Secondly, the diplomatic record with respect to settlement activity is analyzed. Finally, the analysis will then turn to the full implications of the linkage between a

58

cessation of violence and a settlement freeze. Should this linkage be accepted, it will be argued that remaining chances for a future negotiated settlement between Israel and the Palestinians could be seriously undermined.

The Repudiation of Violence and Terrorism: The Heart of the Oslo Process

The Oslo Process that began with the September 13, 1993, Declaration of Principles between Israel and the PLO was founded upon the renunciation of violence and terrorism by the Palestinian leadership. This explicit prohibition on resorting to violence ran throughout the various letters and implementation agreements that accompanied this entire Oslo process from 1993 through 1999.

Just before going off to the Washington signing ceremony with Prime Minister Yitzhak Rabin and President Bill Clinton, Yasser Arafat wrote a letter of recognition of Israel to Prime Minister Rabin on September 9, 1993, in which he stated: "[T]he PLO renounces the use of terrorism and other acts of violence and will assume responsibility over all PLO elements and personnel in order to assure their compliance, prevent violations and discipline violators." Thus, the abandonment of terrorism and violence by the PLO served as the cornerstone of the mutual recognition between the two parties that was a pre-requisite for signing the first Oslo Agreement. Notably, Rabin's reciprocal letter to Arafat was much shorter and only dealt with Israel's recognition of the PLO as the representative of the Palestinian people, with no additional undertaking on the part of the State of Israel.

This built-in asymmetry had understandable historical reasons. The constituent organizations of the PLO previously had engaged in widespread international terrorism. Moreover, the PLO had once before renounced terrorism five years earlier in 1988, earning a political dialogue with the U.S. as a result, only to relapse into terrorism in 1990 which brought an end to its new relationship with Washington. In short, the PLO had a long track record of employing violence for political purposes. Thus, when Israel and the PLO signed their first Oslo implementation agreement in 1994, it included a specific Palestinian obligation to adopt "all necessary measures to prevent acts of terrorism, crime, and hostilities, and taking of legal measures against offenders" (Gaza-Jericho Agreement, Article XVIII).

Even when the Oslo II Interim Agreement was completed on September 28, 1995, it continued to make very specific security demands of the PLO, including the arrest and prosecution of individuals suspected of perpetrating acts of terror. At the same time, Oslo II detailed clear-cut limitations on the size (30,000 policemen), deployment, and weapons that would be permitted to the Palestinian police. In 1996 when Palestinian Authority security personnel opened fire on Israeli soldiers for the first time since the Oslo Agreement's implementation, these restrictions on Palestinian capabilities to engage in such violence became even more important. The 1999 Note for the Record attached to the Hebron Protocol obligated the PLO "to systematically and effectively combat terrorist organizations and infrastructure in Palestinian-controlled areas," while the 1998 Wye River Memorandum contained a detailed work-plan for the implementation of this requirement. Wye also specifically required that "the Palestinian side will make known its policy of zero tolerance for terror."

Oslo Allows Israeli Right of Re-entry into Area A

To their credit, the negotiators of the Oslo Agreements did not curtail Israel's legal rights to defend Israeli citizens from acts of violence and terrorism that might continue to transpire in the West Bank and Gaza Strip. Israel retained exclusive responsibility for defense against external threats -- i.e., the traditional Israeli concern over coalitions of Arab state armies to Israel's east. Furthermore, no restrictions were placed on the size or character of Israel's forces. The Oslo Agreements more generally entailed the gradual transfer of various powers and responsibilities from Israel's military government in the West Bank and Gaza Strip to the Palestinian Authority.

However, residual powers, at every stage of implementation, were retained by Israel. As Oslo II stated, "Israel shall continue to exercise powers and responsibilities not transferred" (Article I, 1). Besides external security, these powers included Israel's responsibility for "the overall security of Israelis." Article XII of Oslo II added that Israel would "have all the powers to take steps necessary to meet this responsibility." These included, according to Article XI of Annex 1, Israeli military engagement steps "within the territory under the security responsibility of the (Palestinian) Council." In other words, the Oslo Agreements did not even rule out Israeli military activities in Area A, the areas of full Palestinian security jurisdiction, for the defense of Israelis or for purposes of external defense. These powers were re-confirmed in the 1997 Hebron Protocol which entitled Israel "to carry out independent security activities for the protection of Israelis in H-1," which was the functional equivalent of Area A in Hebron.[4]

Arafat's Two-Stage Strategy

These residual powers enjoyed by Israel proved to be vital precisely because the Palestinian Authority failed to comply with its Oslo commitments to combat terrorism in two distinct stages. Before 2000 the Palestinian Authority refused to effectively combat the Islamic fundamentalist armed opposition groups of Hamas and Islamic Jihad which engaged in a spate of highly lethal suicide bombings in the heart of Israeli cities. Their organizational infrastructure was never dismantled.

In early 1996, Major-General Moshe Ya'alon, then head of Israeli military intelligence, explained the Palestinian reluctance to dismantle these groups as a form of military pressure on Israel: "Arafat is preserving this situation for final-status negotiations with Israel."[5] In other words, the continuation of bus bombing by Hamas, from Arafat's perspective, would eventually soften Israel's negotiating position. This situation essentially continued. Two years later, in 1998, Ya'alon concluded: "Sadly, I cannot say that at any point since it entered the territory, in May 1994, that the Palestinian Authority acted decisively and in a clear-cut way against the operational capability of Hamas and the Islamic Jihad."[6] This analysis continued under Ya'alon's successor, Major-General Amos Malka, who concluded at the end of 1998 that the Palestinian Authority had not made a strategic decision to combat terrorism or its infrastructure.[7]

With the outbreak of the current intifada in late September 2000, the main source of terrorism in this new stage of violence against Israel emanates not from Arafat's Islamic opposition but from the Palestinian Authority itself. This time, however, Yasser Arafat's own presidential guard, Force-17; the General Intelligence Apparatus in the West Bank of Colonel Tawfiq Tirawi; and Fatah's militia, the Tanzim, are engaged in regular sniping, with automatic weapons, on Israeli road traffic, on neighborhoods in southern Jerusalem, on the Jewish community in Hebron, and on other Jewish towns on both sides of the pre-1967 line.[8] Force-17 in Ramallah additionally formed joint units with Hamas for bomb attacks against Israeli neighborhoods in northern Jerusalem; there was also evidence that Force-17 had created a liaison relationship with Hizballah, which had begun to penetrate the Gaza Strip. Finally, Force-17 operatives were initially responsible for mortar attacks on Israeli settlements in Gaza, and on neighboring Israeli towns and kibbutzim in the Negev.9 Thus, Arafat may not have been directly in control of every instance of violence in the territories, but he certainly controlled his own presidential guard.

Thus, if in the first stage Arafat engaged in a form of proxy terrorism through other organizations, in the second stage he clearly decided that he could engage more directly in acts of terror against Israeli targets. Either way, the PLO was in total breach of its Oslo obligations to renounce violence and effectively combat terrorism.

Settlement Activity Under Oslo

Nothing in the Oslo Agreements specifically prohibits Israeli settlement activity in the West Bank and Gaza Strip; the whole question of the future status of the settlements was put off for permanent status negotiations. Of course, during the negotiations leading up to the signing of the 1993 Declaration of Principles (DOP), the PLO tried to obtain a settlement freeze. According to an internal memorandum dated March 18, 1996, by Yoel Singer, the Israeli legal advisor to the Oslo talks, which was made public some months later: "In the course of the negotiations on the DOP, the representatives of the PLO tried to obtain a clause prohibiting Israel from establishing new settlements. Israel rejected this demand." Nevertheless, while the Oslo Agreements still permitted settlement activity, the PLO signed the DOP and every successive Oslo implementation agreement that was reached.

Why Rabin insisted on resisting a settlement freeze in Oslo requires some interpretation. At the time he distinguished between "security settlements" that were located in parts of the West Bank that Israel might seek to retain for reasons of national defense, and "political settlements" that had been built on land Israel might eventually concede. According to this perspective, Israel had clear territorial claims in the West Bank and Gaza Strip, in accordance with its right to "secure and recognized boundaries" under UN Security Council Resolution 242. A blanket settlement freeze could have undermined Israel's territorial claims, especially if the Palestinians did not undertake limitations on construction in areas that would come under their jurisdiction. In this sense, the struggle over settlements was a reflection of a far more fundamental dispute over territory between Israel and the Palestinians. Simply, the Palestinians sought a total freeze because they really sought a total Israeli withdrawal. Rabin had a different territorial formula.

Rabin himself actually gave pragmatic explanations for his refusal to agree to any settlement freeze: "I am not ready for there to be a law in Israel to forbid building houses in existing settlements, or a kindergarten or a cultural center in a place where people live today."10 Under Rabin, Israel continued to preserve its legal right to engage in settlement activity when it completed the Oslo II Interim Agreement on September 28, 1995. Seeking Knesset approval for Oslo II on October 5, Rabin stated before the vote:

I wish to remind you, we made a commitment, meaning we reached an agreement, we made a commitment to the Knesset not to uproot any settlement in the framework of the Interim Agreement, nor to freeze construction and natural growth.

Some Palestinians and their advocates have attempted to assert that the clause in

Article XXXI of Oslo II that states, "Neither side shall initiate or take any step that will change the status of the West Bank and the Gaza Strip pending the outcome of the permanent status negotiations," entails a settlement freeze. The intent of the clause was to preclude the unilateral declaration of a Palestinian state or Israeli annexations. These actions would involve a "change in the status" of the territories. But given the entire Oslo negotiating history outlined above, it is clear that any attempt to read into this clause some form of settlement freeze involves ascribing an intent to the language that the negotiators did not have in mind.

In short, none of the Oslo Agreements placed limits on Israeli settlement growth, and no such limitation was added to either the 1997 Hebron Protocol or the 1998 Wye River Memorandum, and yet Yasser Arafat consented to all these agreements.

There is good reason to ask if the settlement issue is really as important for the Palestinians as their spokesmen state in the international media. After all, as noted above, Arafat conceded his demand for a settlement freeze in the 1993 Declarations of Principles and in successive Oslo implementation agreements. If it really was such a vital issue, perhaps Arafat would have been more insistent.

Settlements Less than 2 Percent of West Bank

Moreover, while the television pictures of settlement construction leave the impression that Israeli concrete is being poured over every inch of the West Bank, the amount of land involved is actually relatively minuscule. Using data from Peace Now, David Makovsky, writing in Foreign Affairs, reveals that settlements today take up only 1.36 per cent of the entire West Bank (excluding East Jerusalem and access roads).11 Clearly, the addition of a new row of houses in Maaleh Adumim or Givat Ze'ev involves an infinitesimal amount of additional land. True, the Jewish population in the settlements has grown appreciably since 1993; nonetheless, in a territorial dispute, what is significant is the amount of land displaced rather than the growth of the population.

In formal legal terms, the Israeli government certainly has the right to even build new settlements in Area C, where it still enjoys authority over zoning and planning. Nonetheless, the national unity government of Ariel Sharon has adopted as a matter of policy a more limited goal of allowing the natural growth of existing settlements -- in line with the settlement policies of past Labor governments. Thus, rather than violating any Oslo commitments with respect to settlement activity, Israel has actually unilaterally adopted limitations on its settlement policy, without seeking any quid pro quo.

Rewarding Violence

Linkage policies that seek to tie a cessation of Palestinian violence with a freeze on the natural growth of Israeli settlements pose three serious problems: a) rewarding violence, b) rewarding Oslo non-compliance, and c) prejudicing Israel's claims to secure borders.

In a letter to U.S. Secretary of State Colin Powell, Foreign Minister Shimon Peres reportedly wrote that implementing a freeze on Israeli settlements would be "tantamount to rewarding Palestinian violence."12 Clearly, if the PLO gains a new Israeli concession that was not a part of the Oslo Agreements as a result of months of violence against Israel, then Yasser Arafat can only conclude that his use of violence as a negotiating tool has paid off.

The problem created by rewarding violence is not just a matter of principle. Any negotiations that follow a termination of Palestinian violence will be difficult, given the fact that even former Prime Minister Barak's unprecedented concessions to the Palestinians were insufficient for Arafat. The critical question for the post-intifada period in the future will be what Arafat will do when he reaches the first negotiating deadlock with Israel.

Arafat's behavior will largely be a function of his calculus of whether renewed violence could yield additional Israeli concessions. During the period from September 2000 to February 2001, Arafat could have concluded that his intifada violence was working since Israel continued to negotiate under fire and proposed additional concessions at Taba even greater than the concessions previously offered at Camp David. This undoubtedly made bringing about a termination of the violence more difficult. Now, if Israel were to concede a settlement freeze in exchange for a cease-fire from the Palestinians, it could be safely assumed that such a cease-fire would be highly unstable and, hence, break down the moment diplomatic disagreements emerged. Under such conditions, Arafat's propensity to revert to violence as a negotiating tool would likely be reactivated.

Rewarding Non-Compliance

One of the glaring features of the entire period of Oslo implementation from 1994 through 1999 was the fact that the PLO completely failed to comply with its commitments to combat terrorism and violence. As noted earlier, this was repeatedly stated by the chiefs of Israeli military intelligence. The adoption of direct violence against Israel by the Palestinian Authority as a form of political pressure violates the core principles of the Oslo Agreement that were enshrined in the letters of mutual recognition between the parties, just before they signed the Declaration of Principles.

The formula of an Israeli settlement freeze in exchange for a termination of Palestinian violence essentially entails requiring that Israel undertake an obligation beyond the Oslo Agreements, in exchange for the fulfillment of central Palestinian responsibilities within the Oslo process. The Mitchell Report falls right into this trap when it asserts: "The kind of security cooperation desired by the Government of Israel cannot for long co-exist with settlement activity."[13]

In short, this formula requires Israel to pay an additional price for the security to which it is entitled under written agreements. Normally, a party that refuses to undertake its responsibilities under an international agreement finds itself penalized in some fashion. For example, other parties to the same agreement might not fulfill their undertakings, as well, under the doctrine of reciprocity. As a result, non-compliance can sometimes be corrected, and international understandings restored.

But in a case where the PLO massively violates the agreements it signed and then obtains additional, new concessions from Israel, it will prove to be increasingly difficult to assure PLO compliance in the future, whether with respect to an eventual permanent status agreement or even a more limited long-term interim agreement. Should any kind of agreement be reached in the post-intifada period, it is doubtful that it will be sustained, since the PLO will have understood that it faces no negative sanction for its violations of core elements of previous arrangements. This approach could particularly undermine any future peace process if Israelis and Palestinians decide to resume their diplomacy by first implementing all existing agreements. The PLO will assume that it does not really have to fulfill its obligations in such a situation. Such behavior could bring a resumed peace process to a quick collapse.

Prejudicing Israel's Claims to Secure Borders

At the heart of the Israeli-Palestinian dispute over settlements are very different expectations between the parties over the territorial outcome of the peace process. At the United Nations, for example, Palestinian draft resolutions refer to the West Bank and Gaza Strip as "occupied Palestinian territory." Israeli settlement construction, despite its very limited magnitude, is viewed as the imposition of an Israeli presence on Palestinian land. This perception dovetails with the general Arab state interpretation of UN Security Council Resolution 242 as calling for a total withdrawal from all the territories Israel entered in 1967.

Israel views the West Bank and Gaza Strip as disputed territories, to which it has certain claims so that it can achieve "secure and recognized boundaries" under UN Security Council Resolution 242. Israel has been historically concerned with the threat of conventional war coalitions from its eastern neighbors, including large expeditionary armies from Iraq. British and American diplomats back in November 1967 intentionally omitted the definite article "the" before the word "territories" in the resolution's with-drawal clause, for Israel was not expected to pull out of all the territories that it entered in a defensive war. In any case, Israel had legitimate territorial rights it could assert, derived from the British Mandate, which were never suspended because of the loss of these territories in 1948.

The U.S. certainly has supported Israel's view that the West Bank and Gaza in their entirety should not be viewed as Palestinian land. When President Bush launched the peace process in Madrid during 1991, he spoke about the need for "territorial com-promise." Equally, U.S. Ambassador to the UN Madeleine Albright stated in March 1994: "We simply do not support the description of the territories occupied by Israel in the 1967 war as occupied Palestinian territory."14

When elements of the international community insist on a freeze of the natural growth of Israeli settlements, while Palestinian Arab construction continues in Palestinian towns and villages, the foundation of the peace process -- particularly Resolution 242 -- is undermined. Palestinians will interpret this asymmetry as agreement with their view of the entire West Bank and Gaza Strip as Palestinian territory. This clearly pre-judges the outcome of eventual negotiations in the future. The Palestinian readiness to compromise over land, which was barely discernable in the Camp David-Taba period, will become even more negligible.

In summary, both the Egyptian-Jordanian initiative and the Mitchell Committee Report were undeniably motivated by good intentions. Both understand the urgency of ending the current wave of Palestinian violence which Israel now faces. But the sug-gested utilization of a settlement freeze as a quid pro quo for a cessation of these attacks can have further negative implications that must be considered prior to the eventual con-tinuation of the peace process. The international community needs to make an unequiv-ocal and unconditional demand from PLO leader Yasser Arafat to end the violence. Linking the cessation of violence to new Israeli concessions is the best prescription for assuring that a cease-fire will only be short-lived.

Notes

1. Aluf Ben, "Israel Seeks 'Improved' Egypt-Jordanian Peace Plan," Ha'aretz, April 23, 2001.
2. "The Mitchell Report on Israeli-Palestinian Violence," Ha'aretz, May 5, 2001; http://ww2.haaretz.co.il/breaking-news/kuku/362927.stm.

3. Daoud Kuttab, "Mitchell and Settlements," Jerusalem Post, May 10, 2001.

4. Daniel Reisner, "The Hebron Agreement," Justice, no. 12 (March 1997):14.

5. Dore Gold, "No Security, No Peace," New York Times, March 29, 1997.

6. Ma'ariv, April 16, 1998.

7. Gideon Allon, "Military Intelligence Chief: Palestinian Authority is Not Fighting Terror," Ha'aretz, December 16, 1998.

8. Ehud Ya'ari, "A Nuanced Approach: Some of the PA's Security Agencies have Turned into Terror Organizations" in the Jerusalem Report. Tirawi's organization was involved in repeated shooting attacks in the area of Ramallah and Qalqilyah, as well as the killing of an Israeli soldier, Tal Gideon; see Amos Harel, "The Palestinian Authority Leaves Fingerprints," in Ha'aretz, December 15, 2000. For example, Force-17 was responsible for the killing of Arye Hershkowitz on January 29, 2001. See "Sharm el-Sheikh Fact-Finding Committee: Second Statement of the Government of Israel," March 20, 2001, http://www.israel-mfa.gov.il/mfa/go.asp?MFA-H0jb0. A November 20, 2000, roadside bomb against a school bus in Kfar Darom that was filled with children, was detonated by Tanzim, as well, according to former Prime Minister Ehud Barak. See "Statement by Prime Minister and Defense Minister Ehud Barak on School Bus Attack," http://www.israel-mfa.gov.il/mfa/go.asp?MFAH0ifj0. Israel security sources accused Rashid Abu Shabbak, deputy to Gaza Preventive Security Chief Muhammad Dahlan, of actually preparing the Kfar Darom bomb. Dahlan's headquarters was subsequently targeted by Barak. See Isabel Kershner, "One Step Away from Chaos," in the Jerusalem Report. Unfortunately, back articles of the Jerusalem Report are not dated on the magazine's website.

9. Amos Harel, "Palestinians Fire Mortar Into Israel," Ha'aretz, March 19, 2001.

10. Associated Press, January 10, 1995.

11. David Makovsky, "Middle East Peace Through Partition," Foreign Affairs (March/April 2001):35.

12. Aluf Ben, "Sharon and Peres Mount Campaign Against Findings of Mitchell Report," Ha'aretz, May 10, 2001.

13. Mitchell Report; see note 1.
14. Cable News Network, "Text of Amb. Albright's Speech to the UN on Mideast," March 18, 1994.

Jerusalem In International Diplomacy

Dore Gold
Jerusalem Center For Public Affairs
June 2001

The July 2000 Camp David Summit was clearly a diplomatic failure. It resulted largely, though not exclusively, from the insurmountable gap between Israel and the PLO over the issue of Jerusalem. Prime Minister Ehud Barak and President Bill Clinton insisted on holding the summit apparently assuming that the diplomatic gaps between the parties could ultimately be bridged. Were they equipped with a more accurate assessment of the positions of the principal parties on the Jerusalem question, they might have anticipated that the summit would not succeed. For the PLO, the various Clinton proposals were a non-starter. But for Israel, as well, Barak's readiness to even consider concessions on Jerusalem led to the collapse of parliamentary support for his government, a massive public demonstration against the U.S. proposals, and finally, when combined with Palestinian violence, Barak's loss in national elections by an unprecedented majority to Ariel Sharon.

Israel suffered from a more fundamental diplomatic failure of its own, beyond its misreading of the Palestinian position on Jerusalem. The structure of the peace process, whereby Israel has focused all its energies on an abstract, albeit worthy, goal of peace, while the Palestinians' diplomatic energies were concentrated on a concrete goal of achieving a Palestinian state with a capital in Jerusalem, inevitably led the negotiations in the direction of the party with the more articulated objective -- namely, the Palestinian goal of sovereignty in Jerusalem. This diplomatic asymmetry led to a clear-cut erosion of Israel's own claims.

Yet, a careful reading of the historical record of the Jewish presence in Jerusalem and an understanding of the international legal rights of the Jewish people to their historical capital might have led negotiators to take a stronger stand on behalf of Israel's rights in the city. This study was conceived with the purpose of providing both a more realistic understanding of the actual positions of the principal parties to the Jerusalem question and a deeper appreciation of the rights Israel possesses in Jerusalem for any future negotiations.

Prior to 1948

Since its independence in 1948, and indeed even in prior times, Israel's rights to sovereignty in Jerusalem have been firmly grounded in history and international law:

Even before the rise of modern Zionism, a Jewish plurality was restored in Jerusalem under the Ottoman Empire in the early nineteenth century. Since the destruction of the ancient Jewish capital of Jerusalem by the Roman armies in 70 CE, Jews streamed back to their holy city over the centuries, whenever possible. Efforts to restore Jewish political sovereignty were accompanied by the re-establishment of Jerusalem as the national political capital of the Jewish people, even if briefly, in 135 CE and 614 CE.

There has been a Jewish majority in Jerusalem for nearly 150 years since at least 1864, when out of a total population of 15,000 there were 8,000 Jews, 4,500 Muslims and 2,500 Christians, according to British consular sources. By 1914, there were 45,000 Jews in Jerusalem out of a total population of 65,000.

Israel's international legal position in Jerusalem emanates from the Palestine Mandate, by which the League of Nations, the source of international legitimacy prior to the United Nations, recognized "the historic connection of the Jewish people with Palestine" and called for "the establishment in Palestine of a national home for the Jewish people." The League of Nations did not draw a distinction between Jewish rights to Jerusalem and the rest of the area of Palestine.

Despite the fact that the League of Nations was formally terminated in April 1946, the rights of the Jewish people in Palestine (and in Jerusalem particularly) were preserved by the successor organization to the League of Nations, the United Nations, through Article 80 of the UN Charter, which negated efforts "to alter in any manner the rights whatsoever of any states or any peoples (emphasis added) or the terms of existing international instruments" at the time of the UN's creation.

The 1947 UN proposal for internationalizing Jerusalem as a "corpus separatum," under UN General Assembly Resolution 181 (II), was only a non-binding recommendation which was rejected by the Palestinian Arabs and the Arab states by the use of force. The UN did nothing when Jerusalem's Jewish population was placed under siege by invading Arab armies in 1948, so that Israel regarded the internationalization proposals as "null and void." Israel's first prime minister, David Ben-Gurion, established Jerusalem as the capital of Israel in 1950.

After the Six-Day War
The aftermath of the 1967 Six-Day War only reinforced the strength of Israel's claims:

From 1948 to 1967, Jordan denied the Jewish people access to the Western Wall in violation of its Armistice Agreement with Israel; over fifty synagogues in the Old City's Jewish Quarter were destroyed or desecrated; its Jewish residents were expelled. The Christian population of Jordanian Jerusalem fell from 25,000 to 11,000, as restrictive laws were imposed on Christian institutions. Considering that Jordan's position in Jerusalem had resulted from its 1948 invasion of the city, while Israel's standing in Jerusalem in 1967 resulted from a war of self-defense, Israel could claim that it had a superior title to unified Jerusalem.

This line of argument was largely consistent with the analysis of major international legal experts like State Department Legal Advisor Stephen Schwebel, who would later head the International Court of Justice in The Hague. Schwebel indeed argued in 1970 that "Israel has better title in the territory of what was Palestine, including the whole of Jerusalem (emphasis added), than do Jordan and Egypt."

UN Security Council Resolution 242 of November 1967, which began as a British draft resolution, did not even mention Jerusalem and did not insist on a full withdrawal to the pre-1967 lines in the resolution's operative language (only a withdrawal from "territories" to "secure and recognized boundaries"). Britain's Foreign Secretary, George Brown, later noted: "The proposal said 'Israel will withdraw from territories that were occupied,' not from 'the territories,' which means that Israel will not withdraw from all the territories." Writing retrospectively, the U.S. Ambassador to the UN in 1967, Arthur Goldberg, noted: "I never described Jerusalem as occupied territory....Resolution 242 in no way refers to Jerusalem, and this omission was deliberate."

Resolution 242, which was adopted unanimously by the UN Security Council, served as the basis of UN Security Council Resolution 338 of October 1973, that formally launched the Arab-Israeli peace process and continued to provide the only agreed basis for the 1978 Camp David Agreements and the 1991 Madrid Peace Conference.

With the liberation of the Old City of Jerusalem as a result of the Six-Day War, the Eshkol government, with the backing of the Knesset, extended Israeli law, jurisdiction, and administration to the eastern part of Jerusalem on June 27, 1967. While Israeli sovereignty applied to the Temple Mount, nonetheless, Israel agreed that administration of the compound would continue to be maintained by the Jordanian Waqf, under the Jordanian Ministry of Religious Endowments.

From the Oslo Agreement to Camp David

The September 1993 Declaration of Principles between Israel and the PLO – the Oslo Agreement – represented a fundamental change in past policy, for Israel's very willingness to negotiate the Jerusalem issue, as specifically stipulated in Oslo, was not narrowly circumscribed to the religious dimension alone as it had been under past Israeli governments. Yet Prime Minister Yitzhak Rabin himself nonetheless remained firm on retaining Israeli sovereignty over all of Jerusalem; he told a group of Tel Aviv schoolchildren in mid-1995, during his last year in office: "If they told us that peace is the price of giving up on a united Jerusalem under Israeli sovereignty, my reply would be 'let's do without peace.'" Despite the fact that Oslo had made Jerusalem negotiable, it was still based on UN Security Council Resolutions 242 and 338, which did not call for a full Israeli withdrawal.

Seven years after the implementation of the 1993 Oslo Agreement, Prime Minister Ehud Barak became the first Israeli prime minister to consider re-dividing Jerusalem in response to an American proposal at the July 2000 Camp David Summit. The December 2000 Clinton Plan attempted to codify Barak's possible concessions on Jerusalem. Yet Barak's Camp David concessions proved to be insufficient for PLO Chairman Yasser Arafat, who rejected the U.S. proposals for Jerusalem, leading to a breakdown in the peace process and an outburst of Palestinian violence with regional implications:

Arafat's post-summit comments on the negotiations revealed the bottom line of the Palestinian position on Jerusalem: the PLO's demands for sovereignty "not only refer to the Church of the Holy Sepulchre and the Temple Mount mosques, and the Armenian quarter, but it is Jerusalem in its entirety, entirety, entirety."

At Camp David, Arafat denied core Jewish claims in Jerusalem, even insisting that there never were Jewish temples on the Temple Mount. Arafat's claims even extended to the Western Wall: "The British Mandate administration stated as early as 1929 that the Western Wall is the Al-Buraq Wall and that it is considered a Muslim religious endowment (waqf) to which Palestinians hold historic rights." This diplomatic experience demonstrated that there was an unbridgeable gap between the most conciliatory Israeli position on Jerusalem and the PLO position, as articulated by Yasser Arafat.

Yet it would be an error to link these hard line Palestinian positions to Yasser Arafat alone. Palestinian claims to the 1967 lines, including the entire Old City, were widespread among all levels of the PLO leadership. Moreover, there was significant evidence that the local Palestinian leadership in Jerusalem still harbored claims to the western portions of the city. Thus, there was little basis for concluding that, in a post-Arafat era, Palestinian positions on the Jerusalem question would become more flexible.

After rejecting the U.S. proposals at Camp David, Yasser Arafat initiated what the Palestinians called the Al-Aqsa Intifada. In its earliest stages, it began with rock attacks by Palestinian mobs situated on top of the Temple Mount against Jewish worshippers praying at the Western Wall below, on the day before the Jewish holy day of Rosh Hashanah, the Jewish New Year. The Western Wall area had to be evacuated as it became completely covered with stones.

Moreover, since September 2000, the Muslim Waqf closed off the Temple Mount entirely from any archeological oversight by the Israel Antiquities Authority; some 13,000 tons of rubble were removed from the Temple Mount by the Waqf that included archeological remnants from the First and Second Temple periods, so that new underground mosques could be completed. These remains were dumped in city waste sites. The complete disregard that the Waqf demonstrated toward the pre-Islamic ancient Jewish heritage of Jerusalem was reminiscent of the behavior of the Taliban in Afghanistan during 2001 toward the pre-Islamic Buddhist presence in the Bamian Valley. Continuing Palestinian attacks against Jewish holy sites in Nablus (Joseph's Tomb), Jericho, and Rachel's Tomb bordering Bethlehem only reinforced the view among Israelis that the holy sites of Jerusalem could only be protected under continued Israeli sovereignty.

The Clinton Plan's vision for Jerusalem that would have divided the city into a checkerboard of different sovereignties was completely unacceptable to the Israeli security establishment, including the Chief of Staff of the Israel Defense Forces, Lt. General Shaul Mofaz. In fact, Mofaz reportedly stated that the Clinton Plan, if implemented, would "threaten the security of the state."

The Taba Negotiations

The last chapter of Israeli-Palestinian negotiations during the Barak period took place in Taba, Egypt, during the latter part of January 2001. Unlike the Camp David summit and the Clinton Plan, the Taba negotiations were mostly bilateral, with only a low-level American diplomatic presence. The Taba negotiations illustrated the problem Israeli negotiators had in reading Palestinian positions. Foreign Minister Ben-Ami asserted that the parties "had never been closer to an agreement." Yet the Palestinians presented a completely contradictory assessment; Saeb Ereqat said that Taba "emphasized the size of the gap between the positions of the two sides." It appeared that throughout the negotiating process from Camp David to Taba, Israeli and American assessments of the Palestinians were based more on wishful thinking than on hard analysis:

The Palestinians appeared to have taken a harder line on many issues in comparison to what Israeli negotiators had anticipated, including settlement blocs. Israeli negotiators tested with the Palestinians the idea of creating a special international regime for the "Holy Basin" -- an area including the Old City and some areas outside the walls including the Mount of Olives cemetery. The Palestinians rejected the proposal, insisting on Palestinian sovereignty instead.

U.S. and Israeli negotiators discerned from their private discussions with some of Arafat's closest advisors that the PLO could be more flexible on some of these Jerusalem issues. Yet this purported flexibility was not borne out in repeated Palestinian public statements made at all levels since the end of the Camp David Summit. Clearly, there was a vast discrepancy between these private diplomatic discussions and repeated public remarks; ultimately, the failure of the Jerusalem negotiations indicated that the public Palestinian positions represented the real policy of the PLO.

Unfortunately, there was increasing evidence that mainstream Palestinian spokesmen ultimately rejected any compromise at all; thus Faysal al-Husseini declared in March 2001: "We may lose or win [tactically] but our eyes will continue to aspire to the strategic goal, namely, to Palestine from the river to the sea." A month earlier, Salim Za'anun, the Chairman of the Palestine National Council, stated that the PLO Covenant, calling for Israel's destruction, was never changed, despite actions taken in 1996 and 1998, so that it remained in force.

At least the failed Clinton Plan and the Israeli proposals at the Taba talks did not bind future Israeli governments or U.S. administrations, leaving open the possibility of new diplomatic alternatives. Only by avoiding premature negotiation over an unbridgeable issue such as Jerusalem can the U.S., Israel, and the Palestinians stabilize the volatile situation that has emerged and restore hope that a political process can be resumed in the future. Given its fundamental rights in Jerusalem, as well as its recent experiences with the Al-Aqsa Intifada, Israel must continue to preserve Jerusalem as its unified capital under Israel's exclusive sovereignty. This will not only best protect the interests of the Jewish people in Jerusalem, but also the interests and access of all faiths, as well.

No Democracy Under Arafat

Jack Kemp
Copley News Service
June 7, 2001

An old Jewish proverb says, "What you don't see with your eyes, don't invent with your mouth." Since Israel imposed a unilateral cease-fire on itself on May 23, all eyes have been trained on the Palestinian Authority looking in vain for evidence that "peace" is more than just a word to be mouthed in the propaganda war against Israel.

The Islamic Resistance Movement, or Hamas as it's popularly known, responded to Israel's courageous gesture of peace with renewed terrorist attacks on Israel civilians, innocent women and children. Since Israel began its self-imposed cease-fire, Israelis have continued to die by terrorist attacks, 23 last week alone.

In the eight months prior to Israel's unilateral cease-fire, the death tolls in this most recent Intifada had increased beyond anything seen in over a decade: a bomb planted on a bus one day, a suicide bomber in a crowded market the next, and this past weekend another suicide bomber in a disco filled with young people. Targets of Hamas terror are almost always civilian women, children, young people and old people. Israeli reprisals are forceful but always at military targets in response to a terror attack.

Finally last week, Israeli President Moshe Katsav said enough is enough: "People are fed up. Our patience is not unlimited." He warned that if Yasir Arafat didn't end the violence within a couple of days, Israel would respond with a sharply escalated military response. Within 48 hours there was another suicide bombing so horrendous that Arafat was forced under pressure from the US, finally, to call for a Palestinian cease fire. The world watches to see whether he follows up his words with deeds such as re-arresting Islamic militants whom he released from Palestinian prison last fall. On Sunday, Israeli Prime Minister Sharon said, "I don't believe in words or in declarations, I believe in actions."

Israel has been opposed with war and terror since it was founded. Just last month, as Israel was celebrating its 53rd anniversary, Palestinian radio, television and bullhorns in the street declaimed against the 53-year-old "Al Nakba" (catastrophe). The state of Israel does not appear on official Palestinian maps. To the radical Palestinian leadership and its followers, Israel's very existence is a "catastrophe."

When daily bombings, knifings and shootings against civilians back up these claims of illegitimacy, it's hard to make peace. The cycle of violence and suspicion escalates, borders are closed, commerce shuts down and the tempering commercial ties between people that ordinarily prevent their radicalization fray and eventually rupture. As Adam Smith taught us, the legitimate aspirations of all people is to improve their lot in life, and Palestinians are no different from Americans or Israelis in seeking economic prosperity, a good education for their children, access to capital, personal dignity, freedom, security and justice under the law. Economic opportunity, jobs and a rising standard of living for the Palestinian people cannot guarantee peace but without them we can be sure there will be no peace.

The U.S. State Department has called for a return to the negotiating table, echoing the moral equivalence argument of the report put out by the investigating team led by former Sen. George Mitchell on the causes of the Israeli-Palestinian violence that broke out in September 2000. But the negotiating table with Arafat at the other end of it has always led to more violence and more bloodshed.

Last year Arafat stormed out of Camp David when he was promised only 90 percent of what he wanted, and he unleashed the Intifada currently taking place. In Arabic, Arafat fulminates about destroying Israel in phases; in English he speaks the language of democracy: peaceful negotiation. But his goals are always the same: jihad, destruction and a non-acceptance of Israel's right to exist.

We should not be confused about Arafat's demands or pretenses. While the Munich analogy is one of the most abused of all historical lessons, it is almost perfectly analogous to the "land-for-peace" chimera in Israel today. In 1938, when Prime Minister Neville Chamberlain ceded the Sudetenland to Adolf Hitler, he proclaimed that he achieved "peace in our time." As political scientist Harry Jaffa has recently pointed out in this context, what Chamberlain actually accomplished was to "guarantee the outbreak of the greatest war in all human history." We should be exceedingly wary of following that example.

Israel is a democratic country, and it guarantees a judicial system closer to ours than almost any other nation. Arabs are routinely democratically elected to Israel's parliament. No Arab country has anything close to this, and no Arab country allows Jews to become citizens, much less partake in their government. Of course, no Arab democracy exists, either.

As Jaffa points out, more Palestinians have been murdered by their own government for expressing dissent than have died in action against the Israeli Defense Forces in the Intifada. Ask the families of Majdi Makawi and Alam Odeh how Arafat's "judicial system" treats his own people. This past January, the Palestinian Authority put these two men on trial for collaborating with Israel. They were each found guilty after a one-hour trial, no appeal was allowed and, within 24 hours, they were summarily tied to posts in the streets and killed by firing squads.

My colleague at Empower America, Jeane Kirkpatrick, once pointed out that democracies do not start wars with democracies. Until the seeds of democracy are sown in the Palestinian Authority, peace will be difficult to achieve in the Middle East. We all hope this latest cease fire will hold but with Arafat in power, there will be no democracy in the Palestinian Authority and thus no true peace in the Middle East. Until Palestinian leadership comes to power that understands democratic norms of civility, Israel will continue to be in a fight for her very existence.

Mideast Myths Exploded

Michael Kelly

The events of the past 11 months in Israel have been remarkably clarifying. When the Palestinians, on the pretext of a visit by Ariel Sharon to Jerusalem's Temple Mount, began the second intifada last fall, it was still possible for the aggressively delusional to pretend that the Israelis and the Palestinians equally desired a workable peace. That belief shattered under repeated, murderous attacks on Israelis that clearly occurred with at least the tacit blessing of the Palestinian leadership.

Now the other great founding myth of the peace process is also dead. This is the great falsehood of relative morality. For decades, the European left has maintained that the Palestinians held a morally superior position to the Israelis: They were an illegally subjugated people who were striking back in what may have been violent but were also appropriate ways. The claim of Palestinian moral superiority ended when the world saw Palestinians cheer in the street a young man holding up hands red with the blood of an Israeli soldier beaten to death, or perhaps it was when Palestinians stomped two boys, one a U.S. citizen, to death in a cave, or perhaps it was some other moment of gross and gleeful murder.

What remained -- the left's final feeble resort -- was a claim of moral equivalency: The Palestinians might be engaged in terrible acts but so too were the Israelis. Both sides were killing; indeed, the Israelis, with their better arms and soldiers, had killed far more than had the Palestinians.

Now this too has gasped its last breath. It is not possible to pretend any more that there is anything like a moral equivalency at work in this conflict. The facts are indisputable.

One: The Palestinians are the aggressor; they started the conflict, and they purposely drive it forward with fresh killing on almost a daily basis. Two: The Palestinians regard this second intifada not as a sporadically violent protest movement but as a war, with the clear strategic aim of forcing a scared and emotionally exhausted Israel to surrender on terms that would threaten Israel's viability. Three: As a tactic in this strategy, the Palestinians will not fight Israeli forces directly but instead have concentrated their efforts on murdering Israeli civilians. The greater the number, the more pathetically vulnerable the victims -- disco-goers, women and children in a pizza restaurant -- the better. Four: Israel has acted defensively in this conflict; and while Israeli forces accidentally killed Palestinian civilians, their planned lethal attacks have all been aimed only at Palestinian military and terror-group leaders.

Since the Oslo accords were signed in 1993, Palestinian terrorists have killed more than 400 Israelis. In June a bomber killed 21 teenagers at a Tel Aviv disco; last week, a bomber killed 15 and maimed as many as a hundred in a Sbarro pizzeria in Jerusalem; three days later, another suicide-bomber wounded 20 persons at another restaurant.

After the Sbarro bombing, Secretary of State Colin Powell, astonishingly, lectured the Israelis in the language of the literally exploded idea of moral equivalency. "I hope that both sides will act with restraint," Powell said. "They both have to do everything they can to restrain the violence, restrain the provocation and the counter-response to the provocation."

This official U.S. policy statement is beyond stupid. It is immoral, hypocritical, obscene. It is indefensible. Israel is at war with an enemy that declines, in its shrewdness and its cowardice, to fight Israel's soldiers but is instead murdering its civilians, its women and children.

This enemy promises, credibly, more murders. In the face of this, in the aftermath of an attack expressly and successfully designed to blow children to bits, how dare a smug, safe-in-his-bed American secretary of state urge "restraint" by "both sides?" How does the secretary imagine his own country would respond to such a "provocation" as the Sbarro mass murder? (His own country bombed Serbia to its knees for killing ethnic Albanians in distant Kosovo, let alone Americans on American soil.)

And when you get down to it, why, exactly, should Israel continue to exercise restraint? Why shouldn't it go right ahead and escalate the violence? The only point to waging war is to win. Israel is at war, and losing. It can win only by fighting the war on its terms, unleashing an overwhelming force (gosh, just what is called for in the Powell Doctrine) to destroy, kill, capture and expel the armed Palestinian forces that have declared war on Israel.

So far, Israel has indeed chosen to practice restraint. But, at this point, it has every moral right to abandon that policy and to engage in the war on terms more advantageous to military victory. This is a matter for Israel, at war, to decide one way or the other. Whether Secretary Powell purses his lips or not.

Occupied Territories Or Disputed Territories?

Dore Gold
Jerusalem Center For Public Affairs
September 2, 2001

Last month's Palestinian draft resolution at the UN Security Council again described the West Bank and Gaza Strip as "occupied Palestinian territories." References to Israel's "foreign occupation" also appear in the Durban Draft Declaration of the UN World Conference Against Racism. This language was not just chosen for rhetorical purposes but in order to invoke specific legal claims: For example, Palestinian insistence on using the term "occupied territories" is usually connected to the assertion that they fall under the 1949 Fourth Geneva Convention. Yet, Palestinian spokesmen also speak about Israeli military action in Area A as an infringement on Palestinian sovereignty: If Israel "invaded Palestinian territories," then they cannot be regarded as "occupied"; however, if the territories are defined as "occupied," Israel cannot be "invading" them.

Israel's Traditional Definitions

Israel entered the West Bank and Gaza Strip in the 1967 Six-Day War. Israeli legal experts traditionally resisted efforts to define the West Bank and Gaza Strip as "occupied" or falling under the main international treaties dealing with military occupation. Former Chief Justice of the Supreme Court Meir Shamgar wrote in the 1970s that there is no de jure applicability of the 1949 Fourth Geneva Convention regarding occupied territories to the case of the West Bank and Gaza Strip since the Convention "is based on the assumption that there had been a sovereign who was ousted and that he had been a legitimate sovereign." In fact, prior to 1967, Jordan had occupied the West Bank and Egypt had occupied the Gaza Strip; their presence in those territories was the result of their illegal invasion in 1948. Jordan's 1950 annexation of the West Bank was recognized only by Great Britain and Pakistan and rejected by the vast majority of the international community, including the Arab states.

International jurists generally draw a distinction between situations of "aggressive conquest" and territorial disputes that arise after a war of self-defense. Former State Department Legal Advisor Stephen Schwebel, who later headed the International Court of Justice in the Hague, wrote in 1970 regarding Israel's case: "Where the prior holder of territory had seized that territory unlawfully, the state which subsequently takes that territory in the lawful exercise of self-defense has, against that prior holder, better title." Israel only entered the West Bank after repeated Jordanian artillery fire and ground movements across the previous armistice lines; additionally, Iraqi forces crossed Jordanian territory and were poised to enter the West Bank. Under such circumstances, even the UN rejected Soviet efforts to have Israel branded as the aggressor in the Six-Day War.

In any case, under UN Security Council Resolution 242 from November 1967, that has served as the basis of the 1991 Madrid Conference and the 1993 Declaration of Principles, Israel is only expected to withdraw "from territories" to "secure and recognized boundaries" and not from "all the territories" captured in the Six-Day War. This language resulted from months of painstaking diplomacy. Thus, the UN Security Council recognized that Israel was entitled to part of these territories for new defensible borders. Taken together with UN Security Council Resolution 338, it became clear that only negotiations would determine which portion of these territories would eventually become "Israeli territories" or territories to be retained by Israel's Arab counterpart.

The last international legal allocation of territory that includes those strategic zones of what is today the West Bank and Gaza Strip occurred with the 1922 League of Nations Mandate for Palestine which recognized Jewish national rights in the whole of the Mandated territory. Moreover, these rights were preserved under the United Nations as well, according to Article 80 of the UN Charter, despite the termination of the League of Nations in 1946. Given these fundamental sources of international legality, Israel cannot be characterized as a "foreign occupier" with respect to the West Bank and Gaza Strip.

The Impact of Oslo: Are the West Bank and Gaza Strip "Occupied" From a Legal Standpoint?

Under the Oslo Agreements, Israel transferred specific powers from its military government in the West Bank and Gaza to the newly created Palestinian Authority. Already in 1994, the legal advisor to the International Red Cross, Dr. Hans-Peter Gasser, concluded that his organization had no reason to monitor Israeli compliance with the Fourth Geneva Convention in the Gaza Strip and Jericho area, since the Convention no longer applied with the advent of Palestinian administration in those areas. Since that time, 98 percent of the Palestinian population in the West Bank and Gaza Strip have come under Palestinian jurisdiction. Israel transferred 40 spheres of civilian authority, as well as responsibility for security and public order, to the Palestinian Authority, while retaining powers for Israel's external security and the security of Israeli citizens. These residual powers have only been employed extensively, in recent months, in response to the escalation of violence and armed attacks imposed on Israel by the decision of the Palestinian Authority.

The 1949 Fourth Geneva Convention itself (Article 6) states that the Occupying Power would only be bound to its terms "to the extent that such Power exercises the functions of government in such territory...." Under the earlier 1907 Hague Regulations, as well, a territory can only be considered occupied when it is under the effective and actual control of the occupier. Thus, according to the main international agreements dealing with military occupation, Israel's transfer of powers to the Palestinian Authority under the Oslo Agreements has made it difficult to continue to characterize the West Bank and Gaza as occupied territories.

It is not surprising that at the United Nations, the U.S. has opposed the phraseology of "occupied Palestinian territories." In March 1994, U.S. Ambassador to the UN Madeleine Albright stated: "We simply do not support the description of the territories occupied by Israel in the 1967 War as occupied Palestinian territory."

Describing the West Bank and Gaza Strip as "occupied Palestinian territories" is incorrect and misleading. Israel's transfer of government functions under the Oslo Agreements greatly strengthens Israel's case that the main international conventions relevant to military occupations do not apply. Describing these territories as "Palestinian" may serve the Palestinians' political agenda but prejudges the outcome of future territorial negotiations that were envisioned under UN Security Council Resolution 242. It also serves the current Palestinian effort to obtain international affirmation of Palestinian claims and a total denial of Israel's fundamental rights in every international forum. It would be far more accurate to describe the West Bank and Gaza Strip as "disputed territories" to which both Israelis and Palestinians have claims. Additionally, UN resolutions that characterize these territories as "Palestinian" clearly undermine the foundations of the peace process for the future.

First, Accept Israel

Daniel Pipes
New York Post
September 10, 2001

Accusations fly rapidly back and forth: Israelis complain about suicide bombers, Arabs protest the occupation of their lands. No wonder a recent poll finds 78% of Americans blaming both sides for the crisis in the Middle East.
But "a plague on both your houses" makes for poor understanding and yet weaker policy. To understand the Arab-Israeli conflict and the proper U.S. role toward it requires stepping back from the daily rush of details and looking at the big picture. That picture is surprisingly simple, for since the birth of Israel in 1948, the core issue has remained remarkably unchanged: Should Israel exist?

In reply, most Arabs at most times have emphatically replied with a "no." This attitude -- what I call rejectionism -- stubbornly holds that the Jewish state must be destroyed, with its inhabitants either subjugated, exiled or killed.

Rejectionism has varied in strength from one period to another. It reached a low point in 1993 when the Israeli and Palestinian leaders shook hands on the White House lawn. Since last September it has again peaked, returning with a terrible fury and spewing forth ubiquitously from political speeches, the media, mosque sermons, poetry, school textbooks and even crossword puzzle clues.

Some examples: The Syrian vice president portrays the current Palestinian violence as the "countdown for the destruction of Israel" and a Lebanese leader claims that the present time offers "an exceptional historic opportunity to finish off the entire cancerous Zionist project."

"We were forced to leave Jaffa, Haifa and Tel Aviv," says a leader of Hamas, the Palestinian fundamentalist organization, "and recovering from that can only be achieved when war returns and forces the invaders out." A children's poem in a Palestinian magazine addresses Israelis: "You can choose the sea like cowards, or you can choose us, and we will rip you to shreds."

Rejectionist sentiments are sometimes expressed by Arabs in the West too, even if softened. The Guardian, a London newspaper, recently carried an opinion piece declaring that Israel "has no moral right to exist."

The revival of Arab rejectionism is clearly a tragic development for Israel, whose people are being constantly murdered and where a Western, democratic, liberal and affluent country finds itself reluctantly and repeatedly forced to assert its own existence through military force. However, Arabs, ironically, are even more harmed by their own rejectionism, for the obsession with destroying Israel obstructs skilled and dignified peoples from modernizing. Dictatorship, poverty and backwardness are the wretched results. Release will come only when Arabs accept the permanent existence of a sovereign Jewish state in the Middle East. Then the Arab-Israeli conflict can end and the former combatants can be liberated to achieve their potentials.

Understanding the central role of Arab rejectionism offers important insights into the current dispute. So long as rejectionism prevails:

All other Arab-Israeli issues are unsolvable. Israel's control of the lands it occupied in 1967, the Jews living on those lands, Arab refugees, the final borders of Israel, water and Jerusalem -- none can be addressed until Arabs accept Israel.

Arab-Israeli diplomacy cannot work. How can there be negotiations over the details of a settlement when the Arabs are planning to eradicate Israel?
Israel should make no concessions. Recent experience shows that prematurely made concessions are not just useless but actually counterproductive. Arabs interpret them as a sign of weakness, which causes rejectionism to surge.

The demise of Arab rejectionism would reverse all these points. Then the parties will no longer have irreconcilable differences, Arab-Israeli diplomacy could fruitfully begin, details could be hammered out and Israeli magnanimity would become useful.

When rejectionism expires, a settlement is possible.

How, then, to end Arab rejectionism? Perhaps one day the Arabs themselves will shuck off this cursed legacy, but in the meantime, Israel and the U.S. must take the lead roles. Israel's burden was eloquently described already in 1923, when the Zionist leader Ze'ev Jabotinsky explained, "So long as the Arabs have a glimmer of hope to rid themselves of our presence, they will not give it up for all the sweet words and far-reaching promises in the world."

Israel's burden, then, is to be strong and to persevere, until Arabs eventually recognize the futility of rejectionism and give it up. For Americans, the equation is simple: The more we stand by Israel, the stronger it is and the sooner the Arabs will abandon rejectionism in favor of more constructive ventures.

One Year Of Yasser Arafat's Intifada: How It Started And How It Might End

Dore Gold
Jerusalem Center For Public Affairs
October 1, 2001

The first anniversary of the current Palestinian Intifada was marked on September 28, 2001, throughout parts of the Arab world. The date was chosen to correspond to Ariel Sharon's visit to the Temple Mount one year ago, when he served as head of Israel's parliamentary opposition. Because of the alleged proximity of his visit to the Al-Aqsa Mosque (he actually did not get near the Muslim shrines), the Palestinians called their uprising: the Al-Aqsa Intifada. But clearly this name was chosen in order to mobilize Arab and Islamic public opinion for a more general struggle over Jerusalem rather than over the Palestinian cause alone.

"Whoever thinks the Intifada broke out because of the despised Sharon's visit to the Al-Aqsa Mosque is wrong....This Intifada was planned in advance, ever since President Arafat's return from the Camp David Negotiations," admitted Palestinian Communications Minister 'Imad Al-Faluji six months ago (Al-Safir, March 3, 2001, trans. MEMRI). Even earlier, Al-Faluji had explained that the Intifada was initiated as the result of a strategic decision made by the Palestinians (Al-Ayyam, December 6, 2000). By forgetting that the present Intifada violence resulted from a strategic decision taken by Yasser Arafat, most diplomatic initiatives over the last year have been misdirected, focusing evenhandedly on both Israel and the PLO. As a result, these efforts have largely failed.

These previously-noted statements are matched by additional overwhelming evidence that the Intifada was planned in advance and was not a spontaneous popular response to the Sharon visit:

Arafat began to call for a new Intifada in the first few months of the year 2000. Speaking before Fatah youth in Ramallah, Arafat "hinted that the Palestinian people are likely to turn to the Intifada option" (Al-Mujahid, April 3, 2000).

Marwan Barguti, the head of Fatah in the West Bank, explained in early March 2000: "We must wage a battle in the field alongside of the negotiating battle...I mean confrontation" (Ahbar Al-Halil, March 8, 2000). During the summer of 2000, Fatah trained Palestinian youths for the upcoming violence in 40 training camps.

The July 2000 edition of Al-Shuhada monthly, distributed among the Palestinian Security Services, states: "From the negotiating delegation led by the commander and symbol, Abu Amar (Yasser Arafat) to the brave Palestinian people, be ready. The Battle for Jerusalem has begun." One month later, the commander of the Palestinian police told the official Palestinian newspaper Al-Hayat Al-Jadida: "The Palestinian police will lead together with the noble sons of the Palestinian people, when the hour of confrontation arrives." Freih Abu Middein, the PA Justice Minister, warned that same month: "Violence is near and the Palestinian people are willing to sacrifice even 5,000 casualties." (Al-Hayut al-Jadida, August 24, 2000 -- MEMRI).

Another official publication of the Palestinian Authority, Al-Sabah, dated September 11, 2000 -- more than two weeks before the Sharon visit -- declared: "We will advance and declare a general Intifada for Jerusalem. The time for the Intifada has arrived, the time for Intifada has arrived, the time for Jihad has arrived."

Arafat advisor Mamduh Nufal told the French Nouvel Observateur (March 1, 2001): "A few days before the Sharon visit to the Mosque, when Arafat requested that we be ready to initiate a clash, I supported mass demonstrations and opposed the use of firearms." Of course, Arafat ultimately adopted the use of firearms and bomb attacks against Israeli civilians and military personnel. On September 30, 2001, Nufal detailed in al-Ayyam that Arafat actually issued orders to field commanders for violent confrontations with Israel on September 28, 2000.

Since the Intifada was deliberately initiated by Yasser Arafat, the question remains: what exactly did he hope to achieve through this pre-mediated escalation of violence against Israel? It should be remembered that when the Camp David Summit broke down in July 2000, Arafat was blamed for the failure. Thus, his advisor, Hani al-Hasan, admitted on October 12, 2000 (Al-Ayyam, MEMRI): "The present Intifada permitted the Palestinians to change the rules of the game, damaging Barak's attempts to place responsibility for the deadlock in the peace process (on the Palestinians)."

Arafat's advisors hoped that by combining violence with negotiations, the Palestinian Authority could force Israel to make further tangible concessions. Moreover, they expected that excessive Israeli firepower would bring about the kind of international intervention that would externally impose new political arrangements on Israel that would be to the Palestinians' advantage.

Ending the Intifada: Demonstrating that Arafat's Strategy Failed and is Self-Defeating

Arafat's continuing pursuit of the Intifada option, including the use of his own security forces in attacks against Israeli civilians, is based on his assessment that he is succeeding in converting the violence into tangible gains. For this reason, Arafat has refrained from taking action to prevent Hamas and Islamic Jihad suicide attacks launched from areas under his control. Clearly comparing the U.S. Camp David proposals of July 2000 to the December 2000 Clinton parameters and then to the final Taba negotiations of January 2001, Israel demonstrated its willingness to make further concessions at the negotiating table, despite the Intifada attacks. While this was not Israel's intention, Arafat could have concluded that the pressure of the Intifada violence succeeded in altering Israel's negotiating position.

This process ended once the Sharon government resolved not to engage in substantive peace negotiations while Israelis continued to be under fire. Nonetheless, a variety of international actors may have given Arafat the impression that his adoption of violence was working. For example, the Mitchell Committee recommended a settlement freeze, a unilateral Israeli concession that did not previously exist in the Oslo Agreements. At least the settlement freeze was not an explicit condition for a Palestinian cease-fire, but only appeared at a later stage of the Mitchell sequence, after a "cooling-off period."

Subsequently, from the G-8 to the U.S. Department of State, a variety of international actors over the last six months have suggested the deployment of international observers or monitors in the West Bank and Gaza Strip, in order to verify the implementation of any cease-fire. These international forces would serve Arafat's intent of internationalizing the Israeli-Palestinian confrontation. The net impact of these various international interventions was to give Arafat the sense that important elements of the international community contemplated providing him with a quid pro quo for stopping his campaign of violence against Israel. If Arafat perceives that violence is regarded as an accepted instrument for achieving political ends, then there is no reason why he should permanently terminate the Intifada. It is not surprising, under such circumstances, that every cease-fire initiative with Yasser Arafat has failed.

The problem Israel faces is not the lack of a political initiative at present that would only reward Arafat's violence with some new Israeli political concession. A new U.S. Mideast envoy is also not required. What is needed is Arafat's compliance with cease-fire commitments that he has already made but not fulfilled. This message requires new international political will.

America's new war against terrorism presents an opportunity for bringing an end to the year-long Intifada. If Arafat internalizes that there is now a universal norm in the international community renouncing terrorism as a political instrument, it might be possible to alter his cost/benefit calculus as he engages in the present-day violence. That new norm would have to clearly establish that no political grievance can justify the resort to violence and terrorism. Indeed, political movements that adopt terrorism should find their cause to be losing international support because of its reliance on such means. However, if Arafat understands that the new international consensus applies restrictively to the Bin Laden case alone, but not to the terrorism emanating from areas under his jurisdiction, then, unfortunately, the Intifada will likely be prolonged, with all its escalatory potential.

Standing Up For Israel Is Standing Up For Our Principles

William J. Bennett And Jack Kemp
Copley News Service
October 19, 2001

Since Sept. 11, some observers have pointed to the United States' support of Israel as the reason for the terrorists' attacks. Although such comments still are somewhat isolated, the sentiment is likely to become more common in the event of more terrorist attacks or a protracted war.

The rush to blame Israel, of course, is nothing new. It also is nothing more than an attempt to pressure the U.S. government into withdrawing long-standing support for Israel. It would be tragic if such efforts succeeded.

Let us be unambiguously clear: Even if Israel and the Palestinians settled their differences, Osama bin Laden and his network of fanatical Islamic revolutionaries wouldn't cease their drive to destroy Israel and impose a perverted form of Islamic theocracy throughout the Muslim world. Nor would they call off their unholy war to kill as many Americans as possible.

Like Adolf Hitler during his rise to power, Osama bin Laden produces an expanding list of "grievances" against the United States to incite the Muslim masses and foster guilt and uncertainty among us. Hitler shed crocodile tears for displaced Germans and demanded the return of the Sudetenland, the Rhineland, and Danzig to mask his real strategic objectives and deter Europe and America from stopping his expansionism. Today, Osama bin Laden uses so-called disputed territories, Palestinian deaths in the intifada, and the suffering of innocent Iraqi civilians under the embargo to manipulate Americans and tempt us to believe we can appease his evil ambitions.

In that context, Israeli Prime Minister Ariel Sharon has reason to fear Israel will end up being a de facto Czechoslovakia. And that is why broaching the question of a Palestinian state at this critical juncture is wrong. It gives the appearance of rewarding the intifada. Even though we are absolutely confident the Bush administration has no intention of abandoning Israel, one must fully appreciate Israeli sensitivity to any suggestion that the United States might change policy during such perilous times.

That said, both Israel and the United States, and indeed the Palestinians themselves, would be well advised to look through Osama bin Laden's surface demands - contrived to drive a wedge between us - to his real agenda: topple the Saudi monarchy and return to Saudi Arabia a hero, use the vast Saudi wealth to topple Pakistan and gain access to Islamic nuclear weapons, and, from there, prosecute a worldwide nuclear guerrilla war against the "infidel" West.

While it is clear that Israel and the United States have a common enemy in those who celebrated the attacks of Sept. 11, those who blame the attacks on our support for Israel miss this simple fact: Osama bin Laden has been criticized by some in his den of terror for being insufficiently concerned with Israel. In the videotaped speech given after U.S. planes struck Afghanistan, Osama bin Laden certainly indicated an interest in the Palestinians but not nearly as much as some news reports have indicated.

As former Israeli Prime Minister Benjamin Netanyahu put it, "They [radical Muslims] call Israel the Little Satan, to distinguish it from the country that has always been and will always be the Great Satan - the United States of America." What the radical Muslims hate about Israel is precisely what they hate about America: democracy, democratic capitalism, individual freedom, and the dignity of human beings. The liberal, tolerant, and secular principles for which Israel stands are anathema to the Islamic fanatics who constitute al-Qaeda and other radical Islamic groups, which is why they seek to destroy Israel as they seek to destroy us.

Our support for Israel must not be shaken by the attacks of Sept. 11. Israel is a nation that shares our ideals, our beliefs, and our principles. If we were to sacrifice our support for Israel, we would be sacrificing everything in which we believe. By standing up for Israel, we do nothing more than stand up for ourselves and our most fundamental and important principles.

How Arafat's Palestinian Authority Became An "Entity Supporting Terrorism"

Dore Gold
Jerusalem Center For Public Affairs
December 9, 2001

In the aftermath of the December 1-2 Hamas bombings in Jerusalem and Haifa that left 27 Israeli civilians dead and 175 wounded, the Israeli government designated the Palestinian Authority "an entity that supports terrorism." This determination, even if only declaratory, closed a chapter in Israeli-Palestinian relations.

At the time of the signing of the first Oslo Agreement on September 13, 1993, Israel viewed the Palestine Liberation Organization (PLO) as a bulwark against the militant fundamentalist challenge of Hamas -- an offshoot of the Muslim Brotherhood, and Islamic Jihad -- disciples of Iran's Ayatollah Khomeini. In the 1980s and 1990s a region-wide struggle between the older forces of Arab nationalism and the rising forces of Islamic fundamentalism took place in Algeria, Egypt, and Syria. The PLO was similarly expected to ruthlessly fight Palestinian fundamentalist organizations "without Bagatz and without Betselem" (the Israeli Supreme Court and Israeli human rights organizations).

Indeed, U.S. and Israeli diplomats drew a distinction between their PLO peace partners and the fundamentalist "enemies of peace" whom, it was assumed, were trying to undermine the Palestinian Authority. Yet, while PLO and Hamas were competitors for influence among the Palestinians, their evolving relations appeared to be characterized by increasing collusion rather than confrontation, as described below:

The PLO Reconciles with Hamas

From the very outset of the Oslo process, the PLO refused to assume the role Israel had assigned it vis-a-vis Hamas and other militant Islamic elements. During 1993 the PLO undertook two negotiating efforts with Hamas: in Khartoum, Sudan, in January and in Gaza during September. A six-point agreement was signed between the military wings of the two movements on April 22, 1994, in the Gaza Strip. A third set of talks was held in Cairo on December 17-21, 1995.

The Palestinian Authority Prefers to Harbor Hamas Rather than Dismantle its Capabilities

In January 1996, it was reported throughout the Israeli press that the Chief of Israeli Military Intelligence, Major-General Moshe Ya'alon, warned the Knesset Foreign Affairs and Defense Committee that Yasser Arafat refused to dismantle the military potential of his Islamic opposition: "The organizational infrastructure of Hamas continues to be built, whether with weaponry or the mobilization of activists." Ya'alon then explained Arafat's motivation: "Arafat is preserving this situation for final-status negotiations with Israel." In other words, Arafat judged that he benefited from the Hamas and Islamic Jihad attacks on Israel because they provided him with negotiating leverage. After 58 Israelis were killed in Hamas and Islamic Jihad bombings during February-March 1996, Arafat briefly imprisoned their operatives, but began releasing them toward the end of 1996.

Arafat Gives a "Green Light" to Hamas to Attack Israel

In a series of four meetings during March 9-13, 1997, Arafat met with the leaders of Hamas and other militant groups; these opposition elements walked away from the meetings with the clear impression that they had a "green light" to start terrorist attacks against Israel. Summarizing Israel's reading of the March meetings, Chief of Staff Lt. General Amnon Shahak told Israel Radio on March 23: "Organizations such as Hamas and Islamic Jihad have an understanding from the Palestinian Authority to carry out attacks." Ya'alon concluded a year later: "Sadly, I cannot say that at any point since it entered the territory in May 1994, that the Palestinian Authority acted decisively or in a clear-cut way against the operational capability of Hamas and Islamic Jihad" (Ma'ariv, April 16, 1998).

Arafat's Own Security Forces Join Terrorist Attacks Against Israel

Perhaps the most significant military development during the Israeli-Palestinian struggle that began in 2000 was the involvement of forces over which Arafat had direct command in the terrorist violence against Israel. This first occurred in September 1996, when the Palestinian security services suddenly opened fire on Israeli soldiers throughout the West Bank and Gaza, killing 15 Israeli soldiers, some days after Israel opened a narrow wall at the end of a pre-existing archeological tunnel from the Maccabean period, adjacent to the northwestern corner of the Temple Mount. Arafat's forces fired on Israelis again in May 2000 during the al-Naqba riots. But their participation in terrorism became a regular feature of Arafat's intifada since September 2000:

Force 17 -- Yasser Arafat's personal bodyguard became regularly involved in sniping attacks against Israeli civilian traffic along main roads crossing the West Bank. Force 17 was initially responsible for mortar attacks on Israeli settlements in the Gaza Strip and on Israeli civilian towns and kibbutzim in the Negev. Force 17 was established during the years of the PLO presence in Lebanon; its name was taken from the last two digits of its Beirut telephone number.

Fatah Tanzim Militia -- Fatah, Yasser Arafat's component of the PLO, became the principal force behind sniping attacks at Israeli civilians living in Hebron and in the southern Jerusalem suburb of Gilo, opposite the Arab town of Beit Jalla. Initially, Fatah and Hamas tried to preserve a division of responsibility in their attacks against Israelis: Fatah killed Israelis beyond the 1967 boundaries in the West Bank and Gaza Strip while Hamas concentrated on pre-1967 Israel. By September 2001, both engaged in terrorism everywhere, yet at least fifty percent of terrorist attacks against Israelis were conducted by Force-17 or Tanzim, forces directly loyal to Yasser Arafat.

Other Palestinian Authority Security Agencies Take Part in Attacks -- Rashid Abu Shabak, Deputy to Gaza Preventive Security Chief Muhammad Dahlan, masterminded the bombing of an Israeli school bus in Kfar Darom on November 20, 2000. Colonel Taufiq Tirawi's General Intelligence Apparatus in the West Bank joined in the sniping incidents against Israeli civilian traffic. Over the weekend of December 7-8, 2001, Israel destroyed an illegal Palestinian mortar factory that was hidden beneath the offices of Gaza Palestinian Police Chief Brig.-General Ghazi Jabali.

Joint Operations between Arafat Forces and Hamas/Islamic Jihad -- During the intifada, joint multi-organizational units became common: a joint Hamas/Force-17 unit in Ramallah was formed in March 2001 that planned bomb attacks in northern

Jerusalem, while a joint Islamic Jihad/Fatah unit from the Jenin area attacked Israeli civilians in Afula in late November 2001. At the end of June 2001, a spokesman for the "Popular Resistance Committees" of the Fatah organization admitted that there was operational cooperation between Fatah, Hamas, Islamic Jihad, and the Popular Front for the Liberation of Palestine (PFLP) (Sabiron website, June 30, 2001).

A Broadening International Consortium of Terrorism

Force-17/Hizbullah Cooperation -- In February 2001, Israeli helicopters struck the car of Lt.-Colonel Masoud Iyyad, an officer in Arafat's Force-17, who also belonged to the Lebanese terrorist organization, Hizbullah. Iyyad had ordered mortar attacks on Israeli settlements such as Netzarim. The Gaza branch of Hizbullah was called "Bader Forces." Force-17/Hizbullah connections date back to the 1980s in Beirut when Imad Mughniyeh, the head of special overseas operations for Hizbullah, served in Force-17 before joining Hizbullah.

Iraqi Involvement and Collaboration -- Israeli security services revealed on November 25, 2001, that they had uncovered a 15-man Palestinian cell belonging to the Palestine Liberation Front (PLF) of Abul Abbas, an Iraqi-based component of the PLO. The members of the cell had been trained in the al-Quds military camp outside of Baghdad by Iraqi officers. The PLF unit worked closely with Iraqi intelligence. Its weaponry was smuggled in the car of a key Palestinian Authority Security Chief, General Abdul Razek Yehiye, who also serves as an aide to Yasser Arafat and has benefited from immunity at Israeli checkpoints due to his VIP pass (Ma'ariv, November 26, 2001). The pro-Iraqi unit, whose members came from Ramallah, had been planning bombing attacks at Ben-Gurion Airport, Dizengoff Street in Tel Aviv, and Afula.

Conclusions

Moving Yasser Arafat to arrest, interrogate, and imprison military operatives of Hamas and Islamic Jihad involves overturning many years of close coordination between the Palestinian Authority and the militant Palestinian fundamentalist organizations. Given the escalating bombing attacks against Israeli cities emanating from the vast terrorist infrastructure that has grown in the areas under Palestinian jurisdiction, Israel has no choice but to strike directly at the network of terrorism operating within the Palestinian Authority -- including forces loyal to Yasser Arafat.

President Bush declared on September 20, 2001, that "Every nation, in every region, now has a decision to make. Either you are with us or with the terrorists." Bush specifically stated that "any nation that continues to harbor or support terrorism will be regarded by the U.S. as a hostile regime." Arafat's failure to close down the terrorist organizations that have spread in his domain will require both the U.S. and Israel to follow a very different course of action in dealing with the Palestinian Authority in the months ahead.

A New Round Of Anger And Humiliation:
Islam After 9/11

Daniel Pipes
Our Brave New World: Essays on the Impact of September 11
Stanford: Hoover Institution Press, 2002

"The world has changed," Westerners often say, commenting on the events of September 11, but few Muslims echo that view. In dueling statements issued on October 7, the day the war in Afghanistan began, President George W. Bush and Osama bin Laden exemplified this contrast. While the former referred to the "sudden terror" that had descended on the United States just twenty-seven days earlier, the latter reported that the Muslim world had experienced more than eighty years of "humiliation and disgrace" at American hands, during which its sons were killed and its sanctities defiled. Twenty-seven days versus eighty years sums up the difference between a stunned American sense of ruptured innocence and the brooding militant Islamic feeling of epochal betrayal and trauma. For this and other reasons, the Muslim world was not nearly so jolted by the death of over three thousand Americans as was the West.

More broadly, to understand the impact of September 11 on the Muslim world requires putting aside the response in the West and immersing oneself in Muslim sensibilities. The best place to begin is with an understanding of the deep resentment against the West that bin Laden articulates and so many Muslims share.

Islamic History and Hostility to the West

This anger has deep roots. From the Islamic religion's origins in the seventh century and for roughly the next millennium, the career of Muslims was one of consistent worldly success. By whatever standard one judged - power, wealth, health, or education -Muslims stood at the pinnacle of global achievement. This connection between accepting the Islamic message and apparent reward by God endured in so many aspects of life in so many places for such a long time that Muslims readily came to assume that mundane well-being was their due as a sign of God's favor. To be Muslim meant to be on the winning team.

But then, starting about 1800, things went awry. Power, wealth, health, and education moved elsewhere, and specifically to Europe, a place long scorned as backward. For two long centuries, Muslims have watched as other peoples, especially Christians, surged ahead. Not only did France, England, and the United States do so on the grandest scale, but more recently East Asia has outpaced the Muslim world. As a result, a sense of failure has suffused Muslim life. If Islam brings God's grace, many Muslims have asked themselves, why then do Muslims fare so poorly? This traumatic history of things going all wrong is the key to understanding modern Islam.

It has spurred deep questions about what needs to be done to find the right direction but few satisfying answers. Despite extensive soul-searching, Muslims have not yet found an answer to the question "what went wrong?" Instead, they have bounced from one scheme to another, finding satisfaction in none of them. A succession of false starts have left Muslims deeply perplexed about their predicament, and not a little frustrated. In all,

Muslims sense their own conspicuous lack of success in emerging from the humiliation of their current circumstances.

This sense of failure goes far to explain the acute hostility to the West that prevails in most Muslim societies. Muslims vaguely realize that a thousand years ago, as Martin Kramer puts it, "the Middle East was the crucible of world civilization" whereas today, it "sulks on the margins of a world civilization forged in the West."[1] That sulking has translated into anger, envy, hostility, irrational fears, conspiracy theories, and political extremism. These emotions go far to account for the appeal of a host of radical ideologies, both imported (fascism, Leninism) and home-grown (Pan-Arabism, Pan-Syrianism). Each of these movements in turn confirms the sense that the West is the enemy.

These days, the strongest vehicle for such emotions is militant Islam (also known as Islamism), a political movement that takes the religion of Islam and turns it into the basis of a totalitarian ideology that shares much with prior versions, namely fascism and Marxism-Leninism. Like them, for example, it seeks to replace capitalism and liberalism as the reigning world system. The appeal of militant Islam goes far to account for the anti-Western hatred coming from Muslims in many places around the world, including Muslims resident in the West itself.

Islamists discern a long list of countries - Algeria, Turkey, Egypt, and Malaysia are prominent examples - where they believe local Muslim rulers are doing the West's dirty business in suppressing their movement. They also have another list - Kashmir, Afghanistan, Chechnya and Sudan rank high here - where they see the West actively suppressing noble Islamist efforts to establish a just society. Whenever Muslims move toward the emergence of an Islamic State, an Islamist explains, the "treacherous hands of the secular West are always there in the Muslim world to bring about the defeat of the Islamic forces."[2] Islamists see themselves surrounded and besieged by the West. Around the world, they feel, they are stymied by an arrogant and imperialist West.

Hatred of the United States

In particular, Islamists see the United States as an aggressive force that seeks to steal Muslims' resources, exploit their labor, and undermine their religion. A wide consensus exists that Washington and Hollywood have joined forces to establish a hegemony over the world (the "new world order"). In the words of Ayatollah Khomeini, perhaps the most influential modern interpreter of Islam: "The danger that America poses is so great that if you commit the smallest oversight, you will be destroyed. . . . America plans to destroy us, all of us."[3] In the words of an Egyptian, the Americans "have us by the throat."

This outlook has the crucial implication that violence against Americans is viewed as defensive in nature. That in turn justifies Muslim attempts to harm Americans or even destroy the United States. Ikrama Sabri, Yasir Arafat's man running the Palestinian Authority's religious hierarchy in Jerusalem, often inveighs against the United States in his Friday sermon at Al-Aqsa mosque, a prestigious and influential position. For example, he made this choice plea to God in 1997: "Oh Allah, destroy America, her agents and her allies!"[4]

To dehumanize Americans, fundamentalists portray them in beast-like terms - vermin, dogs, and bacteria - thereby making these into enemies deserving of extermination.

The Westerner, in the view of 'Adil Husayn, a leading Egyptian writer, is "nothing but an animal whose major concern is to fill his belly."[5] Immoral, consumerist, and threatening, he deserves to die. The conspiracy theories that so many Middle Eastern religious establishments espouse also dehumanize Americans, turning them into cunning plotters grasping at Muslim lands, wealth, and women.

One result is the expression of delight on hearing about American fatalities. Ahmad Jibril, a Palestinian leader, publicly shared his joy on hearing about the loss of life due to the San Francisco earthquake in 1989, then added: "I don't know how I would have managed to take revenge on the United States, but it seems that God did it for me."[6] One also finds such vicious views expressed by Muslims living in the United States itself: responding to the news of a U.S. Air Force accident not long after, Islam Report, a San Diego-based publication, published a headline that read, "O ALLAH, LOCK THEIR THROATS IN THEIR OWN TRAPS!"[7]

This litany of statements points to two facts: Osama bin Laden is not a unique figure but echoes views promoted by some of the most authoritative and influential Islamic authorities; and this viewpoint resonates among Muslims around the world, even including some living in the West.

This context helps explain why the Muslim world responded as it did to the September 11 atrocities, even before it was clear who had perpetrated them. In most of the world, initial reactions to this news was mournful. Peoples and governments alike responded with heartfelt grief and with the sense of common humanity. But among Muslims, the killing of thousands of Americans prompted less a sense of grief than one of pleasure.

"Bull's-eye," commented Egyptian taxi drivers as they watched reruns of the World Trade Center collapse. "It's payback time," said a Cairene. Other Egyptians expressed a wish for George W. Bush to have been buried in the buildings or exulted that this was their most happy moment in decades. And so it went around the Middle East. In Lebanon and the West Bank, Palestinians shot guns into the air, a common way of showing delight. "We're ecstatic," said a Lebanese. In Jordan, Palestinians handed out sweets in another expression of joy.

Outside the Middle East, a good many Muslims expressed the view that Americans got what they deserved. Nigerian papers reported that the Islamic Youth Organisation in Zamfara province organized an event to celebrate the attacks. "Whatever destruction America is facing, as a Muslim I am happy," came a typical quote from Afghanistan. A Pakistani leader said that Washington is paying for its policies against Palestinian, Iraqi, Bosnian, and other Muslims, then warned that the "worst is still to come."

Around the Muslim world, nearly identical anti-American slogans were heard over the next weeks: "U.S., Go to Hell!" (Indonesia), "Go To Hell America" (Malaysia), "Death to America" (Bangladesh), "Death to America" (India), "America is the enemy of God" (Oman). "America is a great Satan" (Yemen), "U.S. go to hell" (Egypt), "Down, down USA!" (Sudan).

Most Muslim governments were on best behavior after September 11, decrying the loss of American lives. But here too, there were cracks. Iranian officialdom, for example, found it very hard to be sympathetic to Americans and insisted on bringing the Arab-Israeli conflict into the discussion. Some analyses connected the terrorism to America's "blind support of the Zionist regime" and others actually accused Israel of organizing the attacks, in a supposed effort to deflect world opinion from its own conflict with the Palestinians. (This subsequently became an accepted verity in many Muslim countries, with elaborate conspiracy theories about the Mossad's role.) In Iraq, not surprisingly, the state-controlled media approved of the violence, commenting that the "the American cowboys are reaping the fruit of their crimes against humanity." It also announced that the "myth of America was destroyed along with the World Trade Center."

Love of bin Laden

Even before September 11, Osama bin Laden enjoyed a very high reputation due to his unremitting hostility to the United States. His biographer, Simon Reeve, wrote in 1999 that "Many who had never met him, whose only contact was through one of his interviews, a radio broadcast or Internet homepage, pronounced themselves ready to die for his cause."[8] Hasan at-Turabi, the powerful Sudanese leader, found that bin Laden had developed "as a champion, as a symbol of Islam for all young people, in the whole Muslim world."[9]

When he emerged as the man behind the September 11 attacks, his reputation soared to extraordinary heights around the Muslim world. "Long live bin Laden" shouted five thousand demonstrators in the southern Philippines. In Pakistan, bin Laden's face sold merchandise and massive street rallies left two persons dead. Ten thousand marched in the capitals of Bangladesh and Indonesia. In northern Nigeria, Bin Laden had (according to Reuters) "achieved iconic status"[10] and his partisans set off religious riots leading to two hundred deaths.[11] Pro-bin Laden demonstrations took place even in Mecca, where overt political activism is unheard of.

Everywhere, the Washington Post reported, Muslims cheered on bin Laden "with almost a single voice."[12] The Internet buzzed with odes to him as a man "of solid faith and power of will."[13] A Saudi explained that "Osama is a very, very, very, very good Muslim."[14] A Kenyan added: "Every Muslim is Osama bin Laden."[15] "Osama is not an individual, but a name of a holy war," read a banner in Kashmir.[16] In perhaps the most extravagant statement, one Pakistani declared that "Bin Laden is Islam. He represents Islam."[17] In France, Muslim youths chanted bin Laden's name as they threw rocks at non-Muslims.

Palestinians were especially enamored. According to Hussam Khadir, a member of Arafat's Fatah party, "Bin Laden today is the most popular figure in the West Bank and Gaza, second only to Arafat."[18] A 10-year-old girl announced that she loves him like a father.[19] Nor was she alone. "Everybody loves Osama bin Laden at this time. He is the most righteous man in the whole world," declared a Palestinian woman.[20] A Palestinian Authority policeman called him "the greatest man in the world ... our Messiah" even as he (reluctantly) dispersed students who marched in solidarity with the Saudi.[21]

Survey research helps understand these sentiments. In the Palestinian Authority, a Bir Zeit poll found that 26 percent of Palestinians considered the September 11 attacks consistent with Islamic law.[22] In Pakistan, a Gallup found a nearly identical 24 percent reaching this conclusion.[23] Even those who consider the attacks on September 11 an act of terrorism (64 percent of both Palestinians and Pakistanis) showed respect for these as acts of political defiance and technical prowess. "Of course we're upset that so many died in New

York. But at the same time, we're in awe of what happened," said a young Cairene woman.[24] An online survey of Indonesians found 50 per cent seeing bin Laden as a "justice fighter" and 35 per cent a terrorist.[25] More broadly, I estimate that bin Laden enjoyed in those first weeks the emotional support of half the Muslim world.

With the exception of one government-staged anti-bin Laden demonstration in Pakistan and very few prominent Islamic scholars, hardly anyone publicly denounced him in September or October 2001. The only Islamic scholar in Egypt who unreservedly condemned the September 11 suicide operations admitted that he is completely isolated. [26] Further, not a single Muslim government came out publicly in support of the American bombings against him. American officials were waiting in vain for Muslim politicians to speak up. "It'd be nice if some leaders came out and said that the idea the U.S. is targeting Islam is absurd," notes one U.S. diplomat.[27] They did not do so because to do so meant to contradict bin Laden's wide adulation.

But then a remarkable change took place.

Disappointment with bin Laden

The U.S. government began its military campaign in Afghanistan on October 7. For a month, there were no visible results. As late as the morning of November 9, the Taliban regime still ruled the territories that had been under its control for several years - or almost 95 percent of Afghanistan. But then the Taliban rule collapsed. Days later it controlled just 15 percent of the country and by December 7, it had lost control of Kandahar, its last city, and was on the run in the hills and the caves of Afghanistan, a spent force repudiated widely by joyous Afghans.

This quick change of fortunes resulted in large part from the powerful use of air power by the United States, but also to the lack of perseverance on the part of Taliban troops. Awed by American power, many of them switched sides to the U.S.-backed Northern Alliance. According to one analyst, "Defections, even in mid-battle, are proving key to the rapid collapse across Afghanistan of the formerly ruling Taliban militia."[28] American muscle and will made militant Islam a losing proposition. The force that had ruled their country was disintegrating before their eyes and the Taliban's own forces realized they were on the losing side, having no desire to go down with it, and decided to do something.

This readiness to switch sides fit into a larger pattern that became evident within days of November 11; Muslims around the world sensed the same shift of power away from militant Islam and they responded similarly.

This was especially evident in Pakistan, where enthusiasm for the Taliban cause had been extremely high in September and October 2001. Here is a report, in the Los Angeles Times, starting with an account of the scene in Quetta, near the border with Afghanistan, on Oct. 8, or one day after hostilities began. After demonstrators "burned effigies of the American and Pakistani presidents, set fire to cars, stormed the police station and smashed shop windows," firebrand religious leaders addressed 10,000 people in Ayub Stadium each Friday. They had vengeance in their bellies, they had outrage in their hearts, their anger came out in such a flood of words that some of them got hoarse. "The time will come when the American heads are on one side and our guns are on the other!" one shouted. "Prepare yourself for jihad, and I assure you that success will be ours!" But then, as

American military success became clear, the anti- American zealots lost their nerve. The same stadium that a month earlier held 10,000 two months later had less than 500 people. "A lone, badly wrinkled poster of Osama bin Laden bobbed in the front row. After a parade of religious leaders fumed at the microphone about jihad, or holy war, the crowd, which had sat almost silent through two hours of speeches, could barely muster a chorus of Allahu akbar (God is great) at the end." In Swat Valley, some 20 percent of the 10 to 15 thousand men who were inspired by cries of jihad to go off to fight the United States in Afghanistan did not return. In some cases, the losses were much higher: one Pakistani reported that 41 out of 43 of his comrades lost their lives in Afghanistan.[29] These losses generated intense resentment of the militant Islamic leaders who prodded them to go off to war, unprepared and even unwelcome, while they themselves stayed back in the comfort of their native villages.

Pakistanis turned against the militant Islamic groups, especially those that encouraged devout Muslims to travel to Afghanistan and help the Taliban. For example, Tehrik Nifaz Shariat-e-Mohammedi has acknowledged that two to three thousand of its volunteers are missing and feared dead; the organization's leader, Sufi Muhammad, found himself jailed by the Pakistani authorities when he returned from Afghanistan in November. There is also a widespread anger against him. "We curse Sufi Muhammad for sacrificing so many innocent lives," said one tribal elder. "It is because of him that so many children have become orphans and women widows."[30] More broadly, the battle fervor that swept this region at the beginning of the war has largely evaporated, as thousands of foreign volunteer fighters - many of them Pakistani - were left in the gun sights. … In these frontier communities, where the mullahs have always had more pull than the government, there is a deepening resentment of the religious leaders who called away so many young men to a certain death.[31]

To put it mildly, this is hardly the expected reaction to the American air campaign in Afghanistan, which many analysts predicted would convulse Pakistani society and perhaps even lead to an overthrow of the government by those sympathetic to militant Islam. Instead, a convincing demonstration of U.S. power led to the cowering and retreat of militant Islam.

A similar sequence can be seen in the Arabic-speaking countries. Martin Indyk, the former U.S. ambassador to Israel, noted that in the first week after the U.S. airstrikes began on Oct. 7, nine anti-American demonstrations took place. The second week saw three of them, the third week one, the fourth week, two. "Then - nothing," observes Indyk. "The Arab street is quiet."[32] This is all the more remarkable given that the Arab-Israeli conflict, perhaps the most emotional touchstone of Arab life, heated up considerably at about the same time. A well-traveled reporter came to a similar conclusion:nearly two months into an intense military campaign, and halfway through the Muslim holy month of Ramadan, the Arab "street," or public opinion, appears to have responded to bin Laden's call for an anti-Western uprising in the same way it has reacted to similar calls in the past from Islamic militants, Iraqi President Saddam Hussein and others - by changing the channel and proceeding with business.[33]

In fact, the mood rapidly shifted in the opposite direction. For example, in Kuwait, where the law code was close to being brought into line with Islamic requirements and punishments before September 11, the reality of U.S. strength led to a rapid change in mood. "America's swift reaction to the Sept. 11 terror attacks, and the scenes of Afghan joy at abolishing the very same religious restrictions, quickly damped enthusiasm" for such rightly acknowledged the connection: "The secular people, they are triumphant now, they feel they are getting power.… Now, the secular people want to abolish all Islamic rules that are applied in Kuwait or Saudi Arabia. There are even some voices about permitting alcohol."[34]

In similar fashion, the Arab media turned on bin Laden when he began looking like a loser. Generalizing about this trend, the Washington Post found that "there has been a clear effort to discredit bin Laden in religious terms and shed light on his criminal bent, political aspirations and pretensions of piety."[35] Indeed, some analysts went so far as to suspect that the damage bin Laden had caused Islam was an Israeli plot! "If world Zionism spent billions of dollars to tarnish the image of Islam, it will not accomplish what the terrorists have done with their actions and words."[36] So far had bin Laden fallen that he was now no better than a tool of the alleged Jewish conspiracy.

The same patterns can be found throughout the Muslim world, in such countries as Indonesia, India, and Nigeria, where the overwrought passions of September quickly became distant memories.

American military success so encouraged the authorities that they began, finally, to crack down. This was again most evident in Pakistan. "There has been a profound shift in the politics of religious extremism in Pakistan over the last few weeks," reported the Los Angeles Times, which went on to explain that the government for years had permitted militant Islamic groups to operate with almost total freedom, seeing which way the wind was now blowing, it began to "rein in the jihad organizations and check their pervasive influence on the nation's educational, political and social welfare systems." Those Swat Valley preachers, for example, found themselves behind bars. The most significant step came on 12 January 2002, when President Pervez Musharraf attacked militant Islam in a major speech ("The day of reckoning has come. Do we want Pakistan to become a theocratic state?") that one observer suggested "has the potential - the potential - to be the kind of mind-set-shattering breakthrough for the Muslim world that has not been seen since Anwar el-Sadat's 1977 visit to Israel."[37] Making good on his word, in just the first week after this historic speech, Musharraf had government forces close hundreds of religious offices and arrest over two thousand people. Militant Islamic groups aired much displeasure with these steps but did almost nothing to obstruct them ("We cannot fight against our own state, we can only wait for a better time").[38]

This pattern was replicated in other countries. The effective ruler of Saudi Arabia admonished religious leaders to be careful and responsible in their statements ("weigh each word before saying it")[39] after he saw that Washington meant business. Likewise, the Egyptian government moved more aggressively against its militant Islamic elements. In Yemen, the government cracked down on the Islamist foreigners coming into the country. Similarly, in China, the government prohibited the selling of badges celebrating Osama bin Laden ("I am bin Laden. Who should I fear?")[40] only after the U.S. victories began. Ironically, the same strengthening of resolve could be seen even in the United States itself; after monitoring the Holy Land Foundation, an Islamic "charitable" foundation, since 1993, the federal authorities only closed it down in December 2001 when it felt the confidence that came from its own successful military campaign.

9/11 vs. 11/9

The events of the brief three-month period following September 11 send a powerful and unambiguous message about the fortunes of militant Islam and the exercise of power.

If militant Islam achieved the acme of its achievement on 9/11, then 11/9 could be when the movement began its descent. The first date marked the peak of militant Islam, its day of greatest success in humiliating the West, causing death and panic. The second date, when the Taliban lost their first major city, marked an apparent turning point, with the West finding its resolve and its strength to deal with its new main enemy.

The marked contrast between these two dates has several implications for understanding the Muslim world. First, public opinion in the Muslim world is volatile, responding to developing events in an emotional, superficial, and changeable way. Second, as the Los Angeles Times notes, "popular support for militant Islam is not nearly so broad as was once believed."[41] The movement is loud and it is vociferous, but it does not command more than a small minority of the Muslim world's active support. Third, that militant Islam is a bit of a paper tiger - ferocious when unopposed but quite easily intimidated. Fourth, the so-called street has little bearing on developments. It rises up with much noise but without much consequence, unable to force governments to take its preferred actions. It dies down when its favorite causes fare poorly.

This is not to deny that much anger continues to be directed against the United States ("Jihad will continue until doomsday, or until America is defeated, either way")[42] or that in some circles bin Laden retains his appeal (one Afghan: "to me, he is a god").[43] It is only to say that American strength and resolve makes these sentiments less likely to become operational.

U.S. Policy Implications

For two decades - from the time Ayatollah Khomeini reached power in Iran in 1979 with "Death to America" as his slogan - U.S. embassies, planes, ships, and barracks were assaulted, leading to hundreds of American deaths. These attacks took place around the world, especially the Middle East and Europe, but also in the United States itself. In the face of this persistent assault, Washington barely responded. The policy through those years was to view the attacks as no more than a sequence of discrete criminal incidents, and not as part of a sustained military assault on the country. This approach had several consequences. It meant:

Focusing on the arrest and trial of the dispensable characters who actually carried out violent acts, leaving the funders, planners, organizers, and commanders of terrorism to continue their work unscathed, prepared to carry out more attacks.

Relying primarily on such defensive measures as metal detectors, security guards, bunkers, police arrests, and prosecutorial eloquence - rather than on such offensive tools as soldiers, aircraft, and ships. Seeing the terrorists' motivations as criminal, ignoring the extremist ideologues involved.

Ignoring the fact that terrorist groups (and the states that support them) have declared war on the United States (sometimes publicly). Requiring that the U.S. government have levels of proof that can stand up in a U.S. court of justice before deploying military force, assuring that in the vast majority of cases there would be a subdued response to the killing of Americans.

As Muslims watched militant Islam hammer away at Americans and American interests, they could not but conclude that the United States, for all its resources, was tired and soft. Not knowing the nature of democracy - slow to be aroused but relentless when angered - they marveled at the audacity of militant Islam and its ability to get away with its attacks. This awe culminating in the aftermath of September 11, when Osama bin Laden and the Taliban leader called openly for nothing less than the "extinction of America."[44] At that time, this did not seem beyond reach.

These ambitious claims shed light on the goals of the September 11 attacks. Although one cannot be sure of their purpose, it makes sense that they were intended severely to weaken the United States. Judging from militant Islam's previous successes, Al-Qaeda must have thought that it would get away with this attack with no more than the usual criminal probe. Further, having seen both the American unwillingness to absorb casualties and the damage the Afghanistan-based Islamists did to the Soviet Union a decade and more earlier, Al-Qaeda probably thought that its hits would demoralize the American population and lead to civil unrest, perhaps even beginning a sequence of events that would eventually lead to the U.S. government's collapse. If this was their thinking, they probably counted on the American police protecting government buildings, not tracking down Al-Qaeda operatives.

How could bin Laden and his colleagues know that their acts would lead to a rousing call to arms? Why should 240 deaths in a Beirut barracks lead to no retaliation and just over three thousand deaths on the east coast mobilize the country in a way not seen since Pearl Harbor? One can hardly fault them for not having foreseen this shift. It has something to do with the mysterious forces of democracy and public opinion, about which they are highly ignorant.

Even less could they have understood that a paradigm shift took place on September 11, whereby terrorism left the domain of criminality and entered that of warfare. This change had many implications. It meant no longer targeting just the foot soldiers who actually carry out the violence but the organizations and governments standing behind them. It meant relying on the armed forces, not policemen. It meant defense overseas rather than in American courtrooms. It meant organizations and governments sponsoring terrorism would pay a price, not just the foot-soldiers who carry it out. It meant dispensing with the unrealistically high expectations of proof so that when reasonable evidence points to a regime or organization having harmed Americans, U.S. military force can be deployed. It meant using force so that the punishment is disproportionately greater than the attack. It also meant that, as in conventional war, America's military need not know the names and specific actions of enemy soldiers before fighting them. There is no need to know the precise identity of a perpetrator; in war, there are times when one strikes first and asks questions later.

It might seem mysterious that the military model was not adopted earlier, it being so obviously more appropriate than the criminal one. But the fact it, it is also much more demanding of Americans, requiring a readiness to spend money and lose lives over a long period. Force works only if part of sustained policy, not a one-time event. Throwing a few bombs (such as was done against the Libyan regime in 1986 and against sites in Afghanistan and Sudan in 1998) does not amount to a serious policy. Going the military route requires a long-term commitment that demands much from Americans over many years.

The pattern is clear: So long as Americans submitted passively to murderous attacks by militant Islam, this movement gained support among Muslims. When Americans finally took up arms to fight militant Islam, its forces were overwhelmed and its appeal quickly diminished. Victory on the battlefield, in other words, has not only the obvious advantage of protecting the United States but also the important side-effect of lancing the anti-American boil that spawned those attacks in the first place.

The implication is clear: There is no substitute for victory. If the U.S. government wishes to weaken its strategic enemy, militant Islam, it must take two steps. First, continue the war on terror globally, using appropriate means, starting with Afghanistan but going on to wherever militant Islam poses a threat, in Muslim-majority countries (such as Saudi Arabia), in Muslim-minority countries (such as the Philippines), and even in the United States itself. As this effort brings success, secondly Washington should promote moderate Muslims. Not only will they represent a wholesome change from the totalitarianism of militant Islam but they, and they alone, can address the trauma of Islam and propose ideas that will ease the way for one sixth of humanity fully to modernize.

Ironically, while Muslims did not feel the impact of September 11 as intensely as did Westerners, it is they in the long run who might well be far more profoundly affected by it.

---

1 Martin Kramer, "Islam's Sober Millennium," 31 December 1999.
2 Shamim A. Siddiqi, Methodology of Dawah Ilallah in American Perspective (Brooklyn, N.Y.: The Forum for Islamic Work, 1989), pp. ix-x.
3 Imam Khomeini, Islam and Revolution trans. Hamid Algar, (Berkeley, Calif.: Mizan Press, 1981), pp. 286, 306.
4 Voice of Palestine, on 12 September 1997.#1e
5 Ash-Sha`b (Cairo), 22 July 1994. #101
6 The Sunday Independent, 26 November 1989. #37
7 Quoted in Steven Emerson, "The Other Fundamentalists," The New Republic, 12 June 1995, p. 30.
8 Simon Reeve,The New Jackals: Ramzi Yousef, Osama bin Laden, and the Future of Terrorism (Boston: Northeastern University Press, 1999), p. 203.
9 Quoted in Reeve, The New Jackals, p. 213.
10 Reuters, 19 October 2001.
11 Reuters, 14 October 2001,
12 The Washington Post, 9 October 2001.
13 Reuters, 8 October 2001.
14 Time, 15 October 2001.
15 The New York Times, 13 October 2001.
16 Reuters, 11 October 2001.
17 The New York Times, 30 September 2001
18 The Boston Globe, 10 October 2001.
19 The Independent, 11 October 2001.
20 The Guardian, 9 October 2001.

21 The Independent, 11 October 2001.

22 IRI, 11 October 2001.

23 Newsweek, 14 October 2001.

24 The Washington Post, 9 October 2001.

25 Reuters, 17? October 2001.
http://straitstimes.asia1.com.sg/asia/story/0,1870,77031,00.html

26 Newsweek, 15 October 2001.

27 The Washington Post, 9 October 2001.

28 Associated Press, 17 November 2001.

29 The New York Times, 27 January 2002.

30 Associated Press, 11 December 2001.

31 Los Angeles Times, 3, 10 December 2001.

32 Newhouse News Service, 16 November 2001.

33 Howard Schneider, "Arab 'Street' Unmoved by News," The Washington Post, 30 November 2001.

34 31 December 2001.

35 The Washington Post, 23 November 2001.

36 Nabil Luka Bibawi in Al-Ahram, cited in The Washington Post, 23 November 2001.

37 Thomas L. Friedman, "Pakistan's Constitution Avenue," The New York Times, 20 January 2002.

38 Reuters, 18 January 2002.

39 Arab News, 15 November 2001.

40 Associated Press, 17 November 2001, quoting Beijing Youth Daily.

41 Los Angeles Times, 3, 10 December 2001.

42 The New York Times, 27 January 2002.

43 The Times (London),, 19 January 2002.

44 Associated Press, 15 November 2001.

The Myth Of The Palestinian People

Yehezkel Bin-Nun
Israel Insider
January 7, 2002

"Palestinians doubt Blair can deliver," announces the BBC. "Four Palestinians die in West Bank," reports CNN. "Many Palestinian families divided," says NBC. The modern media is filled with stories about the Palestinians, their plight, their dilemmas and their struggles. All aspects of their lives seem to have been put under the microscope. Only one question never seems to be addressed: Who are the Palestinians? Who are these people who claim the Holy Land as their own? What is their history? Where did they come from? And how did they arrive at the country they call Palestine? Now that both U.S. President George Bush and Israeli Prime Minister Ariel Sharon (in direct opposition to the platform he was elected on) have come out in favor of a Palestinian state, it would be prudent to seek answers to these questions. After all, for all we know, Palestine could be as real as Disneyland.

The general impression given in the media is that Palestinians have lived in the Holy Land for hundreds, if not thousands of years. But curiously, when it comes to giving the history of this "ancient" people most news outlets find it harder to go back more than the early nineteen hundreds.

CNN, a news outlet which has devoted countless hours of airtime to the "plight" of the Palestinians, has a website which features a special section on the Middle East conflict called "Struggle For Peace." In it, is included a promising sounding section entitled "Lands Through The Ages" which assures us it will detail the history of the region using maps. But strangely, it turns out, the maps displayed start no earlier than the ancient date of 1917. The CBS News website has a background section called "A Struggle For Middle East Peace." Its history timeline starts no earlier than 1897. The NBC News background section called "Searching for Peace" has a timeline which starts in 1916. BBC's timeline starts in 1948.

But the clincher must certainly be the Palestinian National Authority's own website. While it is top heavy on such phrases as "Israeli occupation" and "Israeli human rights violations" the site offers practically nothing on the history of the so-called Palestinian people. The only article on the site with any historical content is called "Palestinian History - 20th Century Milestones" which seems only to confirm that prior to 1900 there was no such concept as a Palestinian people.

While the modern media maybe short on information about the history of the "Palestinian people" the historical record is not. Books, such as "Battleground" by Samuel Katz and "From Time Immemorial by" Joan Peters long ago detailed the history of the region.

Far from being settled by Palestinians for hundreds, if not thousands of years, the Land of Israel, according to dozens of visitors to the land, was, until the beginning of the last century, practically empty. Alphonse de Lamartine visited the land in 1835. In his book, "Recollections of the East," he writes "Outside the gates of Jerusalem we saw no living object, heard no living sound...." None other than the famous American author Mark Twain, who visited the Land of Israel in 1867, confirms this. In his book "The Innocents Abroad" he writes, "A desolation is here that not even imagination can grace with the pomp of life and action.

98

We reached Tabor safely.... We never saw a human being on the whole journey." Even the British Consul in Palestine reported in 1857, "The country is in a considerable degree empty of inhabitants and therefore its greatest need is that of a body of population..."

In fact, according to official Ottoman Turk census figures, in 1882, in the entire Land of Israel, there were only 141 000 Muslims, both Arab and non-Arab. This number was to skyrocket to 650 000 Arabs by 1922, a 450% increase in only 40 years. By 1938 that number would become over 1 million or an 800% increase in only 56 years. Population growth was especially high in areas where Jews lived. Where did all these Arabs come from?

According to the Arabs the huge increase in their numbers was due to natural childbirth. In 1944, for example, they alleged that the natural increase (births minus deaths) of Arabs in the Land of Israel was the astounding figure of 334 per 1000. That would make it roughly three times the corresponding rate for the same year of Lebanon and Syria and almost four times that of Egypt, considered amongst the highest in the world. Unlikely, to say the least. But if the massive increase was not due to natural births, then were did all these Arabs come from?

All the evidence points to the neighboring Arab states of Egypt, Syria, Lebanon and Jordan. In 1922 the British Governor of the Sinai noted that "illegal immigration was not only going on from the Sinai, but also from Transjordan and Syria."

In 1930 the British Mandate sponsored Hope-Simpson Report noted that "unemployment lists are being swollen by immigrants from Trans-Jordania" and "illicit immigration through Syria and across the northern frontier of Palestine is material." Indeed the Arabs themselves bare witness to this trend. For example, the governor of the Syrian district of Hauran, Tewfik Bey el Hurani, admitted in 1934 that in a single period of only a few months over 30 000 Syrians from Hauran had moved to the Land of Israel. Even British Prime Minister Winston Churchill noted the Arab influx. Churchill, a veteran of the early years of the British mandate in the Land of Israel, noted in 1939 that "far from being persecuted the Arabs have crowded into the country and multiplied."

Far from displacing the Arabs, as they claimed, the Jews were the very reason the Arabs chose to settle in the Land of Israel. Jobs provided by newly established Zionist industry and agriculture lured them there just as Israeli construction and industry provides most Land of Israel Arabs with their main source of income today. Malcolm MacDonald, one of the principal authors of the British White Paper of 1939, which restricted Jewish immigration to the Land of Israel admitted (conservatively) that were it not for a Jewish presence the Arab population would have been little more than half of what it actually was. Today, when due to the latest "Intifada", Arabs from the territories under 35 are no longer allowed into pre-1967 Israel to work, unemployment has skyrocketed to over 40% and most rely on European aid packages to survive.

But not only pre-state Arabs lied about being indigenous. Even today, many prominent so-called Palestinians, it turns out, are foreign born. Edward Said, an Ivy League Professor of Literature and a major Palestinian propagandist, long claimed to have been raised in Jerusalem. But in an article in the September 1999 issue of Commentary Magazine, Justus Reid Weiner revealed that Said actually grew up in Cairo, Egypt, a fact which Said himself was later forced to admit to.

But why bother with Said? PLO chief Yasser Arafat himself, and self-declared "leader of the Palestinian people," has always claimed to have born and raised in "Palestine." In fact, according to his official biographer Richard Hart as well as the BBC, Arafat was born in Cairo on August 24, 1929 and that's where he grew up.

To maintain the charade of being an indigenous population, Arab propagandists have had to do more than a little rewriting of history. A major part of this rewriting involves the renaming of geography. For two thousand years the central mountainous region of Israel was known as Judea and Samaria, as any medieval map of the area testifies. But ever since Jordan occupied the area in 1948 they renamed it the West Bank. This is a funny name for a region which actually lies in the eastern portion of the land and can only be called "West" in reference to Jordan. This does not seem to bother the majority of news outlets, which cover the region and universally refer to the region by its recent Jordanian name.

The term "Palestinian" is itself a masterful twisting of history. To portray themselves as indigenous, Arab settlers adopted the name of an ancient Canaanite tribe, the Philistines, that died out over almost 3000 years ago. The connection between this tribe and modern day Arabs is nil. But who is to know the difference?

Given the absence of any historical record, one begins to understand why Yasser Arafat claims that Jesus Christ, a Jewish carpenter from the Galilee, was a Palestinian. Every year at Christmas time Arafat goes to Bethlehem and tells worshippers that Jesus was in fact "the first Palestinian."

In spite of the historical evidence, the media has succeeded in implanting the idea that there is a people called the Palestinians. No wonder then that a recent poll of French citizens shows that the majority believe (falsely) that prior to the establishment of the State of Israel an independent Arab Palestinian state existed in its place. In fact, no independent Arab state ever existed in the geographic area Arabs call Palestine. Nor was there ever, throughout human history, a country called Palestine. The last independent state to exist in the region, prior to the establishment of the modern State of Israel in 1948, was the ancient Jewish State of Judea 2000 years ago.

If the Palestinians are indeed a myth, then the real question becomes "Why?" Why invent an imaginary people? The answer is, the myth of the Palestinian people serves as the justification for the Arab occupation of the Land of Israel. While the Arabs already possess 21 sovereign countries of their own (more than any other people on earth) and control a land mass 800 times the size of the Land of Israel, this is apparently not enough for them. They therefore feel the need to rob the Jews of their one and only country, one of the smallest on the planet. Unfortunately, many people ignorant of the history of the region, including much of the world media, are only too willing to help.

It All Points To Arafat

Michael Kelly

(c)2001, 2002, *The Washington Post*. Reprinted with permission
January 9, 2002

At 4:45 in the morning of Jan. 3, the 4,000-ton freighter Karine A was cruising in the Red Sea less than 300 miles from Israel. The Karine A's captain, Omar Akawi, an officer in Yasser Arafat's Palestinian Authority miniature navy, was asleep in his bunk, as was most of the 13-man crew. He heard a noise, he later told Israeli interrogators, and woke up to find himself staring at armed commandos of the Israeli navy.

In the holds of the Karine A the Israelis discovered more than 50 tons of military arms, including long-range Katyusha rockets, high explosives, anti-tank missiles, mortars, sniper rifles and mines. All of this -- reportedly between $10 million and $15 million of materiel -- was packed in 83 crates sealed in watertight plastic, ready for offloading in coastal waters.

Despite the personal publicity efforts of Israeli Prime Minister Ariel Sharon, the seizure of the Karine A made relatively little news. This was due in part to some confusion about for whom the arms of the Karine A were intended. The Israeli government claimed to have "unequivocal, clear and undeniable" proof that the Palestinian Authority was responsible for the smuggling. Palestinian Authority officials denied any involvement and suggested that the shipment had been intended for the Lebanese terrorist force Hezbollah. U.S. officials seemed at first to support that suggestion.

The picture by now has become a great deal clearer. The evidence is close to overwhelming that the Karine A mission was financed and organized at the highest levels of the Palestinian Authority, most likely sanctioned by Arafat himself -- and that Arafat allowed the mission to proceed after he called for cessation of all armed actions against Israel on Dec. 16.

As the Palestinian Authority has confirmed, Capt. Akawi is an officer in the tiny fleet of coastal patrol boats the Palestinian Authority calls its navy. In jailhouse interviews arranged on Monday with Western news agencies, Akawi identified himself as "a Palestine officer of the Authority," adding "I am taking my salary and [am an] employee of the Palestinian Authority." He said that he had been a member of Arafat's own group Fatah since 1976 and that "Abu Amar [Arafat's nom de guerre] is my president and my commander and chief." He said he was acting directly on the orders of the Authority: "I'm a soldier. I have to obey my orders." He said he expected to be ordered to stop the mission after Arafat called for a truce, but the order never came.

Akawi further said that the operation was organized and supervised by senior Palestinian Authority official Adel Awadallah, also known as Adel Mughrabi, who is based in Greece. He said that Awadallah had arranged the purchase of the Karine A for $400,000 and that Awadallah had personally given him his initial orders. Israeli Defense Minister Binyamin Ben-Eliezer testified Monday before the Knesset Foreign Affairs and Defense Committee that Israel has "incontrovertible evidence" that the Palestinian Authority purchased the ship on Oct. 10, "a month after the attack on the twin towers in New York."

Akawi said subsequent control of the mission was in the hands of Fathi El-Razem, who is known by the nickname Fathi El-Bahriyeh (The Navy) because he is the deputy commander of the Palestinian Authority navy: "I took my orders from Fathi El-Bahriyeh," said Akawi. "He took his orders from Adel Awadallah." The Montreal Gazette reported Tuesday that El-Razem, "who has been Arafat's chief weapons smuggler since the 1970s," was captured with Akawi aboard the Karine A.

Akawi affirmed that the munitions were headed for Gaza, and for the Palestinian Authority, not for Lebanon and Hezbollah: "I knew that the weapons were intended for the Gaza Strip," he said. The plan had been to transfer the crates to three smaller boats at a location near the Egyptian port of Alexandria; the small boats would carry the arms to a spot off the Gaza coast or just south of it, off the Sinai, where they would be picked up by Palestinian navy officers disguised as fishermen.

Akawi said that he thought Arafat himself did not know of the mission. This seems more of a politic statement than a heartfelt one, given the amount of money involved and given that the men who commanded Akawi answered directly to Arafat.

Not surprisingly, Arafat supports the rogue operation theory. He reportedly tried to sell it to U.S. envoy Anthony Zinni that the whole thing was a renegade affair, not under his control. The Jerusalem Post said Zinni was "very unconvinced." Yes.

On Israel, Dr. King's Wisdom Endures

Congressman John Lewis
Senate Floor Statement
January 21, 2002

Dr. Martin Luther King, Jr. understood the meaning of discrimination and oppression. He sought ways to achieve liberation and peace, and he thus understood that a special relationship exists between African Americans and American Jews. This message was true in his time and is true today.

He knew that both peoples were uprooted involuntarily from their homelands. He knew that both peoples were shaped by the tragic experience of slavery. He knew that both peoples were forced to live in Ghettoes, victims of segregation. He knew that both peoples were subject to laws passed with the particular intent of oppressing them simply because they were Jewish or Black. He knew that both peoples have been subjected to oppression and genocide on a level unprecedented in history.

Dr. King understood how important it is not to stand by in the face of injustice. He understood the cry, "Let my people go." Long before the plight of the Jews in the Soviet Union was on the front pages, he raised his voice. " I cannot stand idly by, even though I happen to live in the United States and even though I happen to be an American Negro and not be concerned about what happens to the Jews in Soviet Russia. For what happens to them happens to me and you, and we must be concerned."

During his lifetime Dr. King witnessed the birth of Israel and the continuing struggle to build a nation. He consistently reiterated his stand on the Israel-Arab conflict, stating "Israel's right to exist as a state in security is uncontestable." It was no accident that Dr. King emphasized "security" in his statements on the Middle East.

On March 25, 1968, less than two weeks before his tragic death, he spoke out with clarity and directness stating, "peace for Israel means security, and we must stand with all our might to protect its right to exist, its territorial integrity. I see Israel as one of the great outposts of democracy in the world, and a marvelous example of what can be done, how desert land can be transformed into an oasis of brotherhood and democracy. Peace for Israel means security and that security must be a reality."

During the recent United Nations Conference on Racism held in Durban, South Africa, we were all shocked by the attacks on Jews, Israel and Zionism. The United States of America stood up against these vicious attacks. Once again the words of Dr. King ran through my memory, "I solemnly pledge to do my utmost to uphold the fair name of the Jews...because bigotry in any form is an affront to us all." During an appearance at Harvard University shortly before his death, a student stood up and asked Dr. King to address himself to the issue of Zionism. The question was clearly hostile. Dr. King responded, "When people criticize Zionists they mean Jews, you are talking anti-Semitism."

Martin Luther King Jr. taught us many lessons. As turbulence continues to grip the Middle East his words should continue to serve as our guide. I am convinced that were he alive today he would speak clearly calling for an end to the violence between Israelis and Arabs. He would call upon his fellow Nobel Peace Prize winner, Yasser Arafat, to fulfill the dream of peace and do all that is within his power to stop the violence. He would urge continuing negotiations to reduce tensions and bring about the first steps toward genuine peace. Dr. King had a dream of an "oasis of brotherhood and democracy" in the Middle East. As we celebrate his life and legacy let us work for the day when Israeli and Palestinian, Jew and Muslim, will be able to sit in peace "under his vine and fig tree and none shall make him afraid."

Israel's Debate Is A Sign Of Strength

Steve Huntley, Editorial Page Editor
Chicago Sun Times
February 25, 2002

Israel is engaged in something normal for a democracy: a vigorous, emotional, and public debate over the direction of national policy. An unusually murderous week in what already has been the "most violent year and a half in Israeli history spurred Prime Minister Ariel Sharon to go before the Knesset last week to outline a new direction in his nation's war on terrorism. The surge in deaths came as terrorists redirected their campaign to end the "occupation" of the West Bank and Gaza Strip by having gunmen attack vulnerable Israeli army checkpoints and by successfully employing a powerful explosive to knock out an Israeli tank. (Of course, if the goal is to attack the cause of occupation, then Palestinian rage should be directed at Yassar Arafat because he's the one who wrecked the Oslo Peace process through which Israel intended to turn over land taken from Jordan in the 1967 war to the Palestinians for them to create their own state.)

Sharon's response is to begin digging trenches and building electronic fences to establish "buffer zones" to keep terrorists out of Israel. This appears to be a partial adaptation of the Israeli Left's proposal of "unilateral separation." That would have Israel separate from the Palestinians by establishing defensible frontiers and leave remote Israeli settlements outside the boundary lines. Sharon would not be pinned down on the extent of the buffer zones or their relationship to widely scattered settlements.

Perhaps in the category of grasping for straws is the State Department's embrace of, well, it's hard to say exactly what it is. Interviewing Crown Prince Abdullah bin Abdul Aziz al-Saud of Saudi Arabia, columnist Thomas Friedman of the New York Times offered his own ideas for peace: Saudi Arabia woul dgrant diplomatic relations, normalize trade and guarentee Israel's security if the Israelis withdrew from all territories won in 1967. Apparently, the prince's face lit up, and he exclaimed that these very ideas were contained in a speech in his desk drawer! Just like that, more than half a century of the Saudis' unrelenting campaign against Israel woudl be gone. The prince hasn't actually made this speech. But the Times' editorial page and the State Department latched on to his "thinking" and are pushing it as a peace plan. The suspicion, of course, is that Saudi Arabia is trying to earn some good will to counter all the bad press it's been getting, deservedly, since Sept. 11. But it's going to take more than words, especially unspoken words. The Israelis proved at Camp David in 2000 that they were willing to go the extra mile for peace. Saudi Arabia, Egypt -- which gets billions in U.S. aid and plows some of it back into the official media's vitriolic anti-American tirades -- and other Arab nations must do so now.

Nothing could be more dangerous than for Arafat, the Palestinians and the Arab world to mistake the current Israeli debate as a sign of weakness. In fact, this kind of noisy democracy is part of what makes Israel strong. As historian Victor Davis Hanson demonstrates in his brilliant new book *Carnage and Culture*, the western way of conducting war has been so successful because of the value the West puts on "civic militarism"-- meaning consensual government, free speech, dissent, individual freedom and initiative -- which only strengthens the will and means to wage wars. As Hanson reminds us, in five wars, Israel, a tiny nation of only a few million, faced Arab allies with a total population of more than 100 million, and Israel won every time.

The Only Solution Is Military

Daniel Pipes
New York Post
February 26, 2002

"We are in a war," Israel's Prime Minister Ariel Sharon said last week, referring to his country's fight with the Palestinians. The Palestinians agree: "This is war," responded Al-Fatah's commander on the West Bank, Hussein Sheikh.

In fact, Israelis and Palestinians have already been at war for over a year, but their leaders finally acknowledging this fact makes it easier squarely to assess the situation. War has clearly established patterns, and these provide insights into the Levantine situation:

* What each side seeks - to achieve victory and avoid defeat - is primarily psychological in nature. Victory consists of imposing one's will on the enemy (Israel wants its neighbors to leave it alone; the Palestinians want to destroy Israel) by convincing it that his cause is hopeless. Defeat means accepting that one's cause is hopeless.

* Will, fortitude and morale are often more important for victory than are objective factors such as the economy, technology, arsenal, the number of casualties or votes at the United Nations. In many cases, these latter count mainly in so far as they affect a combatant's mood.

* Resolution occurs when one party realizes it can no longer pursue its aims and gives them up. This usually follows its unambiguous vanquishment, either a military collapse (as in World War II) or internal rot (as in the Cold War).

"In every case I can think of," writes strategist Michael Ledeen, "peace has come about at the end of a war in which there was a winner and a loser. The winner imposed terms on the loser, and those terms were called 'peace.'"

Resolution can follow from other reasons - e.g., when a bigger enemy turns up. Worried about the common German menace, Britain and France buried their historic enmity in 1904.

* Stalemate, conversely, keeps conflict alive by letting both sides hope to win another day. The Germans lost too narrowly to give up in their first attempt to dominate Europe (World War I), so they tried again (World War II), when they got decisively defeated and give up.

Many unresolved conflicts loom in today's world. The Korean War ended inconclusively in 1953; a half century later, another round remains likely - unless the North Korean regime collapses first. The Iran-Iraq conflict ended in 1988 with neither side feeling defeated, so more hostilities are likely - again, unless one regime first disappears.

So too in the Arab-Israeli conflict: The Arabs lost many rounds (1948-49, 1956, 1967, 1970, 1973, 1982) but never felt defeated, so they keep coming back to try again.

* Diplomacy rarely ends conflicts. Hardly a single major interstate conflict has concluded due to some one's clever schema. The idea that a "peace process" can take the place of the dirty work of war is a conceit.

Again, to quote Ledeen, "Peace cannot be accomplished simply because some visiting envoy, with or without an advanced degree in negotiating from the Harvard Business School, sits everyone down around a table so they can all reason together." The oft-heard mantra that "there is no military solution" (repeated recently, for example, by former Sen. George J. Mitchell), in short, has things exactly wrong.

Applying these rules of war to the Palestinian-Israeli conflict offers some useful insights. Palestinians were winning until about a year ago, now Israel is.

Until Prime Minister Ariel Sharon took over, Israel was politically divided and militarily demoralized, avoiding reality and indulging in escapism (like "post-Zionism"). Meanwhile, Palestinians exulted in their successes. Smelling victory, they showed impressive stamina and great capacity for self-sacrifice.

A year later, circumstances have flipped. Palestinian violence had the unintended effect of uniting, mobilizing and fortifying Israelis. "Specialists in terrorism have been surprised - some of us are even amazed," admits Ely Carmon of the Interdisciplinary Center in Herzliya, "by the endurance, the patience, the relative calm of the Israeli public to what has happened in last year and a half."

Contrarily, the Palestinians' morale is plummeting and despair is setting as Yasser Arafat's ruinous leadership locks them into a conflict they cannot win.

History teaches that what appears to be endless carnage does come to an end when one side gives up. It appears increasingly likely that the Palestinians are approaching that point, suggesting that if Israel persists in its present policies it will get closer to victory.

Peace In The Middle East

U.S. Sen. James M. Inhofe (R-Okla)
Senate Floor Statement
March 4, 2002

I was interested the other day when I heard that the de facto ruler, Saudi Arabian Crown Prince Abdullah, made a statement which was received by many in this country as if it were a statement of fact, as if it were something new, a concept for peace in the Middle East that no one had ever heard of before. I was kind of shocked that it was so well received by many people who had been down this road before.

I suggest to you that what Crown Prince Abdullah talked about a few days ago was not new at all. He talked about the fact that under the Abdullah plan, Arabs would normalize relations with Israel in exchange for the Jewish state surrendering the territory it received after the 1967 Six-Day War as if that were something new. He went on to talk about other land that had been acquired and had been taken by Israel.

I remember so well on December 4 when we covered all of this and the fact that there isn't anything new about the prospect of giving up land that is rightfully Israel's land in order to have peace.

When it gets right down to it, the land doesn't make that much difference because Yasser Arafat and others don't recognize Israel's right to any of the land. They do not recognize Israel's right to exist.

I will discuss seven reasons, which I mentioned once before, why Israel is entitled to the land they have and that it should not be a part of the peace process.

If this is something that Israel wants to do, it is their business to do it. But anyone who has tried to put the pressure on Israel to do this is wrong.

We are going to be hit by skeptics who are going to say we will be attacked because of our support for Israel, and if we get out of the Middle East--that is us--all the problems will go away. That is just not true. If we withdraw, all of these problems will again come to our door.

I have some observations to make about that. But I would like to reemphasize once again the seven reasons that Israel has the right to their land. The first reason is that Israel has the right to the land because of all of the archeological evidence. That is reason, No. 1. All the archeological evidence supports it.

Every time there is a dig in Israel, it does nothing but support the fact that Israelis have had a presence there for 3,000 years. They have been there for a long time. The coins, the cities, the pottery, the culture--there are other people, groups that are there, but there is no mistaking the fact that Israelis have been present in that land for 3,000 years.

It predates any claims that other peoples in the regions may have. The ancient Philistines are extinct. Many other ancient peoples are extinct. They do not have the unbroken line to this date that the Israelis have.

Even the Egyptians of today are not racial Egyptians of 2,000, 3,000 years ago. They are primarily an Arab people. The land is called Egypt, but they are not the same racial and ethnic stock as the old Egyptians of the ancient world. The first Israelis are in fact descended from the original Israelites. The first proof, then, is the archeology.

The second proof of Israel's right to the land is the historic right. History supports it totally and completely. We know there has been an Israel up until the time of the Roman Empire. The Romans conquered the land. Israel had no homeland, although Jews were allowed to live there. They were driven from the land in two dispersions: One was in 70 A,.D. and the other was in 135 A.D. But there was always a Jewish presence in the land.

The Turks, who took over about 700 years ago and ruled the land up until about World War I, had control. Then the land was conquered by the British. The Turks entered World War I on the side of Germany. The British knew they had to do something to punish Turkey, and also to break up that empire that was going to be a part of the whole effort of Germany in World War I. So the British sent troops against the Turks in the Holy Land.

One of the generals who was leading the British armies was a man named Allenby. Allenby was a Bible-believing Christian. He carried a Bible with him everywhere he went and he knew the significance of Jerusalem.

The night before the attack against Jerusalem to drive out the Turks, Allenby prayed that God would allow him to capture the city without doing damage to the holy places.

That day, Allenby sent World War I biplanes over the city of Jerusalem to do a reconnaissance mission. You have to understand that the Turks had at that time never seen an airplane. So there they were, flying around. They looked in the sky and saw these fascinating inventions and did not know what they were, and they were terrified by them. Then they were told they were going to be opposed by a man named Allenby the next day, which means, in their language, ``man sent from God'' or ``prophet from God.'' They dared not fight against a prophet from God, so the next morning, when Allenby went to take Jerusalem, he went in and captured it without firing a single shot.

The British Government was grateful to Jewish people around the world, particularly to one Jewish chemist who helped them manufacture niter. Niter is an ingredient that was used in nitroglycerin which was sent over from the New World. But they did not have a way of getting it to England. The German U-boats were shooting on the boats, so most of the niter they were trying to import to make nitroglycerin was at the bottom of the ocean. But a man named Weitzman, a Jewish chemist, discovered a way to make it from materials that existed in England. As a result, they were able to continue that supply.

The British at that time said they were going to give the Jewish people a homeland. That is all a part of history. It is all written down in history. They were gratified that the Jewish people, the bankers, came through and helped finance the war.

The homeland that Britain said it would set aside consisted of all of what is now Israel and all of what was then the nation of Jordan--the whole thing. That was what Britain promised to give the Jews in 1917.

In the beginning, there was some Arab support for this action. There was not a huge Arab population in the land at that time, and there is a reason for that. The land was not able to sustain a large population of people. It just did not have the development it needed to handle those people, and the land was not really wanted by anybody. Nobody really wanted this land. It was considered to be worthless land.

I want the Presiding Officer to hear what Mark Twain said. And, of course, you may have read ``Huckleberry Finn'' and ``Tom Sawyer.'' Mark Twain--Samuel Clemens--took a tour of Palestine in 1867. This is how he described that land. We are talking about Israel now. He said:

A desolate country whose soil is rich enough but is given over wholly to weeds. A silent, mournful expanse. We never saw a human being on the whole route. There was hardly a tree or a shrub anywhere. Even the olive and the cactus, those fast friends of a worthless soil, had almost deserted the country.

Where was this great Palestinian nation? It did not exist. It was not there. Palestinians were not there. Palestine was a region named by the Romans, but at that time it was under the control of Turkey, and there was no large mass of people there because the land would not support them.

This is the report that the Palestinian Royal Commission, created by the British, made. It quotes an account of the conditions on the coastal plain along the Mediterranean Sea in 1913. This is the Palestinian Royal Commission. They said:

The road leading from Gaza to the north was only a summer track, suitable for transport by camels or carts. No orange groves, orchards or vineyards were to be seen until one reached the Yavnev village. Houses were mud. Schools did not exist. The western part toward the sea was almost a desert. The villages in this area were few and thinly populated. Many villages were deserted by their inhabitants.

That was 1913.

The French author Voltaire described Palestine as ``a hopeless, dreary place.''

In short, under the Turks the land suffered from neglect and low population. That is a historic fact. The nation became populated by both Jews and Arabs because the land came to prosper when Jews came back and began to reclaim it. Historically, they began to reclaim it. If there had never been any archaeological evidence to support the rights of the Israelis to the territory, it is also important to recognize that other nations in the area have no longstanding claim to the country either.

Did you know that Saudi Arabia was not created until 1913, Lebanon until 1920? Iraq did not exist as a nation until 1932, Syria until 1941; the borders of Jordan were established in 1946 and Kuwait in 1961. Any of these nations that would say Israel is only a recent arrival would have to deny their own rights as recent arrivals as well. They did not exist as countries. They were all under the control of the Turks.

Historically, Israel gained its independence in 1948.

The third reason that land belongs to Israel is the practical value of the Israelis being there. Israel today is a modern marvel of agriculture. Israel is able to bring more food out of a desert environment than any other country in the world. The Arab nations ought to make Israel their friend and import technology from Israel that would allow all the Middle East, not just Israel, to become an exporter of food. Israel has unarguable success in its agriculture.

The fourth reason I believe Israel has the right to the land is on the grounds of humanitarian concern. You see, there were 6 million Jews slaughtered in Europe in World War II. The persecution against the Jews had been very strong in Russia since the advent of communism. It was against them even before then under the Czars.

These people have a right to their homeland. If we are not going to allow them a homeland in the Middle East, then where? What other nation on Earth is going to cede territory, is going to give up land?

They are not asking for a great deal. The whole nation of Israel would fit into my home State of Oklahoma seven times. It would fit into the Presiding Officer's State of Georgia seven times. They are not asking for a great deal. The whole nation of Israel is very small. It is a nation that, up until the time that claims started coming in, was not desired by anybody.

The fifth reason Israel ought to have their land is that she is a strategic ally of the United States. Whether we realize it or not, Israel is a detriment, an impediment, to certain groups hostile to democracies and hostile to what we believe in, hostile to that which makes us the greatest nation in the history of the world. They have kept them from taking complete control of the Middle East. If it were not for Israel, they would overrun the region. They are our strategic ally.

It is good to know we have a friend in the Middle East on whom we can count. They vote with us in the United Nations more than England, more than Canada, more than France, more than Germany--more than any other country in the world.

The sixth reason is that Israel is a roadblock to terrorism. The war we are now facing is not against a sovereign nation; it is against a group of terrorists who are very fluid, moving from one country to another. They are almost invisible. That is whom we are fighting against today.

We need every ally we can get. If we do not stop terrorism in the Middle East, it will be on our shores. We have said this again and again and again, and it is true.

One of the reasons I believe the spiritual door was opened for an attack against the United States of America is that the policy of our Government has been to ask the Israelis, and demand it with pressure, not to retaliate in a significant way against the terrorist strikes that have been launched against them.

Since its independence in 1948, Israel has fought four wars: The war in 1948 and 1949--that was the war for independence--the war in 1956, the Sinai campaign; the Six-Day War in 1967; and in 1973, the Yom Kippur War, the holiest day of the year, and that was with Egypt and Syria.

You have to understand that in all four cases, Israel was attacked. They were not the aggressor. Some people may argue that this was not true because they went in first in 1956, but they knew at that time that Egypt was building a huge military to become the aggressor. Israel, in fact, was not the aggressor and has not been the aggressor in any of the four wars.

Also, they won all four wars against impossible odds. They are great warriors. They consider a level playing field being outnumbered 2 to 1.

There were 39 Scud missiles that landed on Israeli soil during the gulf war. Our President asked Israel not to respond. In order to have the Arab nations on board, we asked Israel not to participate in the war. They showed tremendous restraint and did not. Now we have asked them to stand back and not do anything over these last several attacks.

We have criticized them. We have criticized them in our media. Local people in television and radio often criticize Israel, not knowing the true facts. We need to be informed.

I was so thrilled when I heard a reporter pose a question to our Secretary of State, Colin Powell. He said:

Mr. Powell, the United States has advocated a policy of restraint in the Middle East. We have discouraged Israel from retaliation again and again and again because we've said it leads to continued escalation--that it escalates the violence. Are we going to follow that preaching ourselves?

Mr. Powell indicated we would strike back. In other words, we can tell Israel not to do it, but when it hits us, we are going to do something.

But all that changed in December when the Israelis went into the Gaza with gunships and into the West Bank with F-16s. With the exception of last May, the Israelis had not used F-16s since the 1967 6-Day War. And I am so proud of them because we have to stop terrorism. It is not going to go away. If Israel were driven into the sea tomorrow, if every Jew in the Middle East were killed, terrorism would not end. You know that in your heart. Terrorism would continue.

It is not just a matter of Israel in the Middle East. It is the heart of the very people who are perpetrating this stuff. Should they be successful in overrunning Israel-- which they won't be--but should they be, it would not be enough. They will never be satisfied.

No. 7, I believe very strongly that we ought to support Israel; that it has a right to the land. This is the most important reason: Because God said so. As I said a minute ago, look it up in the book of Genesis. It is right up there on the desk.

In Genesis 13:14-17, the Bible says:

The Lord said to Abram, ``Lift up now your eyes, and look from the place where you are northward, and southward, and eastward and westward: for all the land which you see, to you will I give it, and to your seed forever. ..... Arise, walk through the land in the length of it and in the breadth of it; for I will give it to thee.''

That is God talking.

The Bible says that Abram removed his tent and came and dwelt in the plain of Mamre, which is in Hebron, and built there an altar before the Lord. Hebron is in the West Bank. It is at this place where God appeared to Abram and said, ``I am giving you this land,''--the West Bank.

This is not a political battle at all. It is a contest over whether or not the word of God is true. The seven reasons, I am convinced, clearly establish that Israel has a right to the land.

Eight years ago on the lawn of the White House, Yitzhak Rabin shook hands with PLO Chairman Yasser Arafat. It was a historic occasion. It was a tragic occasion.

At that time, the official policy of the Government of Israel began to be, ``Let us appease the terrorists. Let us begin to trade the land for peace.'' This process continued unabated up until last year. Here in our own Nation, at Camp David, in the summer of 2000, then Prime Minister of Israel Ehud Barak offered the most generous concessions to Yasser Arafat that had ever been laid on the table.

He offered him more than 90 percent of all the West Bank territory, sovereign control of it. There were some parts he did not want to offer, but in exchange for that he said he would give up land in Israel proper that the PLO had not even asked for.

And he also did the unthinkable. He even spoke of dividing Jerusalem and allowing the Palestinians to have their capital there in the East. Yasser Arafat stormed out of the meeting. Why did he storm out of the meeting? Everything he had said he wanted was offered there. It was put into his hands. Why did he storm out of the meeting?

A couple of months later, there began to be riots, terrorism. The riots began when now Prime Minister Ariel Sharon went to the Temple Mount. And this was used as the thing that lit the fire and that caused the explosion.

Did you know that Sharon did not go unannounced and that he contacted the Islamic authorities before he went and secured their permission and had permission to be there? It was no surprise.

The response was very carefully calculated. They knew the world would not pay attention to the details.

They would portray this in the Arab world as an attack upon the holy mosque. They would portray it as an attack upon that mosque and use it as an excuse to riot. Over the last 8 years, during this time of the peace process, where the Israeli public has pressured its leaders to give up land for peace because they are tired of fighting, there has been increased terror.

In fact, it has been greater in the last 8 years than any other time in Israel's history. Showing restraint and giving in has not produced any kind of peace. It is so much so that today the leftist peace movement in Israel does not exist because the people feel they were deceived.

They did offer a hand of peace, and it was not taken. That is why the politics of Israel have changed drastically over the past 12 months. The Israelis have come to see that, ``No matter what we do, these people do not want to deal with us. ..... They want to destroy us.'' That is why even yet today the stationery of the PLO still has upon it the map of the entire state of Israel, not just the tiny little part they call the West Bank that they want. They want it all.

We have to get out of this mind set that somehow you can buy peace in the Middle East by giving little plots of land. It has not worked before when it has been offered.

These seven reasons show why Israel is entitled to that land.

Suicidal Lies

Thomas L. Friedman
New York Times
March 31, 2002

The outcome of the war now under way between the Israelis and Palestinians is vital to the security of every American, and indeed, I believe, to all of civilization. Why? Quite simply because Palestinians are testing out a whole new form of warfare, using suicide bombers strapped with dynamite and dressed as Israelis to achieve their political aims. And it is working.

Israelis are terrified. And Palestinians, although this strategy has wrecked their society, feel a rising sense of empowerment. They feel they finally have a weapon that creates a balance of power with Israel, and maybe, in their fantasies, can defeat Israel. As Ismail Haniya, a Hamas leader, said in The Washington Post, Palestinians have Israelis on the run now because they have found their weak spot. Jews, he said, "love life more than any other people, and they prefer not to die." So Palestinian suicide bombers are ideal for dealing with them. That is really sick.

The world must understand that the Palestinians have not chosen suicide bombing out of "desperation" stemming from the Israeli occupation. That is a huge lie. Why? To begin with, a lot of other people in the world are desperate, yet they have not gone around strapping dynamite to themselves. More important, President Clinton offered the Palestinians a peace plan that could have ended their "desperate" occupation, and Yasir Arafat walked away. Still more important, the Palestinians have long had a tactical alternative to suicide: nonviolent resistance, à la Gandhi. A nonviolent Palestinian movement appealing to the conscience of the Israeli silent majority would have delivered a Palestinian state 30 years ago, but they have rejected that strategy, too.

The reason the Palestinians have not adopted these alternatives is because they actually want to win their independence in blood and fire. All they can agree on as a community is what they want to destroy, not what they want to build. Have you ever heard Mr. Arafat talk about what sort of education system or economy he would prefer, what sort of constitution he wants? No, because Mr. Arafat is not interested in the content of a Palestinian state, only the contours.

Let's be very clear: Palestinians have adopted suicide bombing as a strategic choice, not out of desperation. This threatens all civilization because if suicide bombing is allowed to work in Israel, then, like hijacking and airplane bombing, it will be copied and will eventually lead to a bomber strapped with a nuclear device threatening entire nations. That is why the whole world must see this Palestinian suicide strategy defeated.

But how? This kind of terrorism can be curbed only by self-restraint and repudiation by the community itself. No foreign army can stop small groups ready to kill themselves. How do we produce that deterrence among Palestinians? First, Israel needs to deliver a military blow that clearly shows terror will not pay. Second, America needs to make clear that suicide bombing is not Israel's problem alone. To that end, the U.S. should declare that while it respects the legitimacy of Palestinian nationalism, it will

115

have no dealings with the Palestinian leadership as long as it tolerates suicide bombings. Further, should make clear that Arab leaders whose media call suicide bombers "martyrs" aren't welcome in the U.S.

Third, Israel must tell the Palestinian people that it is ready to resume talks where they left off with Mr. Clinton, before this intifada. Those talks were 90 percent of the way toward ending the occupation and creating a Palestinian state. Fourth, U.S. or NATO troops must guarantee any Israeli-Palestinian border.

"The Spanish Civil War was the place where the major powers all tested out their new weapons before World War II," said the Israeli political theorist Yaron Ezrahi. "Well, the Israeli-Palestinian conflict today is the Spanish Civil War for the 21st century. A big test is taking place of whether suicide terrorism can succeed as a strategy for liberation. It must be defeated, but that requires more than a military strategy."

The Palestinians are so blinded by their narcissistic rage that they have lost sight of the basic truth civilization is built on: the sacredness of every human life, starting with your own. If America, the only reality check left, doesn't use every ounce of energy to halt this madness and call it by its real name, then it will spread. The Devil is dancing in the Middle East, and he's dancing our way.

Lessons Of History Bedevil The Mideast
Desperate Acts Of Self-Destruction
Will Not Achieve Palestinians' Goals

Alan Keyes
www.msnbc.com
April 8, 2002

The fretting of the international community, now joined by the United States, over Israel's attempt to defend itself from suicide bombing, treats the situation in the Middle East as though history, and moral reality, are irrelevant. Such is not the way to peace, or justice, in the region.

In negotiations with the PLO, the Palestinian Authority and Arafat, the Israelis have made concessions, reached agreements, signed on the dotted line and followed through on those agreements. Israel turned substantial authority in the West Bank and Gaza over to Yasser Arafat as a result of such an agreement.

And from the Palestinians has come lip service to peace and preparation for war. The one thing - the one thing - that was required of their side has never been delivered. And that is to stop killing Israelis. The Palestinians have been unwilling to cease manipulating the peace process through deadly destruction of civilians.

The Israelis, as a result, face the same situation we do in our war on terror. No defensive action will actually forestall the death-dealing blow of suicidal terror. The only possible step is to attack those who have incited, equipped and financed those who are determined to kill you.

America understands this when we are attacked. We must acknowledge the same imperative in the policies that the Israelis are now pursuing.

REAL SELF-GOVERNMENT

I have long supported the legitimate demand for Palestinian self-government. But the first prerequisite of self-government is to govern one's own passions, resentment and anger. Martin Luther King made the 20th century's racial progress possible by teaching us that even the victims of terrible oppression still are responsible for not contributing to the very culture of violence that oppresses them.

The Palestinian people need that kind of leadership now. But they aren't getting it. Instead, they are being led into desperate acts of self-destruction. Suicide bombing symbolizes all that such leadership offers. It accomplishes nothing except national immolation on the altar of prideful leaders preaching the martyrdom of despair.

Arafat's leadership consists precisely of inciting his people to martyrdom. But "martyr" means "witness." And the Palestinian people don't need more witnesses to violence, incitement, reprisal and revenge. They desperately need witnesses to hope, leaders who will look at Israel's record with Egypt, Jordan and others.

Israel has kept its bargains. That is an offer of hope. The Palestinian choice for life and dignity is to challenge Israel with new, real offers of legitimate peaceful coexistence. The Palestinians can have reasonable hope that such offers will be met with honorable reply from Israel. But this can't happen until the Palestinians reject the leadership now pushing them over the desperate precipice of revenge and self-destruction.

America can help by repudiating the plea of victimization as excuse for the surrender to evil. We do not relieve Palestinian suffering by coddling a leadership which is seeking quite consciously to incite self-destruction. If we have the toughness to join Israel in refusing to deal with such leadership, we will open the door to hope. We will help spark the Palestinian people to turn away from the cult of revenge, and to look for leaders willing to offer something better than the pointless destruction of the innocent.

Netanyahu Speech Before The US Senate

Binyamin Netanyahu
www.netanyahu.com
April 10, 2002

Distinguished Senators,

I have come here to voice what I believe is an urgently needed reminder: That the war on terror can be won with clarity and courage or lost with confusion and vacillation.

Seven months ago, on a clear day in the capital of freedom, I was given the opportunity to address you, the guardians of liberty

I will never forget that day - a day when words that will echo for ages pierced the conscience of the free world:

Words that lifted the spirits of an American nation that had been savagely attacked by evil. Words that looked that evil straight in the eye and boldly declared that it would be utterly destroyed. Most important, words that charted a bold course for victory.

Those words were not mine. They were the words of the President of the United States.

In an historic speech to the world last September and with determined action in the crucial months that followed, President Bush and his administration outlined a vision that had the moral and strategic clarity necessary to win the war on terror.

The moral clarity emanated from an ironclad definition of terror and an impregnable moral truth. Terrorism was understood to be the deliberate targeting of civilians in order to achieve political ends. And it was always unjustifiable. With a few powerful words, President Bush said all that needed to be said: 'Terrorism is never justified.'

The strategic clarity emanated from the recognition that international terrorism depends on the support of sovereign states, and that fighting it demands that these regimes be either deterred or dismantled.

In one clear sentence, President Bush expressed this principle: 'No distinction will be made between the terrorists and the regimes that harbor them.'

This moral and strategic clarity was applied with devastating effect to the Taliban regime in Afghanistan that supported Al Qaeda terrorism.

No false moral equivalence was drawn between the thousands of Afghan civilians who were the unintentional casualties of America's just war and the thousands of American civilians deliberately targeted on September 11.

No strategic confusion lead America to pursue Al Qaeda terrorists while leaving the Taliban regime in place. Soon after the war began, the American victory over the forces of terror in Afghanistan brought to light the third principle in the war on terror - namely, that the best way to defeat terror is to defeat it.

At first, this seemingly trite observation was not fully understood. Contrary to popular belief, the motivating force behind terror is neither desperation nor destitution. It is hope - the hope of terrorists systematically brainwashed by the ideologues who manipulate them that their savagery will break the will of their enemies and help them achieve their objectives - political, religious, or otherwise.

Defeat this hope and you defeat terrorism. Convince terrorists, their sponsors, and potential new recruits that terrorism will be thoroughly uprooted and severely punished and you will stop it cold in its tracks.

By adhering to these three principles - moral clarity, strategic clarity and the imperative of victory - the forces of freedom, led by America, are well on their way to victory against terror from Afghanistan.

But that is only the first step in dismantling the global terrorist network. The other terrorist regimes must now be rapidly dealt with in similar fashion.

Yet today, just seven months into the war, it is far from certain that this will be done.

Faced with the quintessential terrorist regime of our time - a regime that both harbors and perpetrates terror on an unimaginable scale - the free world is muddling its principles, losing its nerve, and thereby endangering the successful prosecution of this war.

The question many in my country are now asking is this: Will America apply its principles consistently and win this war, or will it selectively abandon those principles and thereby ultimately lose the war?

My countrymen ask this question because they believe that terrorism is an indivisible evil and that the war against terror must be fought indivisibly. They believe that if moral clarity is obfuscated, or if you allow one part of the terror network to survive, much less be rewarded for its crimes, then the forces of terror will regroup and rise again.

Until last week, I was certain that the United States would adhere to its principles and lead the free world to a decisive victory. Today, I too have my concerns.

I am concerned that when it comes to terror directed against Israel, the moral and strategic clarity that is so crucial for victory is being twisted beyond recognition.

I am concerned that the imperative of defeating terror everywhere is being ignored when the main engine of Palestinian terror is allowed to remain intact.

I am concerned that the State of Israel, that has for decades bravely manned the front lines against terror, is being pressed to back down just when it is on the verge of uprooting Palestinian terror.

These concerns first surfaced with the appearance of a reprehensible moral symmetry that equates Israel, a democratic government that is defending itself against

120

terror, with the Palestinian dictatorship that is perpetrating it

The deliberate targeting of Israeli civilians is shamefully equated with the unintentional loss of Palestinian life that is the tragic but unavoidable consequence of legitimate warfare.

Worse, since Palestinian terrorists both deliberately target civilians and hide behind them, Israel is cast as the guilty party because more Palestinians have been killed in Arafat's terrorist war than Israelis.

No one, of course, would dare suggest that the United States was the guilty party in World War II because German casualties, which included millions of civilians, were twenty times higher then American casualties.

So too, only a twisted and corrupt logic would paint America and Britain as the aggressors in the current war because Afghan casualties are reported to have well exceeded the death toll of September 11.

My concern deepened when, incredibly, Israel was asked to stop fighting terror and return to a negotiating table with a regime that is committed to the destruction of the Jewish State and openly embraces terror.

Yasser Arafat brazenly pursues an ideology of policide - the destruction of a state -and meticulously promotes a cult of suicide.

With total control of the media, the schools, and ghoulish kindergarten camps for children that glorifies suicide martyrdom, Arafat's dictatorship has indoctrinated a generation of Palestinians in a culture of death, producing waves of human bombs that massacre Jews in buses, discos, supermarkets, pizza shops, cafés - everywhere and anywhere.

Israel has not experienced a terrorist attack like the one the world witnessed on that horrific day in September. That unprecedented act of barbarism will never be forgotten.

But in the last eighteen months, Israel's six million citizens have buried over four hundred victims of terror - a per capita toll equivalent to half a dozen September 11ths. This daily, hourly carnage is also unprecedented in terrorism's bloody history.

Yet at the very moment when support for Israel's war against terror should be stronger than ever, my nation is being asked to stop fighting.
Though we are assured by friends that we have the right to defend ourselves, we are effectively asked not to exercise that right.

But our friends should have no illusions. With or without international support, the government of Israel must fight not only to defend its people, restore a dangerously eroded deterrence and secure the Jewish State, but also to ensure that the free world wins the war against terror in this pivotal arena in the heart of the Middle East.

Israel must now do three things. First, it must dismantle Arafat's terrorist regime and expel Arafat from the region. As long as the engineer of Palestinian terror remains in the territories, terror will never stop and the promise of peace will never be realized.

Second, Israel must clean out terrorists, weapons, and explosives from all Palestinian controlled areas. No place, whether it is a refugee camp in Gaza or an office in Ramallah can be allowed to remain a haven for terror.

Third, Israel must establish physical barriers separating the main Palestinian population centers from Israeli towns and cities. This will prevent any residual terrorists from reaching Israel.

Done together, these three measures will dramatically reduce terrorism, bring security to the people of Israel and restore stability to the region.

Last week, the government of Israel began to take the second of these vital steps. Rather than bomb Palestinian populated cities and towns from the air - an operation that would have claimed thousands of civilian casualties - the Israeli army is taking on greater risk by using ground forces that painstakingly make their way through the hornet's nests of Palestinian terror.

But instead of praising Israel for seeking to minimize civilian casualties through careful and deliberate action, most of the world's governments shamelessly condemn it.

For seven months, many of these governments have rightly supported the war against Afghan terror. Yet after only seven days, their patience for the war against Palestinian terror ran out.

The explanations that are offered for this double standard are not convincing.

First it is said that war on Palestinian terror is different because a political process exists that can restore security and advance peace.

This is not so. There can never be a political solution for terror. The grievance of terrorists can never be redressed through diplomacy. That will only encourage more terror.

Yasser Arafat's terrorist regime must be toppled, not courted. The Oslo agreements are dead. Yasser Arafat killed them.

He tore it to shreds and soaked it in Jewish blood by violating every one of its provisions, including the two core commitments he made at Oslo: to recognize the State of Israel and to permanently renounce terrorism

With such a regime and such failure of leadership, no political process is possible. In fact, a political process can only begin when this terrorist regime is dismantled.

Second, it is said that waging war on Palestinian terror today will destabilize the region and cripple the imminent war against Sadaam Hussein.

This concern is also misplaced.

Clearly, the urgent need to topple Sadaam is paramount. The commitment of America and Britain to dismantle this terrorist dictatorship before it obtains nuclear weapons deserves the unconditional support of all sane governments.

But contrary to conventional wisdom, what has destabilized the region is not Israeli action against Palestinian terror, but rather, the constant pressure exerted on Israel to show restraint.

It is precisely the exceptional restraint shown by Israel for over a year and a half that has unwittingly emboldened its enemies and inadvertently increased the threat of a wider conflict.

If Israeli restraint were to continue, the thousands that are now clamoring for war in Arab capitals will turn into millions, and an avoidable war will become inevitable.

Half-measures against terrorists will leave their grievances intact, fueled by the hope of future victory. Full- measures will not redress those grievances, but it will convince them that pursuing terror is a prescription for certain defeat.

America must show that it will not heed the international call to stop Israel from exercising its right to defend itself. If America compromises its principles and joins in the chorus of those who demand that Israel disengage, the war on terror will be undermined.

For if the world begins to believe that America may deviate from its principles, then terrorist regimes that might have otherwise been deterred will not be deterred. Those that might have crumbled under the weight of American resolve will not crumble. As a result, winning the war will prove far more difficult, perhaps impossible.

But my friends, I must also tell you that the charge that Israel, of all countries, is hindering the war against Sadaam is woefully unjust.

For my country has done more than any other to make victory over Sadaam possible.

Twenty-one years ago, Prime Minister Menachem Begin sent the Israeli air force on a predawn raid hundreds of miles away on one of the most dangerous military missions in our nation's history.

When our pilots returned, we had successfully destroyed Sadaam's atomic bomb factory and crippled his capacity to build nuclear weapons.

Israel was safer - and so was the world.

But rather than thanking us for safeguarding freedom, the entire world condemned us.

Ten years later, when American troops expelled Iraqi forces in the Gulf War, then secretary of Defense Richard Cheney, expressed a debt of gratitude to Israel for the bold and determined action a decade earlier that had made victory possible.

Indeed, I am confident that in time those who would condemn Israel now will understand that rooting out Palestinian terror today will also make both Israel and the world safer tomorrow.

For if we do not immediately shut down the terror factories where Arafat is producing human bombs, it is only a matter of time before suicide bombers will terrorize your cities.

If not destroyed, this madness will strike in your buses, in your supermarkets, in your pizza parlors, in your cafes. Eventually, these human bombs will supplement their murderous force with suitcases equipped with devices of mass death that could make the horrors of September 11 pale by comparison.

That is why there is no alternative to winning this war without delay. No part of the terrorist network can be left intact. For if not fully eradicated, like the most malignant cancer, it will regroup and attack again with even greater ferocity. Only by dismantling the entire network will we be assured of victory.

But to assure that this evil does not reemerge a decade or two from now, we must not merely uproot terror, but also plant the seeds of freedom

Because only under tyranny can a diseased totalitarian mindset be widely cultivated. This totalitarian mindset, which is essential for terrorists to suspend the normal rules that govern a man's conscience and prevents him from committing these grisly acts, does not breed in a climate of democracy and freedom.

The open debate and plurality of ideas that buttress all genuine democracies and the respect for human rights and the sanctity of life that are the shared values of all free societies are a permanent antidote to the poison that the sponsors of terror seek to inject into the minds of their recruits. That is why it is also imperative that once the terrorist regimes in the Middle East are swept away, the free world, led by America, must begin to build democracy in their place.

We simply can no longer afford to allow this region to remain cloistered by a fanatic militancy. We must let the winds of freedom and independence finally penetrate the one region in the world that clings to unreformed tyranny.

That in exercising our basic right to defend ourselves Israel is condemned by Arab dictatorships is predictable.

That today a Europe which sixty years ago refused to lift a finger to save millions of Jews has turned its collective back on the Jewish State is downright shameful.

But my friends, I must admit. I expected no better from them.

Yet the America I know has always been different.

History has entrusted this nation with carrying the torch of freedom. And time and time again, through both war and peace, America has carried that torch with courage and with honor, combining a might the world has never known with a sense of justice that no power in history has possessed.

I have come before you today to ask you to continue to courageously and honorably carry that torch by standing by an outpost of freedom that is resisting an unprecedented terrorist assault. I ask you to stand by Israel's side in its fight against Arafat's tyranny of terror, and thereby help defeat an evil that threatens all of mankind.

Evil Triumphs When Good Men Do Nothing

Jack Kemp
Copley News Service
April 10, 2002

Just before he left for the Middle East, Secretary of State Colin Powell went on "Meet the Press" to say, "I'm going to consult with our Arab friends to reinforce to them that they have a role to play. They have to do much more in the future, with respect to encouraging Palestinian leaders to take more responsible action to bring this kind of violence under control, to speak of peace, not incite people to violence."

Although President George W. Bush is asking Israel to cease its military operations in the West Bank, he and Powell also understand there is absolutely no moral equivalence between that operation and the Palestinian suicide bombings that provoked it. Before he left for the Middle East, Powell said of the Palestinian bombings, "Violence of this kind is not justified, no matter how aggrieved the people may feel, no matter how humiliated they may feel, no matter how much they yearn for a political solution, no matter they want to have their own state."

Edmund Burke, the great 18th-century Scottish philosopher and British parliamentarian, said, "Evil triumphs when good men do nothing." Last Friday, Saudi Arabia's Ambassador to the United States, Bandar bin Sultan, demonstrated his willingness to let evil triumph in the Middle East when, in a Washington Post op-ed, he refused to condemn targeted Palestinian suicide bombing attacks against innocent Israeli civilians and failed to call for their immediate cessation.

The day before the prince's op-ed, Bush had the moral clarity to call suicide bombers of innocents "murderers," not martyrs. He also called on all governments in the region to "do everything in their power to stop terrorist activities, to disrupt terrorist financing, and to stop inciting violence by glorifying terror in state-owned media or telling suicide bombers they are martyrs." Bandar did just the opposite. He ridiculed as "senseless" Bush's call on Arafat to insist that his people end the suicide bombings and to do whatever else he can to stop the violence.

The ambassador did so much more in his column, though, than simply "do nothing" to stop the intentional killing of innocent Israelis. He leveled an unambiguous threat to America when he labeled Israel a "burden" to America, proclaimed that "America's worldwide interests are victims of the Israeli occupation" and foresaw a disruption to the war on terrorism unless the United States turns against Israel.

Bandar's column is both confusing and confounding. He professes to justify the unjustifiable by drawing a false "moral equivalence" between the intentional Palestinian murder of innocent Israeli civilians and the accidental and unavoidable deaths of Palestinian civilians that result when careful Israeli military responses to those murders attempt to root out terrorists and uproot their infrastructure. He condemns Israel's refusal to allow itself to be destroyed as "Israeli oppression of Palestinians." The ambassador labels Israeli acts of self-defense as "terrorism," and he condones cold-blooded Palestinian murder of innocents as legitimate "resistance" to Israel's so-called occupation of Palestinian territory.

125

Bandar and others in the Arab world fabricate a false image of a "cycle of violence," contending that Yasser Arafat cannot be expected to call for an end to Palestinian violence until Israel ceases its own military response to the violence, which he neglects to acknowledge is always in direct response to violence that the Palestinian terrorists began in the first place. But this notion of a "cycle of violence" is nothing but the handmaiden of "moral equivalence." There is no "cycle" of violence; there is "perpetual" violence kept in motion by radical Palestinians intent on driving Israel into the sea, and screeds like the Bandar column are the fuel that keeps the perpetual violence in motion.

To appreciate just how disingenuous and calculated this endless string of excuses for Palestinian violence is, recall that just a few weeks ago, when the Israelis had imposed a unilateral cease-fire on themselves and were calling on the Palestinians to respond in kind, the response was then that Palestinian violence could not be stopped until the Israeli "occupation" ended. No matter what Israel does, the Palestinians, and now Bandar, have an excuse for why Palestinian violence cannot stop. And remember, when Arafat says, "... until the occupation is over," he means not just until the West Bank and Gaza are given over, he means until all of that territory identified on Arab and Palestinian maps as "Occupied Territory" is given over, and that means all of Israel.

This kind of distorted and belligerent rhetoric is carefully conceived within a pretense of friendship for America to stir up Arab hatred against Jews and the United States and to whip up a whirlwind of confusion among non-Arabs everywhere.

Nobel Prize-winning author Elie Wiesel once pondered how "Shoah" -- which means whirlwind or confusion in Hebrew -- comes about in the affairs of man. It happens, Wiesel concluded, "When good and bad are put on the same plane, and the evil receive the approval of the just."

Ten Tips On How To Be An Arafat Apologist

Jamie Glazov
www.frontpagemagazine.com
April 11, 2002

With all of the empirical evidence that has now confirmed, beyond any reasonable doubt, Arafat's terrorist connections and duplicitous behavior vis-à-vis Israel, it has become impossible for Arafat's apologists to make any legitimate excuses for their hero. I know a number of academics and writers that have become extremely depressed because of this situation. Having based their entire lives and professional careers on blaming Israel for any and every sparrow that fell from the sky, they have now lost the will to live. I feel sorry for these pathetic people.

I have decided to come forward to help the individuals who want to continue championing Yasser Arafat but simply don't know how.

Seeing that I have dedicated most of my adult life to observing and dissecting the psychotic mindset that it takes to blame Israel for the conflict in Palestine, I know exactly what it takes to be an Arafat supporter. Even in these difficult times, I can teach an individual how to effectively defend Arafat and the Palestinian Authority -- even if the entire charade is filled with specious nonsense and lies.

I have created ten tips on how to be an Arafat apologist. They come with an easy to follow step-by-step guide. All you have to do is fertilize your personal dedication to anti-Semitism and then simply allow yourself to become as delusional as humanly possible.

The video infomercial for these tips should be coming out next month on television stations across the United States. Meanwhile, here is the basic outline for all those Jew-haters who have dedicated their lives to blaming Israel for every Arab terrorist act but thought that doing so was no longer possible:

Tip #1 - Imagine that the Palestinians are fighting for a homeland that was taken away from them by the evil Jews.

That's right. The foundation to becoming and remaining a faithful pro-Arafat enthusiast is to intoxicate yourself with the belief that the Palestinians actually once owned a homeland that was, in turn, stolen by the greedy and parasitic Jews.

While trying to convince yourself of this fantasy, ignore the historical fact that the Palestine Mandate was never a nation, let alone even a political entity of any kind. It was a "mandate" that was created by the British from the remnants of the Turkish Empire after World War I. 10% of it was given to the Jews and 90% was given to the Palestinian Arabs.

The key here is that you should never worry about where 90% of Palestine actually is. Just obsess with the miniscule tiny bit of land that the Israelis "occupy" now. It's not important that this land was never officially "owned" by anyone in the first place.

You should also never reflect on whether all of your rage and hatred on this issue is proportional to the fact that Israel consists of 1% of the land in the Middle East.

Just get really angry that Israel is on territory that you think should be given to the Palestinians. And because you think this, then it automatically makes it right and historically correct.

You should never wonder how your moral indignation on this issue fits with your complete indifference to the fact that Jordan occupies 80% of the land that made up the original Palestine Mandate. So if you really cared about the Palestinians, you would obviously be focusing your energy on protesting the crime being perpetrated by the Jordanians against the Palestinians. But the key here is that, well, deep down, you don't really care about the Palestinians -- and neither should you. You must never admit this, but the Palestinians are only there for you to cynically exploit as pawns in your contributory effort to finish off what Adolph Hitler started.

That's right. You know what I'm talking about. And even the Palestinians are in on this with you. I mean, think about it: if the Palestinians themselves really cared about getting a homeland, don't you think that they would be screaming about -- and fighting for -- the land that Jordan occupies? Don't you think it is somewhat curious that Jordan has never, even for a second, been the target of a Palestine liberation movement?

Don't you think it is a little bit curious that, in 1948, the Palestinian Arabs rejected an international resolution that would have established a Palestinian state, and instead focused all of their energies on destroying the new Jewish state?

You're starting to get the picture now, right?

So be a smart and clever Arafat apologist. The overall objective of your life should be facilitating the killing of Jews and destroying the state of Israel. The last thing you should be doing is worrying about the Palestinians. At the same time, however, in terms of what you actually say in public, you must always discuss the Middle East "problem" on the assumption that you are agonizing over the Palestinians' plight and how their entire "homeland" somehow lies in tiny little Israel.

It is also a very good idea that you always refer to the myth of how the Jews "stole" the Palestinian "homeland" in passing, because then it makes its reality appear to be a given. You can't believe how effective this ploy can be, especially in the midst of people who know nothing about Middle East history.

So believe in yourself and just do it!

Tip #2 - Never question the cause of Palestinian terror.

Every time that a Palestinian blows himself up along with innocent Jewish civilians, including babies in carriages, you should shake your head in despair and say things like, "That poor Palestinian. But he simply had no choice. The Israelis have pushed his people beyond their means."

You should always say things like this with a tone that implies that the "Israeli occupation" is the most oppressive reality in the world. Say things like, "The Israelis are doing to the Palestinians what the Nazis did to them." Follow this up with sentences like, "The Jews have obviously forced the Palestinians into terrorism."

When you mouth these slogans, make sure to have a serious and sincere look on your face, otherwise the asininity of what you are saying might become more easily discernable. Maintaining a sober facial expression can be made easier if you convince yourself that the wars of 1973 and 1967 are irrelevant to the subject at hand.

Before Israel was attacked in 1973, it occupied less of the land that is now in dispute, and before 1967, it occupied none of it. In other words, the Arab terror that was unleashed against Israel in 1967 had nothing to do with the Israeli "occupation" of the West Bank and Gaza Strip because the "occupation" did not exist.

From 1949-1967, Jordan had occupied the West Bank while Egypt controlled the Gaza Strip. But instead of the Arabs using terror against Egypt and Jordan to get them off of the Palestinians' "land,", an Arab war of terror against Israel was launched in 1967. Israel won that war and grabbed both the West Bank and Gaza Strip as a security measure.

So why is it, you think, that Jordan's annexation of the West Bank and Egypt's annexation of the Gaza Strip from 1949-67 didn't trigger any emotions in the Palestinians who lived in those territories? Why is it that not once, in all of those 18 years, was there even a sentence of indignation uttered by the Palestinians or by their "liberation" organization about the injustice done to the inhabitants of the West Bank and Gaza Strip? Why did other Arab states say nothing about it?

You know why. And this means that the terror against Israel has always been, and still is, caused by something other than Israelis being on any kind of "territory." I'll give you six hints about what the real cause is connected to:

Hint #1: Hitler formulated the Final Solution because of it.

Hint #2: It has something to do with why Israel cannot be found on a map in Palestinian geography classes. It's also connected to why Palestinian textbooks teach Palestinian children that Jews are evil thieves who have taken Arab land and who must therefore be killed. The textbooks also tell the kiddies that suicide bombing is what Allah loves most, since that noble and holy activity is the most effective way of murdering Jews and "liberating" Palestine.

Hint #3: It's why the Palestinian Authority has published the Arabic translation of Mein Kampf, and why that tract has reached number six on its best-seller list.

Hint #4: It is connected to why, in 1960, when the Israelis captured Adolph Eichmann, the government-run Saudi Arabian newspaper ran a story headlined: "Arrest Of Eichmann, Who Had The Honor Of Killing Six Million Jews."

Hint #5: It has something to do with the great honor and respect that is bestowed in the Middle East upon anyone who succeeds in killing Jews. For instance, if you blow yourself up along with some innocent Jewish mothers and babies, your picture will be plastered on posters throughout your hometown. Your family will acquire a revered place in society and will also receive $25,000 in American currency from Saddam Hussein. You, meanwhile, will get to fulfill all of your wildest and repressed sexual fantasies with 72 virgins in heaven.

Hint #6: The whole matter is related to why Hashemi Rafsanjani, the eminent representative of "Iranian moderation," has boasted that once the Muslim world gets a hold of nuclear weapons, which he assures will be very soon, the Jewish "question" will be solved forever.

Now that you know what the real cause of Palestinian terror is, make sure to always deny it. Instead, consistently maintain to others that it is the result of Israelis being on "Palestinian territory."

Tip #3 - Ignore the words of Palestinians.

When you make your arguments for the Palestinian right to a homeland, always make sure to emphasize that the Palestinians acknowledge the right of Israel to exist. To make sure this works effectively, never mention, or ever even think about, what the Palestinians actually say themselves.

For instance, never talk about the Palestinian Covenant of 1968, because it embodies the philosophical principles of the Palestinians themselves and says things that would shatter the foundation to all of your arguments. For instance, Article 19 affirms that, "The partition of Palestine in 1947 and the establishment of Israel is fundamentally null and void, whatever time has elapsed, because it is contrary to the wish of the people of Palestine and its natural right to its homeland."

Article 15 states that, "The liberation of Palestine, from the Arab viewpoint, is a national duty to repulse the Zionist, Imperialist invasion from the great Arab homeland and to purge the Zionist presence from Palestine."

Also ignore Articles 20 and 22, because they reject even the historical and religious ties of Jews to the Holy Land itself. And that is precisely why Palestinian children are yet to find the state of Israel on any maps in their geography classes.

You also shouldn't worry that Arafat has never repudiated the Articles in the Palestinian Covenant of 1968. This explains why, when speaking English to Western audiences, he always talks about how he acknowledges the right of Israel to exist. But when he speaks Arabic to Arab audiences, he does little else but boast about his successes in working toward the Palestinians' most ambitious goal: to destroy the state of Israel. One only has to briefly listen to the Arab media, mosque sermons, and classroom and cafe conversations to gauge that this disposition represents a wide consensus in Arab society in general and in Palestinian society in particular.

Thus, when you are trying to persuade someone about the good intentions of Arafat and the Palestinian Authority, and how they accept the existence of Israel, never mention what the Palestinians themselves talk about. You should most definitely stay away from the subject of the 1968 Palestinian Covenant, because this could cause you problems. If someone else brings it up, change topics immediately.

Tip #4 - Imagine that Palestinians were, and are better off without Israel and the Israeli "occupation."

You should be constantly angry about the suffering of Palestinians and be convinced that it is the fault of Israel. Palestinian suffering should always be equated with

Israeli responsibility. These two notions must be inseparable in your mind.

Palestinian suffering is definitely not the fault of Arafat or of all the Arab states - even though they have done everything in their power to make sure that the Palestinians do not receive a homeland.

That's right. So try not to reflect too much on why the Palestinians of the West Bank are barred from becoming citizens in the Arab world. When the Gaza Strip was under Egyptian administration, for instance, the Palestinians there were denied Egyptian citizenship and thereby remained stateless. This is exactly why the Palestinians are known as "refugees."

The Arabs love their Palestinian brothers. It's just that, well, they love them from a distance.

In any case, you should try your hardest to convince yourself that the Palestinians' life under the Israeli "occupation" is the worst experience of any people under any regime in the history of the human race. The first step to believing this notion is to ignore the fact that Palestinians are much worse off in occupied Lebanon, where they are denied basic rights to employment, healthcare and government services -- unlike the Palestinians in Israel and in the "occupied" territories.

You should also avoid the subject of how Kuwait ethnically cleansed all Palestinians (about 300,000 of them) just a decade ago, and how Jordanians slaughtered thousands of them after the 1967 war.

Try to imagine that all of this isn't very relevant. And neither is the fact that the world community never said too much about these Arab atrocities. It's okay when Muslim Arabs practice genocide against Palestinians. It's only wrong when the Israelis oppress Palestinians in the effort to defend themselves from terror.

You also shouldn't stress yourself about the racism against Arabs that this whole double standard implies. Indeed, by holding Jews up to a higher moral accountability than Arabs, the view that lets Arabs off the hook for oppressing their own brethren implies a civilizational inferiority to them -- and a civilizational superiority to Jews. But don't think through this too much. You might get depressed after realizing that, deep down, just like a Leftist despises the "underclass" people for whom he purports to speak, so too you have smug contempt for the Arabs that you believe you represent in your self-alienated imagination.

The key, in general, is that you should just avoid the whole issue of how the Jews have treated the Palestinians much better than the Arabs have.

It is also a very good idea for you to ignore the fact that Israel has given birth to an Arab citizenry inside Israel of more than one million people. This way you won't have to wonder how it is that, as Israeli citizens, Arabs have more rights, privileges and opportunities than the citizens of any Arab state in the Middle East. Unlike their Arab brothers and sisters, Arab citizens in Israel vote in free elections and are themselves elected to the Israeli parliament. In other words, the only place where Arabs know democracy and a high standard of living is in a Jewish nation.

This is a hard pill to swallow for a person like you, who aspires to demonize Israel and to glorify the Arab world as the embodiment of true democracy and stupendous progress in world civilization.

So what you have to do is visualize images of how Israel is the most evil nation on the face of the earth and how Arabs and Palestinians have endured unspeakable suffering because of it.

Tip #5 - Imagine that Israel controls the "occupied" territories for some bizarre, vague and sinister reason.

That's right: imagine that Israel controls the "occupied" territories because Jews have nothing better to do than to inflict pain. They think it's in their interest to trigger terrorism against themselves, as well as to ignite the hatred of a large portion of the world's population.

With great moral indignation, you should say things like, "the Israelis need to get out of the occupied territories." Say this as if it is a really easy, simple and safe thing for the Israelis to do.

Never consider that the Israeli "occupation" of the territories in question might actually not be the greatest crime in world history. It might also not deserve immediate rectification. Sometimes land is confiscated when aggressive and terrorist states repeatedly attack their neighbors -- and lose.

But this should not be your concern.

What should be your concern is to say things that make Israel look as if it controls areas like the West Bank because Israelis need to fill the void of no longer being allowed to sacrifice and eat gentile babies in their religious rituals.

Tip #6 - Say that Arafat isn't a terrorist.

You should always say things like: "One man's terrorist is another man's freedom-fighter." After that, say things like, "Arafat is a freedom-fighter."

You must always ignore that Arafat has provided sanctuary and support to Palestinian suicide bombers and terrorists of all stripes. Be very open-minded about how he has personally endorsed suicide bombings rhetorically and celebrated the cult of "martyrdom" and other forms of homicide.

And always make sure to announce things like, "Arafat has imprisoned militants." When you say this, don't worry that the Palestinian "jails" that Arafat places "militants" in are notorious for their bars in the front and revolving doors at the back. Just tell people that Arafat is really trying to get terrorism under control.

Don't lose any sleep over the fact that explosives of the specific type used by Palestinian suicide bombers have been found in Palestinian police stations all over the "occupied" territories. Also don't concern yourself with the fact that 500 Palestinians were just recently arrested in and around Arafat's compound and that dozens of them were on Israel's lists of most-wanted terrorists. Arafat was obviously still trying his best to track these people down. The reason he couldn't find them was that they were clever-ly hiding in his office while he was desperately patrolling the West Bank looking for them.

And by all means, deny to others, as well as to yourself, that connections between the Palestinian Authority and international Islamic terror organizations, includ-ing al-Qaeda, have now been established beyond any reasonable doubt. If you accept this reality, then your whole belief system will come crashing down.

Just look really sure of yourself and say things like, "Arafat isn't a terrorist. He is a freedom fighter."

Tip #7 - Imagine that Arafat has the interests of his own people in mind.

This is the key to being an effective apologist for Arafat. You must always tell people that your hero truly cares about his own people -- even though the history of his every move negates the possibility of this being the case.

A person that truly wanted the best for the Palestinian people would have embraced an offer that accepted 95% of the Palestinians' negotiating demands and would have given the Palestinians their own sovereign state in Judea, Samaria and the Gaza Strip, more than 90 percent of the West Bank, and a capital in Jerusalem. That's what Israeli Prime Minister Ehud Barak offered Arafat in 2000. But Arafat rejected the proposal, demanding, instead, the flooding of Israel with millions of Palestinians. He knew, as Israelis did, that such a development would destroy Israel as a Jewish state.

Arafat shrewdly understood that Israel could not, and would not, engage in self-destruction and this is how he succeeded in his main objective: to avoid the cre-ation of a new Arab state and to annihilate the only Jewish one. That's what the "Palestinian uprising," after all, is really all about.

It is obvious, therefore, why Arafat has consistently stifled all Israeli efforts to improve the prosperity of the Palestinian people. He wants his people to bleed in mis-ery and destitution. That way their suffering can be exploited in the Arabs' suicide wars against Israel.

Now the key for you, therefore, is to deny the obvious.

You know that the "Palestinian problem" is far more useful to Arafat than its solution will ever be. Arafat knows that peace with Jews is his own political suicide at best -- and his own death warrant at worst.

What you have to do is look people in the eyes as honestly as you can and say things like, "Arafat is really trying to help his people." Say this as if you yourself have been talking to Arafat and that he tells you things that he wouldn't confide in most people.

Tip #8 - Say that Arab terrorism has nothing to do with jealousy.

It is absolutely crucial that you consistently tell anyone you talk to that Israel is vehemently hated by the Arabs because of something that Israel has done to the Arabs.

Never consider what the Arabs of the Middle East would do with all of their time if there were no Israel.

Never suspect that Middle Eastern Arabs spend such an inordinate amount of their daily life hating a nation that takes up 1% of land in the Middle East because they might have a little problem with envy and jealousy.

It might not be the easiest thing for Arabs to reconcile themselves with the reality that their culture has yet to produce one prosperous, functional and democratic society. Yet they see that the Jews have accomplished exactly that - in a tiny piece of land that was a desert fifty years ago. Indeed, the Jews have built the most powerful economy and the only industrial and democratic nation in the entire Middle East.

This is a very painful truth for Middle Eastern Arabs to accept. So as an Arafat apologist, your job is to completely ignore this phenomenon. You must fantasize that when Arabs jump up and down with ferocious rage for hours on end every day screaming "Death to Israel," that the solution to their rage is definitely not to get a job, let alone a life of any kind. The solution lies in the Jews smartening up and stopping being so evil. If they did that, then obviously Arabs would find better things to do than spend ten hours a day, seven days a week, hollering at the top of their lungs and foaming at their mouths in the middle of the barren deserts that they have lived in for centuries.

You see: Arabs don't fail in making progress because of any serious pathology in their personal lives and culture. No, they mope around in long robes and headscarves in medieval societies because of what the Jews are doing to the Palestinians. And yes, ok, these same Arabs never lifted a finger or mouthed a word of protest when the Palestinians received much harsher treatment from Arabs. But don't think this through. Actually, if anyone ever points this out to you, just say that the Arabs did protest the persecution of the Palestinians by other Arabs but that the Western press just didn't report it.

Tip #9 - Say it's in Israel's interest to pursue "peace".

You should constantly say that it is in Israel's interest to pursue "peace," even though all of the evidence suggests the exact opposite. More Israelis have died from terrorism since the signing of Oslo in 1993 than in the four decades before it. There have been more than 80 suicide bombings against Israel since the "peace process" began. Before Oslo, suicide bombings were almost non-existent. Each new atrocity against Israelis since 1993, meanwhile, has been hailed by the Palestinian media and the Palestinian Authority that controls it.

You should ignore facts such as these and make it a daily habit to say things like, "The Israelis should really try to make peace with Arafat. It's in their interest."

Tip #10 - Shed yourself of any integrity you might have ever had.

In order for you to practice the previous nine tips successfully, you need to make sure that you rid yourself of any personal dignity or integrity that might ever have been a part of your character and personality. You have to be absolutely shameless and live by absolutely no ethical or moral standard of any kind. Otherwise you will not be able to lie to others, and to yourself, the way I instruct you to. Arafat supporters have done it effectively before you. But now you can do it the best. Be the best liar you can be. That way, you might yet become the best Arafat apologist on earth. You can do it!

Poison: The Use Of Blood Libel In The War Against Israel

Raphael Israeli
Jerusalem Center For Public Affairs
April 15, 2002

An Epidemic on the West Bank

On the morning of March 21, 1983, one week before Pesach, in a high school in the town of Arrabeh in the Jenin area of the West Bank, Palestinian girls (between the ages of 15 and 17) were sitting in several classrooms when they suddenly began to faint, one after the other. They were taken to hospital and checked, but no medical reason was found for their fainting. Yet they had fainted, so a search began in order to find the reason.

Then other girls of the same age began fainting in other villages on the West Bank, in Bethlehem, and afterwards in Hebron and Halhul, Tulkarem and Nablus. Over a period of a few days approximately 1,000 girls ended up in hospital at the same time, seemingly victims of an epidemic.

Since all this occurred just before Pesach, the motif of blood libel and mass poisoning was raised. The rumors began that it was the Israelis who had poisoned the girls.

The Arab Tradition of Miracle Literature

The famous Japanese director Akira Kurasawa made a classic film in 1950, "Rashomon," based on a Japanese folk tale from the twelfth century. It told the story of the family of a Samurai who were attacked by thieves. Afterward, there are four different stories of the incident. The dead Samurai's spirit tells what happened from his point of view. There are also the stories of his wife, one of the servants, and a woodcutter who happened to witness the attack. The film is a fascinating depiction of four different points of view of the same event, and Kurasawa's message is that there is no objective truth. The truth can be given different interpretations, and everyone can see the truth from a different angle.

In the Middle Ages there was a genre in Arabic literature known as miracle literature. The author would describe his adventures on the way to China or India. He would tell fantastic stories about places with all kinds of amazing things, about diamonds, silver, and gold, about eagles that would fly with him, and afterwards it came together in the wonderful stories we know in the collection of A Thousand and One Nights.

The Palestinian-Arab-Muslim stories about what happens here simply remind one of the miracle literature. Stories come out of the imagination and are strengthened by new inventions. This is what interests the people, and whether it happened or not is not that important. In the political reality, the invented story is believed in the Palestinian-Arab-Muslim consciousness as the truth.

Accusing the Israelis

After the mass fainting epidemic in 1983, the girls claimed that they had been poisoned, although the doctors who checked them found no evidence of this. Then the Arabs began to make charges that maybe, and then certainly, it was Israelis who had poisoned the girls. They also presented the reason -- the fantastic story that the Jews have an interest in countering the high Palestinian birthrate so they specifically targeted young girls approaching the age of marriage. The poisoning was done to harm this most fertile age group in order to limit Arab demographic growth. They even said they had found medical proof, claiming that urine tests showed a high protein level, which means that something is abnormal in the fertility system.

They began to build all kinds of theories and enlisted statements from Arab doctors. Then, amazingly, the Israeli newspapers began asking why the Jews, who were killed in the gas chambers, would do something like this, and there were calls for an investigation of the actions of the then-Likud government of Menachem Begin. The Arabs saw the Israelis themselves accusing their own government and raised the tone of their accusations even higher.

Baruch Modan, the director-general of the Health Ministry and one of the leading epidemiologists in Israel, headed an investigation team and, of course, found nothing. At a press conference he announced that there was no evidence of poisoning and that this was nothing more than a case of mass hysteria. But in this case the foreign journalists refused to accept the professional opinion of a well-respected doctor.

The Palestinians became bolder and offered still more proof. Yellow powder was found on the window sills. Dr. Modan and his team had checked the powder and found it to be from nearby pine trees, but this did not convince the foreign journalists who kept on saying that the Israelis were guilty.

However, the Israeli media started to backtrack because Dr. Modan is indeed a respected authority. Suddenly a spate of articles began appearing on the history of blood libels and protesting that here, too, on the eve of Pesach, they are acting toward us just as they did in the Middle Ages, with accusations of poisoning the wells. It was amazing -- within ten days the Israeli press went from self-accusation to massive self-defense. That is the Israeli side of Rashomon.

The Story Grows

On the Palestinian side, doctors reported on the signs which indicated that there must have been mass poisoning. The accusations increased and were adopted by the leadership of the PLO, which in 1983 had been deported from Lebanon to Tunisia.

The Palestinians then took out their secret weapon. They saw the massive damage this negative publicity was doing to Israel and they received international encouragement, so they began to send girls to pretend to faint. They prepared trucks in advance, and when the girls got to school they would be put on the trucks, with the journalists and photographers following them to the hospital. As soon as the foreign journalists left, according to Israeli journalists who were following the story, the girls would get up out of bed. Yet the Arabs saw how much they could get out of this hoax and turned it into a true story which they encouraged.

The International Perspective

The third side of this Rashomon story is the interest of the international organizations and the international media. The French newspapers Liberation and Le Monde headlined that there was evidence that Israel had poisoned the children. The presentation of Dr. Modan was called a weak attempt by the Israelis to hide their crime. In the UN, the Security Council came out with a harsh statement against Israel -- how could Israel allow such a thing to happen? The entire story was taken as based on reality and the entire affair just got bigger, involving the Arab League and the Islamic Conference.

Finally, Israel formally asked the International Red Cross and the World Health Organization to come and investigate. The International Red Cross representative came and issued a weak statement that he did not find evidence. When he was asked why he did not make a stronger statement, and thus let the hoax stand, he replied that this is not the job of the International Red Cross. If the Palestinians suffered, they must have suffered from something real, and if they did not suffer from poisoning, then they suffered from the "poison of occupation." Afterwards, the International Red Cross was asked to publicize its findings. They wrote back saying that it was not their policy to publicize their findings, although if they had been against Israel, the findings would have been publicized immediately.

Eventually, the world-renowned Center for Disease Control in Atlanta reported on the results of its investigation. The U.S. experts concluded that this was indeed a case of mass hysteria, a phenomenon similar to teenage girls fainting at rock concerts.

Apart from the New York Times, which buried a retraction of its accusations against Israel in the back pages, no other newspaper bothered to do even that. Israeli ambassadors in a number of countries asked local newspapers to print a story of correction, but they were ignored. So a case of mass hysteria was exploited by the Palestinians into a major international affair, with great success.

The Politics of Human Rights

A while after this event, the Palestinian representative to the Human Rights Commission in Geneva declared to the Commission that Israelis had spread the AIDS virus to 300 Palestinian children in order to destroy an entire generation as part of an Israeli plan of genocide. This is the very same claim as in the poisoning episode. Of course no member of the Commission, except for the Israeli representative, protested or said anything. Then the Israeli representative asked the chairman of the Commission, who was Czech, how he could allow the body which he headed to remain silent in the face of such an accusation, which becomes a part of the minutes of the UN. The chairman then wrote a letter to the members of the Commission saying that the accusation was never proven and that all members of the Commission should avoid making unsubstantiated charges in the future.

The same evening, five members of the Commission from countries famous for human rights such as Iraq and Sudan demanded that the chairman retract his letter, claiming he had no authority to annul what any representative had said, and warned him that he would be removed from office if he did not comply. So he wrote another letter canceling his original letter.

The Sterilizing Bubble Gum

In 1997 the Palestinians exposed yet another Israeli "plot to suppress Arab population growth." They claimed to have tested packets of strawberry-flavored bubble gum which were found to be spiked with sex hormones and sold at low prices near schoolhouses in the West Bank and Gaza Strip. It was claimed that the gum aroused irresistible sexual appetites in women, then it sterilized them. According to Palestinian Supply Minister Abdel Aziz Shaheen, it was capable of "completely destroying the genetic system of young boys," as well.

In this case, Palestinians allege, Israel came with chewing gum laced with progesterone, one of the two hormones of femaleness. The hormone, they say inaccurately, drives women wild with desire and serves as a contraceptive, too -- corrupting Arab women while ensuring they cannot reproduce. The story was reminiscent of a furor over Israeli chewing gum a year earlier in Egypt. The story grew with the retelling. Shaheen contended that the gum was sold "only at the gates of primary schools or kindergartens," because Israelis "want to destroy our genetic system" by giving sex hormones to children before their bodies can cope with them. By the time the story reached Hebron in the West Bank, local health official Mahmoud Batarna claimed to have captured 200 tons of gum.

The Washington Post commissioned a test of allegedly contaminated chewing gum provided by Palestinian health officials. Dan Gibson, professor of pharmaceutical chemistry at Hebrew University and a member of the left-wing lobby group Peace Now, said that, using a mass spectrometer capable of detecting as little as a microgram of progesterone, he found none in the gum.[1]

More Poison

The pattern of miracle literature is repeated time and time again in the Arab world and there is no end to it. There are two Israeli teams in Egypt that have been doing exceptional work developing desert agriculture in that country, and they have produced amazing results. Yet the hostile Egyptian media have accused the Israelis of poisoning the land and destroying Egyptian agriculture.

In June 1997, the Palestinian El Quds newspaper reported the accusation by the head of the Criminal Division of the Palestinian Police in Nablus that the Israeli security services operated a ring of AIDS-infected Israeli prostitutes sent to infect the Palestinian people.[2]

These are just a few of the hoaxes that have been used as propaganda tools against Israel. Some twenty such events are detailed and explained in Poison: Modern Manifestations of the Blood Libel, a new book just released by Lexington Books. It documents the story of modern blood libel against the Jews and Israel, involving not only Arabs and Muslims but also the European media and world organizations.

Blood Libel as a Form of Warfare

During the current Palestinian offensive, Yasser Arafat has for many months been accusing Israel of using weapons of depleted uranium against Palestinians, and told the French paper l'Humanite (21 Feb 2002) that this information was confirmed by the U.S., although the U.S. has never confirmed any such claims. In a speech broadcast by El-Jezira TV on 27 March 2002, Arafat charged Israel's army with using depleted uranium gasses and even toxic waste. Israel was also accused of distributing booby trapped or poisoned sweets across the West Bank to kill children.

The international calls for an investigation into Israel's conduct in Jenin, during its offensive in response to Palestinian "Islamikaze"3 bombings in Israeli cities, follow all too closely the pattern of world support for the Palestinian fabrications described above. Sadly, we are once again witness to yet another round of blood libel as part of the ongoing Arab war against Israel.

*   *   *

Notes
1. Barton Gellman, "Pop! Went the Tale of the Bubble Gum Spiked With Sex Hormones," Washington Post, July 28, 1997, p. A14.

2. Maariv, Shabbat, 27 June 1997, p. 19.

3. "Islamikaze" is a word coined by the author combining the words "kamikaze" and "Islam," to signify that the so-called "suicide" bombers have nothing suicidal about them, but that they, just like the Japanese kamikaze before them, are intent on mass killing of the enemy, with the difference being that the kamikaze operated against military targets while the Islamikaze acts mainly against innocent civilians.

The Litmus Test For Authentic 'Freedom Fighters'

Binyamin Netanyahu
Prepared remarks to the pro-Israel rally at Washington, DC Mall
April 15, 2002

At this very hour, the entire nation of Israel is silent. The Jewish state is commemorating the 20,000 soldiers who gave their lives to defend the state of Israel and the thousands of civilians struck down by the forces of terror in our long battle for freedom. Just a few months ago, America too lost thousands of its citizens to terrorist savagery. And we stand here today to honor these fallen sons and daughters of liberty.

But I've also come here today, my dear friends, to give thanks, to thank all of you for standing up for the Jewish state when so many outside America stood silent -- -- to thank the American people and their government for remembering the difference between freedom and tyranny, between right and wrong, between good and evil, to thank President Bush for boldly declaring that terrorism, the deliberate attack on civilians, is never justified; it's always evil -- -- and for bravely charting a course that will lead the free world to victory.

No greater friend of Israel has ever been in the White House, and no president has ever championed a cause that was more just. Israel and the United States are today fighting the same battle, waging the same war, confronting the same evil. Like the United States, Israel did not seek this war. It was forced on us by a savage enemy that glorifies in a culture of death, a culture where murderers are called martyrs and where suicide is sanctified.

My friends, an enemy that sends children to die and to kill other children is an enemy that cannot be placated. An enemy that openly preaches the destruction of our state is not a partner for peace. With such evil, there can be no negotiations and no concessions -- -- because the only way to confront -- to fight such evil is to confront it. The only way to defeat it is to destroy it. And once terror is defeated, I believe other Palestinians will come to the fore with whom we will forge a genuine and lasting peace.

Now, I don't want you to be fooled by the apologists of terror. They tell us that the way to end terror is to appease it, to meet or give in to the terrorists' demands -- because -- listen to their argument -- because, they tell us, the root cause of terrorism - - did you ever hear that? -- the root cause of terrorism is the deprivation of national and civic rights.

Well, let's examine that proposition. If that were the case, then in the thousands of conflicts and struggles for national and civil rights in modern times, we would expect to have found endless examples of terrorism. But guess what: We don't.

Mahatma Gandhi did not use terrorism in fighting for the independence of India. The peoples of Eastern Europe did not resort to terrorism to bring down the Berlin Wall. But one other example; one other example. Martin Luther King did not resort to terrorism in fighting for equal rights for all Americans. In fact, speaking in this city, in this very place, four decades ago, Martin Luther King preached a creed that was the very opposite of terrorism -- not violence, non-violence; completely the opposite.

So now we must ask ourselves, why did all these people pursue their cause without resorting to terror? Because they believed in the sanctity of each human life, because they were committed to the ideals of liberty, because they championed the values of democracy; simply put, because they were democrats, not terrorists. That's why.

But, you see, those who practice terrorism do not believe in these ideals. In fact, they believe the very opposite. They believe that the cause they espouse is so all-encompassing, so total, that it justifies anything and everything. They believe that it allows them to break any law, to discard any moral code, to trample all human rights into the dust. They believe that their cause permits them to indiscriminately murder and maim innocent men and women. They believe that it lets them blow up a bus full of babies.

My friends, there's a name for the mindset that produces this evil. It is called totalitarianism. Indeed, this is the root cause of terrorism. The root cause of terrorism is the totalitarian mindset, a tyranny that systematically brainwashes the minds of its subjects, to suspend all moral constraints for the sake of a twisted cause. And this is why, from its inception, totalitarianism has always been wedded to terrorism, from Lenin to Stalin to Hitler to the ayatollahs to Saddam Hussein to Osama bin Laden to Yasser Arafat.

My friends, I want you to listen to me carefully, because I want to say something else. It is not merely that the goals of terrorists do not justify the means they use. It is that the means that they choose tell you what their real goals are, because those who target the innocent will never protect freedom and human rights.

And how can we see that? We can see that clearly every time terrorists come to power. Those who fight as terrorists rule as terrorists, setting up dark dictatorships, whether in Iraq or in Iran or in Afghanistan or in Arafatistan.

And indeed, Yasser Arafat is the quintessential terrorist. Both his means and his goals are illegitimate. Arafat pursues a goal of policide, the destruction of a state, by employing the means of suicide, suicide and mass terror. Arafat does not want a Palestinian state next to Israel. He wants a Palestinian state instead of Israel.

But my friends, any time that Israel was confronted with an Arab leader who was genuinely interested in peace and delivered a message of peace to his own people in Arabic, every time we were confronted with such a leader, we made peace.

Menachem Begin made peace with Egypt's Anwar Sadat, and Yitzhak Rabin made peace with Jordan's King Hussein. But five Israeli prime ministers have been unable to make peace with Arafat. Do you know why? For a simple reason: Because Arafat does not want peace.

Now, let me show you the difference between one leader and another. Until the day I die, I will not forget the day that King Hussein came with me to visit the bereaved families of seven young Israeli school girls, 12 years old, gunned down by a deranged Jordanian soldier. He knelt before the families, before the mothers and fathers. He was weeping. There were tears streaming down his eyes and he said, "Please, please forgive me. Please forgive me."

Now, contrast that to Yasser Arafat. Do you know what he does? He glorifies these mass killers. He calls public squares after them. He names buildings, streets in their honor. He has suicide kindergarten camps. He has suicide universities. He has suicide museums. For G-d's sake, this is the man who pays the checks. He signs the checks for the explosives of the suicides. He is a terrorist, if there ever was one.

Now, you may remember that many right here, right here in this town, and many in Israel, many in Washington and many in Jerusalem, had hoped, at the beginning of the Oslo accords, that Arafat would prove to be a statesman, a Palestinian King Hussein. Instead he's proved to be a Palestinian Saddam Hussein.

And I ask you, what do you do with Saddam Hussein? Do you negotiate with him? Do you make concessions to him? Do you appease him? No, exactly. You do the same thing to him that the U.S. just did to the Taliban. You defeat him.

America rightly defeated the Taliban. And today, in an historic mission that deserves the support of civilized peoples and nations everywhere, President Bush is courageously leading the free world to dismantle Saddam's regime before it acquires nuclear weapons.

Well, if we're to end terror and begin peace in our own part of the world, Israel must too now dismantle Arafat's regime, a mission also worthy of support from all foes of terror and all friends of liberty.

I think that garnering this support is much easier now than it was a year ago. I think that the face of Palestinian terror has finally been unmasked. The people of this great nation are not fooled by Yasser Arafat and the con artists he employs on American television. Americans know that Yasser Arafat is nothing more than Osama bin Laden with good PR. Americans know that if it looks like a duck, it walks like a duck, it talks like a duck, it's a terrorist.

Today, gathered in the capital of liberty, we send a powerful message to the entire world. To those in Europe who 60 years ago did nothing to prevent the slaughters of millions of Jews and who today side with the mass killers who seek to destroy the Jewish state, we send this message: History's shame will once again fall on you.

To the anti-Semites of the world, we send a message of defiance. The Jewish people are not afraid. We will roll back the savage assaults, those assaults that you direct against us. We will courageously stand up to you and to all other enemies. And to the terrorists and terror regimes that support them, we send a warning: The free world, led by President Bush, has awoken to your evil. Terror will be given no quarter, no peace, until it is wiped out from our world.

My friends, I want to congratulate all of you on the largest rally in support of Israel in Israel's history. I want to assure you that standing tall, standing proud, we will win this war. We will secure our states and we'll preserve our liberty. And in defending the Jewish state, all of you here today in Washington, Jews and non-Jews alike, are defending the cause of liberty, a cause that has once again made America, Israel and the defenders of freedom the last, best hope on earth.

We shall win.

Whosoever Blesses Them
The Intifada And Its Defenders.

Larry Miller
Daily Standard
April 22, 2002

I was watching Greta Van Facelift on Fox the other night, and she and her guests made me talk back to the TV. Shout back, actually. Nothing witty or trenchant, you understand, just something like, "Oh, come on!" Now, to be honest, it was late, and I was downstairs alone, and I was a little, what's the word . . . loaded, yes, that's the word. I was a little shined up. A little spiffed and a little miffed, and I shouted something and angrily turned off the remote. I don't know exactly how angrily a remote can be turned off, but as angrily as you can push a pfennig-sized piece of round plastic, that's how angrily I did it. Then I walked back to the bar, made myself one-for-the-stairs (as opposed to one-for-the-road) and read some P.G. Wodehouse to restore my cheery nature. But back to the freshly-tightened Greta.

Her guests were (INSERT INDISTINGUISHABLE ARAB NAME), from Hamas, and their attorney, Stanley Cohen. No, that's not a joke. Would that it were. Stanley Cohen, the attorney for Hamas. Check that handle again: Stanley Cohen. I mean, if you tried to make up a better name than that, you couldn't do it. Let's give it a shot, though, shall we? Irving Lefkowitz. Nah, too obvious. Lew Fishman. No, no, sounds like a carpet salesman. Isaac Bashevis Singer? Now I'm reaching. Nope, you just can't beat good ol' Stan Cohen. Yes, Stanley Cohen, folks, a hard-left, righteously indignant true-believer, an honors grad-uate from the William Kunstler School of Just-Not-Getting-It-And-Never-Will, who had flown all the way from New York to sit next to his wonderful client over there in not the land of milk and honey. Stanley Cohen. A man who, if he listened very carefully, would no doubt hear voices in the next room planning to blow the eyes out of more of his nieces and nephews. Stanley Cohen, and even typing that name right now and remem-bering this horrible man damning his own people again and again and again, I crack a nervous smile, because they're my people, too, and, God help me, if I didn't laugh, I think I might cry.

Oddly enough, out of the three of them, the homunculus from Hamas didn't bother me at all. I mean, if you think about it, why should he bother any American? We know exactly who he is and, in a way, we should be grateful for that. Because if we're only willing to absorb their own words--nevermind their demonic deeds--he and his brethren have a perfectly uncomplicated point of view and agenda, and their clarity should give us our own clarity, and wouldn't that be refreshing? You want us dead? Well, now, isn't that a funny coincidence. Guess what we want?

My point is, if American TV calls up and wants to put these philanthropists on, who could blame them for saying, "Sure!" I can just see them bursting out laughing and slapping each other on the back. ("They're going to put us on Fox TV! I told you terror works! And I'll bet their Green Room beats the snot out of Al Jazeera. I mean, please, how many olives can you eat?") If we're stupid enough to do that, I don't blame them for taking us up on it. All they have to do is take a few minutes away from packing rusty nails around the C4, pick one of their guys who looks, relatively, the least like a vicious scumbag, borrow a suit, and send him forth to smile for the cameras. With Stanley Cohen.

144

But let's leave the newly-stretched Greta for a moment, as well as our friends Stanley and Ishmael (no joke, his real name). A brief overview of the situation is always valuable, so as a service to all Americans who still don't get it, I now offer you the story of the Middle East in just a few paragraphs, which is all you really need. Don't thank me. I'm a giver. Here we go:

The Palestinians want their own country. There's just one thing about that: There are no Palestinians. It's a made up word. Israel was called Palestine for two thousand years. Like "Wiccan," "Palestinian" sounds ancient but is really a modern invention. Before the Israelis won the land in war, Gaza was owned by Egypt, and there were no "Palestinians" then, and the West Bank was owned by Jordan, and there were no "Palestinians" then. As soon as the Jews took over and started growing oranges as big as basketballs, what do you know, say hello to the "Palestinians," weeping for their deep bond with their lost "land" and "nation." So for the sake of honesty, let's not use the word "Palestinian" any more to describe these delight-ful folks, who dance for joy at our deaths until someone points out they're being taped. Instead, let's call them what they are: "Other Arabs From The Same General Area Who Are In Deep Denial About Never Being Able To Accomplish Anything In Life And Would Rather Wrap Themselves In The Seductive Melodrama Of Eternal Struggle And Death." I know that's a bit unwieldy to expect to see on CNN. How about this, then: "Adjacent Jew-Haters."

Okay, so the Adjacent Jew-Haters want their own country. Oops, just one more thing. No, they don't. They could've had their own country any time in the last thirty years, especially two years ago at Camp David. But if you have your own country, you have to have traffic lights and garbage trucks and Chambers of Commerce, and, worse, you actual-ly have to figure out some way to make a living. That's no fun. No, they want what all the other Jew-Haters in the region want: Israel. They also want a big pile of dead Jews, of course--that's where the real fun is--but mostly they want Israel. Why? For one thing, trying to destroy Israel--or "The Zionist Entity" as their textbooks call it--for the last fifty years has allowed the rulers of Arab countries to divert the attention of their own people away from the fact that they're the blue-ribbon most illiterate, poorest, and tribally backward on God's Earth, and if you've ever been around God's Earth, you know that's really saying something. It makes me roll my eyes every time one of our pundits waxes poetic about the great histo-ry and culture of the Muslim Mideast. Unless I'm missing something, the Arabs haven't given anything to the world since Algebra, and, by the way, thanks a hell of a lot for that one.

Chew this around and spit it out: Five hundred million Arabs; five million Jews. Think of all the Arab countries as a football field, and Israel as a pack of matches sitting in the middle of it. And now these same folks swear that if Israel gives them half of that pack of matches, everyone will be pals. Really? Wow, what neat news. Hey, but what about the string of wars to obliterate the tiny country and the constant din of rabid blood oaths to drive every Jew into the sea? Oh, that? We were just kidding.

My friend Kevin Rooney made a gorgeous point the other day: Just reverse the num-bers. Imagine five hundred million Jews and five million Arabs. I was stunned at the simple brilliance of it. Can anyone picture the Jews strapping belts of razor blades and dynamite to themselves? Of course not. Or marshalling every fiber and force at their disposal for gener-ations to drive a tiny Arab state into the sea? Nonsense. Or dancing for joy at the murder of innocents? Impossible. Or spreading and believing horrible lies about the Arabs baking their bread with the blood of children? Disgusting. No, as you know, left to themselves in a world of peace, the worst Jews would ever do to people is debate them to death.

Mr. Bush, God bless him, is walking a tightrope. I understand that with vital operations coming up against Iraq and others, it's in our interest, as Americans, to try to stabilize our Arab allies as much as possible, and, after all, that can't be much harder than stabilizing a roomful of supermodels who've just had their drugs taken away. However, in any big-picture strategy, there's always a danger of losing moral weight. We've already lost some. After September 11 our president told us and the world he was going to root out all terrorists and the countries that supported them. Beautiful. Then the Israelis, after months and months of having the equivalent of an Oklahoma City every week (and then every day) start to do the same thing we did, and we tell them to show restraint. If America were being attacked with an Oklahoma City every day, we would all very shortly be screaming for the administration to just be done with it and kill everything south of the Mediterranean and east of the Jordan. (Hey, wait a minute, that's actually not such a bad id . . . uh, that is, what a horrible thought, yeah, horrible.)

There's bad news on the losing moral weight front, and the signs are out there. Last week, the day after Secretary Powell left on his mission (whatever that was), the Los Angeles Times ran its lead editorial in one hundred percent support of the trip and the pressure he and President Bush were putting on Israel. Here's a good rule of thumb: If the Los Angeles Times thinks you're doing a great job, everything you're doing is wrong, stupid and mortally dangerous. If they think everything you're doing is wrong, stupid and mortally dangerous, you're doing a great job, and, in fact, your chances are probably very good for getting on the fast track for sainthood.

So, now, back to Greta. You know what made me mad enough to shout? You might not even think it was that big a thing.

After the show she said to these guys, "Thank you, gentlemen, for being my guests." "Gentlemen." "Guests." "My guests." That's what it's come to with these nonjudgmental hosts and hostesses. Nice, huh? "Thank you, Mr. Stalin, sir, for being so gracious in giving us your valuable time." "My eternal gratitude, Chairman Mao, for taking precious moments away from your splendid Five-Year Plan and visiting with us in this most convivial way."

And I winced, and grunted, and shouted. Oh, yeah, and made that drink.

I mean, please, folks. In 1941, did reporters feel it was their duty to give equal time to Hitler and Hirohito? Would Stanley Cohen have represented them? Ok, Stanley probably would have, but would any American have stood still while he told us about it?

The Canary In Europe's Mine

Jeff Jacoby
The Boston Globe
April 28, 2002

The rocks have been lifted all over Europe, and the snakes of Jew-hatred are slithering free.

In Belgium, thugs beat up the chief rabbi, kicking him in the face and calling him "a dirty Jew." Two synagogues in Brussels were firebombed; a third, in Charleroi, was sprayed with automatic weapons fire.

In Britain, the cover of the New Statesman, a left-wing magazine, depicted a large Star of David stabbing the Union Jack. Oxford professor Tom Paulin, a noted poet, told an Egyptian interviewer that American Jews who move to the West Bank and Gaza "should be shot dead." A Jewish yeshiva student reading the Psalms was stabbed 27 times on a London bus. Antisemitism, wrote a columnist in The Spectator, "has become respectable . . . at London dinner tables." She quoted one member of the House of Lords: "The Jews have been asking for it and now, thank God, we can say what we think at last."

In Italy, the daily paper La Stampa published a Page 1 cartoon: A tank emblazoned with a Jewish star points its gun at the baby Jesus, who pleads, "Surely they don't want to kill me again?" In Corriere Della Sera, another cartoon showed Jesus trapped in his tomb, unable to rise, because Ariel Sharon, with rifle in hand, is sitting on the sepulchre. The caption: "Non resurrexit."

In Germany, a rabbinical student was beaten up in downtown Berlin and a grenade was thrown into a Jewish cemetery. Thousands of neo-Nazis held a rally, marching near a synagogue on the Jewish sabbath. Graffiti appeared on a synagogue in the western town of Herford: "Six million were not enough."

In Ukraine, skinheads attacked Jewish worshippers and smashed the windows of Kiev's main synagogue. Ukrainian police denied that the attack was anti-Jewish.

In Greece, Jewish graves were desecrated in Ioannina and vandals hurled paint at the Holocaust memorial in Salonica. In Holland, an anti-Israel demonstration featured swastikas, photos of Hitler, and chants of "Sieg Heil" and "Jews into the sea." In Slovakia, the Jewish cemetery of Kosice was invaded and 135 tombstones destroyed.

But nowhere have the flames of antisemitism burned more furiously than in France.

In Lyon, a car was rammed into a synagogue and set on fire. In Montpellier, the Jewish religious center was firebombed; so were synagogues in Strasbourg and Marseille; so was a Jewish school in Creteil. A Jewish sports club in Toulouse was attacked with Molotov cocktails, and on the statue of Alfred Dreyfus in Paris, the words "Dirty Jew" were painted. In Bondy, 15 men beat up members of a Jewish football team with sticks and metal bars. The bus that takes Jewish children to school in Aubervilliers has been attacked three times in the last 14 months. According to the police, metropolitan Paris has seen 10 to 12 anti-Jewish incidents per day since Easter.

147

Walls in Jewish neighborhoods have been defaced with slogans proclaiming "Jews to the gas chambers" and "Death to the Jews." The weekly journal Le Nouvel Observateur published an appalling libel: It said Israeli soldiers rape Palestinian women, so that their relatives will kill them to preserve "family honor." The French ambassador to Great Britain was not sacked -- and did not apologize -- when it was learned that he had told guests at a London dinner that the world's troubles were the fault of "that shitty little country, Israel."

"At the start of the 21st century," writes Pierre-Andre Taguieff, a well-known social scientist, in a new book, "we are discovering that Jews are once again select targets of violence. . . . Hatred of the Jews has returned to France."

But of course, it never left. Not France; not Europe. Antisemitism, the oldest bigotry known to man, has been a part of European society since time immemorial. In the aftermath of the Holocaust, open Jew-hatred became unfashionable; but fashions change, and Europe is reverting to type.

To be sure, some Europeans are shocked by the re-emergence of Jew-hatred all over their continent. But the more common reaction has been complacency. "Stop saying that there is antisemitism in France," President Jacques Chirac scolded a Jewish editor in January. "There is no antisemitism in France." The European media have been vicious in condemning Israel's self-defense against Palestinian terrorism in the West Bank; they have been far less agitated about anti-Jewish terror in their own backyard.

They are making a grievous mistake. For if today the violence and vitriol are aimed at the Jews, tomorrow they will be aimed at the Christians.

A timeless lesson of history is that it rarely ends with the Jews. Militant Islamist extremists were attacking and killing Jews long before they attacked and killed Americans on Sept. 11. The Nazis first set out to incinerate the Jews; in the end, all of Europe was ablaze.

Jews, it is often said, are the canary in the coal mine of civilization. When they become the objects of savagery and hate, it means the air has been poisoned and an explosion is soon to come. If Europeans don't rise up and turn against the Jew-haters, it is only a matter of time until the Jew-haters rise up and turn against them.

From Defeat To Reconciliation To Peace
But Only In That Order

Victor Davis Hanson
National Review Online
April 30, 2002

Anytime we see screaming anti-American crowds full of hate, with pathetic banners and frothing demagogues, we should be skeptical that such raw enmity represents a real threat to our security - or even any enduring and irreconcilable antipathy to the United States. The fact is that almost any people, at almost any time, can be whipped into a frenzy and yet very soon afterwards also be convinced to drop its fanaticism and recognize its errors - once war and subsequent military defeat bring home to them the wages of such lunatic bellicosity.

Note the now suddenly subdued Afghani and Pakistani streets - for much of last fall, both, we were told, were the engines that drove anti-Americanism in the region. Neither U.N. negotiations with the Taliban nor globetrotting Nobel Peace prizewinners nor injunctions from the Arab or Islamic Leagues would have brought calm. Only force, or the threat of force, brought by the United States could do that.

Fifth-century Athens flourished on the principles of radical democracy and overseas imperialism - a devil's bargain that empowered the underclass at home by extracting capital for it from subject states abroad. Yet the bitter defeat at Aegospotami at the end of the Peloponnesian War - and the final dismantling of the Athenian navy - disabused Athenians of their credence in the once-grand overseas imperialism that had slaughtered Melians and attempted the same to Syracusans. Their subsequent reconstituted postbellum democracy engaged in neither ethnic cleansing nor capital expropriation abroad - so cognizant were they of the past follies that led finally to Spartan triremes docked at their Piraeus.

A review of Confederate rhetoric between 1850 and 1860 might suggest not only that an entire generation was nursed on hatred of the North, but that such a recalcitrant, proud, and militarily capable people could never be reconciled to the Union, could never be defeated, and thus would have to exist as an independent slave society - forever. Yet by 1864 beleaguered Georgians were telling Sherman's Army of the West to "hurry up" and get over to the Carolinians to punish those "who started this damn war." Negotiating with Jefferson Davis in 1863, electing George McClellan in 1864, or restraining William Tecumseh Sherman would not have saved lives and brought peace, but rather would have ensured a nightmare whose consequences would be frightening even today.

Seeing old newsreel footage of civilian rallies in Tokyo in 1938 and at Nuremberg at about the same time is still chilling. Millions of Japanese and Germans - the elderly, children, women young and old - seem to be blood-drunk on militarism, screaming chants of victory, mesmerized with the belief that their armies in China and in eastern Germany were invincible, the vanguard of even greater victories to come. Indeed, in late 1941 the Japanese, flush with victory, declared December 8 to be forever a national holiday. But by 1945 humbled diplomats huddled in a burned-out Tokyo and Berlin with their American advisors to craft democratic constitutions - humane blueprints still in force today.

Safety for London was not obtained by asking Mr. Hitler to curb his use of V-1s; Pearl Harbor was not left unconquered on account of Mr. Yamamato's leniency; nor did the Communist Koreans leave the South through negotiations. Instead dour men like Bomber Harris, Curtis LeMay, and Matthew Ridgeway were unleashed to ensure that their enemies were no longer able to inflict the mayhem they desired.

Force, then, has a way of making people change. Even the most militant citizenries can be disabused of their rather dangerous ideas - but only after they understand that the logical consequences of their extremism are impoverishment, ruin, and humiliation. Currently in the Middle East we are shown glimpses of small boys with plastic replicas of bomb-belts, and then told that "an entire generation will grow up to despair and anger." CNN reporters stick microphones into the faces of angry residents of Jenin, and logically get the response they hoped for - pledges of undying hatred for Israel "and the Jews." Pundits wrinkle their brows and then pontificate that "violence breeds violence," and that hatred has become so deeply embedded that real peace is impossible. In fact, peace in the region has never been more likely than it is at the present moment.

Both our own war against the terrorists and the Israeli response on the West Bank - if conducted forcefully and coupled with the clear intention to help the defeated to rebuild their societies - can prompt real peace rather than breed endless war. Already the fragile Afghani government not only is far better than the Taliban, but in many ways offers more hope than anything in the region - from Syria to Pakistan. We pray to prompt a similar metamorphosis in Iraq, where the most evil nation in the Islamic world might transmogrify into the most promising. And it would not be naïve to envision that, after the current Mideast war, a newly regrouped Palestine - under far better and real democratic leadership - could have a more liberal and humane government than its thuggish neighbors such as Syria and Lebanon.

As the smoke clears from Jenin, many Palestinians slowly - but still privately - will begin to assess the catastrophe. What will they learn? That murdering bombers ultimately draw a devastating Israeli response. That their own leadership that condoned and at times sponsored the terror, and so prompted the war, allows neither dissent nor freedom in formulating its policy - and thus is solely responsible for its own failure. Most will grudgingly admit that 97 percent of the West Bank was a better deal than Jenin and Israeli tanks.

The Palestinian Authority's state-run propaganda that "ten thousand were murdered" and that the fighting "was a real Holocaust" proved deceitful and ultimately lost, rather than gained, credibility for the Palestinians. The very spokesmen who allege an unending war against the Israelis also know that their own youths mined streets and homes that magnified the carnage in Jenin; and they know those murderers whom they now cherish as martyrs are also the culprits who brought them weeks of misery.

So there will be a bitter recognition of what rests ahead as well: Another round of suicide bombings will bring the Israelis into Gaza and any other cities so far left unscathed. More government hysterics and lying, without an independent press to verify events, will only erode even European support. Occupying Christian shrines, murdering bound and gagged prisoners, machine-gunning Israeli children in their beds, assassinating Israeli cabinet members, sending out more suicide murderers, and booby-trapping houses are the policies of a failed, not merely a desperate, regime. And so out of the conundrum - should the Israelis remain firm - will slowly come an awakening that the Palestinians can have their own state and live far better in it without, rather than with, Mr. Arafat.

What, then, can Israel really hope for? And how can it translate tactical success to long-term strategic victory? Its continued policy of deterrence is working - most of the Arab world knows better now than to try a fifth invasion with conventional forces. Strong incursions against the nests and infrastructure of terrorism are also making it clear that such murdering brings the perpetrators and their abettors misery, not concessions.

Quiet will occur not with more Nobel Peace prizes spread about to those who either cannot deliver peace or actively thwart it, not with more bottled piety from Mr. Carter, and not with more threats from subsidized intellectuals in the European Union - but only when unsavory men like Mr. Sharon's make it clear to the real killers who surround Mr. Arafat that war is hell and cannot be refined.

Yet at the same time, Israel must envision some type of Palestinian autonomous state on its borders. This is its dilemma - one that is unfortunately inescapable. Thus its only long-term hope, as we learned after World War II and Korea, but did not fully not grasp in Vietnam, is to continue to defeat the Palestinian terrorists and then to renovate a broken enemy into a proud, but democratic, state with a real market economy - and in a region with no history of consensual government or liberal institutions, no less!

Such a massive evolution could take years - but again, given world opinion and the vast array of Israel's enemies, it is Israel's only chance at some future of peace. Like the free world in the Cold War, Israel must maintain its army ever-ready to strike back, even as its entire society mobilizes to promote moderate Palestinians, to hope that thousands rethink their support for terrorists, and to encourage wherever possible economic and political liberalization among a population which, if it had its way right now, would destroy Israel itself.

It is not an easy thing first to crush a deadly adversary, then help the defeated, and finally join in with that former enemy - but it is the only way to peace. And because Israel remains a democratic, magnanimous, and militarily strong society, there is more hope in all this gloom than pessimists think - as long as the historical order of events that lead to lasting peace is not allowed to be subverted by well-meaning but ultimately reckless outsiders, who seek to impose their own self-serving and often utopian policies from a safe distance.

The U.N.'s Israel Obsession: A Primer

David Tell
www.weeklystandard.com
April 30, 2002

In 1948, when the armies of five surrounding Arab dictatorships invaded tiny, newborn Israel--in what the secretary general of the Arab League announced was a "war of extermination" against "the Jews"--the United Nations sat on its ass. And did not send a fact-finding mission.

But, oh, how the U.N. has been making up for that oversight ever since. For more than 50 years now, the Jews have been its favorite subject.

Among the nearly 200 nations represented at the U.N., only Israel has ever been assigned special--reduced--membership privileges, its ambassadors formally barred, for 53 straight years ending only recently, from election to the Security Council. Meanwhile, and right up to the present day, that same Security Council has devoted fully a third of its energy and criticism to the policies of a single country: Israel. The U.N. Commission on Human Rights, which regularly--and unreprovingly--accepts delegations from any number of homicidal tyrannies across the globe, has issued fully a quarter of its official condemnations to a single (democratic) country: Israel.

There has been a genocide in Rwanda, an ethnic cleansing in Yugoslavia, periodic and horrifying communal "strife" in Indonesia's East Timor, the "disappearance" of a few hundred thousand refugees in the Congo, a decades-long and culturally devastating occupation of Tibet by the People's Republic of China . . . but none of those U.N. member states has ever been subjected to the rebuke of a General Assembly "emergency special session." Israel has, though, repeatedly, simply for refusing to surrender in the face of terrorist attacks that have killed hundreds and injured thousands of its citizens--murders that no U.N. resolution has ever so much as mentioned.

No fewer than four separate administrative units within the U.N.--two of them directly supervised by Kofi Annan's governing secretariat--do nothing but spend millions of dollars annually on the production and worldwide distribution of propaganda questioning Israel's right to exist. The "Special Committee to Investigate Israeli Practices Affecting the Human Rights of the Palestinian People and other Arabs of the Occupied Territories," for example, "investigates" Israel's continued "practice" of "occupying" not just the territory taken in the 1967 war, but also the land within its internationally recognized, pre-1967 borders.

And then there is the United Nations Relief and Works Agency, an operation originally established in December 1949 to assist those Palestinian refugees created by the Arab world's botched attempt at a second Final Solution. UNRWA, as it happens, is centrally relevant to its parent organization's latest outburst of naked Israelophobia. Because UNRWA wholly funds and largely administers the West Bank refugee camp in Jenin where the Israeli army is purported--by various Palestinian militants and local U.N. officials--to have just perpetrated a "massacre" of "unarmed civilians." It is to the site of this alleged "atrocity" that Kofi Annan now intends to dispatch a commission of inquiry chaired by Yasser Arafat's favorite European diplomat, former president Martti

152

Ahtisaari of Finland, and seconded by Cornelio Sommaruga, retired chief of the International Red Cross, a man who once likened the Star of David to a swastika.

All by themselves, Annan's personnel choices here are a genuine scandal, and as this issue of The Weekly Standard goes to press, Israel's understandable objections, to Sommaruga in particular, have left it a still open question when and whether the secretary general's designees will ever be allowed to reach their destination. And if, at the end of the day, they aren't? That will be perfect justice, we think. The "world community" will howl, of course, and Israel's many enemies will believe the worst. But they believe the worst already. And they will continue to believe the worst no matter what. And, quite apart from the controversy over what its staff should look like, the whole idea of a U.N. fact-finding mission to Jenin is scandalous to begin with, it seems to us--an assault on Israel's honor, even its basic legitimacy as an independent nation, that no similarly situated democracy would ever be expected to endure.

Assuming Annan's investigators do eventually make their way to Jenin, is it possible they might actually find the "facts" they are looking for? No, almost certainly not. Media accounts of Israel's incursion into a football-field-sized sector of the camp have bubbled over with lurid details worthy of a medieval peasant's worst anti-Semitic fantasies. And the peasant-in-chief has been a U.N. official, UNRWA commissioner general Peter Hansen, who has given dozens of lip-smacking interviews recounting "wholesale obliteration," "a human catastrophe that has few parallels in recent history," "helicopters . . . strafing civilian residential areas," and "bodies . . . piling up" in "mass graves." Some of this carnage Hansen even claims to have seen "with my own eyes." But he is a bald-faced liar. The Israelis have been out of Jenin--and foreign journalists and other international observers have been back in--for more than a week. And no evidence, literally nothing that would indicate the presence of a civilian "massacre," has yet emerged.

Quite the contrary, rescue workers in Jenin have so far recovered the bodies of six--not the rumored six hundred, but six--women, children, and elderly Palestinians. This, in a now ruined central area of the camp where countless armed gunmen rained days of nonstop sniper fire on Israeli foot patrols from the windows of still-occupied residences they had booby-trapped with high explosives. This is a "massacre"?

And why, even if its death toll had proved a hundred times higher, would it warrant a U.N. fact-finding mission? In 1993, just after the events lately made famous by Hollywood's "Black Hawk Down," a two-week U.S. bombing campaign against Mogadishu killed a thousand Somali civilians. During the whole of the present intifada, now six months old, far fewer Palestinians than that have died as Israel has attempted to rescue itself from a national security threat far graver and more immediate than any America faced in East Africa. But did it ever occur to the United Nations to convene an inquest into the "human catastrophe" that was Somalia? It did not.

Maybe the U.N. picks on Israel simply because it can. Or maybe, just maybe, there is a darker impulse at play.

Which would explain why the U.N. has spent decades, in the guise of refugee assistance, providing active, organized, and enthusiastic auxiliary services to the most delusional and violent strains of Jew-hating Palestinian irredentism. It bears mentioning, though one rarely hears it mentioned, that the UNRWA camp at Jenin has been for years what the Palestinians call a'simat al-istashidin, the "suiciders' capital," from which dozens of Hamas, Islamic Jihad, Fatah, Al Aksa, and Tanzim terrorist attacks have been launched, killing hundreds of Israelis.

UNRWA funds and staffs the schools of Jenin, where, from fall through spring each year, children are taught that all of "Palestine," from the Jordan River to the Mediterranean Sea, belongs to them. During summer vacation, those very same schools host training camps in which those very same students are instructed in the arts of kidnapping and rock-throwing and bomb-manufacturing and martyrdom. UNRWA rents the buses that regularly take residents of Jenin on tours of the Israeli countryside-- where "their" property, "stolen" by the Jews, is carefully pointed out. UNRWA allows its food warehouses in Jenin to do double duty as munitions dumps. UNRWA pretends not to know that explosives and counterfeit currency factories are housed in the public shelters it has constructed in Jenin. UNRWA cannot understand how it might be that its own administrative offices in Jenin are festooned with graffiti celebrating some of the world's most notorious terrorist organizations. Or how some of the world's most notorious terrorists might have found their way onto the agency's payroll--to the point where the Popular Front for the Liberation of Palestine, extreme even in the context of Palestinian extremism, now openly controls the UNRWA workers' union.

This same United Nations, the blood of Israeli civilians still wet on its hands, now dares to question the morality of a modest, defensive, and long-overdue Israeli reprisal?

In curricular materials published by the Palestinian Authority's Ministry of Education, "Objective Five" for high school history teachers reads as follows: "The student will understand why the people of the world hate the Jews." It is a question for the ages. Zionism may no longer be racism at the United Nations. But anti-Semitism is forever.

Anti-Semitism Abides

George F. Will
The Sacramento Bee
May 2, 2002

Such is the richness of European culture, even its decadence is creative. Since 1945 it has produced the truly remarkable phenomenon of anti-Semitism without Jews. How does Europe do that?

Now it offers Christian anti-Semitism without the Christianity. An example of this is the recent cartoon in La Stampa -- a liberal Italian newspaper -- depicting the infant Jesus in a manger, menaced by an Israeli tank and saying "Don't tell me they want to kill me again." This reprise of that hardy perennial, Jews as Christ-killers, clearly still strikes a chord in contemporary Italy, where the culture is as secular as a supermarket.

In Britain the climate created by much of the intelligentsia, including the elite press, is so toxic that the Sun, a tabloid with more readers than any other British newspaper, recently was moved to offer a contrapuntal editorial headlined "The Jewish faith is not an evil religion." Contrary to what Europeans are encouraged to think. And Ron Rosenbaum, author of the brilliant book "Explaining Hitler," acidly notes the scandal of European leaders supporting the Palestinians' "right of return" -- the right to inundate and eliminate the state created in response to European genocide -- "when so many Europeans are still living in homes stolen from Jews they helped murder."

It is time to face a sickening fact that is much more obvious today than it was 11 years ago when Ruth R. Wisse asserted it. In a dark and brilliant essay in Commentary magazine, she argued that anti-Semitism has proved to be "the most durable and successful" ideology of the ideology-besotted 20th century.

Successful? Did not Hitler, the foremost avatar of anti-Semitism, fail? No, he did not. Yes, his 1,000-year Reich fell 988 years short. But its primary work was mostly done. Hitler's primary objective, as he made clear in words and deeds, was the destruction of European Jewry.

Wisse, who in 1991 was a professor of Yiddish literature at McGill University and who now is at Harvard, noted that many fighting faiths, including socialism and communism, had arisen in the 19th century to "explain and to rectify the problems" of modern society. Fascism soon followed. But communism is a cold intellectual corpse. Socialism, born and raised in France, is unpersuasive even to the promiscuously persuadable French: The socialist presidential candidate has suffered the condign humiliation of failing to qualify for this Sunday's runoff, having been defeated by an anti-Semitic "populist" preaching watery fascism.

Meanwhile, anti-Semitism is a stronger force in world affairs than it has been since it went into a remarkably brief eclipse after the liberation of the Nazi extermination camps in 1945. The United Nations, supposedly an embodiment of lessons learned from the war that ended in 1945, is now the instrument for lending spurious legitimacy to the anti-Semites' war against the Jewish state founded by survivors of that war.

Anti-Semitism's malignant strength derives from its simplicity -- its stupidity, actually. It is a primitivism which, Wisse wrote, makes up in vigor what it lacks in philosophic heft, and does so precisely because it "has no prescription for the improvement of society beyond the elimination of part of society." This howl of negation has no more affirmative content than did the scream of the airliner tearing down the Hudson, heading for the World Trade Center.

Today many people say that the Arabs and their European echoes would be mollified if Israel would change its behavior. People who say that do not understand the centrality of anti-Semitism in the current crisis. This crisis has become the second -- and final? -- phase of the struggle for a "final solution to the Jewish question." As Wisse said 11 years ago, and as cannot be said too often, anti-Semitism is not directed against the behavior of the Jews but against the existence of the Jews.

If the percentage of the world's population that was Jewish in the era of the Roman Empire were Jewish today, there would be 200 million Jews. There are 13 million. Five million are clustered in an embattled salient on the eastern shore of the Mediterranean, facing hundreds of millions of enemies. Ron Rosenbaum writes, "The concentration of so many Jews in one place -- and I use the word 'concentration' advisedly -- gives the world a chance to kill the Jews en masse again."

Israel holds just one one-thousandth of the world's population, but holds all the hopes for the continuation of the Jewish experience as a portion of the human narrative. Will Israel be more durable than anti-Semitism? Few things have been.

Jenin: The Truth

Charles Krauthammer
May 3, 2002

"Jenin Camp Is a Scene of Devastation But Yields No Evidence of a Massacre."
Headline, front page, The Washington Post, April 16.

"There is simply no evidence of a massacre."
Peter Bouckaert, senior researcher, Human Rights Watch, Jenin. Jerusalem Post, April 28.

"Holley told Agence France-Presse that he did not see 'any evidence of a massacre. The Israeli army was fighting against some desperate [Palestinian] fighters here.'"
Agence France-Presse, quoting Maj. David Holley, British military adviser to Amnesty International, April 28.

A massacre is the deliberate mass murder of the defenseless. The "Jenin massacre" is more than a fiction. It is a hoax. "Palestinian Authority allegations," reported the Boston Globe (April 29), ". . . appear to be crumbling under the weight of eyewitness accounts from Palestinian fighters who participated in the battle and camp residents who remained in their homes until the final hours of the fighting. . . . All said they were allowed to surrender or evacuate."

And yet for weeks the world has been seized with the question of the "Jenin massacre." The U.N. Security Council called emergency meetings. The secretary general appointed a special investigating committee (now disbanded). The European press published the most lurid allegations. To say nothing, of course, of al-Jazeera TV.

All this for a phantom massacre. Yet this same Middle East conflict yields no shortage of real massacres:

o April 27: Adora, Palestinian gunmen enter residential quarters shooting everyone, including a 5-year-old girl shot through the head in her bed.

o April 12: Jerusalem, suicide bombing at a bus stop, 6 murdered.

o April 10: Yagor, suicide bombing on a bus, 8 murdered.

o March 31: Haifa, suicide bombing in a restaurant, 15 murdered.

o March 28: Eilon Moreh, shooting attack, 4 murdered.

o March 27: Netanya, suicide bombing at a Passover seder, 28 murdered.

These are massacres -- actual, recent massacres. Massacres for which the evidence is hard. Massacres for which the perpetrators claimed credit. Where was the Security Council? Where was the Kofi Annan commission? Where was the world?

The United Nations' excuse will be that these murders were perpetrated not by states but by groups. But this is nonsense. The Palestinian Authority is a recognized government. The links of its top leadership to these murders is precisely the kind of question that warrants investigation. Yet the very idea that the United Nations would investigate Palestinian massacres is absurd.

The fact that such an undertaking is unimaginable is what has made the past several months so deeply, despairingly troubling. The despair comes from the bewilderment of living in a world of monstrous moral inversion.

Take Jenin. What was the real story? That hand-to-hand, door-to-door combat, in an intensely built-up shantytown, among dozens of houses booby-trapped by Palestinian fighters, should have yielded somewhere between seven and 21 scattered civilian casualties is nothing less than astonishing. It testifies to the extraordinary scrupulousness of the Israeli army, which lost 23 soldiers in the battle, precisely because it did not want to cause the civilian casualties that come with aerial bombardment, as has happened everywhere from Grozny to Kabul. And yet Israel was investigated precisely for defending itself against massacres that warrant no investigation.

Palestinian apologists wave away this double standard with the magic mantra of "occupation."

More nonsense. Twenty-one months ago, Israel offered a total end to the occupation, ceding 100 percent of Gaza and 97 percent of the West Bank to the first Palestinian state ever. The Palestinians turned that down and took up the suicide bomb. By the Orwellian logic of today, the Palestinians are justified in perpetrating one massacre after another to end an occupation that Israel offered to remove almost two years ago.

For the "international community," as embodied by the United Nations, such inverted moral logic is the norm. This is what it must have been like living in the false consciousness of Soviet communism, where everyone had to publicly and constantly pretend to believe the official lies, all the while knowing they were lies. This is what it must have been like living in the 1930s, as the necessities of appeasement created a gradual inversion of right and wrong -- the Czechs, for example, pilloried by official opinion in Britain and France for selfishly standing in the way of peace at Munich.

Churchill's great gift to civilization was not just that he rallied good against evil but also that he pierced a suffocating fog of self-deception by speaking truth to lies. Where is the Churchill of today, the official of any government, prepared to tell the United Nations that its frantic hunt for a phantom massacre by Jews -- while ignoring massacre after massacre of Jews -- is grotesque and perverse?

America Must Stand With Israel Against Arab Tyranny And Terror

John McCain
On The Record
May 6, 2002

There will always be an Israel. The terrorist onslaught against her people represents not progress towards a refoundation of historic Palestine but a
plunge into an abyss of moral decay perpetrated in the name of the Palestinian people by their own leaders. There will always be an Israel, because the Israeli people will defend their homeland against murderers who pose as martyrs, and will never accept justice imposed on them by leaders who send children to kill their children.

There will always be an Israel, strong and free, because Israel, and her supporters in this country, will never allow the depravity of her enemies to obscure the moral clarity that inspired her founding, 54 years ago last week, as the homeland of a people who understood evil long before Americans
saw its more recent expression on September 11.

Terrorism is terrorism, whether in the form of professional killers who crash civilian aircraft into buildings or amateur murderers undistinguished by anything other than their willingness to take innocent lives.

A political solution to the conflict with the Palestinians is the best answer to Israeli insecurity, of course. But no moral nation--neither Israel nor America--can allow terrorists to chart the political course of its people. No freedom-loving nation can tolerate a terrorist state on its border. And no great nation can abandon the obligations of moral clarity for the convenience of situational ethics.

If we are serious about the values we in America and Israel live by, and
the opportunities we would like all people in the Middle East to enjoy, we can allow terrorists no role in the political process.

Indeed, we must work to spread our values in the Middle East, first by
opposing tyranny in the Arab world. The celebration of freedom in the streets of liberated Baghdad will serve as a counterpoint to the state-directed Arab media's distortion of the Palestinian conflict. It will be a reminder to other Arab tyrants that the United States is a natural ally of Arab people who aspire to freedom. Freeing Arabs from repression by tyrannical regimes is the priority of neither Yasser Arafat nor the dictators he counts as his allies. But bringing liberty's blessings to Arab peoples will do much more to improve their lives than will their jihad against Israel.

Unfortunately, when it comes to advocating freedom and opportunity in the Arab world, our values know few champions. In the monarchies and dictatorships of the Middle East, cynicism is the essence of statecraft. Americans find ourselves handicapped in our Middle East diplomacy by a native regard for moral clarity.

It is our fidelity to the values Arab leaders reject that makes it unmistakably clear to Americans who destroyed the peace process begun in Oslo. The authors of that disaster were the Palestinians themselves--and the Arab leaders who encouraged or accepted Yasser Arafat's rejection of the sweeping settlement offered by former Prime Minister Barak at Camp David, and provided rhetorical and material support for the ensuing intifada waged by suicide bombers.

I don't think our cultural differences with Arab states are so vast that a common recognition of what constitutes real peace and a just settlement is unattainable. I think Arab leaders know exactly what it will take to achieve real peace between Palestinians and Israelis, and that what they currently offer serves only to perpetuate the conflict.

Telethons and poems glorifying suicide bombers are not steps toward peace. Cash payments to the families of suicide bombers are not steps toward peace. Communiqués glorifying the murder of innocents are not stepstoward peace. All of this is evil, pure and simple.

It is not peace, but fear of each other that motivates Arab dictators, and fear of their own populations, whose resentments toward Israel and America have been inflamed for generations to distract them from grievances against their own rulers for the economic and political inequities they are expected to endure permanently.

It is the unenlightened rule of Arab dictators, not the plight of the Palestinians, that condemns the Arab world to the civilizational crisis in which it finds itself. Which Middle Eastern nation grants its Arab citizens the most political freedom? Israel. Which countries' leadershave the blood of innocents on their hands but hear nothing about it from the Arab League? Iraq, Syria, and Sudan, for starters. Which country has the most egregious record of occupying another today? Syria, in Lebanon. In which countries do Palestinian refugees suffer without rights and the most basic freedoms? Other than Israel, only Jordan has treated these people with any dignity. Which nation in the region has matched its payments to the families of Palestinian murderers with money for health care, education, and other development in the territories? Not one.

How Arab leaders can abide their own hypocrisy is one question. Why they expect us to do so is a better one.

Arab leaders recoil in mock indignation from any suggestion that they have a responsibility to discourage Palestinian treachery. Instead, they demand that the United States pressure the government of Israel into forsaking its obligation to defend its citizens from terrorism that Arab governments celebrate and support.

I'm also distressed that some of our European allies are dismissing Israel's legitimate security concerns. In some quarters, Jews are once again threatened with attacks on their institutions. We are witnessing once again the torching of European synagogues. All world leaders must condemn, in the strongest terms, such despicable behavior.

Israel has proved its willingness to risk its strategic interests by returning territories captured in war, and living cheek by jowl with a Palestinian state in exchange for peace and acceptance of Israel's right to exist by its Arab neighbors. Yasser Arafat and the Palestinian Authority he claims to lead insist on a settlement that would threaten the eventual extinction of a Jewish state in the Middle East, and accept and support murder as a means to achieve it. Official sponsorship of Palestinian terror is a self-induced mockery of the Palestinian leadership's moral authority, and that of its Nobel Peace Prize-winning chairman.

The Oslo peace process was premised on the notion that Israelis and Palestinians could live together. I believe it is now time to exploreways in which they can live apart. It is time to consider alternatives such as that proposed by former Prime Minister Barak--to erect a security barrier between the Israelis and the Palestinians. This is not to accept the hopelessness of a political solution, but to embrace the hope that Israel's people can live in safety until a Palestinian leadership truly committed to peace emerges from the chaos and despair inflicted on Palestinians for generations by leaders who lack the courage and compassion and wisdom to make a better life for their people.

Friends, I make no claim to wisdom on how to resolve the crisis in the Middle East. Like you, I look for guidance in the values we share with the only democracy in the region. I know this: no American leader should be expected to sell a false peace to our ally, consider Israel's right to self-defense less legitimate than ours, or insist that Israel negotiate a political settlement while terrorism remains the Palestinians' preferred bargaining tool.

The moral clarity you bring to American understanding of Israel's plight is the most effective antidote to the cynicism and hostility that parade as Arab diplomacy in the Middle East today. We will defeat terrorism against America, and we will stand with Israel as she fights the same enemy.

One of the great privileges of my life was the friendship that I developed with the late Sen. Henry "Scoop" Jackson. I got to know Scoop when I was the Navy liaison to the Senate in the late '70s. Scoop was and remains the model of what an American statesman should be.

In 1979, I traveled to Israel with Scoop, where I knew he was considered a hero. I had no idea how great a hero he was until we landed in Tel Aviv. When we arrived, we were transferred to a bus big enough to accommodate our large delegation, as well as the U.S. Ambassador in Israel and several of his staff. About a hundred yards outside the airport, the bus was surrounded by a crowd of seven or eight hundred Israelis screaming for Jackson, waving signs that read "God Bless you, Scoop," "SenatorJackson, thank you," and dozens of other tributes. For a patriot like Scoop,their affection for him was nothing less than affection for America.

Scoop understood a deep truth. The bond between America and Israel is not just a strategic one, though that is important. Today, in the war against terror, we have no stronger ally than Israel. The more profound tie between our two countries, however, is a moral one. We are two democracies whose alliance is forged in our common values. To be proudly pro-American and pro-Israeli is not to hold conflicting loyalties. As Scoop understood, it is about defending the principles that both countries hold dear.

And I stand before you today, proudly pro-American and pro-Israel.

Washington Misled: Saudi Arabia's Financial Backing Of Terrorism

Dore Gold
Jerusalem Center For Public Affairs
May 6, 2001

As a result of Israel's Operation "Defensive Shield," new documents have been uncovered from Palestinian offices that directly link the Kingdom of Saudi Arabia with financial backing of terrorist attacks against Israel. The Saudis have repeatedly denied such connections. Last month, for example, Saudi state television held a telethon for the families of "Palestinian martyrs" that raised over $100 million.

Responding to charges that with the telethon Saudi Arabia was backing terrorism, Adel Al-Jubeir, foreign policy adviser to Saudi Crown Prince Abdullah, told Fox television: "We have made it very clear in terms of where Saudi funding has gone to provide humanitarian assistance to the families who have suffered as a result of the Israeli occupation and the recent Israeli aggression." Adel Al-Jubeir added: "We do not support suicide bombers. Our objective is to put food on people's tables and medicine in their pharmacies" (Fox News, April 28, 2002).

Earlier in the month, the U.S. government was apparently given similar assurances by the Saudis. Thus, White House spokesman Ari Fleischer responded to a press briefing on April 12 by saying: "As I said, we have received assurances from the Saudi Arabian government that the money is going to the Palestinian people, and not to support terrorism." Fleisher was sufficiently confident about Saudi assurances that he even compared the Saudi aid from the telethon to U.S. financial assistance to the Palestinian people.

One new Saudi document found in Palestinian offices demonstrates that the Saudis were not providing general humanitarian aid as they told the U.S. government and explained to American television audiences. Riyadh had misled Washington, for the Saudis itemized their allocations line by line, detailing the circumstances of the death of Palestinians whose families received assistance; the Saudis themselves explain that the allocation was for suicide attacks.

Rewarding Suicide Bombers

Among the documents found in Tulkarm was a table from Saudi Arabia itemizing the tenth set of payments to the "Martyrs of the Al-Aqsa Intifada." The table details how $545,000 was allocated to 102 families. The logo at the top of the table reads: "Kingdom of Saudi Arabia, the Saudi Committee for Aid to the Al-Quds Intifada." This committee was established in the fall of 2000 under the Saudi Minister of the Interior, Prince Nayef bin 'Abd al-Aziz. Prince Nayef's organization was also responsible for collecting Saudi contributions during the April 11 telethon for Palestinian "martyrs" on Saudi state television.

The table explains the type of activity that entitled a family to receive Saudi assistance:

162

According to the document, Abd al-Fatah Muhammad Musalah Rashid, number 15 on the list, died in a "martyrdom act." The individual involved was a member of the pro-Iranian Islamic Jihad who died in a car-bomb attack at Beit Lid on September 9, 2001, for which he was responsible. Eight Israelis were wounded.

Abd al-Karim Amr Muhammad Abu Na'sa, who appears as number 17 in the Saudi table, is described as having died in a "martyrdom act in Afula." This is a reference to his suicide bombing on behalf of Islamic Jihad and the Al Aqsa Martyrs Brigades in Afula on November 27, 2001. Forty-six Israelis were wounded.

There is no doubt that when the document refers to a "martyrdom act" -- amliyya itishaddiyya -- it is referring to suicide attacks. A martyr, or "shahid" in Arabic, is an individual who gave his life in a holy war -- or in a Jihad -- and is therefore entitled to automatic entry into Paradise after his death, according to Islamic tradition. The term "martyr" has thus become synonymous with suicide bombers or those who died attacking Israelis. Israel has been able to determine that at least eight of the beneficiaries of Saudi aid are the families of suicide bombers.

Other "martyrs" on the Saudi list may not have been suicide bombers, but were well known for their past involvement in terrorism. Thus, number 68, Mahmud Abu Hanud, was the commander of Hamas for the West Bank. Number 8, Atef Abiyat, commanded the Al-Aqsa Martyrs Brigades in Bethlehem. His name was well known to those who engaged in peace process matters since Yasser Arafat promised the European Union that he was in prison while he moved about freely until his death.

When a potential suicide bomber knows that his family will be handsomely rewarded with financial aid after his death, his motivation to undertake suicide operations increases. Thus, Saudi aid promotes terrorism directly.

Implications of Israeli Revelations about Saudi Arabia for the U.S. War on Terrorism

First Evidence of Direct Saudi Aid to Terrorism: Prior to the discovery of the Saudi document, attempts to trace the Saudi money trail in backing international terrorism focused on Saudi-backed charities. For example, on March 11, 2002, the U.S. Treasury identified the Al-Haramain Islamic Foundation, based in Saudi Arabia, as an organization with which U.S. citizens are prohibited from making any transactions because of its suspected support for terrorism. Al-Haramain receives millions of dollars per year from the Saudi government; some of this aid may indirectly reach terrorist organizations. The Saudi documents found with the Palestinians point to a direct link between Saudi funds and suicide bombing attacks.

Saudis Not Involved in Humanitarian Aid but Rather in Assistance to Recognized International Terrorist Groups: The specificity of the Saudi table allows the Saudis to monitor in detail the identity of each recipient family. Matching the names in the table to its own information, Israel was able to link suicide bombers with specific organizations -- Hamas, Islamic Jihad, Al Aqsa Martyrs Brigades -- that have been declared by the U.S. to be indisputable international terrorist organizations. Had there just been a Saudi grant for families who had lost relatives, without the details of the table, then Saudi advocates could argue that the money was provided as general aid to the Palestinian people.

The official Saudi table itemizing allocations to the families of "martyrs" was not the only document found by Israel in Palestinian offices during Operation "Defensive Shield." According to additional captured documents, which were Palestinian intelligence reports, the Saudis also transferred direct aid to Palestinian Islamic terrorist groups - both to Hamas and Islamic Jihad.[1]

Saudi Arabian financial aid to terrorist groups is not just an Israeli problem. During October 2001, NATO forces entered the offices of the Saudi High Commission for Aid to Bosnia. Surveillance photographs of possible American targets were found. A former employee of the Saudi Commission is now in Guantanamo Bay, suspected of plotting an attack against the U.S. Embassy in Sarajevo. Saudi-sponsored charities have been tied to other terrorist attacks, including the U.S. embassy bombings in East Africa in 1998.[2] Unless Saudi Arabia ceases all assistance, direct or indirect, for acts of international terrorism, it cannot play any role to stabilize the Middle East and advance Arab-Israeli peace.

1 Minister for Parliamentary Affairs Dan Naveh, "The Involvement of Arafat, PA Senior Officials, and Apparatuses in Terrorism Against Israel, Corruption, and Crime," May 2002, p. 67.

2 Matthew Levitt, Senior Fellow, "Tackling the Financing of Terrorism in Saudi Arabia," in Policywatch, No. 609, March 11, 2002, Washington Institute of Near East Policy.

Why I Stand With Israel

William J. Bennett
Jerusalem Post
May 7, 2002

The first piece I ever published in the popular press was a 1977 "My Turn" column in Newsweek. There I lamented the fact that children were no longer identifying with heroes. I pointed out that to find a hero, to see heroism, one had to look no farther than Yonatan Netanyahu who died at Entebbe the previous year. Netanyahu was a hero, to be sure - but so, too, is the State of Israel a hero to many of us, even if so many others still think it appropriate to condemn, criticize, and investigate it.

One of the premier political philosophers of our age said that Winston Churchill taught us to "see things as they are, and this means above all in seeing their greatness and their misery, their excellence and their vileness." When one looks at Israel and the Middle East, no task can be more important and, through the lens of moral clarity, no task can be more easily accomplished.

It did not take a great deal to see things as they really were on September 11 nor on the days and weeks that followed. On September 11, Israelis lowered their flags to half staff in empathy with the US. By contrast, Palestinians in the West Bank were cheering in the streets.

On September 11, we in the United States were forced to stare into the face, and feel the hand, of evil - our very existence demanded that we fight back, not only to punish the wrong done to us, not only to protect our citizens and institutions, but to vindicate our democratic virtues.

Just after the slaughter that took place on September 11, many Israelis said, "We are all Americans now." The truth is, after September 11, we all became Israelis. Israel has been fighting a war against terrorism since the day it was founded, and this has been a war for the state's survival. It is not difficult to see that those who want to do Israel in - from Iran and Iraq to Hamas and the PLO - want to do the US in as well. And, as is true in the case of Israel, our war on terrorism became, had to become, a war for our survival. Israel's war is our war, just as Israel's cause is our cause.

I am a Catholic, and many have speculated that Christian interpretations of the Torah are the reason many Christians support Israel. There may be something to that. But that is not my reason for standing with Israel, nor is it the reason the US does and should stand with Israel.

We stand with Israel because Israel is a beacon of freedom and hope - to the world, generally, and, in a more important sense, to the Middle East. In its very Declaration of Independence, Israel proclaimed that it would "ensure complete equality of social and political rights to all its inhabitants irrespective of religion, race, or sex; it will guarantee freedom of religion, conscience, language, education, and culture; it will safeguard the holy places of all religions." Israel has kept faith with the promise of its founding, a founding more similar to America's than perhaps any other nation's.

Israel is the only country in the region that permits citizens of all faiths to worship freely and openly. We need to remember that 20 percent of Israeli citizens are not Jewish. While Jews are not permitted to live in many Arab countries, Arabs are granted full citizenship and have the right to vote in Israel. (Arabs not only comprise a faction within the Knesset, but routinely side with Israel's enemies.) Arabs living in Israel have more rights and are freer than most Arabs living in Arab countries. Israel, in short, has shown the way in the Middle East, it has shown - the way for freedom, for democracy, and for education.

And Israel has done all this while under continued pressure aimed at undermining and extinguishing its very existence. It was invaded by five armies upon its founding and has been threatened with annihilation ever since. Milan Kundera once wrote that a small nation is "one whose very existence may be put into question at any moment; a small nation can disappear, and knows it." Israel is a small nation.

It should not have been surprising or worthy of condemnation that just after Yasser Arafat attempted to smuggle 50 tons of weapons into his Palestinian Authority, and just as his Fatah-affiliated Al-Aksa Martyrs Brigades were perfecting their human-bomb-making capabilities, Israel finally said, "Enough!"

Israel then went into the territories to root out terrorists, to do what Arafat over the years had refused to do. That mission was of a piece with what the US did in Afghanistan in rooting out the Taliban and al-Qaida. The pressure on Israel to cease that operation amounted to perhaps the greatest blurring of our moral clarity since September 11. That pressure was imposed on Israel in order to appease nations like Saudi Arabia, a repressive dictatorship that owes the US a great many explanations, that deserves from the US nothing.

Nor, by contrast, was it surprising that the first sentences uttered by Arafat upon his release from confinement were libels against Israel as a "terrorist, Nazi, and racist" regime. This is what he always said. Lies pervade his speech, and those lies have trickled down and out into the common criticisms of Israel heard elsewhere. One of them is that the Jewish settlements in the disputed territories are the greatest obstacle to peace in the Middle East. When I hear this, I am reminded of a lie from another context and another time: that blacks living as minorities in all-white neighborhoods in the American South were the cause of racial strife. They weren't - racists were the cause of racial strife.

There is no reason Jews should not be able to live in the West Bank unless there is a reason Arabs should not be able to live in Tel Aviv - which is to say, there is no reason at all. The freedoms to travel and live are fundamental. To claim that certain lands should be free of Jews is to claim that the Third Reich had a moral point.

While many may prefer to forget their ugly history, I think it critical to remember it, for nowhere more than in the Middle East is history a prelude. Because of their animus against Jews, many leaders of the Palestinian cause have long supported our enemies. The grand mufti of Jerusalem allied himself with Adolf Hitler during World War II. Yasser Arafat has repeatedly targeted and killed Americans.

Arafat was very closely aligned with the Soviet Union and other enemies of ours throughout the Cold War. In 1991, during the Gulf War, Arafat aligned himself with Saddam Hussein, whom he praised as "the defender of the Arab nation, of Muslims, and of free men everywhere." Israel, by contrast, has always been on the side of the US, both as a strategic and as a moral ally. And the civilized world will never be able to pay its debt to Israel for bombing Iraq's nuclear reactor in 1981.

Today, more than ever, we cannot afford to criticize Israel for its war against terrorism, as we ignominiously did in that episode in 1981. Now more than ever we need to see things for their "excellence and for their vileness."

Those searching for heroes of democracy need look no farther than Israel, a country that has done more, for more people, with fewer resources and under greater threat, than almost any other. We must never ignore the fact that if Israel loses its war against terrorism, it will lose its existence. To vindicate our own virtues and cherished beliefs, we should stand foursquare with Israel and apply pressure to the dictatorships in its neighborhood, not the other way around.

Moral clarity demands standing with Israel in its still unfinished war against terrorism, in its still unfinished work for survival. It is for these reasons and more, far more, that I count myself among the millions of Americans who see America's fate and Israel's fate as one.

Calling Arabs' Bluff

William Safire
New York Times
May 23, 2002

After American diplomatic persuasion, Israel has (1) withdrawn its forces sent into the West Bank to hunt down the terrorists the Palestinian "Authority" not only condoned but supplied and incited; (2) freed Yasir Arafat, whose first response was to call Israelis "Nazis"; (3) freed the armed terrorists who broke into a Christian church to escape capture in Bethlehem; and (4) held back from retaliating for the bloody suicide attack timed to disrupt the Bush-Sharon meeting in Washington.

If terrorists see this pattern of restraint as a sign of weakness and take it as an invitation to wear down the Israeli will, Israel will be forced to respond mightily. Prepared to strike into Hamas headquarters and suicide-bomb factories in Gaza, Israel waits to see if President Bush can get the Saudis and Egyptians to deliver on their side of the "pressure bargain."

That places the war-ending ball squarely in the royal court. Arab rulers in Riyadh, Amman and Cairo, pledged to exert pressure on Palestinians to defeat Hamas and related terror centers, now face their moment of truth. Arafat's phony arrests, revolving-door jails and pious condemnations no longer fool anybody. Only an internal crackdown will end the killing and impose order. If Arabs cannot prevail on a Palestinian leadership to deliver this, talk of peace and statehood is a waste of lives.

In an interview with three U.S. columnists just before hurrying home last week, Prime Minister Ariel Sharon was curiously confident that what he called the moderate Arab states would carry out their promises to Bush to lean on Arafat to share power.

"To reach a peace agreement," he told us, "comprehensive reform of the Palestinian Authority is a precondition. We know that key members inside that authority are calling for change. They will cooperate with an approach by moderate Arab leaders to bring Arafat to the status of 'symbolic leader' whose hold on the levers of power will gradually diminish."

Why would Arafat agree to that? "Only if he is pressured by the U.S., the European Union, Russia and Arab countries. We are in contact with Jordanians and Egyptians, in concept not in details." Not the Saudis? "The problem with the Saudis is that they come with a vision of peace between the Arab world and Israel, but documents we have captured show how their interior minister is supporting Hamas terror even after Sept. 11. They must stop it." What would convince him that Palestinian reform was real? "Pressure must be applied to reorganize not just the security bodies but the economic system," Sharon replied. "All financial means should not be in the hands of one man.

Institute legal and law enforcement systems with a prime minister ostensibly subordinate to Arafat but the sole point of contact with foreign aid and security officials."

Jim Hoagland of The Washington Post wanted to know if negotiation with

168

Palestinians at a regional meeting could take place first. "Implement reform immediately. Arafat should be told, 'Look, we won't provide you with financial means unless you agree to these reforms.' Now is the time for the coalition of war-- Iran, Iraq and Syria--to be countered with a coalition of peace--Israel, Egypt, Jordan, the Saudis after they stop supplying terrorist organizations, one or two of the emirates, maybe Morocco and peace-minded Palestinians. Bush and I agreed that reform of the Palestinian Authority was the most important thing."

Sharon really wants the Arabs to come up with a Palestinian leadership he can do business with. Back in Israel, his Likud compatriots have voted against acceptance of a Palestinian state. They point out that a "demilitarized state" is a fiction, as shown by Germany after Versailles, and that a Palestine capable of making treaties with Iran and Iraq, and of importing arms as on the terror ship Karine A, and of blocking Israeli planes from tight turnarounds in its air space, would be one dangerous state.

That positions Sharon as a centrist. He will stick to his plan: cessation of terror, interim agreements, compromises on land, steady establishment of trust. The former general is confident he can handle both his soft-left and hard-right flanks. Now he is putting it up to Arabs to come up with a real partner for peace.

Nine Wars Too Many

Thomas L. Friedman
New York Times
May 15, 2002

If I were making a movie of the Arab-Israeli conflict today I would call it "Ten Wars and a Funeral."

Because the biggest problem in resolving this conflict is that there are at least 10 different wars being fought over Israel-Palestine, and we need to reduce them to just one to have any chance of making peace.

Let's run down the list: A majority of Israelis are fighting a war for the right of a Jewish state to exist in the Middle East, roughly along the pre-1967 borders. But a minority in Israel today want a Jewish state within the pre-1967 lines and a Jewish state in the West Bank and Gaza.

This was amply demonstrated by Bibi Netanyahu's stunt at the recent Likud Party convention, where he tried to advance his political career and embarrass Ariel Sharon by getting the lunatic core of the Likud to reject any Palestinian state ever in the West Bank.

These Israeli rightists and settlers deliberately label any Palestinian resistance to the Israeli occupation of the West Bank as "terrorism" to rope the United States into supporting Israel's continued hold on the occupied territories as part of America's global war on terrorism. Beware.

The same is true inside the Bush administration. The State Department sees the Mideast war as a fight over Israel's 1967 boundaries, and its focus is "conflict resolution" - diplomacy aimed at getting Israel to trade occupied land for peace.

But over at the Pentagon, the view is that Yasser Arafat is no different from Osama bin Laden, and the other Arab leaders are worthy only of contempt.

The Pentagon sees the Israeli war to crush Arafat as an extension of the U.S. war on terrorism and believes the most you can do with Arabs and Israelis today is "conflict management," not conflict resolution.

This view is reinforced by the fact that the Palestinians are fighting two wars.

Yes, many Palestinians are simply fighting to get Israel out of the West Bank, Gaza and East Jerusalem so they can establish a state there - not because they acknowledge the legitimacy of a Jewish homeland in pre-1967 Israel, but because they know they lack the power to eliminate it.

But some Palestinians, and Arafat is among them, have not abandoned hope of establishing a Palestinian state in the West Bank and Gaza today - through diplomacy and armed struggle - and a Palestinian state in pre-1967 Israel tomorrow - through a baby boom and securing the right of return of millions of Palestinian refugees.

170

Israel still does not appear on many of Arafat's maps. So let's cut the nonsense that the only thing that all Palestinians want is an "end to the Israeli occupation." I wish that were true.

Ditto the Arabs. Egypt, Saudi Arabia and Syria all claim they just want Israel to withdraw to the pre-1967 borders, but anyone reading their official media, which regularly spew articles comparing Israel to Nazi Germany and extolling the virtues of Palestinian girls who commit suicide amid Israeli civilians in Tel Aviv, would hardly be assured that for them the only problem is the Israeli occupation - and not the Jewish people's right to a homeland in the Middle East.

And ditto-ditto the Europeans. Yes, yes, many Europeans really do just want an end to the Israeli occupation, but the anti-Semitism coming out of Europe today suggests that deep down some Europeans want a lot more:

They want Sharon to commit a massacre against Palestinians, or they want to describe what he did in Jenin as a massacre, so that the Europeans can finally get the guilt of the Holocaust off their backs and be able to shout: "Look at these Jews - they're worse than we were!"

Frankly, I'm happy President Bush is getting more involved in Mideast peace-making.

But he'll get nowhere unless he can get the parties (including his own aides) to abandon all the other wars they're fighting and to tell their own people, and each other, that there's only one war left - a war to determine the border between a Jewish state and a Palestinian state.

Anyone who's fighting any other war is an enemy of peace and an enemy of America's national interest.

Twenty Facts About Israel And The Middle East

William J. Bennett, Jack Kemp, and Jeanne Kirkpatrick
Copley News Service
May 21, 2002

The world's attention has been focused on the Middle East. We are confronted daily with scenes of carnage and destruction. Can we understand such violence? Yes, but only if we come to the situation with a solid grounding in the facts of the matter—facts that too often are forgotten, if ever they were learned. Below are twenty facts that we think are useful in understanding the current situation, how we arrived here, and how we might eventually arrive at a solution.

ROOTS OF THE CONFLICT

When the United Nations proposed the establishment of two states in the region—one Jewish, one Arab—the Jews accepted the proposal and declared their independence in 1948. The Jewish state constituted only 1/6 of one percent of what was known as "the Arab world." The Arab states, however, rejected the UN plan and since then have waged war against Israel repeatedly, both all-out wars and wars of terrorism and attrition. In 1948, five Arab armies invaded Israel in an effort to eradicate it. Jamal Husseini of the Arab Higher Committee spoke for many in vowing to soak "the soil of our beloved country with the last drop of our blood."

The Palestine Liberation Organization (PLO) was founded in 1964—three years before Israel controlled the West Bank and Gaza. The PLO's declared purpose was to eliminate the State of Israel by means of armed struggle. To this day, the Web site of Yasir Arafat's Palestinian Authority (PA) claims that the entirety of Israel is "occupied" territory.* It is impossible to square this with the PLO and PA assertions to Western audiences that the root of the conflict is Israel's occupation of the West Bank and Gaza.

The West Bank and Gaza (controlled by Jordan and Egypt from 1948 to 1967) came under Israeli control during the Six Day War of 1967 that started when Egypt closed the Straits of Tiran and Arab armies amassed on Israel's borders to invade and liquidate the state. It is important to note that during their 19-year rule, neither Jordan nor Egypt had made any effort to establish a Palestinian state on those lands. Just before the Arab nations launched their war of aggression against the State of Israel in 1967, Syrian Defense Minister (later President) Hafez Assad stated, "Our forces are now entirely ready . . . to initiate the act of liberation itself, and to explode the Zionist presence in the Arab homeland . . . the time has come to enter into a battle of annihilation." On the brink of the 1967 war, Egyptian President Gamal Nassar declared, "Our basic objective will be the destruction of Israel."

Because of their animus against Jews, many leaders of the Palestinian cause have long supported our enemies. The Grand Mufti of Jerusalem allied himself with Adolf Hitler during WWII. Yasir Arafat, chairman of the PLO and president of the PA, has repeatedly targeted and killed Americans. In 1973, Arafat ordered the execution of Cleo Noel, the American ambassador to the Sudan. Arafat was very closely aligned with the Soviet Union and other enemies of the United States throughout the Cold War. In 1991, during the Gulf War, Arafat aligned himself with Saddam Hussein, whom he praised as "the defender of the Arab nation, of Muslims, and of free men everywhere."

172

Israel has, in fact, returned most of the land that it captured during the 1967 war and right after that war offered to return all of it in exchange for peace and normal relations; the offer was rejected. As a result of the 1978 Camp David accords—in which Egypt recognized the right of Israel to exist and normal relations were established between the two countries—Israel returned the Sinai desert, a territory three times the size of Israel and 91 percent of the territory Israel took control of in the 1967 war.

In 2000, as part of negotiations for a comprehensive and durable peace, Israel offered to turn over all but the smallest portion of the remaining territories to Yasir Arafat. But Israel was rebuffed when Arafat walked out of Camp David and launched the current intifada.

Yasir Arafat has never been less than clear about his goals—at least not in Arabic. On the very day that he signed the Oslo accords in 1993—in which he promised to renounce terrorism and recognize Israel—he addressed the Palestinian people on Jordanian television and declared that he had taken the first step "in the 1974 plan." This was a thinly-veiled reference to the "phased plan," according to which any territorial gain was acceptable as a means toward the ultimate goal of Israel's destruction.

The recently deceased Faisal al-Husseini, a leading Palestinian spokesman, made the same point in 2001 when he declared that the West Bank and Gaza represented only "22 percent of Palestine" and that the Oslo process was a "Trojan horse." He explained, "When we are asking all the Palestinian forces and factions to look at the Oslo Agreement and at other agreements as 'temporary' procedures, or phased goals, this means that we are ambushing the Israelis and cheating them." The goal, he continued, was "the liberation of Palestine from the river to the sea," i.e., the Jordan River to the Mediterranean Sea—all of Israel.

To this day, the Fatah wing of the PLO (the "moderate" wing that was founded and is controlled by Arafat himself) has as its official emblem the entire state of Israel covered by two rifles and a hand grenade—another fact that belies the claim that Arafat desires nothing more than the West Bank and Gaza.

While criticism of Israel is not necessarily the same as "anti-Semitism," it must be remembered that the Middle East press is, in fact, rife with anti-Semitism. More than fifteen years ago the eminent scholar Bernard Lewis could point out that "The demonization of Jews [in Arabic literature] goes further than it had ever done in Western literature, with the exception of Germany during the period of Nazi rule." Since then, and through all the years of the "peace process," things have become much worse. Depictions of Jews in Arab and Muslim media are akin to those of Nazi Germany, and medieval blood libels—including claims that Jews use Christian and Muslim blood in preparing their holiday foods—have become prominent and routine. One example is a sermon broadcast on PA television where Sheik Ahmad Halabaya stated, "They [the Jews] must be butchered and killed, as Allah the Almighty said: 'Fight them: Allah will torture them at your hands.' Have no mercy on the Jews, no matter where they are, in any country. Fight them, wherever you are. Wherever you meet them, kill them." Over three-quarters of Palestinians approve of suicide bombings—an appalling statistic but, in light of the above facts, an unsurprising one.

THE STATE OF ISRAEL

There are 21 Arab countries in the Middle East and only one Jewish state:

Israel, which is also the only democracy in the region.

Israel is the only country in the region that permits citizens of all faiths to worship freely and openly. Twenty percent of Israeli citizens are not Jewish.

While Jews are not permitted to live in many Arab countries, Arabs are granted full citizenship and have the right to vote in Israel. Arabs are also free to become members of the Israeli parliament (the Knesset). In fact, several Arabs have been democratically elected to the Knesset and have been serving there for years. Arabs living in Israel have more rights and are freer than most Arabs living in Arab countries.

Israel is smaller than the state of New Hampshire and is surrounded by nations hostile to her existence. Some peace proposals—including the recent Saudi proposal—demand withdrawal from the entire West Bank, which would leave Israel 9 miles wide at its most vulnerable point.

The oft-cited UN Resolution 242 (passed in the wake of the 1967 war) does not, in fact, require a complete withdrawal from the West Bank. As legal scholar Eugene Rostow put it, "Resolution 242, which as undersecretary of state for political affairs between 1966 and 1969 I helped produce, calls on the parties to make peace and allows Israel to administer the territories it occupied in 1967 until 'a just and lasting peace in the Middle East' is achieved. When such a peace is made, Israel is required to withdraw its armed forces 'from territories' it occupied during the Six-Day War—not from 'the' territories nor from 'all' the territories, but from some of the territories."

Israel has, of course, conceded that the Palestinians have legitimate claims to the disputed territories and is willing to engage in negotiations on the matter. As noted above, Israeli Prime Minister Ehud Barak offered almost all of the territories to Arafat at Camp David in 2000.

Despite claims that the Israeli settlements in the West Bank are the obstacle to peace, Jews lived there for centuries before being massacred or driven out by invading Arab armies in 1948-49. And contrary to common misperceptions, Israeli settlements—which constitute less than two percent of the territories—almost never displace Palestinians.

The area of the West Bank includes some of the most important sites in Jewish history, among them Hebron, Bethlehem, and Jericho. East Jerusalem, often cited as an "Arab city" or "occupied territory," is the site of Judaism's holiest monument. While under Arab rule (1948-67), this area was entirely closed to Jews. Since Israel took control, it has been open to people of all faiths.

Finally, let us consider the demand that certain territories in the Muslim world must be off-limits to Jews. This demand is of a piece with Hitler's proclamation that German land had to be "Judenrein" (empty of Jews). Arabs can live freely throughout Israel, and as full citizens. Why should Jews be forbidden to live or to own land in an area like the West Bank simply because the majority of people is Arab?

In sum, a fair and balanced portrayal of the Middle East will reveal that one nation stands far above the others in its commitment to human rights and democracy as well as in its commitment to peace and mutual security. That nation is Israel.

How Did The Infidels Win?

Bernard Lewis
Reprinted with permission of National Post
National Post
June 1, 2002

In the enormously rich historical literature developed during 14 centuries of Islamic history, until very recent times, there were no histories of countries or nations. Rather, there are histories of Islam and histories of particular dynasties or states within Islam. We think, for example, of the long wars involving the Muslims and the Europeans, the Moors in Spain, the Tartars in Russia or the Turks in Europe. But in the Muslim world, they do not describe encounters in these terms. They never use the words "Arab" or "Moors" or "Tartars" or "Turks" in this context. The division is always the wars between the Muslims and the unbelievers.

In the West, the nation is seen as the natural unit of identify and allegiance. But until recently, this was not so in the Muslim world. In modern times, the Arab world has been chopped up into what would apparently seem to be nation-states. But if you look at them closely, you can see their artificiality. Look at the borders. Most of North America's borders are straight lines. That's understandable because they were drawn with pencils and rulers on maps. The borders of Europe are different. They are not straight lines. They are the result of a thousand years of struggle. You would expect the same to be the case in the Middle East, where the entities are even more ancient than those of Europe. But no, their borders are straight lines drawn by Europeans. Perhaps even more remarkably, there is no word in Arabic for Arabia. This is not because Arabic is a poor language. On the contrary, Arabic is an incredibly rich language. It is because the Muslims simply did not think in terms of territorial ethnic identity. I mention this point because I think it's important in understanding Muslim perceptions of what is going on.

In the Muslim perception, the world took a new turn in the 7th century when Islam was born and spread rapidly in all directions with enormous success. This was seen at the time, with some justification, as a challenge to other faiths. Anyone who has been to Jerusalem will surely have visited the Dome of the Rock. That magnificent structure is the oldest surviving Muslim religious building outside Arabia. If you go inside, you will see inscriptions written on the dome. One says "He is God. He is one. He does not beget. He is not begotten." This is an explicit rejection of certain basic Christian dogmas. By building this structure in Jerusalem of all places, which at that time was not yet regarded as a Muslim Holy City, by putting up this building with these inscriptions in Jerusalem, the Muslims were in effect saying to the Christian world -- and, in particular to the Christian emperor in Constantinople, "Your time has passed. Now we are here. Move over."

There has been a lot of talk of late about the clash of civilizations. Most of the civilizations known to history -- such as those of China, India, Greece, Rome, Egypt and Babylon -- have been regional. Christianity and Islam are different. These are the only two civilizations whose underlying religions claim not only that their truths are universal -- all religions claim that -- but also that their truths are exclusive. Both believe that they are the fortunate recipients of God's final revelation to mankind, and it is therefore their duty to bring it to the rest of the world. It is inevitable that you will have a clash between two religions that are geographically adjacent, historical consecutive, theologically akin.

For a long time, Islam got the better of this clash. For a period of centuries, the civilization of Islam was by far the most advanced and the most creative in the world. It was enormously successful in every material sense. Its armies coming out of Arabia conquered everything across the Middle East and North Africa. They invaded Europe, conquering Spain, Portugal, Southern Italy and even advancing into France. Eastwards, they advanced across to Central Asia and India. Muslims also developed a highly sophisticated economic system of production and exchange with a remarkably advanced system of banking and credit. As far back as the 10th century, a Muslim merchant or a non-Muslim merchant living under Muslim rule could draw a cheque in Southern Iraq and cash it in Morocco.

From the perspective of Muslims, Western Europe was a kind of outer darkness of barbarism and unbelief, a primitive tribe beyond the border to which they gave understandably little attention. There was nothing to fear and nothing to learn. On the contrary, it was the Europeans who went to the great Muslim universities in Spain, in Sicily and in the East. In those centuries, Europe -- meaning Christendom as Muslims saw it -- was a poor benighted backwater.

Then things changed. The change was gradual, and took place over a vast area and a long period. But what brought the change home were rather dramatic single events. One of those events was the second Turkish siege of Vienna in 1683.

It is important to remember that, in the 17th century, Islam was still threatening Europe, not the other way around. Turkish pashas were still ruling in Budapest and in Belgrade. Corsairs from North Africa were still raiding the European coasts, including the coasts of England and Ireland and, on one occasion, even Iceland -- collecting human booty for sale in the slave markets of Algiers.

The first Turkish siege of Vienna ended in a sort of draw. But the second siege, in 1683, was a disaster. A Turkish historian of the time, describing the episode, said: "This is the most calamitous defeat that we have suffered since the foundation of our state." One must admire his candour and regret that similar candour is rarely to be found among present day historians of the region.

The defeat outside Vienna was followed by a headlong retreat through the Balkans and a peace treaty, the Treaty of Karlowitz in 1699, the first ever imposed on a defeated Ottoman empire by victorious Christian European enemies.

The lessons of history are often taught on the battlefield. In this case, the lesson was clear.

Among Muslims, the debate began at the beginning of the 18th century, and has been going on ever since. The main question: What went wrong?

There was a growing awareness that Muslims, who had always been victorious, were now losing on the battlefield, in the marketplace and, in fact, in every significant field of human endeavor. The debate became increasingly agonized, and continues to the present day.

176

When you become aware that things are going wrong, there are two ways you can approach the problem. First, you can ask "What are they doing right?" There were many Muslims who followed this line of inquiry, and experimented with Western forms of warfare and weaponry, Western-style factories, parliaments and the like.

The second approach is to say "Who did this to us?" This of course leads into a twilight world of anti-Western conspiracy theories and neurotic fantasies. Unfortunately, this approach has prevailed in many parts of the Muslim world to the present day.

In answering the question, "Who did this to us?" Muslims have often blamed "Imperialists." (Of course, when Muslims were invading Europe, imperialist expansionism was seen as natural and good because the invaders were bringing the word of God to the heathens. When the Europeans, after centuries of Muslim domination, counterattacked on the other hand, this was wicked.) In this regard, the United States has now inherited the role of its Christian predecessors. As many Muslims see it, the world continues to be divided between the Islamic world and its age-old imperialist rival, the Christian world. This division is at the heart of the writings of Osama Bin Laden and his complaints about the "crusader" presence in Saudi Arabia and so forth.

- - -

Even after the second siege of Vienna, the Arab world was largely shielded from reality by Ottoman power, even in the era of Ottoman decline and retreat. But eventually, that came to an end.

The modern history of the Arab world is generally held to begin at the end of the 18th century, when the French Republic sent a small expeditionary force commanded by a young general called Napoleon Bonaparte to Egypt. To the utter shock and horror of the Egyptians and everyone else in the region, this small army from France was able to invade, conquer, occupy and govern Egypt without the slightest difficulty. The fact that an army from the West managed to penetrate one of the heartlands of the Islamic world -- not just Vienna or the Balkans -- was a terrible shock.

But if the arrival of the French was a shock, their departure was a second and perhaps more salutary shock. The eviction of the French was accomplished not by the Egyptians, nor by the Turks, but by a small squadron of the Royal Navy commanded by a young Admiral called Horatio Nelson.

The lesson was clear: A European power could come to the region and do what it pleased, and only another European power could get them out. Thus began the game, so to speak, of playing European powers off against one another.

For two centuries or more, the scenario remained the same -- though the players were sometimes different. In the final phase, the players were the two superpowers, the Soviet Union and the United States; and Middle Eastern leaders used the skills they had perfected over two centuries in playing them off against each other.

Then, suddenly, it came to an end. The phase in history that had been initiated by Bonaparte and Nelson was terminated by Bush and Gorbachev. Suddenly, there was no rivalry; there were no rival powers. First one and then the other seemed disinclined to play the Imperial role -- the Russians because they couldn't and the Americans because they wouldn't.

Some Muslim leaders are trying to keep playing the old game, and so are seeking another power to play off against the West, as it is embodied by the United States. The prime candidate is the European Union, or at least some parts of the European Union where there is a negative sentiment regarding America. Unfortunately, for those who pursue this policy, even if the Europeans have the will to play this role, they lack the ability.

The other, and at first sightly more promising response to the end of the Cold War, was that of Osama bin Laden. He and his followers make it perfectly clear in their writings that they regard the defeat of the Soviet Union as their achievement -- through their long struggle in Afghanistan. I think you must agree it is not by any means an implausible explanation of what happened.

- - -

Where are we now? Within the Islamic world, more particularly the Middle Eastern world, I think one must divide countries in terms of their attitude to the West into three zones. One zone comprises those countries that have governments that we are pleased to regard as pro-Western and pro-American. These governments are therefore, and I stress the word "therefore," cordially detested by their people. They are detested not because they are pro-West but because they are regarded as Western puppets and therefore the West is held responsible for the corruption and tyranny of these regimes. It is no accident that most of the hijackers and terrorists on Sept. 11 came from countries with Western-friendly governments.

A second group are countries with hostile governments. I am thinking in particular of Iraq and Iran, perhaps also Syria. These are bitterly anti-American and anti-Western; and therefore their peoples are very pro-Western and pro-American. Let me relate an Iranian joke that I heard only last week from an Iranian, which I think captures the mood. (Jokes are often the only uncensored form of comment in these countries.) When American planes began to fly over Afghanistan, many Iranians put out notices over their houses saying, "This way, please."

In these countries whose governments detest the West, all the indications are that there is general goodwill toward the West among the people. In Iran, for example, after 9/11, great numbers of people went out into the streets and lit candles in sympathy vigils. This did not happen in nominally U.S.-friendly countries like Saudi Arabia; quite the reverse.

The third group comprises the Middle Eastern countries where both the government and the people are friendly. There are just two countries in this categories: Turkey and Israel, which happen to be the only two countries with functioning democracies.

- - -

Let me end with a discussion about Western influence in the Middle East. We tend to think of modernization and Westernization as good things. And, in many ways, they have been good things. But they have also done tremendous damage to Muslim societies. They have, for example, strengthened dictatorship to a degree that was never possible previously.

Modernization has strengthened the central power, and given the government new means of surveillance and repression. This has made possible that ultimate example of Westernization -- the one-party dictatorship. It flourishes in Syria and in Iraq at the present time in a way that combines the Nazi and Soviet models.

Westernization also has the effect of enfeebling or eliminating the limiting powers within a society. In traditional societies, there were many limiting powers that acted as constraints on government power. There were the urban patricians, the country nobility, the religious establishment, the military establishment and others. All these were enfeebled or abolished and made subject to the central authority.

There was a time when socialism and nationalism were the two most widely accepted creeds in the Middle East -- particularly after the end of the Second World War, when the Soviets had won great victories in Eastern Europe. The British Labour Party had won a great electoral victory, throwing out the mighty Winston Churchill. Socialism was seen as the wave of the future. So they brought in a whole series of socialist governments all over the Arab world. There was some debate. Some said that we must have Arab socialism; that is to say socialism, but adjusted to the different Arab cultural context. Others said, "No, that's nonsense. We must have scientific socialism," meaning the Moscow Marxists' variety. By now, I think they would all agree that socialism is neither Arab nor scientific.

The other great slogan of the time was nationalism, which was supposed to bring freedom, throwing off the foreign yoke. Unfortunately, there was some confusion between freedom and independence. Indeed, in most of the places that had previously been under Imperial rule, they had less freedom under independence than they had under foreign rule. So you had the two ideas discredited -- socialism discredited by its failure; nationalism discredited by its success. These were the two great movements that dominated public discourse and public life in these countries for half a century. Both are dead. Both are gone. So, where do they turn now?

Basically there are two alternative approaches. One is the approach of those who ask, "What did we do wrong?" and who feel that the way forward is to modernize their societies but to do it properly and, most important of all, with a measure of democratization of their political institutions and liberalization of their economies.

On the other hand you have those who say: "The source of all our troubles was the West" -- either what Westerners themselves did or, more frequently and more importantly, what Westernizing local "puppets" or imitators did. And the remedy, therefore, is to go back to back in time to the true, authentic, original Islam. This is the remedy proposed by the Islamic Republic in Iran and also by the various terrorist movements.

The choice between the two approaches is an awe-inspiring one; and, at this point, I would not like to predict which way it will go. It is, of course, going both ways at the present time.

The Culture Of Martyrdom
How Suicide Bombing Became Not Just A Means But An End

David Brooks
The Atlantic
June 1, 2002

Suicide bombing is the crack cocaine of warfare. It doesn't just inflict death and terror on its victims; it intoxicates the people who sponsor it. It unleashes the deepest and most addictive human passions-the thirst for vengeance, the desire for religious purity, the longing for earthly glory and eternal salvation. Suicide bombing isn't just a tactic in a larger war; it overwhelms the political goals it is meant to serve. It creates its own logic and transforms the culture of those who employ it. This is what has happened in the Arab-Israeli dispute. Over the past year suicide bombing has dramatically changed the nature of the conflict.

Before 1983 there were few suicide bombings. The Koran forbids the taking of one's own life, and this prohibition was still generally observed. But when the United States stationed Marines in Beirut, the leaders of the Islamic resistance movement Hizbollah began to discuss turning to this ultimate terrorist weapon. Religious authorities in Iran gave it their blessing, and a wave of suicide bombings began, starting with the attacks that killed about sixty U.S. embassy workers in April of 1983 and about 240 people in the Marine compound at the airport in October. The bombings proved so successful at driving the United States and, later, Israel out of Lebanon that most lingering religious concerns were set aside.

The tactic was introduced into Palestinian areas only gradually. In 1988 Fathi Shiqaqi, the founder of the Palestinian Islamic Jihad, wrote a set of guidelines (aimed at countering religious objections to the truck bombings of the 1980s) for the use of explosives in individual bombings; nevertheless, he characterized operations calling for martyrdom as "exceptional." But by the mid-1990s the group Hamas was using suicide bombers as a way of derailing the Oslo peace process. The assassination of the master Palestinian bomb maker Yahya Ayyash, presumably by Israeli agents, in January of 1996, set off a series of suicide bombings in retaliation. Suicide bombings nonetheless remained relatively unusual until two years ago, after the Palestinian leader Yasir Arafat walked out of the peace conference at Camp David-a conference at which Israel's Prime Minister, Ehud Barak, had offered to return to the Palestinians parts of Jerusalem and almost all of the West Bank.

At that point the psychology shifted. We will not see peace soon, many Palestinians concluded, but when it eventually comes, we will get everything we want. We will endure, we will fight, and we will suffer for that final victory. From then on the struggle (at least from the Palestinian point of view) was no longer about negotiation and compromise-about who would get which piece of land, which road or river. The red passions of the bombers obliterated the grays of the peace process. Suicide bombing became the tactic of choice, even in circumstances where a terrorist could have planted a bomb and then escaped without injury. Martyrdom became not just a means but an end.

Suicide bombing is a highly communitarian enterprise. According to Ariel

Merari, the director of the Political Violence Research Center, at Tel Aviv University, and a leading expert on the phenomenon, in not one instance has a lone, crazed Palestinian gotten hold of a bomb and gone off to kill Israelis. Suicide bombings are initiated by tightly run organizations that recruit, indoctrinate, train, and reward the bombers. Those organizations do not seek depressed or mentally unstable people for their missions. From 1996 to 1999 the Pakistani journalist Nasra Hassan interviewed almost 250 people who were either recruiting and training bombers or preparing to go on a suicide mission themselves. "None of the suicide bombers-they ranged in age from eighteen to thirty-eight-conformed to the typical profile of the suicidal personality," Hassan wrote in The New Yorker. "None of them were uneducated, desperately poor, simple-minded, or depressed." The Palestinian bombers tend to be devout, but religious fanaticism does not explain their motivation. Nor does lack of opportunity, because they also tend to be well educated.

Often a bomber believes that a close friend or a member of his family has been killed by Israeli troops, and this is part of his motivation. According to most experts, though, the crucial factor informing the behavior of suicide bombers is loyalty to the group. Suicide bombers go through indoctrination processes similar to the ones that were used by the leaders of the Jim Jones and Solar Temple cults. The bombers are organized into small cells and given countless hours of intense and intimate spiritual training. They are instructed in the details of jihad, reminded of the need for revenge, and reassured about the rewards they can expect in the afterlife. They are told that their families will be guaranteed a place with God, and that there are also considerable rewards for their families in this life, including cash bonuses of several thousand dollars donated by the government of Iraq, some individual Saudis, and various groups sympathetic to the cause. Finally, the bombers are told that paradise lies just on the other side of the detonator, that death will feel like nothing more than a pinch.

Members of such groups re-enact past operations. Recruits are sometimes made to lie in empty graves, so that they can see how peaceful death will be; they are reminded that life will bring sickness, old age, and betrayal. "We were in a constant state of worship," one suicide bomber (who somehow managed to survive his mission) told Hassan. "We told each other that if the Israelis only knew how joyful we were they would whip us to death! Those were the happiest days of my life!"

The bombers are instructed to write or videotape final testimony. (A typical note, from 1995: "I am going to take revenge upon the sons of the monkeys and the pigs, the Zionist infidels and the enemies of humanity. I am going to meet my holy brother Hisham Hamed and all the other martyrs and saints in paradise.") Once a bomber has completed his declaration, it would be humiliating for him to back out of the mission. He undergoes a last round of cleansing and prayer and is sent off with his bomb to the appointed pizzeria, coffee shop, disco, or bus.

For many Israelis and Westerners, the strangest aspect of the phenomenon is the televised interview with a bomber's parents after a massacre. These people have just been told that their child has killed himself and others, and yet they seem happy, proud, and-should the opportunity present itself-ready to send another child off to the afterlife. There are two ways to look at this: One, the parents feel so wronged and humiliated by the Israelis that they would rather sacrifice their children than continue passively to endure. Two, the cult of suicide bombing has infected the broader culture to the point where large parts of society, including the bombers' parents, are addicted to the adrenaline rush of vengeance and murder. Both explanations may be true.

It is certainly the case that vast segments of Palestinian culture have been given over to the creation and nurturing of suicide bombers. Martyrdom has replaced Palestinian independence as the main focus of the Arab media. Suicide bombing is, after all, perfectly suited to the television age. The bombers' farewell videos provide compelling footage, as do the interviews with families. The bombings themselves produce graphic images of body parts and devastated buildings. Then there are the "weddings" between the martyrs and dark-eyed virgins in paradise (announcements that read like wedding invitations are printed in local newspapers so that friends and neighbors can join in the festivities), the marches and celebrations after each attack, and the displays of things bought with the cash rewards to the families. Woven together, these images make gripping packages that can be aired again and again.

Activities in support of the bombings are increasingly widespread. Last year the BBC shot a segment about so-called Paradise Camps-summer camps in which children as young as eight are trained in military drills and taught about suicide bombers. Rallies commonly feature children wearing bombers' belts. Fifth- and sixth-graders have studied poems that celebrate the bombers. At Al Najah University, in the West Bank, a student exhibition last September included a re-created scene of the Sbarro pizzeria in Jerusalem after the suicide bombing there last August: "blood" was splattered everywhere, and mock body parts hung from the ceiling as if blown through the air.

Thus suicide bombing has become phenomenally popular. According to polls, 70 to 80 percent of Palestinians now support it-making the act more popular than Hamas, the Palestinian Islamic Jihad, Fatah, or any of the other groups that sponsor it, and far more popular than the peace process ever was. In addition to satisfying visceral emotions, suicide bombing gives average Palestinians, not just PLO elites, a chance to play a glorified role in the fight against Israel.

Opponents of suicide bombings sometimes do raise their heads. Over the last couple of years educators have moderated the tone of textbooks to reduce and in many cases eliminate the rhetoric of holy war. After the BBC report aired, Palestinian officials vowed to close the Paradise Camps. Nonetheless, Palestinian children grow up in a culture in which suicide bombers are rock stars, sports heroes, and religious idols rolled into one. Reporters who speak with Palestinians about the bombers notice the fire and pride in their eyes.

"I'd be very happy if my daughter killed Sharon," one mother told a reporter from The San Diego Union-Tribune last November. "Even if she killed two or three Israelis, I would be happy." Last year I attended a dinner party in Amman at which six distinguished Jordanians-former cabinet ministers and supreme-court justices and a journalist-talked about the Tel Aviv disco bombing, which had occurred a few months earlier. They had some religious qualms about the suicide, but the moral aspect of killing teenage girls-future breeders of Israelis-was not even worth discussing. They spoke of the attack with a quiet sense of satisfaction.

It's hard to know how Israel, and the world, should respond to the rash of suicide bombings and to their embrace by the Palestinian people. To take any action that could be viewed as a concession would be to provoke further attacks, as the U.S. and Israeli withdrawals from Lebanon in the 1980s demonstrated. On the other hand, the Israeli raids on the refugee camps give the suicide bombers a propaganda victory. After Yasir Arafat walked out of the Camp David meetings, he became a pariah to most governments, for killing the peace process. Now, amid Israeli retaliation for the bombings, the global community rises to condemn Israel's actions.

Somehow conditions must be established that would allow the frenzy of suicide bombings to burn itself out. To begin with, the Palestinian and Israeli populations would have to be separated; contact between them inflames the passions that feed the attacks. That would mean shutting down the vast majority of Israeli settlements in the West Bank and Gaza and creating a buffer zone between the two populations. Palestinian life would then no longer be dominated by checkpoints and celebrations of martyrdom; it would be dominated by quotidian issues such as commerce, administration, and garbage collection.

The idea of a buffer zone, which is gaining momentum in Israel, is not without problems. Where, exactly, would the buffer be? Terrorist groups could shoot missiles over it. But it's time to face the reality that the best resource the terrorists have is the culture of martyrdom. This culture is presently powerful, but it is potentially fragile. If it can be interrupted, if the passions can be made to recede, then the Palestinians and the Israelis might go back to hating each other in the normal way, and at a distance. As with many addictions, the solution is to go cold turkey.

Israel Can't Do Business With Terrorists
Violence Against Civilians Must Be Forcibly Stopped, Not Forgiven

Ehud Olmert

Reprinted from the Wall Street Journal©
June 3, 2002, Dow Jones Company, Inc. All rights reserved.

State Department envoy William Burns's return to the Middle East promoting the American-backed regional peace summit tragically coincides with the resumption of the daily Palestinian suicide bombings. As Israeli civilians are being murdered in cities all across the Jewish State, the Palestinian leadership is once again damning these new peace initiatives to failure. Terrorism is still part of their tactical plan.

Despite all the tough talk, well-wishing and demand for reform, Arafat's entrenched Palestinian Authority regime is constitutionally unable and morally unwilling to abandon its violent struggle against Israel.

The majority of the Israeli public had naively accepted the basic premises of the Oslo Accords when they were signed in the fall of 1993 because we received a guarantee that the Palestinian police and security forces would put an end to terrorism and bring about a true peace. Yitzhak Rabin, then prime minister, assured us that Arafat would personally order the arrest of the Hamas and Islamic Jihad leaders and eradicate their terrorist infrastructure. Instead of Israeli troops carrying out dangerous patrols in Ramallah, Jenin and Gaza, we were promised, the Palestinian forces would do it for us. In those innocent Oslo days, many truly believed that terrorism could be fought by proxy and we need merely give Arafat the weapons to do it.

Over the next few years, that optimism began to dissipate. If anyone in Israel still had faith in Arafat and his Palestinian security services by October 2000, the Arab violence that commenced that month put it to rest forever. The forces under Arafat's command became both the catalyst and vanguard of the terrorist attacks. Arafat's Fatah Tanzim and Force 17 units were transformed into full-fledged terrorist groups, with their members competing with Hamas to see how many Jews they could kill.

As the violence accelerated, and as more and more Israeli families were being destroyed, the new line touted by both our allies and enemies was that Arafat could not actually assert any influence over the terrorist organizations. The 40,000 armed guerillas that were brought in from PLO bases in Tunis, Syria and south Lebanon were now operating without any restraints against Israel from the Palestinian territories.

The new American plan being presented calls for a reorganization of the Palestinian security forces with the intention of placing them under a unified command. The hope is that they will miraculously be transformed into a law-abiding legion that will root out terrorists. Once again we Israelis are being assured with a straight face that Arafat and his gunmen will fight Hamas and Islamic Jihad for us. Israeli troops are currently being restrained from entering Gaza, while Arafat's forces are supposedly being given yet another makeover.

Hundreds of members of the Palestinian police forces have engaged in terrorist attacks against Israeli civilians, including American citizens, during the last 21 months.

184

Israeli security services and our military are actively hunting these criminals and our Justice Ministry is busy filing their indictments. Thousands of individuals with PA-authorized guns are active members of the Fatah Tanzim terrorist group. And barely a day goes by without another suicide bomber from the Tanzim destroying himself and innocent bystanders in a public center.

The terrorist leaders and their activists cannot suddenly be forgiven or pardoned just because a new political initiative is underway. Israel, like every other Western state, has an obligation to continue to arrest and prosecute those who sought to advance their unacceptable political goal by targeting civilians. Justice dictates that there be no clemency for these rogue police officials.

Many are placing their new hopes on Gaza preventive security service boss Mohammed Dahlan. Mr. Dahlan, a rising star on the Palestinian stage, is being presented as the man who can unify all of Arafat's security forces and bring order to the PA. Word has it that he just returned from a trip to Washington where he got high marks from the National Security Council. (Mr. Dahlan denies ever going.) Either way, Mr. Dahlan is the man who has presided over an ever-fortified terrorist network. Gaza, the home to Hamas and Islamic Jihad, became a base for some of the most heinous terrorist attacks unleashed against Israel.

On his watch, Mr. Dahlan permitted Gaza to become a safe haven for the hundreds of fugitive terrorists fleeing Israeli forces. Among those being sheltered is his childhood friend Mohammed Dief, a leading Hamas mastermind with the blood of scores of Israelis on his hands. In the meantime, Mr. Dahlan's district became the primary launching grounds for the hundreds of Kessem missiles fired at Israel.

Mr. Dahlan's involvement in terrorism has not been confined to mere nonfeasance but, rather, gross malfeasance as well. Mr. Dahlan, along with his assistant Rashid Abu-Shabak, are the primary suspects in the terror attack on an Israeli school bus in Kfar Darom in November 2000. The bombing of the bus left half a dozen children maimed, and seriously injured an American citizen, Rachel Asaroff. In response to this brutal terror attack on Jewish school children, then-Prime Minister Ehud Barak dispatched Israeli planes to strafe Mr. Dahlan's Gaza headquarters.

In Israel, we are frequently lectured that we must do business with the unsavory assortment of dictators, strongmen and criminals that surround us. This, we are told, is the nature of the neighborhood we live in. As mayor of Jerusalem, I have in my public duties the unfortunate experience of sitting down with many individuals I do not necessarily like. But the current thinking that Mr. Dahlan can bring reform and law enforcement to the Palestinians is totally misguided. No democratic state should ever allow itself to do business with those individuals who deliberately target a school bus.

While the State Department and envoy Burns are to be admired for their determination to forge a peace agreement on Israel's behalf, their zealousness is beginning to chafe. Seeking a "regional conference at all costs," and hanging hopes on a reorganized Palestinian security force under the sole leadership of one who has himself been involved in serious terrorist attacks sends an unacceptable message. Criminals such as Mr. Dahlan and Arafat can never be reformed; they must be eradicated by force.

6 Days of War

Daniel Pipes
New York Post
June 4, 2002

The most overwhelming victory in the annals of warfare took place in June 35 years ago, when Israeli forces defeated the Egyptian, Jordanian and Syrian armies in a mere six days. And this June is marked by the publication of "Six Days of War: June 1967 and the Making of the Modern Middle East" (Oxford University Press) by Michael Oren, the finest book ever on this topic.

Oren, an Israeli scholar of American origins, tells his story in a spare, direct and gripping way, replete with punchy quotations.

"Six Days of War" benefits from sources in six languages and is the first account to rely on recently opened state archives, which let the account provide the previously unknown inside story, including a number of scoops (such as the Arab plans for conquering Israel; or how Defense Minister Moshe Dayan's orders to seize the Golan Heights violated his terms of office). No wonder it is a U.S. bestseller even before its formal release.

Several questions still endure about the '67 war, and Oren provides helpful information for answering them. Here are three key ones:

* Why did the war take place? The question arises because, like World War I, no one planned for or wanted this war. Oren's research offers insights into its thoroughly accidental quality.

In November 1966, for example, after the killing of three Israeli policemen at the hands of Jordan-based terrorists, the usually efficient U.S. ambassador to Israel waited a few days to transmit a message of condolence from Jordan's King Hussein to the Israeli prime minister. His delay prompted the Israelis to retaliate, and that retaliation in turn became a major episode in the escalation to war.

The role of accidents needs to be kept in mind these days, as the winds of war again blow in the Middle East: Even the slightest misstep could cause a blow-up.

* How did the Israel Defense Forces win so overwhelmingly? By meticulous practice and absolute realism, in contrast to the Arab militaries, which lived in a fantasy world.

If the Israelis were all nerves on approaching war - Chief of Staff Yitzhak Rabin suffered a breakdown - the Arab leaders were supremely overconfident. A Syrian general predicted a victory over Israel in four days "at most." Egypt's President Gamal Abdel Nasser showed no signs of concern, insisting that Israelis were incapable of mounting precisely the surprise air attack that they in fact pulled off.

More broadly, one high Egyptian official said about his side's leadership that it believed "the destruction of Israel was a child's game that only required believed "the destruction of Israel was a child's game that only required the hooking up of a few telephone lines at the commander's house and the writing of victory slogans."

(Washington, ironically, was more confident than Tel Aviv of an Israeli victory; two weeks before war broke out, Oren shows, the U.S. secretary of defense predicted that if Israel pre-empted, it would defeat its three enemies within the week - precisely what happened.)

* How did the war affect Arab-Israeli diplomacy? It fundamentally changed the terms.

Already in mid-May, weeks before hostilities started, the Middle East hand at the White House, Harold Saunders, suggested that Israel should be allowed the time to trounce its enemies, seeing in this a way "of settling borders and, maybe even refugees."

By the second day of warfare, President Lyndon Johnson had formulated the outline of the land-for-peace policy that 35 years later still drives U.S. diplomacy toward the Arab-Israeli conflict: Israel should return the land it conquered in 1967 in exchange for its recognition by the Arabs.

Americans expected the scale of Israel's military triumph to show the Arabs the futility of their hopes to destroy the Jewish state, an analysis that found immediate agreement among some Israelis (including Yitzhak Rabin, later the prime minister who initiated the Oslo negotiations, which was premised on precisely this assumption).

But, as recent events have so vividly proved, the land-for-peace premise was false. With just a few exceptions (such as Egypt's President Anwar as-Sadat), Israel's willingness to make this exchange precipitated violence against it, not acceptance, by the Arabs.

Oren shows how land-for-peace was based on American hopes, not Middle Eastern realities; his research points to this failed policy needing finally to be replaced by a more realistic approach.

As Oren's subtitle suggests, those six days of war had truly profound consequences.

What's Wrong With Israel's Hasbara?

Bret Stephens
Jerusalem Post
June 6, 2002

What's wrong with Israel's hasbara? Why can't Israel better make its case in the court of public opinion? Why does the country routinely get such shabby treatment in the media?

Speaking at a conference on "Democracy and Limited War" organized by the Begin-Sadat Center of Bar-Ilan University, Brigadier General and IDF spokesman Ron Kitrey offered some answers. There are, he says, "the limitations of the TV frame," which offers the illusion of perfect transparency but in fact serves to obscure broader issues of context and scope. There is the "replay effect," in which limited IDF actions are infinitely magnified through repeated airings of the same clip. And there are the "boundaries of public affairs" - the reluctance of the IDF and the Government Press Office to disseminate graphic photos of terror attack victims in the same way that Palestinians invite camera crews to film the scenes of their "massacres."

All of this is surely right, and one can easily say more. Excepting Binyamin Netanyahu, Ehud Olmert and recently my colleague David Horovitz of The Jerusalem Report, Israel fields no spokesmen of Hanan Ashrawi's or Sari Nusseibeh's caliber. The quality of their spoken English tends to be mediocre. They are a remarkably untelegenic bunch. And time and again, they seem to miss their cues, muddle their arguments, botch their points.

Yet the problem of poor spokesmanship - an easily remediable one - hardly goes to the heart of the matter. Indeed, in seeking the cause for our bad press on the failure of our own efforts, we run the risk of succumbing to the old habit of blaming ourselves for that which is done to us. If we are going to assess the hasbara question rightly, we must first take stock of those things we are powerless to change.

Begin with the fact that, for reasons general, particular and peculiar, Israel's public-relations efforts are hobbled by the basic parameters of modern-day news coverage.

Parameter One is the demand by Western media for "balanced" news coverage, meaning equal time and equal play to both sides. In October 2000, following the lynching of two Israeli reservists in Ramallah, ABC's Nightline delivered a report offering the view that Palestinians had raised "reasonable questions" about just what those two soldiers were doing in Ramallah in the first place. To be sure, Nightline also allowed that Israelis had "reasonable questions." But in seeking to inject balance, ABC gave tacit credence to the Palestinian claim that these slaughtered reservists were in fact Mossad agents. That the claim was preposterous on its face never made the broadcast.

Parameter Two is the fetish for objectivity, which seeks to eliminate the most basic moral judgments from all reporting. Thus ordinary distinctions between aggressors and victims, and between random terrorist acts and targeted military reprisal, are submerged in the catch-all word "violence," as if violence belongs to the same category as the weather.

More egregious still is the substitution of the words "extremist" or "militant" for terrorist, on the theory that terrorism is an "emotive term," or the use of quotation marks around the term "terrorist infrastructure," which hints at a kind of mocking skepticism that a terrorist infrastructure actually exists.

Parameter Three is the general preference for snapshots and soundbites, two categories where Palestinians have the upper hand. Ariel Sharon may talk about defensible borders and strategic depth, but this fares poorly against Palestinian charges of the theft of ancestral land. More potently, televised images of Palestinian boys throwing stones at Israeli tanks makes for a classic David and Goliath fable that Israel can do nothing to counter so long as it fights its battles with Merkavas and F-16s. Which is to say, so long as Israel remains a state.

Beyond these parameters, there's the fact that some Western journalists are personally hostile to Israeli policy and sometimes to Israel itself. No amount of public-relations wizardry, of political concessions of the sort Ehud Barak made at Camp David, is going to win over the likes of Robert Fisk of The Independent to Israel's side, much less have him removed from his post.

Nor is that all. Part of Israel's hasbara problems are inscribed both in the nature of the country, as well as in the nature of the enemy Israelis face. Israel is an open society in conflict with a closed one, and Israelis can be as critical of themselves as are its worst critics in the Western media. So for every Robert Fisk there is a Gidon Levy or Amira Hass to lend credibility to unfavorable reporting by the West. But such pluralism finds no echo in the Palestinian Authority, which can quash dissent and present its case as if it stood at the head of a united front.

Then too, Israel, a country that values truth, confronting an enemy for whom lying (at least when it comes to politics) enjoys religious sanction. From the Kahane Commission of 1983 to the recent prosecution of IDF troops for looting in Ramallah, Israel voluntarily exposes ugly truths about itself in a way that is all but inconceivable among its neighbors - the clampdown on Palestinian celebrations of Sept. 11 being only the most recent case in point.

Both these facts ought to be a boon to Israel's hasbara, and to an extent they are: popular US support for Israel owes largely to the sense that Israel upholds American-style democratic standards. And in the long-term, the habits of truth-telling accrue to Israel's credibility. Yet given the turn-rate of today's news-cycle, getting out your version of the story first is what tends to matter most, and in this respect Israel is usually slow. Thus Jenin becomes a page-one "massacre" long before it becomes a page-two item in the corrections box.

All these things taken into account, it remains the case that Israel's hasbara efforts remain inadequate. Indeed, they are dismal.

The problem is not that Israel has the wrong spokesmen, or that they aren't getting the message across. The problem is, they are getting the wrong message across. For reasons owing largely to the pluralist nature of this society, the Israeli "message" has come down to one low common denominator, which is the argument against terrorism.

And Israel is gradually losing that argument as well.

Let's begin with the basic Palestinian point, which is that they are living under occupation. Once this premise is accepted, there is no way that Israel is going to be able to mount a successful rhetorical counterstrategy. Israelis can yell as loudly as they want that Palestinians are killing "innocent civilians." But if a man were squatting in your apartment, with 20 of his relatives in tow, and the cops refused to haul them away, chances are there's very little you wouldn't eventually do to have them evicted.

The second fundamental hasbara mistake is to harp repeatedly on the point that Palestinians are killing "Jews." This may help make the case that Palestinian politics have become Hitlerite in nature, but it also opens Israel to the charge that it is milking the memory of the Holocaust to pursue policies that ought to be judged by more present-day criteria. Worse, by emphasizing the specifially Jewish angle, Israeli spokesmen transform the conflict into just another ethnic problem, analogous to the conflict between the Yoruba and the Ibo in Nigeria, or the Catholics and the Protestants in Northern Ireland. And who is to say who's right in these ancient blood feuds? This is the perfect recipe for the moral equivalency that so many Israels bemoan today.

Finally, Israeli spokesmen do little to advance Israel's interests with their relentless focus on Palestinian terrorism, which pits an argument about means - the means used by Palestinians to gain a state - against an argument about ends - the right for Palestinians to have a state. The problem with this line of argument is that it tacitly concedes the Palestinian case, so that the moment Palestinians stop the terrorism, Israel will be at an ideological loss to stand in the way.

What sorts of arguments should Israel should be making?
The first step amounts to a kind of reclamation project. Israeli spokesmen must stress that, pace Kofi Annan, the terrritories are not "occupied" but disputed, and that the presence of Israelis on them does not violate the one applicable article of international law as set down by Geneva Convention. Jews in Judea and Samaria, like Arabs in the Gilboa and the Negev, have at least some right to live where they do.

If this seems a stretch, the next line of defense might go as follows: "Yes, the territories are occupied. But Israel came to occupy them in the course of a war it did not start. It continued to occupy them after their return was rejected at the Arab summit in Khartoum. And Israel still occupies them because Israelis have not yet seen on the part of the Arabs any serious sign that a return of the territories will genuinely guarantee our security within the pre-1967 borders. In other words, the occupation is not something Israelis have forced on the Palestinians. It is an occupation they have forced on us."

For the second step, Israeli spokesmen must speak of the conflict not as a battle between Jews and Arabs, but between democrats and dictators. Consant attention must be called to the fact that the PA abides neither by the rule of law nor by the ordinary strictures of human rights, that it suppresses political dissent and press freedom, and that Arafat, far from being the champion of his "people," is just another garden-variety Arab despot foisted on a nation that deserves better.

Above all, the expression "a viable Palestinian state" should not be taken to mean a territorially contiguous entity, but a morally defensible regime, and that it is only with a morally defensible regime that Israel can eventually make peace.

Finally, the argument against terrorism must be placed in the context of an argument for the legitimacy of the state of Israel. For most Israelis, as for those in the West, this may not seem much in doubt. But that legitimacy is very much in doubt among too large a percentage of the Palestinian population, and people in the West need to understand that the dispute over the territories is merely a proxy argument over this larger question.

Why do they murder us in Tel Aviv? Why do they massacre us in Netanya? Why are they blowing up buses at Meggido Junction? Why are they wiping us out in the cafes of Rehavia? And why do such attacks enjoy widespread popularity in one survey of Palestinian opinion after the next? The people who conduct Isael's hasbara efforts must begin to put these questions into the minds of their Western audiences. And they must awaken the West to the danger Israel faces by constantly supplying the answer.

Until they do so, however, I fear that more than just Israel's hasbara will be doomed.

Fact Sheet #2 - The "Right Of Return"

Mitchell Bard
Jewish Virtual Library
June 6, 2002

The Zionists always knew they would have to live with their Arab neighbors and made every effort to reach an agreement to live in peace; however, most Palestinian Arabs were unwilling to live as equal citizens in a Jewish state and abandoned their homes.

Prior to Israel's declaration of independence the Jews of Palestine urged the Arabs to remain in their homes, but most were afraid to be caught in the crossfire of the fighting provoked by the invading Arab armies, or chose to listen to their leaders' promises that they could leave their homes temporarily and then return when the Jews were driven into the sea.

Israel's declaration of independence explicitly called on the Palestinian Arabs to participate in building the state and pledged that they would be accorded equal rights. This promise was fulfilled for the 150,000 Palestinian Arabs who chose to remain in their homes and became Israeli citizens.

For all their rhetorical support for the Palestinians, the Arab states have contributed less than 5% of the budget of the UNRWA. The United States is the largest funder of this international welfare program for Palestinians.

The Palestinian Authority has received billions of dollars in international aid, but has made a tactical decision not to build permanent housing for the refugees, preferring instead to keep them in camps as political tools to breed terrorists and serve as symbols of suffering.

The UN resolved that only those refugees willing to live at peace should be repatriated and that others should be compensated and resettled. The Arab states rejected Resolution 194 because the war had not yet ended and they still expected to destroy Israel. Only after losing the war did they reinterpret the resolution as requiring the return of the refugees.

The UN recognized that Israel could not be expected to repatriate a population that might endanger its security and that the solution to the problem, like all previous refugee problems, would require at least some Palestinians to be resettled in Arab lands.

In the interest of peace, Israeli leaders since 1948 have repeatedly expressed a willingness to accept some refugees as part of a peace agreement, and Israel has already allowed approximately 200,000 to return; however, the Arabs have refused to negotiate and made clear they consider the refugees a weapon in their war against Israel.

Israelis across the political spectrum have made that clear acceptance of a "right of return" would be suicide. If every refugee was allowed to move to Israel, the population would be nearly 10 million and more than 40% Arab. Given the higher Arab birth rate, it would not be long before the Palestinians would be a majority.

Resolution 242 does not mention the Palestinians at all. It calls for "a just settlement of the refugee problem." The use of the generic term "refugee" was a deliberate acknowledgment that two refugee problems were products of the conflict – one Arab and the other Jewish.

Approximately 800,000 Jews fled persecution in Arab countries at about the same time the Palestinians became refugees. The Jews never received any compensation for the property Arab governments stole from them and no international welfare agency was established on their behalf. They were all resettled while the Palestinians were confined to camps by the Arab governments.

When Egypt controlled the Gaza Strip it did not allow the Palestinians into Egypt or permit them to move elsewhere. Today, Palestine refugees in Lebanon do not have social and civil rights, and have very limited access to public health or educational facilities.

Most Palestinian refugees live in the historic territory of Palestine; i.e., Jordan and the West Bank. When they talk of the right of return, they mean to the homes they lived in before they left. A fraction of the 3.7 million refugees on the UN rolls can claim any direct connection to those homes.

The UN repeatedly tried to persuade Arab nations to solve the refugee problem by resettling the Palestinians, but they refused. Modern neighborhoods that were built in the areas of Jenin and Nablus during the 1990's still remain unoccupied because the Palestinian Authority will not allow the refugees to move out of the camps.

To this day, only two Middle East nations grant Palestinians citizenship – Jordan and Israel.

June 1967 Revisited

Jonathan Tobin
Philadelphia Jewish Exponent
June 11, 2002

For all too many journalists, history is yesterday's newspaper. Ask them about stories they worked on last month, let alone last year, and you're likely to get some blank stares.

So it's little wonder that much of the coverage of the current conflict between Israel and the Palestinians is so unsatisfying.

For too many of us, 1967 is just the date that, in the phrase so often used by reporters, Israel "seized Arab lands."

But 35 years ago this week, the Middle East changed profoundly in ways that few then could have predicted. The events of June 5 to June 10, 1967, and the nervous weeks that preceded those days set in motion both ideas and events that determine the situation we struggle with today.

The reality of June 4, 1967, as the world watched and waited to see if Egyptian dictator Gamal Abdul Nasser, and his Syrian and Jordanian allies, would really make good on their boasts of "driving the Jews into the sea" is something few of us seem able to recall, whether we are old enough to remember that time or not.

That makes this anniversary an especially propitious time for the release of a new book on the events of that week. Israeli historian Michael B. Oren's well-researched and beautifully written new "Six Days of War: June 1967 and the Making of the Modern Middle East" ought to be required reading for not only journalists, but everyone else who ventures to express an opinion about the Middle East.

Oren's dispassionate prose and meticulously detailed research provide wonderful examples of what we need badly but too rarely get these days: a work of history that is serious and well-sourced enough to gain the respect of scholars, while at the same time written in an engaging style that should not put off general readers.

Oren, who worked in the administration of the late Israeli Prime Minister Yitzhak Rabin (the Israel Defense Force's commander in the war), has penned a volume that is broad enough in its outlines to give folks who are new to this history a good read, while also providing many nuggets of new information and insights to those who are familiar with the topic.

MYTHS DEBUNKED

That said, it is more than likely that some who pick up this book will be disappointed by its unvarnished account of an event that the author clearly sees as the chance outcome of a host of mistakes and miscalculations on the part of both parties.

Arabs and critics of Israel who wrongly see the events of 1967 as the result of

"Zionist aggression" will be forced to come to terms with the reality of a Jewish state confined to the 1949 armistice lines, the restoration of which they now claim would magically end the fighting. But far from being the formula for peace, the June 4 borders were a constant invitation to Arab terrorism and threats of war aimed, not at ending Israel's "occupation" of the "West Bank," but at the complete destruction of the Jewish state itself.

On the other hand, those Jews who have cherished their own myths about the war also need to understand that the actions of Egypt, Syria and Jordan that precipitated the war in spite of Israel's entreaties for peace were not part of an organized Arab master plan for Israel's end that was averted only by a miracle.

Instead, Oren shows that everything that Egypt did was mostly unintended. Although the war was one of self-defense for Israel, Egypt's eviction of U.N. peacekeeping troops from the Sinai and Gaza, its troop buildup on Israel's borders and the blockade of Israel's port on the Gulf of Aqaba that ensured that war would happen were all the result of gross miscalculations and blunders by Nasser and his underlings and allies.

In fact, as Oren tells us, had the mischief-making Soviet Union not convinced the Egyptians that Israel was about to attack Syria in retaliation for that country's sponsorship of terror attacks on Israel by Yasser Arafat's Fatah, the whole chain of events that led to Israel's triumph might never have happened.

Making sense of what, on the face of it, was perhaps the most amazing military victory in modern history is not easy. Far from presaging Israel's end, the war resulted in the end, at least temporarily, of Israel's fears of destruction. Along with the gain of the Sinai and the Golan Heights, Israel captured the heart of the historic homeland of the Jews in Judea, Samaria and a reunified Jerusalem.

Yet on June 4, many Jews feared that a war between Israel and the Arabs might result in a second Holocaust in a generation.

Israel's Prime Minister Levi Eshkol, as well as Rabin (who suffered something approaching a nervous breakdown in the weeks leading up to the war), spent the previous month as Israel was gradually backed into a corner vacillating between confident boasting and fear that they had led the Jewish state into a war it should not undertake.

At the same time, most of the Arab world was in a state of expectant euphoria as they hoped the coming battle would result in the expunging of the disgrace of Israel's victory in the 1948 War of Independence. The naqba or "disaster" - the term by which Arabs still refer to Israel''s birth - would be revenged, even though none of the Arab leaders actually wanted to fight the tough Israelis. Nasser himself hoped only for a diplomatic victory that would strengthen his regime, not a war he knew his army was ill-prepared to win.

Indeed, as Oren reveals, most military experts on both sides, as well as in the United States, understood that Israel's miraculous victory was not unlikely. The highly motivated Israelis were prepared to fight, while the Arab armies were poorly led and had little idea of the strategy or the tactics that would enable them to stave off disaster. The events of June 1967 should teach us about the laws of unintended consequences. Hoping to merely humiliate the Jews, Nasser was himself humiliated. Israel, too, blundered by alternating between policies that radiated strength and those that undermined its capacity to deter war.

DRAWING CONCLUSIONS

In the years since the war, Israelis and Arabs have tried to correct the mistakes made in 1967. Israel has sought to be open to the possibility of peace, hoping that its military prowess would convince the other side to give up fighting. The Arabs have gradually abandoned the conventional warfare of 1967, and instead used diplomacy mixed with terror to advance their hopes of destroying Israel.

Despite the hopes of many Israelis, far from ensuring peace, their victory was only one more battle among many in the war for the Jewish state's survival.

Looking at current headlines, "Familiar patterns of terror and counterstrike, incursion and retribution, have resurfaced," Oren writes. In truth, the Six-Day War never really ended. It was, just like the War of Independence, the Yom Kippur and Lebanon wars, as well as the current fighting, just one more battle in a war that has never ended.

Israel's survival may or may not have been miraculous, but it was the result of a set of bizarre occurrences that no one could have foreseen. Those pundits and world leaders who think that they have a magic formula for peace in their pockets (paging Tom Friedman of The New York Times) would do well to study this history and learn some humility.

Israel On The Edge

Paul Johnson
Jerusalem Post
June 12, 2002

It is very difficult to combat an enemy that has so few inhibitions about killing either opponents or its own people

In the current Arab-Israeli crisis, the Israelis appear to have forfeited the sympathy of much of the civilized world. Why is this? And what can Israel, and its allies, do about it?

Part of the explanation lies in the failure of Israel's once brilliantly efficient instrument of state to deliver. After half a century of embattlement with the Arab world, Israel has a tired and combat-weary look and seems to be asking, despairingly: "Where will it all end?" Israel's case for its offensive against its neighboring terrorist enclaves is, in essence, excellent and unassailable. It is now clear that the Oslo accords were a mistake and have been used by Arafat - and his foreign backers - merely as a platform from which to launch indiscriminate suicide bombing against Israel's cities. But this case has been poorly presented by officials who seem to have lost heart.

At any rate it has not got through. When Colin Powell was in Israel, most of the horrifying facts presented to him by Ariel Sharon appeared to be news to him. And if Powell does not grasp the strength of Israel's case, how can millions of ordinary TV viewers across the world, who nightly see Israeli tanks trundling through Arab villages, be expected to understand why the Israeli army has had to conduct its campaign? To make matters worse, there has been a manifest decline in the quality and energy of Israeli diplomacy, formerly one of the world's wonders. Israel's ambassadors in key capitals were handpicked for outstanding ability and high profiles, with a superb grasp of English forensic skills. They seized with relish on the smallest chance to provide "bites" for television audiences. Now they tend to be second-raters with limited fluency in English.

These weaknesses on the Israeli side could be removed if the will were there. But is it? Israel has some of the characteristics of a gerontocracy, a state run by old men who have forgotten nothing and learned little in recent decades. It is a genuine democracy - none better - but its multiple-party system makes for a deadly paralysis at the top, where old men never seem to die, or fade away either. The man who tried to break this impasse, Benjamin Netanyahu, was eventually rejected by voters (who are highly conservative, too), but they now seem to be having second thoughts and it may be that a return of Netanyahu to power would be the first decisive step in putting Israel to rights.

However, there are some factors in Israel's present predicament that are outside its control. Here are the most important. First, there is no symmetry in the Arab-Israeli conflict. If the Israelis score a military victory, or a diplomatic one for that matter, the Arabs live to fight another day. Israel, by contrast, cannot afford one serious mistake. If Israel lost control of the air, and her army were overrun, there can be absolutely no doubt that the entire Jewish-Israeli nation would be exterminated. It would be Hitler's Holocaust all over again, conducted not in secrecy and shame but in the open, in a spirit of triumphant exultation as the successful climax of a jihad. This is the nightmare - not distant but proximate - that every Israeli prime minister must face and for which he will be held posthumously responsible ifhe guesses wrongly and fails to use the necessary force in time. By one wrong decision, an Israeli leader cannot only lose the war in one afternoon, he can lose half the Jewish people, too. This helps to explain why the Israeli elite are hag-ridden with anxiety, obstinate, and often closed to argument.

The lack of symmetry between the risks taken by Arabs and by Israelis is one result of a different view of the sanctity of human life. The Jewish faith was the first religion to preach this sanctity and to magnify the value of each individual human being in the eyes of his Creator - hence, equally, in other human beings. This is the main reason that Mosaic law differs so markedly in humanity and reason from all the other fiercely retributive codes of the ancient Near East. The value placed on human life by Jews has steadily increased over the centuries, as a response to persecution and, above all, to the Nazi attempt at extermination of the entire people. Israel itself was created as a refuge and fortress in which Jewish lives would be safe from annihilation. It is thus the physical embodiment of the principle that individual life is sacred.

By contrast, the Islamic-Arab concept of "the war of the martyrs" places no value on human life except as a sacrifice in the holy war. A warrior gains infinitely more by losing his life than by preserving it, for then he gains eternal life, and his status as a martyr is enhanced by the number of dead Israelis - "sons and daughters of Satan" - whom he takes with him.

It is very difficult for the Israelis to know how to straddle this complete lack of symmetry in warfare and to combat an enemy that has so few inhibitions about killing either opponents or its own people. There is, indeed, something Hitlerian about the implacable hatred Israel faces on its own borders. It should come as no surprise that Arabic translations both of Mein Kampf and of the Protocols of the Elders of Zion, that diabolic forgery, are best-sellers in the Arab world. We in the West would be well advised to appreciate the strength of the hatred the Israelis face, for it may soon be turned against us too. (We received a foretaste on September 11.) However, for the moment, the world is unconscious of these deep underlying forces, and tends in its ignorance to see the Arab-Israel conflict as a war like any other, with the faults 50-50. From this perspective it is therefore the Israelis who appear to be guilty of a disproportionate use of force, an impression the nightly TV images seem to confirm.

Thus the Jews, not for the first time in their long and tragic history, are blamed for the persecution they suffer. Like the Israelis themselves, the world is tired of the endless antagonism of the Arabs and wishes that somehow or other the Jews and their state would simply fade away and allow everyone to have some rest. Thus, similarly, in wartime Germany, ordinary Germans, vaguely aware that countless thousands of Jews were being "sent east" - that euphemism employed for Destination Auschwitz - were furious at the rattling of vast trains of cattle-trucks packed with doomed Jews, which disturbed their rest throughout the night, and cursed "those damned Jews, never letting us get a decent night's sleep." (National Review)

The Baby Face Of Hate
MEMRI Releases An Astonishing Example Of The "True Muslim" Faith

David Tell
The Daily Standard
June 12, 2002

If there were justice in the universe, the Middle East Media Research Institute would already have been awarded some kind of special-achievement Pulitzer Prize. MEMRI has pioneered the careful translation, and dissemination to European and American audiences, of print and broadcast news sources in the Arab world. The group's work now pops up everywhere; here in the States, hardly a week goes by when some major daily or cable news show doesn't make use (generally without attribution) of a MEMRI translation. And the cumulative effect of such translations is--or ought to be, at least--roughly analogous to the body blow struck against European philo-communism by the first Western publication of Alexander Solzhenitsyn's novels in the 1960s. Here, really for the first time, non-Arabic speaking Westerners are being given a direct, first-person look into a previously unseen gulag. Only this time there is no barbed wire, the prisoners all serve by choice, and the anti-Semitism is no longer ancillary but central, basic, and paramount. It turns out that the Islamic Middle East, just as the Israelis have been begging us for years to figure out, has got itself trapped in a deep, deep swamp of near-psychotic Jew hatred.

Yesterday morning at the National Press Club here in Washington, MEMRI held a briefing on Arabic-language media coverage of "martyrdom and suicide bombers." Along with all the usual, scrupulously documented newspaper translations, the group also screened an eye-opening videotape compilation (with English subtitles) of recent broadcasts on something called Iqraa Television. Iqraa is one of the global satellite channels packaged by the Arab Radio and Television Network (ART), a Saudi-based company with transmission facilities in Italy which describes itself as "the leading producer of premium Arabic family programming and entertainment worldwide." Iqraa is ART's effort to provide "a focused insight into the teachings of the Quran" to "intellectual, elite, and conservative Islamic markets." It is widely watched.

And it is hair-raisingly insane. The April 25, 2002 interview with Prof. 'Adel Sadeq, head of the psychiatry faculty at 'Ein Shams University in Cairo, for example. Professor Sadeq beams with glee as he explains how Western civilization "has no concepts such as self-sacrifice and honor," which is why Americans fail to understand that the suicide bomber experiences "the height of ecstasy and happiness" just at the moment when, "ten, nine, eight, seven, six, five, four, three, two, one, and then he presses the button to blow himself up." Big smile.

Then there's the May 9, 2002, program on "discipline in the family," featuring one Jasem Al-Mutawah, an "expert on family matters," who patiently describes to his viewers where on her body, how severely, with what weapon, and under what circumstances a man should beat his wife.

And, most harrowing of all, perhaps, especially if you have kids of your own,

199

there is the May 7, 2002 edition of "Muslim Woman Magazine," hosted by Doaa 'Amer, a soft spoken, highly polished anchorlady who might just as well be Joan Lunden or Katie Couric--except that she's wearing a body-length robe. And also that she's a monster. Ms. 'Amer begins as follows:

"Our report today will be a little different, because our guest is a girl, a Muslim girl, but a true Muslim. Allah willing, may our God give us the strength to educate our children the same way, so that the next generation will turn out to be true Muslims who understand that they are Muslims and know who their enemies are. This girl will introduce herself immediately. She is the daughter of my sister in faith and of the artist, Wagdi Al-Arabi. Her name is Basmallah and we will ask her as well."

The camera then begins a low pan downward and to the right as Ms. 'Amer offers a "peace be unto you" welcome to her guest. Who turns out to be . . . a toddler.

Toddler: Allah's mercy and blessing upon you.

'Amer: What's your name?

Toddler: Basmallah.

'Amer: Basmallah, how old are you?

Toddler: Three and a half.

'Amer: Are you a Muslim?

Toddler: Yes.

'Amer: Basmallah, are you familiar with the Jews?

Toddler: Yes.

'Amer: Do you like them?

Toddler: No.

'Amer: Why don't you like them?

Toddler: Because . . .

'Amer: Because they are what?

Toddler: They're apes and pigs.

'Amer: Because they are apes and pigs. Who said they are so?

Toddler: Our God.

'Amer: Where did he say this?

Toddler: In the Koran.

'Amer: Right, he said that about them in the Koran. Okay, Basmallah, what are the Jews doing?

Toddler: The Pepsi company.

'Amer: [Approving laughter.] You also know about the boycott, Basmallah? Did they love our master, Muhammad?

Toddler: No.

'Amer: No. What did the Jews do to him?

Toddler: [Pauses, struggling for the right answer.] The Prophet Muhammad killed someone . . .

'Amer: Obviously, our master Muhammad was strong and could have killed them. All right, you know the traditions about the Jews and what they did to the Prophet Muhammad?

Toddler: [Mumbled assent.]

'Amer: Is there a story you know?

Toddler: Yes, the story about the Jewish woman.

'Amer: The Jewish woman? What did she do to our master, the Prophet Muhammad?

Toddler: The Jewish woman?

'Amer: Yes.

Toddler: There was a Jewish woman who invited the Prophet and his friends. When he asked her, "Did you put poison (in my food)?" she said to him, "Yes." he asked her, "Why did you do this?" and she replied, "If you are a liar you will die and Allah will not protect you; if you speak the truth Allah will protect you."

'Amer: And our God protected the Prophet Muhammad, of course.

Toddler: And he said to his friends, "I will kill this lady."
'Amer: Of course, because she put poison in his food, this Jewess.

Toddler: Oh.

'Amer: [Speaking directly into the camera.] Basmallah, Allah be praised, Basmallah, Allah be praised. May our God bless her. No one could wish Allah could give him a more believing girl than she. May Allah bless her and her father and mother. The next generation of children must be true Muslims. We must educate them now while they are still children so that they will be true Muslims.

Two States Of Mind

Cal Thomas
Jewish World Review
June 13, 2002

The score is 6-0, which represents the number of times Israeli Prime Minister Ariel Sharon has visited President Bush vs. the administration shutout of Palestinian Authority leader Yasser Arafat.

Sharon has gotten what he wants from the president. Bush backs Israel's "right to self defense" as it pursues homicide bombers who target civilians. The president also seems indulgent of Sharon's position not to negotiate with Arafat as long as the violence continues. During Sharon's latest visit to Washington, a "senior Israeli official," speaking only on background, flatly stated that Arafat is becoming "irrelevant" and that he "should be ignored." Israel, he said, may have to wait for Arafat's successor before there are any negotiations about a Palestinian state.

That is not the position taken by Secretary of State Colin Powell, who says that President Bush will announce "in the very near future" how he intends to secure a Palestinian state and that the United States intends to move ahead with a Middle East peace conference this summer.

The senior Israeli official said that while Sharon would like to attend a proposed international peace conference this summer, Israel rejects international involvement in making peace with the Palestinians. "Talks should be bilateral only," said the official, who added, "we won't negotiate under fire and we are tired of promises, lies, talks, declarations and empty words."

President Bush knows the game. He understands that the Palestinians could have had their state at any time over the last 54 years if they had renounced violence and their objective of eradicating Israel. Former Israeli communications and policy official Michael Freund noted in last Wednesday's (June 12) Jerusalem Post that Prime Minister Levi Eshkol proposed opening direct negotiations with the Arab states in 1965 in order to turn the 1949 armistice agreements into full-fledged peace treaties.

The Arab response was the 1967 war, the purpose of which was declared by Egyptian President Nasser: "Our basic aim will be to destroy Israel." Only the strategy for meeting that objective has changed.

Charts were passed out by the official to a small group of journalists. They show the progress made by Israeli forces in their incursions into Jenin and other terrorist strongholds. The official said there would have been far more homicide bombings had not Israel rooted out terrorists in these areas.

There were predictions from the official that Iran will have nuclear weapons by 2005. There are also reports that Iraqi dictator Saddam Hussein (and aren't they all dictators in that region?) will be able to put chemical weapons on his Scud missiles much sooner. Hezbollah, the terrorist group based in Syrian-occupied Lebanon, presents another threat on Israel's northern border, though Israeli withdrawal from the region was supposed to advance the "peace process."

That's the point. Whatever concessions Israel makes for "peace" are reciprocated by war because Israel's enemies hate the existence of the Jewish state and the Jewish people. Nothing the United States does or doesn't do, and nothing that Israel does or doesn't do (short of expiring) will change that. Creating a Palestinian state without a renunciation and cessation of violence will produce sovereignty issues that will do more to threaten the existence of Israel than the five wars and terrorist attacks have done. A Palestinian state without a genuine peace treaty will be a haven for terrorists and for weapons that can, and will, be used for a final assault on Israel.

Since last June, 519 Israelis have been killed and 4,071 wounded in terrorist attacks. The senior official said that is proportional to 31,000 dead Americans and 250,000 wounded, a situation the United States would not tolerate.

The official said, contrary to press reports, that Israel has not been pressured into going easy in its military response to terrorism. He added, "We never received a green light for any military operation and we never asked for one."

The administration ought to give itself a green light to topple Saddam Hussein. That would send a clear message to the Arab world that the United States will fight terrorism anywhere American interests are threatened. Only then might it be possible for a "moderate" leader to replace Arafat and for Israel to have a legitimate negotiating partner. But not before.

Why America Must Support Israel

Bruce S. Thornton
www.frontpagemagazine.com
June 14, 2002

Tell people you support Israel and they often assume that you're either Jewish or a fundamentalist Christian monitoring Israel's starring role in the drama of Apocalypse. As important as ethnic or religious solidarity is, though, supporting Israel is more firmly based on principle, morality, and national interest.

Principle. Israel is a Western society, like ours the heir of Athens and Jerusalem. This means it is a liberal democracy organized politically to protect the rights of individuals and ensure their participation as citizens in the running of the state. Protecting the freedom of the individual person as a person--not as the member of a category--is the primary aim of such a government.

Other features of such a society include: an economic system run to some extent on free-market principles; civilian control of the military; free speech; equality between the sexes; a circumscribed role for religion in government; and a generally secular, rationalist outlook that prizes tolerance and openness rather than the blinkered narrowness of the tribe, clan, or sect. In short, like America Israel is a society of laws rather than powerful men--whether thugs, priests, princes, or bureaucrats-- who monopolize force and run society for their own benefit.

This is the ideal, one that no society, Israel or our own, perfectly realizes. Yet considering that Israel has since its birth lived besieged by incessant aggression against its very existence, the issue is not that Israel compromises on some of these principles in order to survive, but rather that it embodies any of them. An Israeli Arab member of parliament can rise up in the Knesset and publicly criticize the Prime Minister, something he could not do in any other Arab state, at least if he wanted to stay out of jail or survive the night.

As the only liberal democracy in the whole Middle East, then, Israel demands our support-- if we believe in the principle, as we say we do, that such a society is the best way for people to live, no matter what their race, national origin, or religion, for it maximizes the freedom and prosperity of the greatest number of individuals.

Morality. Despite the media's rhetoric of moral equivalence (often the last refuge of the morally bankrupt), there is a clear right and a wrong in this conflict. If we cut through the fog of "checkpoints" and "settlements," we can see clearly the source of the conflict: the Arab attempt to destroy Israel. Does anyone really think that if the Arabs had sincerely accepted Israel in 1948 that the subsequent fifty years would have been as bloody and miserable as they have been for both sides? Quite simply, Israel kills Palestinians and restricts their movements because for fifty years Palestinians have murdered Israelis, egged on by Islamic nations whose populations outnumber Israel 100 to one.

Thus whatever Israel's mistakes or injustices, they have been the byproducts of Israel's attempt to defend its very existence against a sustained, fifty-year assault by terror, guerilla action, and three wholesale military attacks. And whatever the Palestinians have suffered has its ultimate origins in the existence of a critical mass of Arabs who do not accept Israel's right to live and hence compel Israel to defend itself, with all the tragic, unforeseen consequences that always accompany even the just use of force.

The old Greeks understood the moral principle very well: "The doer suffers." He who initiates violence and aggression and threatens another's existence will unleash a defensive response and suffer the consequences. I'm not speaking of the media's "cycle of violence," a phrase that obscures moral responsibility, as though Palestinian murder of civilians and the Israeli defensive response are natural phenomena like the seasons. Violence used to defend is morally different from violence used to destroy.

Finally, there is one critical moral distinction that needs to be affirmed: the inadvertent death of civilians resulting from the use of force to defend one's self is utterly and absolutely different from the planned targeting of civilians to destroy another. A man who shoots at your family while hiding behind his own bears all the responsibility if his family is killed when you defend yourself.

Let us state once more the obvious: if Palestinians stop killing Israelis, Palestinians will stop dying. But the reverse is not true: Oslo has shown that the more Israel accommodates Palestinian aspirations, the more Israelis who will die.

National Interest. In the short-term, defending Israel might appear to be contrary to our national interests. After all, there is no oil in Israel, and supporting her annoys those larger, more strategically placed nations who do possess oil. But this way of thinking is dangerously shortsighted.

Our national interests are more easily served and defended the more liberal democracies there are. Societies of free citizens and free markets are more stable and peaceful, and less prone to aggression against their neighbors. Given that there are no genuinely free societies in the Middle East, it is definitely in our national interest to defend and support a trusted and loyal democratic ally, and to work at creating more such democracies in the region. An ally like Saudi Arabia might serve our short-term interests, but its chronic instability and dysfunctional political order is a time bomb that someday will explode in our faces.

More important, though, after 9/11 we now know that it is very much in our interests to defeat terror, and Israel is the key battleground in the war on terror. Quite simply, if homicide-bombers work in Israel, or even appear to be working, then the rest of the world will regularly suffer from such attacks. Those who think terror is a legitimate instrument for achieving their aims must be utterly and thoroughly defeated and convinced that terror will never result in anything other than their own destruction.

All of us, then, should support Israel--all of us, that is, who believe in a world ruled by law and respectful of individual freedom. As rare and fragile a plant as such freedom has been in human history, principle, morality, and interest all tell us that we cannot afford to see it uprooted anywhere.

Why Our Enemies Are Winning

Naomi Ragen
www.naomiragen.com
June 18, 2002

Today, with the death of 19 Israelis, and over 50 hospitalized; with body parts strewn over the pavement of Jerusalem -- the city all people agree is holy -- I realized why Israel's enemies are winning.

We Israelis are simply too conflicted. We wake up in the morning, and we have to deal with our health system, with unemployment, with caring for our elderly and crippled and deaf. We have to find funding for abused children, and deal with our educational system. We have to worry about our economy, and try to encourage tourism. We worry about appearing well on CNN and BBC, and we worry, sincerely, about hurting innocent people, or even saying untrue or unkind things about the Muslims that live within our borders.

But our enemies have no such conflicts. They don't think about how to feed their people, or get them jobs. They couldn't care less about educating their children to live productive lives, or finding shelters for their abused women (since 99% are abused, there is no point).

No, all our enemies do all day, every day, is figure out how to kill. They work on better bombs. On convincing the gullible to carry them. On transferring funds from Iran and Europe to buy the materials, and securing fax numbers to disseminate the latest baby-killing plan to their numerous cells in Gaza and the West Bank.

They don't worry about bad press. Why should they? They can and have done anything, crossed every red line, broken every rule of civilized behavior without consequence: they've used Red Cross ambulances to ferry suicide bombers and grenades, blown up babies in their carriages, have snipers target the foreheads of 10 month olds in their mothers' arms, blown up schoolbusses, pizza parlors, hotels full of elderly survivors about to celebrate Passover....

Why should they worry? They have their PR plan in place: Saeb Erekat will simply repeat that they are not responsible. They don't have the weapons, the manpower, the you-name it, and CNN and Sky and the BBC will broadcast it like it's news, instead of outdated propaganda. They will broadcast it without questioning a word, as if the PLO didn't use the arms Israel gave them for terrorist attacks, as if they were never aware of the Karin A, as if they never saw the documents with Arafat's signature authorizing suicide bomber payments.

So, with no concern for their people's health care, or education or their economy; with no conscience, no morals, no pressure from a so-called civilized world or an inquiring and independent press, they have the luxury of single-mindedness. All day, every day they are Murder, Inc. supported by the world press, financed by the Saudis and Iranians and Iraqis, who also have nothing better to do with their time. And each day we see the results. More dead. More nails per lung and heart and skull.

More success breeds more money. After all, that's the business they are in. A bloodless day, is a day they don't get paid by their devout Muslim employers. And so, up the corporate ladder they go: thinking up better ways to kill, more effective bombs, more outrageous targets. And doing it full-time.

We Israelis don't have the luxury of ignoring our people's needs. But unless we get rid of some of our complexes, and begin fighting back full-time, we simply can't win.

Wanted: Aggressive Israeli Hasbara

George M. Stanislavski
www.nationalisraelnews.com
June 19, 2002

A few months ago, I met Brad Turrel, a senior CNN executive, at a parlor meeting in North Hollywood, California. After exchanging a few pleasantries, I told him that most Israelis felt that CNN was presenting an anti-Israel bias in its middle-east reporting.

He retorted, " Did you ever pay attention to the material that appears in the Israeli media? Our reporters take these views as representing the Israeli position. We then hear what the Palestinians have to say, and reach the conclusion that the truth is somewhere in between. Get your own media to be more pro-Israeli and CNN will report accordingly."

Turrel's point was valid and I had to agree. If the Israeli press refers to the Jewish residents of communities in Judea, Samaria and Gaza as settlers in "occupied territories" doesn't that weaken our own hasbara argument? When Israeli TV and newspapers give prominent headline coverage to a petition by 50 Israeli reservists who refused to serve in these "occupied territories," doesn't that give the message that Israeli soldiers' presence in Judea, Samaria and Gaza is immoral? When a demonstration by 200 left wing protestors gets the same number of media sound bytes as a rally of tens of thousands of rightwing proponents, is the Israeli public getting a balanced view? Would American talk shows, the bastions of free speech, ever host proponents of Al Quaida after September 11? Yet, our talk shows eagerly interview Jewish Arafat supporters who were holed up in the Mukhata during Operation Defensive Shield. Would the American Congress or any other democratically elected parliament censure its members who openly legitimized the atrocities of that country's enemies? You bet they would. However, most Israeli Arab Knesset members openly justify Palestinian acts of terror with impunity, even when the bombings and shootings are inside Israel's heartland. How can we convince others about the righteousness of our cause if we are getting these muddled messages from our own media. Hasbara like charity begins at home.

Bret Stephens, wrote an excellent essay on What's wrong with Israel's Hasbarah in his Eye on the Media column in the Jerusalem Post . He concluded the article by suggesting the sorts of arguments Israel should be making. He proposed 3 main arguments Israel hasbara should be using:

· Refer to the territories as disputed rather than "occupied" and the presence of Israelis on them does not violate one applicable article of international law set down by the Geneva convention.

· Israeli spokespersons must speak of the conflict between democrats and dictators and not as a battle between Jews and Arabs.

· The argument against terrorism must be placed in the context of an argument for the legitimacy of the State of Israel.

Though I agree with the content of his proposal, I believe method of its presentation must be more aggressive. The Israel Government should fight its information campaign with the same gusto and aggressiveness that a politician uses against an opponent in an election. Top notch pollsters, spin doctors and media mavens must be hired to plan, organize and conduct the campaign. Unlike the classic film Wag the Dog there is no need to fabricate information to demonize the enemy. Israel has enough incriminating evidence against Arafat and the PA as is.

The first job of Israeli Hasbara is to explode the myth that the settlements are the issue in the present war. The PLO was founded 3 years before Israel won back its historic homeland in the Six Day War. The goal of the PLO then is the same as the goal of the PA, namely the destruction of the State of Israel, the only democracy in the middle-east.

Next, people and governments have to be shown that their donations are literally financing terror activities and lining the pockets of a petty dictator. For every dollar given to the Palestinian Authority, a third goes to finance terrorist actions against innocent civilians, another third goes into the private bank accounts of Arafat and company and only the remaining third is split between salaries of the PA apparchniks and the Palestinian people. Similar messages must be directed towards the Palestinian people showing that the cause of their suffering is not the Israelis but their own Palestinian Authority. History has shown that reform in totalitarian regimes only comes about when the change is introduced by the people.

Third, instead of debating whether Arafat should be expelled, Israeli hasbara should shatter the facade of him as a "freedom fighter" and budding statesman:

· He is an Egyptian and not Palestinian. How can he lead the Palestinian people?

· He condemns terrorist actions in English, yet glorifies homicide bombers in Arabic.

· He has broken every agreement he has ever signed with anybody.

· Since he came onto the scene in 1964, he has conducted a reign of terror against Israel, western democracies and his own people.

· In the past 8 years since Israel ceded control of the Palestinian population centers to Arafat, the standard of living has of the average Palestinian family has decreased by 80%.

· He is an abuser of free speech and human rights of his own people. Opponents of his regime simply disappear as in Stalinist Russia

· He has destabilized and caused insurrection against the legitimate governments in every country he has lived in. His present threat is to destabilize the entire region as a form of extortion to pressure western countries to weaken Israel.

Fourth, Israel must equate the bombings of the WTC and the Pentagon with the spate of bombings going on in Israel. Israel's fight is not between Jews and Arabs. It is a fight between freedom and western civilization against totalitarian oppression. There is no difference between the PA and Al Quaida. Both use terror as their main weapon. Terror is the main instrument of feudal totalitarian regimes. Democracies don't use terror as a means to further their ends. The main aim of these regimes is to obliterate Israel. If Israel, the only mid-east democracy falls, the next target will be all other western democracies and their way of life.

Last, there is a great need to personalize the stories of victims of terror attacks and their families and not just quote statistics. Many of the terror victims were citizens of other countries. This fact helps localize the stories and creates greater audience empathy for the Israeli cause.

The time has come for the Israel government to realize that we are facing a life or death situation and act accordingly.

A Guarantee Of More Violence

Charles Krauthammer
June 20, 2002
(c)2001, 2002, The Washington Post. Reprinted with permission.

Whenever a massacre occurs in Israel, Palestinian spokesmen rush out to say: "Yes, this is terrible, but this is what happens when you have a people with no hope for an end to the occupation." Apologists in the West invariably echo this exculpation/explanation.

Of all the mendacity that pollutes Middle Eastern discourse, this is the worst. It assumes that the listener is not only stupid but also amnestic. Two years ago at the Camp David summit, in the presence of the president of the United States, the Palestinians were offered an end to the occupation -- a total end, a final end -- by the prime minister of Israel. They said no. They said no because in return, they were asked to make peace.

Remember? The mantra thrown at the Israelis for decades was "land for peace." It turns out Arafat wanted the land, but at Camp David, as always, he refused to make peace. The reason innocents are dying every day is not because of the occupation but because the Palestinians believe they can get (as Hezbollah got in Lebanon) land without peace.

And why should they not believe it? The State Department wants to give them exactly that. The way out of the Middle East morass, Colin Powell has urged the president, is to give the Palestinians a "light at the end of the tunnel" by giving them their own "interim" or "provisional" Palestinian state -- even as the massacres continue, like the blowing to bits of 26 Jerusalemites in two consecutive suicide bombings this week.

This rewarding of terrorism is not just a moral scandal. It is disastrous diplomacy. What does this provisional state say to the Palestinians? You can reject the state you were offered two years ago, start a war, murder daily and then be re-offered a state -- this time without even having to be asked to make peace.

For an American foreign policy whose major objective is stability and nonviolence (if for no other reason than to give us freedom of action elsewhere in the region to fight terrorism), one could not devise a worse policy. If two years of blood-letting gives the Palestinians an interim state -- without even a simple cease-fire, let alone a real peace -- what possible disincentive do they have to continue the violence?

Statehood before peace is guaranteed to increase the violence. After all, what does "provisional statehood" mean? There has never been a "provisional state." Powell will have to make the concept up as he goes along. But if statehood means anything, it means three things:

(1) Territorial inviolability. Today terrorism is reduced (Israel stops 90 percent of planned attacks) because the Israeli army goes into Palestinian territories to seize and stop terrorists. After statehood, this becomes an invasion of another country. The terrorists will

have sanctuary. Every time Israel pursues them, the Security Council will be called into emergency session, and America will be censured unless it condemns this Israeli "invasion." The net effect will be more terrorism and increased resentment of American diplomacy.

(2) Arms. The basic premise of American policy for 25 years has been that the only way to ensure peace is to have a demilitarized Palestinian entity. Sure, in offering "provisional statehood" the United States will insist on limits to Palestine's buildup of weapons. These limits will be broken as surely as were the limits on the Palestinian "police" that were in the Oslo accords. But it will be worse. Once you have statehood, the Palestinians will say that every self-respecting state has the right to arm itself as it wishes. Why not Palestine? The West Bank will bristle not just with the weapons of guerrilla war (machine guns and car bombs), but the weapons of regional war: Katyusha rockets and antiaircraft missiles. What do you think happens when civilian planes trying to land at Ben Gurion Airport come under fire from such an armed Palestinian state?

(3) Alliances. A basic attribute of statehood is the right to contract alliances. Even before statehood, Arafat secretly allied himself with Iran and Hezbollah. With statehood, he will be able to do so openly. And what do we do when he declares alliance with Syria or Iraq and invites their tank armies into the West Bank to protect Palestine from Israeli "aggression"?

Provisional statehood is folly. For the United States to offer it constitutes a moral and strategic collapse. It is a way to give the Palestinians their goals without even the pretense of asking them to put down the gun.

Statehood for the Palestinians is a foregone conclusion. The only question today is whether they get it while they continue to massacre Jews or only after they have abjured massacres. Land for peace. Remember?

The Killing Mantra

Diana West

A new study tells American mothers that the safest way to get the kids to school is to put them on the bus. Not so in Israel. After another Palestinian terrorist incinerated another Israeli bus, a Netanya mother revealed the painful difference to BBC News: "If my kids end up having to get a bus, I will give them a loving speech before they go in case they never come back" -back from the limb-littered killing fields suicide-bombers have made of Israeli cities and towns.

And Palestinian mothers? They, too, give a loving speech before their children go, sometimes videotaping it, but all too many of them actually hope their youngsters never come back. The sickening fact is, the strongest desire of certain Palestinian parents is for their children to die, killing as many Jews as possible, from infants to old people, in the process.

Take Mariam Farhat. When she got word her 19-year-old son, Mohammed, had been shot dead after murdering five Israeli teens and wounding 23 others, she told the Saudi-owned daily Al-Sharq Al-Awsat: "I began to cry, 'Allah is the greatest,' and prayed and thanked Allah for the success of the operation. I began to utter cries of joy and we declared that we were happy. . . . I encouraged all my sons to die a martyr's death." (Translation by Middle East Media Research Institute.)

The maternal death wish may seem freakish, but Mrs. Farhat is not alone. "May every bullet hit its target and may God give you martyrdom," Naima el Abed tells her son, Mahmoud, on a video released by Hamas that records the 23-year-old college student's preparations for a rampage against Israel. "This," she says, "is the best day of my life."

Almost as good, no doubt, as the day of her son's funeral. This came after Mrs. el Abed's little terrorist was shot dead attempting to infiltrate a Jewish community, killing two Israeli soldiers. Consider the Palestinian scene of bereavement that followed: "All around her were women, clapping and celebrating his death, while his father Hassan quietly received congratulations," the Associated Press reported. "Several of their nine other children handed out candy to visitors. 'I wish all my children would be like him and carry out operations like that,' Naima el Abed said."

Chances are excellent that they will -and not just to please mom. The Palestinian Authority may blindly blame Israel for creating a generation of suicidal maniacs, but it is the PA itself that has helped nurture-if such a word applies-such taboo-breaking evil through its relentless propaganda machine.

With subtitled clips from Palestinian-controlled television (available through WorldNetDaily.com), MSNBC's Alan Keyes this week gave American viewers an eye-popping look at the pernicious role the PA plays in teaching young people to kill and be killed. It starts with state-sponsored sing-alongs for the romper-room set-ditties about blood-drenched soil and warriors of jihad. It continues with shows featuring girls in party dresses delivering bloodthirsty harangues: "When I wander into the entrance of Jerusalem, I'll turn into a suicide warrior! I'll turn into a suicide warrior! In battle-dress! In battle-dress! In battle-dress!" And it goes on through the seemingly continuous loop of government-broadcast sermons. From one tele-imam comes, "Bless those who wired themselves, putting the belt around his waist or his sons, and who enter deeply in the Jewish community and say, 'Allah is great.' " Or: "Wherever you are, kill these Jews and these Americans who are like them and support them." Mr. Keyes pointed out a young boy in one congregation.

Can a child thus indoctrinated ever make peace? This same boy is probably now caught up in the latest Palestinian craze - trading charms, Pokemon-style, that feature the faces of suicide bombers. Maybe he'll go on to Al-Najah University in Nablus, alma mater of this week's bus bomber, Mohammed "How beautiful it is to kill and be killed" al-Ghoul. Al-Najah, it must be noted, was the scene of last fall's commemoration of the Sbarro pizza-parlor attack, complete with fake pizza slices, plastic body parts and play explosions.

That PA sure teaches its children well - only not to create anything except what Ghazi Al-Qusaibi, the Saudi Ambassador to London (infamous for his verses to suicide-bombing), calls "the culture of martyrdom." As he recently told Al Sharq Al Awsat, according to MEMRI, in one of the most chilling statements I have ever read, "When the culture of martyrdom spreads among the Palestinians and the Arabs, the myth of Israel will come to an end." (Not, alas, at the ambassador's own poetry-writing hands. He regrets to say that age and weight disqualify him from personal "martyrdom.")

We hear of the need to reform the PA, from its terror-abetting "security" forces to its corrupt apparatchiks, but the subject of dismantling its poisonous propaganda machine isn't mentioned. As de-Nazification was once required, "de-martyrfication" is one of today's most urgent challenges.

Israel Has A Moral Right To Its Life

Yaron Brook and Peter Schwartz
Israeli Insider, June 23, 2002

Why reason and justice are on Israel's side

As yet another appalling suicide bombing takes place in Israel, killing 19 people and wounding dozens more on a bus packed with schoolchildren in Jerusalem - as Hamas claims credit for the massacre - America's policymakers still insist on seeking an "even-handed," diplomatic solution.

In the past 18 months, Israel's six million citizens have suffered 12,480 terrorist attacks. They have buried more than 400 victims - a per-capita death toll six times that of America on September 11. Yet, in an abhorrent act of injustice, Israel continues to be pressured by the United States into making concessions to Yasser Arafat, the archpatron of those terror attacks. In the long run, this means that Israel is being pressured into sacrificing its basic right to exist.

We should be supporting Israel's right to take whatever military action is needed to defend itself against its nihilistic enemies. Morally and militarily, Israel is America's frontline in the war on terrorism. If America is swayed by Arafat's latest empty rhetoric, and allows him to continue threatening Israel, our own campaign against terrorism becomes sheer hypocrisy and will, ultimately, fail.

Consider the facts and judge for yourself:

The Israelis and the Palestinians are not morally equal Israel is the only free country in a region dominated by Arab monarchies, theocracies and dictatorships. It is only the citizens of Israel - Arabs and Jews alike - who enjoy the right to express their views, to criticize their government, to form political parties, to publish private newspapers, to hold free elections. When Arab authorities deny the most basic freedoms to their own people, it is obscene for them to start claiming that Israel is violating the Palestinians' rights. All Arab citizens who are genuinely concerned with human rights should, as their very first action, seek to oust their own despotic rulers and adopt the type of free society that characterizes Israel.

Since its founding, Israel has been the victim

Since its founding in 1948, Israel has had to fight five wars - all in self-defense - against 22 hostile Arab dictatorships, and has been repeatedly attacked by Palestinian terrorists. Arafat is responsible for the kidnapping and murder of Israeli schoolchildren, the hijacking of airliners and the car bombings and death-squad killings of thousands of Israeli, American, Lebanese and Palestinian civilians. Today he ardently sponsors such terror groups as Hamas, Islamic Jihad and the al Aksa Brigade.

The land Israel is "occupying" was captured in a war initiated by its Arab neighbors. Like any victim of aggression, Israel has a moral right to control as much land as is necessary to safeguard itself against attack. The Palestinians want to annihilate Israel, while Israel wants simply to be left alone. If there is a moral failing on Israel's part, it consists of its reluctance to take stronger military measures. If it is right for America to bomb al-Qaida strongholds in Afghanistan - and it is - then it is equally justifiable for Israel to bomb the terrorist strongholds in the occupied territories.

Hatred of Israel, and of the United States, is hatred for Western values

Like America's war against the Taliban and al-Qaida, the Arab-Israeli dispute is a conflict between opposing philosophies. On the one side are the forces of mysticism, medieval tribalism, dictatorship - and terror; on the other side are the forces of reason, individualism, capitalism - and civilization. Arafat and his sympathizers hate Israel for the same reason that Osama bin Laden and his sympathizers hate America, i.e., for embracing secular, Western values. No "peace process" is possible with such enemies.

This is not an ethnic battle between Jews and Arabs, but a moral battle between those who value the individual's right to be free and those who don't. Those Arabs who value individual freedom are enemies of the Arafat regime and deserve to be embraced by Israel; those Jews who do not value individual freedom deserve to be condemned by Israel.

Israelis have a right to the land

Only Israel has a moral right to establish a government in that area - on the grounds, not of some ethnic or religious heritage, but of a secular, rational principle. Only a state based on political and economic freedom has moral legitimacy. Contrary to what the Palestinians are seeking, there can be no "right" to establish a dictatorship.

As to the rightful owners of particular pieces of property, Israel's founders - like the homesteaders in the American West - earned ownership to the land by developing it. They arrived in a desolate, sparsely populated region and drained the swamps, irrigated the desert, grew crops and built cities. They worked unclaimed land or purchased it from the owners. They introduced industry, libraries, hospitals, art galleries, universities-and the concept of individual rights. Those Arabs who abandoned their land in order to join the military crusade against Israel forfeited all right to their property. And if there are any peaceful Arabs who were forcibly evicted from their property, they may press their claims in the courts of Israel, which, unlike the Arab autocracies, has an independent, objective judiciary - a judiciary that recognizes the principle of property rights.

Palestinians are not "freedom fighters"

The Palestinians want a state, not to secure their freedom, but to perpetuate the dictatorial reign of Arafat's Palestinian Authority. Arafat's "police" brutally expropriate property and silence opposing viewpoints by shutting down radio and TV stations. They systematically arrest, torture and murder peaceful dissenters. To call the militant Palestinians "freedom fighters" - when they support the subjugation of their own people, when they deliberately murder children in the streets or gleefully praise such depravity - is a mind-numbing perversion.

Palestinians have consistently sought to destroy Israel

In 1947 the Palestinians rejected the U.N.'s offer of a state larger than the one they are demanding now. Instead, they joined in a war aimed at wiping Israel from the map. Today, that hostility has only hardened. For example, in a televised public sermon, a Palestinian Imam declared: "God willing, this unjust state [of] Israel, will be erased." Palestinian textbooks are filled with vile, anti-Jewish propaganda, such as this exhortation from a fifth-grade Arabic language text: "Remember: the final and inevitable result will be the victory of the Muslims over the Jews."

A Palestinian state under Arafat would become a base for terrorism

A Palestinian state headed by Arafat would be a launching pad and a training ground for terrorist organizations targeting, not only Israel, but the United States. Forcing Israelis to accept a Palestinian state under Arafat is like forcing Americans to accept a state the size of Mexico, 12 miles from New York City, ruled by Osama bin Laden. As long as the Palestinians sanction aggression, they should not be permitted their own state.

Arafat's meaningless words will not restore life to his terror-victims - past or future

No rhetoric by Arafat can change the fact that he is a hater of freedom and a destroyer of innocent human life. Imagine Osama bin Laden being enticed by American diplomats to announce: "We strongly condemn operations that target American civilians, especially the last one in New York. We equally condemn the massacres that have been, and are still being, committed by U.S. occupation troops against Taliban civilians in Kandahar, Shah-i-Kot and Tora Bora." Would any sane individual thereby endorse an immediate withdrawal of U.S. forces from Afghanistan and the creation of a Taliban state, headed by bin Laden, alongside America? If not, why should Israel be expected to act so suicidally?

America, for its own benefit, must allow Israel to uphold the principle of self-defense

The growing demand for Israel to negotiate with Arafat comes from an unprincipled, range-of-the-moment mentality. Surrendering to extortion - which the "land-for-peace" catechism endorses - is profoundly immoral and impractical. In the 1938 version of "land for peace," Nazi Germany was appeased by being allowed to take over Czechoslovakia as part of the Aryan people's "homeland"; the result was to encourage Hitler to start a world war.

The Arab-Israeli conflict could become a dress rehearsal for a wider, global conflict. If America now stops Israel from retaliating against Arafat, the father of international terrorism, how can it ever justify retaliation against its own enemies? If we force Israel to appease Arafat, we will be broadcasting, loud and clear, that terrorism can bring America too to its knees.

We should urge our government to recognize that there is only one means of achieving long-term Mideast peace: Israel's sweeping retaliation against the scourge of terrorism.

Replacing Arafat Is First Step To Statehood

President George W. Bush
Remarks delivered at the Rose Garden
June 24, 2002

For too long, the citizens of the Middle East have lived in the midst of death and fear. The hatred of a few holds the hopes of many hostage. The forces of extremism and terror are attempting to kill progress and peace by killing the innocent. And this casts a dark shadow over an entire region.

For the sake of all humanity, things must change in the Middle East. It is untenable for Israeli citizens to live in terror. It is untenable for Palestinians to live in squalor and occupation. And the current situation offers no prospect that life will improve. Israeli citizens will continue to be victimized by terrorists, and so Israel will continue to defend herself, and the situation of the Palestinian people will grow more and more miserable.

My vision is two states, living side by side, in peace and security. There is simply no way to achieve that peace until all parties fight terror.

Yet at this critical moment, if all parties will break with the past and set out on a new path, we can overcome the darkness with the light of hope.

Peace requires a new and different Palestinian leadership, so that a Palestinian state can be born. I call on the Palestinian people to elect new leaders, leaders not compromised by terror.

I call upon them to build a practicing democracy based on tolerance and liberty.

If the Palestinian people actively pursue these goals, America and the world will actively support their efforts. If the Palestinian people meet these goals, they will be able to reach agreement with Israel and Egypt and Jordan on security and other arrangements for independence.

And when the Palestinian people have new leaders, new institutions and new security arrangements with their neighbors, the United States of America will support the creation of a Palestinian state, whose borders and certain aspects of its sovereignty will be provisional until resolved as part of a final settlement in the Middle East.

In the work ahead, we all have responsibilities. The Palestinian people are gifted and capable and I'm confident they can achieve a new birth for their nation.

A Palestinian state will never be created by terror. It will be built through reform. And reform must be more than cosmetic change or a veiled attempt to preserve the status quo. True reform will require entirely new political and economic institutions based on democracy, market economics and action against terrorism.

Today the elected Palestinian legislature has no authority and power is concentrated in the hands of an unaccountable few. A Palestinian state can only serve its citizens with a new constitution which separates the powers of government.

218

The Palestinian parliament should have the full authority of a legislative body. Local officials and government ministers need authority of their own and the independence to govern effectively.

The United States, along with the European Union and Arab states, will work with Palestinian leaders to create a new constitutional framework and a working democracy for the Palestinian people. And the United States, along with others in the international community, will help the Palestinians organize and monitor fair, multiparty local elections by the end of the year with national elections to follow.

Today, the Palestinian people live in economic stagnation, made worse by official corruption. A Palestinian state will require a vibrant economy, where honest enterprise is encouraged by honest government.

The United States, the international donor community and the World Bank stand ready to work with Palestinians on a major project of economic reform and development. The United States, the EU, the World Bank and the International Monetary Fund are willing to oversee reforms in Palestinian finances, encouraging transparency and independent auditing. And the United States, along with our partners in the developed world, will increase our humanitarian assistance to relieve Palestinian suffering.

Today, the Palestinian people lack effective courts of law and have no means to defend and vindicate their rights. A Palestinian state will require a system of reliable justice to punish those who prey on the innocent. The United States and members of the international community stand ready to work with Palestinian leaders to establish, finance and monitor a truly independent judiciary.

Today, Palestinian authorities are encouraging, not opposing terrorism.

This is unacceptable. And the United States will not support the establishment of a Palestinian state until its leaders engage in a sustained fight against the terrorists and dismantle their infrastructure.

This will require an externally supervised effort to rebuild and reform the Palestinian security services. The security system must have clear lines of authority and accountability and a unified chain of command.

America is pursuing this reform along with key regional states. The world is prepared to help, yet ultimately these steps toward statehood depend on the Palestinian people and their leaders. If they energetically take the path of reform, the rewards can come quickly. If Palestinians embrace democracy, confront corruption and firmly reject terror, they can count on American support for the creation of a provisional state of Palestine.

With a dedicated effort, this state could rise rapidly, as it comes to terms with Israel, Egypt and Jordan on practical issues such as security. The final borders, the capital and other aspects of this state's sovereignty will be negotiated between the parties as part of a final settlement.

Arab states have offered their help in this process, and their help is needed.

I've said in the past that nations are either with us or against us in the war on terror. To be counted on the side of peace, nations must act. Every leader actually committed to peace will end incitement to violence in official media and publicly denounce homicide bombings. Every nation actually committed to peace will stop the flow of money, equipment and recruits to terrorist groups seeking the destruction of Israel, including Hamas, Islamic Jihad and Hezbollah.

Every nation actually committed to peace must block the shipment of Iranian supplies to these groups and oppose regimes that promote terror, like Iraq.

And Syria must choose the right side in the war on terror by closing terrorist camps and expelling terrorist organizations.

Leaders who want to be included in the peace process must show by their deeds and undivided support for peace.

And as we move toward a peaceful solution, Arab states will be expected to build closer ties of diplomacy and commerce with Israel, leading to full normalization of relations between Israel and the entire Arab world.

Israel also has a large stake in the success of a democratic Palestine. Permanent occupation threatens Israel's identity and democracy. A stable, peaceful Palestinian state is necessary to achieve the security that Israel longs for.

So I challenge Israel to take concrete steps to support the emergence of a viable, credible Palestinian state.

As we make progress toward security, Israel forces need to withdraw fully to positions they held prior to Sept. 28, 2000. And consistent with the recommendations of the Mitchell committee, Israeli settlement activity in the occupied territories must stop.

The Palestinian economy must be allowed to develop. As violence subsides, freedom of movement should be restored, permitting innocent Palestinians to resume work and normal life. Palestinian legislators and officials, humanitarian and international workers, must be allowed to go about the business of building a better future. And Israel should release frozen Palestinian revenues into honest, accountable hands.

I've asked Secretary Powell to work intensively with Middle Eastern and international leaders to realize the vision of a Palestinian state, focusing them on a comprehensive plan to support Palestinian reform and institution building.

Ultimately, Israelis and Palestinians must address the core issues that divide them if there is to be a real peace, resolving all claims and ending the conflict between them.

This means that the Israeli occupation that began in 1967 will be ended through a settlement negotiated between the parties, based on U.N. Resolutions 242 and 338, with Israeli withdrawal to secure and recognized borders.

We must also resolve questions concerning Jerusalem, the plight and future of Palestinian refugees, and a final peace between Israel and Lebanon and Israel and a

Syria that supports peace and fights terror.

All who are familiar with the history of the Middle East realize that there may be setbacks in this process. Trained and determined killers, as we have seen, want to stop it. Yet the Egyptian and Jordanian peace treaties with Israel remind us that, with determined and responsible leadership, progress can come quickly.

As new Palestinian institutions and new leaders emerge, demonstrating real performance on security and reform, I expect Israel to respond and work toward a final status agreement.

With intensive effort by all of us, agreement could be reached within three years from now. And I and my country will actively lead toward that goal.

I can understand the deep anger and anguish of the Israeli people. You've lived too long with fear and funerals, having to avoid markets and public transportation, and forced to put armed guards in kindergarten classrooms. The Palestinian Authority has rejected your offered hand and trafficked with terrorists. You have a right to a normal life. You have a right to security. And I deeply believe that you need a reformed, responsible Palestinian partner to achieve that security.

I can understand the deep anger and despair of the Palestinian people. For decades you've been treated as pawns in the Middle East conflict. Your interests have been held hostage to a comprehensive peace agreement that never seems to come, as your lives get worse year by year.

You deserve democracy and the rule of law. You deserve an open society and a thriving economy. You deserve a life of hope for your children.

An end to occupation and a peaceful democratic Palestinian state may seem distant, but America and our partners throughout the world stand ready to help, help you make them possible as soon as possible.

If liberty can blossom in the rocky soil of the West Bank in Gaza, it will inspire millions of men and women around the globe, who are equally weary of poverty and oppression, equally entitled to the benefits of democratic government.

I have a hope for the people of Muslim countries. Your commitments to morality and learning and tolerance lead to great historical achievements, and those values are alive in the Islamic world today. You have a rich culture, and you share the aspirations of men and women in every culture. Prosperity and freedom and dignity are not just American hopes or Western hopes, they are universal human hopes. And even in the violence and turmoil of the Middle East, America believes those hopes have the power to transform lives and nations.

This moment is both an opportunity and a test for all parties in the Middle East: an opportunity to lay the foundations for future peace, a test to show who's serious about peace and who is not.

The choice here is stark and simple, the Bible says, "I have set before you life and death, therefore choose life." The time has arrived for everyone in this conflict to choose peace and hope --- and life.

Why Does The Left Support The Palestinians?

Dennis Prager
"By permission of Dennis Prager and Creator's Syndicate, Inc."
June 25, 2002

Why does the left support the Palestinians against Israel?

The question is rarely asked. It is simply taken for granted that the left - Europe, the Western news media, the universities, the liberal churches, the arts world - supports the Palestinians and the larger Arab-Muslim worlds in their war against Israel.

But the question does need to be asked. For it is completely inconsistent with the left's professed values to side with Israel's enemies. Just about every value the left claims to uphold, Israel upholds and its enemies do not.

The left speaks about its passion for democracy ("power to the people"). Yet it is Israel that is a fully functioning democracy, as opposed to all of its Arab and Muslim enemies. Yasser Arafat is precisely the self-aggrandizing, corrupt dictator-type that the left claims to hold in contempt.

The left claims to have particular concern for women's rights. Yet it is Israel that has as highly developed a feminist movement as that of any Western country. It is Israel that conscripted women into its armed forces before almost any Western country. At the same time, the state of women's rights among Israel's Muslim enemies is perhaps the lowest in the world.

The left's greatest current preoccupation is with gay rights. Yet it is Israel that has annual gay-pride days, while Egypt and other Arab and Muslim countries arrest homosexuals.

It is Israel that has an independent and highly liberal judiciary. It is Israel that has a leftist press. It is Israel that has been governed more by leftist, even socialist, parties than by rightist ones. Israel's enemies have none of this.

So, why isn't the left out there leading pro-Israel demonstrations?

The answer is as important as it is contemptible.

In general, the left does not care about women, independent judiciaries, minorities, democracy, gays or almost anything else for which it marches. That is why the left opposed America's war in Afghanistan, which liberated women from being treated like animals.

Nearly all the causes the left speaks for are noble-sounding covers for its real agenda - the overthrowing of Western, especially Judeo-Christian and capitalist, values. Remember the chant at Stanford, "Hey, hey, ho, ho, Western civ has got to go"? That is what animates the left.

In psychoanalytic terms, it is antagonism to one's father and his values. In a commencement speech he gave this year, the former president of Dartmouth College, James O. Freedman, a man of the left, said that the purpose of a college education is "to question your father's values." Those of us not on the left believe that the purpose of a college education is to discover what is true and what is good.

America embodies all that the left dislikes. It is the most religious of the industrialized democracies (proudly and uniquely Judeo-Christian). It is also the most capitalist. And, what drives the left especially crazy is that with all this religion and capitalism, America is the most powerful force on earth - economically, militarily and culturally.

Israel is Little America. It, too, is religious (though a secular state like the United States, it is proudly Jewish). It, too, celebrates capitalism. There are no demonstrations in Israel against McDonald's. On the contrary, even before McDonald's opened there, Hebrew replicas like "McDavid's" were established.

And Israel, like America, celebrates its national identity, not the "world" identity that the left affirms. The left loathes nationalism unless it is anti-Western, like Palestinian or Cuban. America does not jump to attention when world treaties are signed and Israel is the U.N.'s pariah, rendering America and Israel the left's "axis of evil," far more reviled than Iran, Iraq and North Korea.

The question, "Why does the left support the Palestinians?" is an extremely important one. At this time in history nothing so illustrates the left's nihilism as does its support of the Palestinians against Israel.

Know The Enemy (And What He Believes)

David Horowitz
www.frontpagemagazine.com
June 25, 2002

The war we have joined is defined by three simple but brutal facts. Our enemy is able to penetrate our borders and strike us in our homes; he can strike us with weapons of mass destruction; and he has made clear his intention is not to change our policies or to force our withdrawal, but to obliterate us and destroy our civilization. Because of these facts, the imperative of defending ourselves as quickly and effectively as possible is more important in this war - by a factor so great as to be impossible to calculate -- than any we have ever fought.

In all wars the first essential is to know your enemy. Everything you can do to thwart his objectives or to protect your life and the lives of your countrymen depends on this knowledge. But if the war is a war of terror, in which stealth warriors target civilians, the importance of this knowledge is even greater still -again by a factor so large as to be impossible to calculate.

Who, then, is the enemy that has struck us and who threatens our destruction? Officially he has been defined in terms that invoke "terror" and "evil," that are generic and that really describe the means by which he has chosen to fight the war, and not why he is fighting or how we have become his enemy. They do not tell us who he is. This failure to name our enemy is already a source of great weakness in erecting our defenses. This ignorance is the most pressing danger to us, after the threat itself. Already, in attempting to establish security perimeters at our borders, and in our airports and harbors, we have denied ourselves the ability to target the specific groups who have targeted us. The policy that will not identify the enemy by name is a policy that asks us to fight in the dark. Yet every terrorist who slips through these nets is capable of killing tens of thousands of innocent Americans.

Yet, we already know who our enemy is, no matter how many choose to deny it. Almost a year has passed since the attacks on Wall Street and the Pentagon -- the twin symbols of American wealth and power. We have seen the face of the enemy, even if we are still reluctant to name him.

We are at war with radical Islam (not all of Islam but with Islamic radicals). And we are - or should be - at war with their allies, the international radical left. Both see us as the embodiment of evil - racism, oppression, on the one hand, and the frustrations of Islamic societies on the other. Both, therefore, seek our destruction.

The publication of a new al-Qaeda manifesto, translated by the Middle East Research Institute (MEMRI) makes its agendas abundantly clear. The statement called, "Why We Fight America," and was issued by al-Qaeda spokesman, Suleiman Abu Gheith and appeared on an al-Qaeda website hosted by Center for Islamic Research and Studies.

The al-Qaeda statement begins by asking why the world is surprised by what happened on 9/11 - pretty much the question that Noam Chomsky, Tariq Ali, Edward Said, Barbara Kingsolver, Arundhati Roy and sundry professors at anti-American rallies on college campuses across the country asked within weeks of the horrific attack. And the answer is pretty much the same for both as well:

"What happened to America [on 9/11] is something natural, an expected event for a country that uses terror, arrogant policy, and suppression against the nations and the peoples, and imposes a single method, thought, and way of life, as if the people of the entire world are clerks in its government offices and employed by its commercial companies and institutions."

Anyone who was surprised by 9/11, the al-Qaeda statement continues, does not understand the root causes of the attack and in particular "the effects of oppression and tyranny on [the victims'] emotions and feelings." Instead, such people must think, "that oppression begets surrender, that repression begets silence, that tyranny leaves only humiliation."

In fact, according to al-Qaeda, humiliation, deprivation and oppression inspire righteous rage against the oppressor. And this righteous indignation is what al-Qaeda's war is about. Of course, unlike the Western left, al-Qaeda does not wage its war in the name of an international proletariat and its goal is not a secular socialist utopia. Al-Qaeda's war is about the future world reign of Islam. The al-Qaeda statement asks: How can a Muslim accept humiliation and inferiority "when he knows that his nation was created to stand at the center of leadership, at the center of hegemony and rule, at the center of ability and sacrifice? … When he knows that the [divine] rule is that the entire earth must be subject to the religion of Allah - not to the East, not to the West - to no ideology and to no path except the path of Allah?…"

Credulous apostles of appeasement in the West like Ted Turner and Cherie Blair (wife of British Prime Minister Tony Blair) are so superior in their own minds to the Muslims who hate them that they don't consider the possibility that the Islamic faithful could actually mean what they say. Justifying Arafat's suicide brigades, Blair said, "As long as young people feel they have got no hope but to blow themselves up you are never going to make progress." This is an inanity heard nightly on cable talk shows from the left. It is the propaganda line of Machiavellian spokesmen for the terrorist cause like PLO spokesman Abudl Rachman and westernized apologists like Hussein Ibish who equate the terrorists' terror with the victims' response. But it ignores what the combatants say about themselves and their inspiration, and patronizes them in the process.

The Middle East Research Institute has also translated an interview given to the Arab press by a mother of a suicide bomber, who has nothing to say about root causes like poverty, or thwarted national desires or "social injustice." (Indeed when the al-Qaeda spokesman speaks of his "nation" he clearly means the entire world of Islam, and not any particular state whether Afghanistan or Palestine or Saudia Arabia or Iraq.) What she says is this:

I am a compassionate mother to my children,… Because I love my son, I encouraged him to die a martyr's death for the sake of Allah… Jihad is a religious obligation incumbent upon us, and we must carry it out. I sacrificed Muhammad as part of my obligation. This is an easy thing. There is no disagreement [among scholars] on such matters. The happiness in this world is an incomplete happiness; eternal happiness is life in the world to come, through martyrdom. Allah be praised, my son has attained this happiness… I prayed from the depths of my heart that Allah would cause the success of his operation. I asked Allah to give me 10 [Israelis] for Muhammad, and Allah granted my request and Muhammad made his dream come true, killing 10 Israeli settlers and soldiers. Our God honored him even more, in that there were many Israelis wounded. When the operation was over, the media broadcast the news. Then Muhammad's brother came to me and informed me of his martyrdom. I began to cry, 'Allah is the greatest,' and prayed and thanked Allah for the success of the operation. I began to utter cries of joy and we declared that we were happy. The young people began to fire into the air out of joy over the success of the operation, as this is what we had hoped for him.

The will to genocide is not specific to the martyrs who blow up little children, but is shared by the community of radical Islam. It comes not from despair, but from a hope of heaven - from extending the territory of Islam and doing Allah's will. Nothing could be more obvious to anyone paying attention. That is, to anyone paying attention without the screen of liberal arrogance, which denies what it has seen in order to explain it. And thereby understand it. And thereby surrender to it.

The hope for heaven - or for the global reign of Islam as the path to heaven -- is generically the same fanatical inspiration that caused believers in socialism (a heaven on earth) to kill tens of millions of innocent unbelievers during the 20th Century. It is the same faith that causes progressive fellow travelers like Ted Turner, Barbara Kingsolver and Edward Said to support the agendas of America's enemies. And of perverse America-haters, like Gore Vidal and Noam Chomsky to support any anti-American war.

The present war against us may be about humiliation and a sense of inferiority stemming from Islam's centuries of eclipse, but it is not about despair. The new statement from al-Qaeda is not addressed to people who have nothing. Quite the opposite It is an incitement to people who have something -- and who might be reluctant to give up what they have -- to sacrifice life itself for the glory of Islam: "As long as the Muslim knows and believes … he will not - even for a single moment -- stop trying to achieve [the universal triumph of Islam], even if it costs him his soul…his time, his property and his son, …"

This is not a war about land in the Middle East or the structure of a Palestinian state, or a U.S. military presence in the Arabian peninsula. It is a war about redemption. In this it exactly parallels the Communist threat from the past. In the eyes of the Communists, America stood in the way of heaven - a socialist paradise in which racism, sexism, and economic inequality would vanish from the earth. In the eyes of radical Islam, America -- the Great Satan -- stands in the way of Islam's rule, and thus of human redemption and it is for this reason America must be destroyed.

Thus, the al-Qaeda proclamation: "America is the head of heresy in our modern world, and it leads an infidel democratic regime that is based upon separation of religion and state and on ruling the people by the people via legislating laws that contradict the way of Allah and permit what Allah has prohibited. This compels the other countries to act in accordance with the same laws in the same ways … and punishes any country [that rebels against these laws] by besieging it, and then by boycotting it. By so doing [America] seeks to impose on the world a religion that is not Allah's…"

Americans wake up! Your enemies hate you for who you are. They hate you because you are democratic, and tolerant and unbelieving. They hate you because you are Christians: "America's standing with the Christians of the world against the Muslims

226

has stripped the camouflague from its face." And they hate you because you are Hindus and Buddhists and secularists and Jews.

This war is not a war we are facing. It is a war we are in. Americans have hardly begun to understand this, but the enemy is already keeping score: "We have not reached parity [with America's alleged attacks on Muslims. [Therefore], we have the right to kill 4 million Americans - 2 million of them children - and to exile twice as many and wound and cripple hundreds of thousands. Furthermore, it is our right to fight them with chemical and biological weapons, so as to afflict them with the fatal maladies that have afflicted Muslims because of the [Americans'] chemical and biological weapons."

Americans have also only begun to understand that if radical Islam is one face of our enemy, the other is the radical left. For two hundred years the radical left has believed in a religion promising a heaven on earth whose end justifies any means. That is why progressives like Lenin and Stalin and Pol Pot killed so many innocent people. That is why radical leftists in America and other European countries have joined in denouncing America's war of self-defense and in abetting the Arab crusade to obliterate Israel and (in the process) exterminate the Jews of the Middle East.

How serious are some American leftists about abetting the war to destroy their own country? Attorney Lynne Stewart is a veteran of the radical left going back to the 1960s and is the lawyer for the "blind sheik" who led the first terrorist attack on the World Trade Center in 1993. Six people were killed in the attack and 1,000 injured. Stewart is associated with the Center for Constitutional Rights and has been a supporter of Communist causes and Arab terrorists for her entire professional life. Recently, the Attorney General indicted Stewart for helping the "blind sheik," who is now in prison, to communicate with his terrorist followers in the Middle East and further their bloody agendas.

A chorus from the left has attacked Attorney General Ashcroft for infringing on the civil liberties of the imprisoned terrorist and his "lawyer." Stewart has been defended as a persecuted civil libertarian by the left-wing National Lawyers Guild, the ACLU, The Nation and other institutions of the "progressive" left.

In 1995, Lynne Stewart was interviewed by the New York Times, which reported her radical beliefs. ""Ms. Stewart suggested that violence and revolution were sometimes necessary to right the economic and racial wrongs of America's capitalist system." Among other things, Lynne Stewart said this: "I don't believe in anarchistic violence, but in directed violence. That would be violence directed at the institutions which perpetuate capitalism, racism, and sexism, and the people who are the appointed guardians of those institutions, and accompanied by popular support."

The World Trade Center is an institution which perpetuates capitalism and -- in the eyes of the left -- racism and sexism as well. According to every leftist - from the Nation magazine to the Chomsky fifth column (the distance is not great) --, America is a land of capitalism, racism and sexism, and the enforcer of capitalism, racism and sexism globally. This is the world that the Islamicists call Dar Al-Harb: The world of darkness. The world that is not socialist (for the leftist believers) and that is not Islam (for the faithful). According to Lynne Stewart and the al-Qaeda spokesman, the people who dwell in Dar Al-Harb and support its profane agendas deserve to die. This is what the present "war on terror" is about. Americans better understand it sooner than later.

How Despair Is Transforming Israel

Yossi Klein Halevi
National Review Online
June 26, 2002

JERUSALEM, ISRAEL

"The world hates us and always will," a neighbor said to me on the stairs before wishing me a good day. "What more do you need than the Holocaust?" He is Sephardi, without familial memory of Europe; but the bitter, new mood of besieged Israel has penetrated everywhere. In a full-page newspaper ad urging Israelis to boycott European nations that now refuse to sell Israel military equipment, employees of the country's military industry wrote, "In the moments of truth, we learn yet again that we can only rely on ourselves." Even the left isn't immune from the growing sense of siege. In a recent interview, the liberal novelist Amos Oz confessed he's haunted by his father's observation that, before the Holocaust, European graffiti read, "JEWS TO PALESTINE," only to be transformed in our time into, "JEWS OUT OF PALESTINE." The message to Jews, noted Oz: "Don't be here and don't be there. That is, don't be."

While international concern is focusing on the physical wall, along the length of the West Bank, that Israel is now building to ward off suicide bombers, Israelis have been increasingly concerned about the invisible wall of isolation that is rising between the Jewish state and much of the world. Israelis haven't felt so alone since the mid-'70s, when the United Nations declared that Zionism equaled racism and when more nations maintained diplomatic relations with the Palestine Liberation Organization (PLO) than with the Jewish state. The eagerness with which most of the world adopted the Palestinian account of the Camp David talks and dismissed Israel's previously unimaginable concessions as irrelevant; the U.N.'s obsessive search for a nonexistent massacre in Jenin even as it ignores the massacres of Israelis; Europe's growing sympathy for suicide killers and its simplistic reduction of the conflict to occupation; anti-Zionism's emergence, since the Durban anti-racism conference, as a defining feature of the anti-globalization movement; the application of traditional Christian anti-Jewish imagery to the Palestinian conflict (like the new mural in a Scottish church depicting a crucified Jesus surrounded by Israeli soldiers)--all have convinced many Israelis that collective Jewish existence is again on probation. Last year, after the collapse of the Camp David talks and the renewal of anti-Jewish frenzy in the Arab world, Israelis began to suspect that the Middle East might never accept a Jewish state, no matter what its borders. After all, denial of the most basic elements of the Jewish story--from the biblical connection to the land of Israel to the existence of the gas chambers--has become routine in much of the Arab world. But in the last few months Israeli despair has broadened. Israelis now fear not only that they will never be accepted in the Middle East, but also that they will never be accepted in the world at large.

Along with returning the Jews to their land, a key Zionist goal was returning the Jews to the community of nations. Addressing the U.N. General Assembly in 1949, Israeli Foreign Minister Moshe Sharett declared that Israel's admission into the world body was "the consummation of a people's transition ... from exclusion to membership in the family of nations."

But today Israelis fear the transition is happening in reverse. "The suspicion slips into the heart that maybe the ultra-Orthodox were right when they warned that a sov-

228

ereign state for Jews would annoy the nations and bring annihilation on the remnant of the Jewish people," wrote Peggy Cidor, a former left-wing activist, in Kol Hazman, a secular Jerusalem newspaper. "The state of Israel, which was intended to give the Jews an entry ticket into the family of nations, didn't deliver the goods. We're still being judged by separate standards; there is still no proportion between our actions and the responses around the world.... It was nice to feel like everyone else for a while, but that seems to be over.... The state of Israel has turned into the `Jew' of the nations."

That last phrase--among the bitterest ever written by a Zionist--was first used by the late Israeli scholar of intellectual history J.L. Talmon in an essay in The New Republic, written in 1976 in response to the "Zionism=Racism" resolution. Now, though, the bitterness may run even deeper, precisely because many Israelis believed international stigmatization of the Jewish state had ended. In the 1990s Israel seemed to finally be realizing the old Zionist dream of normalization; Jews would be neither chosen, nor outcast, but simply a nation among nations. After the collapse of the Soviet Union, the United Nations in 1991 rescinded the Zionism=Racism resolution, and key nations-- including India, China, and the entire former Soviet bloc--resumed relations with the Jewish state. Israelis reciprocated, tempering their defiant independence with a sense of global interdependence. With far greater enthusiasm than in the past, they joined international relief efforts, raising funds for Somali famine victims and Turkish earthquake survivors. The Israeli press even debated whether the Israeli army should participate in international peacekeeping missions. A new prosperity allowed Israelis to become travelers. Tens of thousands of young Israelis participated in the post-army ritual of backpacking in India, and Indian spirituality came to influence Israeli popular culture. In their new identification with far-off places, Israelis displayed a new embrace of the world.

At times Israelis revealed an overeager provincialness, as in 1993 when the local media turned the opening of the country's first McDonald's into a major cultural event. Still, as the world opened up for Israelis, their sense of permanent ostracism began to recede. Many quietly stopped using the ugly word "goy" to describe gentiles or stopped referring to the nations outside Israel as "the world," as if Jews inhabited a separate planet. After the 1982 Sabra and Shatilla massacre, says Aharon Klieman, professor of diplomacy at Tel Aviv University, former Prime Minster Menachem Begin dismissed criticism of Israel by noting, "Goyim kill goyim, and they blame the Jews." "Can you imagine Rabin or even Sharon using the word `goyim'?" asks Klieman. "Israelis learned to make distinctions among nations." Yitzhak Rabin caught the new ethos in his inaugural speech as prime minister in 1992: "No longer is it true that `the whole world is against us,'" he declared. "We must overcome the sense of isolation that has held us in its thrall for almost half a century. We must join the international movement for peace, reconciliation, and cooperation that is spreading over the entire globe these days--lest we be the last to remain, all alone in the station." Israelis were adopting a new national vision; the millennia-old dynamic of Jewish separatism and gentile ostracism seemed about to end.

But now the world is closing up again. I know Israelis who hesitate to write their home address on their luggage when they travel to Europe. When some Norwegian supermarket chains recently announced plans to mark Israeli products so customers could consider boycotting them, a spokesman for the normally understated Israeli Foreign Ministry caustically suggested that the chains use yellow stars. Increasingly, Israelis and the rest of humanity are speaking mutually unintelligible languages of moral outrage. Liberal-minded foreigners can't understand how Israelis elected Ariel Sharon, and many have taken his election as license to view every Israeli act of self-defense as aggression. Israelis can't understand how the world has forgotten the circumstances that produced Sharon's election: Yasir Arafat's terrorist war, launched in September 2000, against the most left-wing government in Israel's history.

He last time Israelis felt this besieged, in the mid-'70s during Zionism=Racism and the widespread severing of diplomatic ties that followed the Yom Kippur War and the Arab oil boycott, the political and social consequences were formidable. In 1977 a right-wing coalition of outsiders, led by Begin, unseated the Labor Party, which since Israel's founding had never lost a national election. The settlement movement, which until the 1973 Yom Kippur War had moved only a few thousand Jews into the West Bank, became an irresistible popular force, luring tens of thousands of Israelis with the promise of cheap, abundant housing and territorial annexation. A back-to-religion movement, attracting some of the country's leading artists and bohemian symbols, emboldened the ultra-Orthodox, who established yeshivas aimed at secular Israelis and grew increasingly aggressive in promoting religious legislation and won massive government subsidies for their insular communities.

True, those trends were directly influenced by factors that had nothing to do with Israel's diplomatic isolation. The Yom Kippur War, Labor Party corruption, Sephardi resentment of Ashkenazi hegemony--all boosted the settlement and back-to-religion movements and especially the Likud Party. Still, it's no coincidence that those three movements shared a contempt for the judgment of the outside world. The seeming failure of Zionism's experiment in normalizing Jewish relations with the world was the incubator in which isolationist movements grew. In the atmosphere of late '70s ghetto Israel, it somehow made sense that the prime minister was a Holocaust refugee whose passion was taunting Europe's leaders as anti-Semites and that Uri Zohar, the country's leading satirical filmmaker and symbol of the Tel Aviv beach culture, would suddenly appear on television wearing a yarmulke.

The settlement and back-to-religion movements have been called a "counter-revolution" against the Zionist vision of integration with the nations. The impact on Israeli Judaism has been particularly devastating. The settlement movement created self-ghettoized West Bank communities where religious stringency became the norm, driving many "modern Orthodox" Jews closer to ultra-Orthodoxy. Even worse, back-to-religion yeshivas transformed a tolerant Sephardi Judaism into a mimicry of Eastern European ultra-Orthodoxy. The most extreme example of this cultural climate was the transformation of the late Rabbi Meir Kahane from political militant into theological racist. Kahane had moved to Israel in 1971 and created a tiny far-right movement that advocated encouraging Israel's Arabs to voluntarily resettle abroad. But after the Yom Kippur War and Israel's growing international isolation, Kahane embraced religious fundamentalism and a policy of forced mass expulsion. Only by adopting anti-Arab policies that would transform Israel into a pariah state, he preached, would Jews prove their contempt for the nations and their trust in God. For Kahane, expelling Israel's Arabs wasn't so much a political as a religious strategy--a crazed bid to push the Jews into a splendid isolation in which they depended on God alone for their salvation. Kahane was a reminder that the great Jewish fear--an incurable otherness--is also a great temptation. And after a hiatus, that temptation is back.

He more that Israelis are treated as pariahs, the greater their tendency toward recklessness. The Likud's recent, self-defeating vote against a Palestinian state wasn't just a political stance but an expression of contempt for the world's judgment of Israel. And one friend, a veteran critic of the occupation, said to me with a terrible casualness, "If the world can't find space for a sliver of a Jewish state, then the world doesn't have the right to exist. And if it blows up because of a nuclear war in the Middle East, maybe that's poetic justice."

One tangible warning is the growing support for transfer of Palestinians from the territories. For now that support is a reflexive reaction to terrorism, not a program. But if Israel's isolation grows, so will the temptation toward extreme, repellent solutions. Earlier this year the National Religious Party (NRP) elected as its new leader a just-retired career combat officer named Effie Eitam. The NRP has long been a mainstay of the settlement movement, but until now it was careful to avoid extremist proclamations that would banish it to the political periphery. In the past, NRP leaders tempered their hard-line politics with compassion, as when the late NRP leader Zevulun Hammer called for a commission of inquiry into the 1982 Sabra and Shatilla massacre. Even Yitzhak Levy, Eitam's immediate predecessor and a rigid ideologue, was careful to repudiate transfer. Eitam, though, is the first NRP leader to flirt with mass expulsion. And Eitam's theological message--that the Jews are a divine people operating beyond normal rules and that the gentile nations matter only as passive recipients for Israel's spiritual greatness--offers a seductive justification for radical policies like transfer that would place the Jewish state outside international norms.

Benign or at least neutral international climate is a key precondition for Israeli willingness to take risks for peace. Though it's widely assumed that the Oslo process restored Israel's diplomatic standing, the sequence of events was actually the opposite. Only after the former Soviet bloc, China, India, and much of the Third World renewed diplomatic relations with Israel in the early '90s, following the Gulf war and the collapse of the Soviet Union, did Israel feel safe enough to begin negotiating with the PLO. The Madrid Peace Conference, precursor to the Oslo process, occurred at the beginning of a new era of reconciliation between Israel and the international community. Now, though, that era has ended. Almost every day the Israeli papers report another attempt to transform Israel into a pariah state--like the recent statement by Swedish Foreign Minister Anna Lind accusing Israel of war crimes. Israel's attorney general, Elyakim Rubenstein, has warned that the new international criminal court about to open in the Hague could begin targeting Israelis for supposed war crimes, including the mere act of moving to a settlement or even a Jewish neighborhood in East Jerusalem. In the current atmosphere, it's ludicrous to assume the Israeli public will feel safe enough to consider returning to the concessions offered by Ehud Barak, let alone the concessions envisioned by the Saudi plan. Barak himself has declared his Camp David offer irrelevant.

In the ongoing if temporarily muted culture war between ultra-Orthodox isolationists and Israelis who embrace the outside world, the burden of proof has shifted to the normalizers. "You might as well oppose the law of gravity," an ultra-Orthodox friend said to me, referring to those of us who believe gentile hatred of Jews is not immutable. While it's too early to see an increase in ultra-Orthodox ranks, the growing hatred of Israel around the world emboldens our theologians of despair.

Crucial to the ultra-Orthodox worldview is that secular Zionism was a false messianism, promoting the absurd idea that the nations would welcome a Jewish state into their club. And so the fact that Israel is the target of more hostile U.N. resolutions than all other countries combined isn't only a political crisis, but also a theological one. Why, indeed, has the state of the Jews, the very instrument intended to end ostracism, become the Jew of the states? The answer is happily provided by dozens of ultra-

Orthodox pirate radio stations operating throughout the country and drawing tens of thousands of listeners. Soft-spoken rabbis offer the beguiling message of Jewish chosenness, an exalted otherness. The word "goy" is constantly evoked, as is this despairing rabbinic quote: "Esau hates Jacob"--that is, it's a law of nature that Esau the gentile hates Jacob the Jew. Rabbi Amnon Yitzhak, a secularist turned ultra-Orthodox preacher who draws packed crowds with his insider's mockery of secular culture, maintains a website that has tracked the world's latest anti-Jewish outbursts--ongoing proof of Zionism's failure to normalize Jewish fate.

"The Israeli debate about our place among the nations is essentially reduced to two alternative worldviews," explains Klieman. "The first is the isolationist position of am l'vad yishkon, a nation that dwells alone. The second is a nation like all others. That's the position of the younger generation, but it's fluid. If Israelis feel they're being given their day in court, they lean toward integrationism. But when they get slapped down, they recoil behind a protective shield. And that's where we are now."

The growing pessimism threatens Zionism's great psychological achievement: protecting the Jews from a fatal, post-Holocaust bitterness. Israel's founding preempted a massive Jewish rejection of the world, allowing survivors to turn rage into reconstruction. Israel even forced the Jews to make their peace with Europe. When David Ben-Gurion negotiated the German reparations agreement in the early '50s, resisting the violent opposition led by Begin, he compelled Israelis to choose pragmatism over history. But that choice should not be taken for granted. Perhaps the Holocaust's deepest long-term wound on the Jewish psyche isn't the actions of the murderers but the passivity of the onlookers. Jews must continually resist the suspicion that even the enlightened world cares little for their survival. The consequences--political, social, and theological--of feeding that suspicion could be shattering.

Most Israelis, of course, still realize that "the world" doesn't hate the Jews. Even now, says Klieman, many Israelis insist on distinctions within the Arab world, let alone the world generally: "We still speak of Egypt and Syria rather than `the Arabs.'" The expansiveness of the '90s remains imprinted on the Israeli psyche and won't be easily forfeited. That's why Israelis seize on every sign of support from abroad. A recent pro-Israel demonstration in Rome, for example, received more coverage in the Israeli press than far larger demonstrations by American Jews, precisely because most of the participants in the Italian protest were reported to have been non-Jews.

Most of all, it's American support that keeps Israelis from total despair. The United States is the great exception that doesn't prove the rule. It challenges the subversive Jewish voice that whispers, "Don't trust the goyim; at the moment of truth, they'll betray you." Israelis know that in moments of truth, the United States has stood with them and presumably will do so again. President George W. Bush's tacit endorsement, in his Rose Garden speech this week, of Sharon's strategy--denying Arafat's terrorist war any political gain--has reinforced Israeli faith in the United States.

Israel's psychological struggle is between the optimism of the '90s and the despair of the '70s. International detractors who turn every Israeli act of war into a war crime and subject the Jewish state to a level of moral judgment not applied to any other nation are inciting the very hard-line forces they deplore. Effie Eitam and Amnon Yitzhak have no better recruiters than Kofi Annan and Javier Solana. Those Israelis who cling to Zionism's promise and insist on remaining part of the world are fighting for their lives.

232

Suicide Bombing

New Republic Editorial Staff
New Republic Online
June 20, 2002

Of course Palestinians went and slaughtered Israelis: The president of the United States was about to propose the creation of a "provisional" Palestinian state. This presented the Palestinians with an emergency. The Palestinian dream was drawing closer to its realization; the possibility of a truce between Palestinians and Israelis was in the air again; territorial compromise with the Jews, and an elementary respect for their lives and their rights, was all that stood between occupation and statehood. Clearly this had to be stopped. The choice between rage and happiness seems to be an easy choice for the Palestinians, and so they regularly choose rage. A bus with schoolchildren, a street corner with baby carriages: Here was the answer to the threat that the resumption of a peace process posed to the Palestinians. But blow the bus and the street corner up and the threat could be averted, and the holy war could continue, and Allah-- or at least Sheikh Ahmad Yassin's Allah--would be gratified.

Actually, the Palestinian depravity of this week was even worse, and more cynical. For no sooner had Hamas exploded the bus in Jerusalem than the Al Aqsa Martyrs Brigade exploded the street corner in Jerusalem: The secularists did not want to suffer in popularity for their failure to murder. In contemporary Palestine, suicide bombing is politically savvy. Yes, yes, the Palestinian community is divided, and there are many decent people who deplore the suicide bombings and aspire to get on with the business of self-government. But Israel cannot be expected to welcome stoically the internecine Palestinian debate while innocent men, women, and children--Jewish and Muslim--are regularly destroyed. The clarification of Palestinian identity is costing too many lives.

So what should Israel do? Strategically speaking, the Israelis may be reaching a breaking point. The Israeli incursions into "Area A" in the wake of the recent atrocities are as justified as the incursions in the wake of the massacre in Netanya a few months ago; but the media is reporting that they are more than that, that the current Israeli action represents a decision to "reoccupy" certain areas for security reasons. If so, it is worth remembering that the West Bank was originally occupied by Israel in the course of defending itself as well. It is not in Israel's interest to stay in "Area A". The last thing that Israel or that most Israelis are seeking is a greater burden of occupation in a hostile territory. They want a fence, not a fiefdom. Anyway, sooner or later the United States and the United Nations and the European Union (Cherie Blair explained about the suicide bombers that they are "young people [who] feel they have got no hope" and Jack Straw expressed his "compassion" for them) will soon force them out. What is taking place on the West Bank now is a police action that is proportionate to the crimes that are being policed; no less, but no more.

What Israel should not do is sacrifice its clarity about security and diplomacy to an obsession with Yasir Arafat. If last week's bombings prove anything, it is that the chairman of the Palestinian Authority has lost control of the Palestinian polity. He is as plainly irrelevant as Ariel Sharon used to say he is. This is bad news, because it means that the problem is not the leader but the community, and this is good news, because it means that the vain and cowardly old man will not stand in the way of diplomacy much longer.

But what should this diplomacy be? The American government, under the leadership of Colin Powell, is readying itself to offer the Palestinians provisional statehood. This is not diplomacy; this is pseudodiplomacy. A provisional Palestinian state is a phony Palestinian state, a chimera, a sop to the violent Palestinian streets, a capitulation to the Riyadh-Cairo analysis of the present crisis. A Palestinian state that is not created in a negotiation with Israel is not a Palestinian state that will live in peace with Israel. The legitimacy of the objective of Palestinian statehood is almost universally acknowledged in Israel; even Sharon speaks of its inevitability. But this great Israeli accommodation to reality should not be mocked by American attempts to appease the Palestinians for their bloody and dogmatic avoidance of negotiations for almost two years now. After all, Israel also has a problem that might be called "homeland security." For their provisional crackdowns on terrorism, will George W. Bush reward the Palestinians with a provisional state? If so, then he is a monumental hypocrite, and no friend of a genuine peace.

Dispensing With Arafat

George F. Will
June 26, 2002
(c)2001, 2002, The Washington Post, Reprinted with permission

President Bush's Monday statement was the most clearsighted U.S. intervention in the Israeli-Palestinian crisis in the 35 years since the 1967 war, and perhaps in the 54 years since the founding of Israel. It enunciated a policy that makes eventual peace at least conceivable, and meanwhile frees the president to pursue the global anti-terrorism agenda articulated in five other speeches in the past year.

Eighty-one days had passed since the president's last intervention, which was the last gasp of the bankrupt policy of attempting to be an "honest broker" between terror and its victims. That April 4 statement was an uncertain trumpet, as in its absurdly mild chastisement of Yasser Arafat for not "consistently" opposing terrorism. Since then, better administration thinking has been signaled by frequent references to the "corruption" of Arafat's Palestinian Authority, a thugocracy that has been the real occupation force since it came from Tunisia to Gaza and the West Bank eight years ago.

The president said Monday that the primary prerequisite for peace is change not in Israel's policy but in Palestinian leadership, and sweeping "reform and institution-building." Almost everyone relevant -- including the president, most Israelis and Prime Minister Ariel Sharon -- believes a Palestinian state is desirable. But it is desirable only if its values are not those of founding fathers who dispatch suicide bombers to school buses, are not the toxic brew of Arafatism -- terror and corruption.

The policy of "land for peace" produced peace -- Israel yielded the Sinai, 91 percent of the land captured in 1967 -- with a peaceful man, Anwar Sadat. But that policy is a sterile irrelevance as a response to Arafatism, which does not disguise its objective of acquiring all the land of Israel.

A slice of Czechoslovakia in September 1938 inflamed the recipient's appetite for the rest of it six months later. Today, only the delusional can believe that gratitude for the powers granted to a "provisional" Palestinian state will predominate over resentment about powers withheld. Furthermore, the withheld powers that would make a Palestinian state provisional will not be withheld for long. Who will enforce any restrictions on the "provisional" state's armaments or diplomacy? The "world community"? The United Nations with its animus against Israel?

So in making even a "provisional" Palestinian state conditional on the selection of new Palestinian leadership "not compromised by terror," and on the establishment of democracy and a market economy, the president has tried to make extreme non-compliance less probable. He also has kicked the can of this crisis down the road. Hence he can devote his attention to the anti-terrorism agenda he has stressed in five major speeches.

In his Jan. 29 State of the Union address, the president said: "We'll be deliberate, yet time is not on our side. I will not wait on events while dangers gather."

On Dec. 11, at the Citadel, he said: "For states that support terror, it's not enough that the consequences be costly -- they must be devastating."

On April 17 at Virginia Military Institute he said that the Taliban was only "the first regime to fall in the war against terror."

On May 23, in Berlin, he said: "Regimes that sponsor terror are developing these weapons [of mass destruction] and the missiles to deliver them. If these regimes and their terrorist allies were to perfect these capabilities, no inner voice of reason, no hint of conscience would prevent their use."

On June 1 at West Point he said that at today's "perilous crossroads of radicalism and technology," Cold War doctrines of containment and deterrence are inadequate: "We must take the battle to the enemy . . . the only path to safety is the path of action."

But for many months the Middle East crisis -- more precisely, the war against Israel's homeland security -- has threatened to paralyze U.S. action on this larger imperative. Paralysis is the aim of terrorists for whom chaos is a strategy.

Writing in Parameters, the journal of the Army War College, P. H. Liotta of the Naval War College warns against enemies who target not America's military but, among other things, America's "national security decision-making process." Such enemies seek to "induce decision paralysis." Liotta cites an adage from India: "One way to kill a tiger is to distract it from so many different sides that it tries to run in every direction at once."

On Monday the president effectively circumscribed the Israeli-Palestinian distraction. The path he has charted to peace through Palestinian regeneration is a long one. Meanwhile, for the president there is, elsewhere, "the path of action."

An End To Pretending

Michael Kelly
June 26, 2002

In the wake of the extraordinary speech George Bush gave in the Rose Garden on Monday afternoon, here are several modest predictions:

o Yasser Arafat will be gone as the leader of the Palestinian Authority within a year -- probably within six months. And he will be gone in the best possible manner: not made a heroic "martyr" by an Israeli bomb or bullet, nor sent into yet another forced exile to wreak more destruction as a heroic leader-in-exile. No, this time the tired, old, failed, disgraced little tyrant without a country will leave as the loser he is; he will be forced into retirement by his own long-suffering people.

o The Palestinians will elect leaders who at least credibly promise a representative government of laws, who at least credibly promise to reject terror and murder and war as the means toward statehood, who at least credibly are committed to achieving a workable two-state, side-by-side peace with Israel. The peace process will begin anew, with some (fragile) hope.

o Israel and the United States will respond by supporting the development of something that has never existed in history, a functioning Palestinian state. While taking heroic measures to protect itself, Israel will support this development with major concessions. The Palestinian people will also support this process. So will the important Arab states. A nascent peace will take hold.

o In a matter of only a few years, Palestine will be one of two new Arab democratic states. The other neonatal Arab democracy will be Iraq. These unthinkable developments will revolutionize the power dynamic in the Middle East, powerfully adding to the effects of the liberation of Afghanistan to force Arab and Islamic regimes to increasingly allow democratic reforms. A majority of Arabs will come to see America as the essential ally in progress toward liberty in their own lands.

Within the boundaries of gambling and guessing, I believe all this might really come to pass. The reason I do is that George Bush believes it might.

There is some limited truth in seeing what Bush is trying to do in the Middle East in traditional terms -- hard-liners vs. State Department softies, etc. -- but this is missing the elephant on the settee. For better or worse -- a great deal better, I think -- Bush has set the Palestinian issue within the context of a larger approach that is fundamentally, historically radical: a rejection of decades of policy, indeed a rejection of the entire philosophy of Middle East diplomacy.

This philosophy has rested on a willingness to accept a U.S. role as a player in a running fraud. In the interests of "stability" and cheap oil and concessions to American military needs, the United States chose to recognize all regimes (except those such as Iran, Libya and Iraq who openly attacked us or the regional status quo) as more or less legitimate. Successive American administrations looked the other way as regimes established gangster states, police states, fascist theocracies; as they erected democracies that were dictatorships; as they looted and tortured and killed vast numbers of their own; as they provided crucial territorial, financial and logistical support to terrorists who murdered Americans. We pretended that these regimes were honorable and that we could do honorable business with them.

The Oslo peace process, which ended in a self-made disaster, was the perfect fruit of this tree. The administrations of Bill Clinton and Yitzhak Rabin knew of course that Arafat was wholly duplicitous, wholly incompetent and a delusional murderous schemer. They knew his people knew this. They knew he was lying when he pretended to want a workable peace. They knew his people knew this too. Yet they treated him as an honest man upon whom could be built a decent peace and a decent state.

To the Palestinians, this said that the Americans were stupid and weak. It also said that they were corrupt. As they had in Saudi Arabia and elsewhere, the freedom-trumpeting Americans were happy to support tyrannies whenever it suited Washington's interests. And so they were doubly worthy of contempt.

In his Monday speech, as in his policy as a whole, Bush is announcing an end to all this. He is saying, repeatedly and clearly, that the United States will -- seriously, on principle -- support all genuine efforts at peace and toward democracy and human rights in a Palestinian state and in all the countries of the Middle East. And the United States will -- seriously, on principle -- support a real Palestinian state, with whatever reasonable concessions from Israel that requires.

But the United States -- for the next three years at least -- is out of the old fraud game. From now on, we do business with people who do honest business with us. That is radical, and it will produce radical results.

On "Hope"

Charlotte West
www.israelnationalnews.com
June 28, 2002

Israeli Defense Minister and Labor Party Chairman Ben Eliezer recently interviewed two failed suicide bombers, concluding that they needed "hope" for their own state, reported Ha'aretz. It wasn't an original observation. In fact, "hope" is the new buzzword. Giving Palestinians "hope" is the new cure-all, the new snake oil. Israelis are charged with dashing that "hope" by settling the very lands Palestinians want and driving them to murder and mayhem. Never mind that Palestinians have repeatedly turned down that land, most recently at Camp David. Many in the world are assuring Israel that offering that land to them AGAIN will provide the necessary "hope" to halt the terror. This time.

What Ben Eliezer overlooked in his past assessment is that these bombers are not suffering from anything that having their own state would cure. One is a foolish impetuous young woman who decided on the spur of the moment to become a bomber and four days later found herself wearing a bomb belt and being hustled to a crowd of Jews, and the other was a fragile personality molded for years by his religious institution. Impetuousness and weakness are personal issues with which individuals must learn to cope without murdering others, whether or not one has one's own state. And as for the society, if impetuousness and weakness in individuals is used by a society to create mass murderers, one must question the legitimacy of that society. I'm sure Hell's Angels, a unique 'people', would love autonomy too (apologies to Hell's Angels for the comparison since their code of ethics do NOT condone mass murders of random individuals based on race, creed, or religion, and I only mention them as an example of a group that would have an awfully tough time convincing anyone to give them a state).

The question that must be asked of those ethnocentrically proposing that "hope" of statehood will exorcise the mass murder demon from Palestinians, is, why did eight years of Oslo not exorcise it, but indeed make it worse? After eight years of Palestinian autonomy and billions of dollars granted their economy, Israel was rudely awakened from its Oslo-fornia dreaming to find Palestinian youth radicalized to such a degree that immediately after being offered everything at Camp David they began excitedly mass murdering those whom they hoped were Jews (they didn't always guess correctly) as if ALL of Israel were their personal shooting gallery. Twelve here, fourteen there, another three, another ten, until the ever spiraling total this hour stands at 558 murdered and 4150 wounded. These were civilians of a democracy, murdered as they shopped, ate, and drove to work. And there are tens of thousands of secondary victims whose lives have been altered by the loss, or caring for the injured. And, the tertiary victim is the society itself - who knows what the murdered might yet have achieved in their lives? Not to mention a shattered economy, fearful citizens … the list is endless.

Obviously Oslo's eight year granting of "hope" topped off by its fulfillment merely ignited their "hope" of gaining ALL of Israel. Ever hear of Maslow's hierarchy of needs? As soon as one is fulfilled one yearns for the next thing up. What ultimately is it that they want? Autonomy? They had more than any Basque or Catalonian. Self rule? They had more than any Kurd or Copt. Religious freedom? They had more than any

Christian Saudi Arabian. Intellectual freedom? They had more than any Columbian . Freedom of speech? They hadmore than any Iranian. Freedom to leave the country? They had more than any Cuban. Freedom to enter the country? They had more than any Jew to Saudi Arabia . Guns? They had more than any Jew in a European ghetto. Billions of dollars in aid? They had more than any IRA terrorists. Friends in high places? Good press? US, England, the Pope, all welcomed Arafat. Right of return? They have right of return to Jordan. Countries where theirs is the dominant culture? They enjoy 5,414,000 square miles in 22 countries from which to choose, all Islamic, all Arab. Which is a whopping twenty two times more in numbers of countries alone than any Jew has.

These recipients had it all, essentially the most the world has to offer in terms of opportunity. And what can one expect but opportunity? Even the American consti-tution does not promise the right to happiness, but only the right to pursue happiness. Palestinians have had all those rights all along. They could have had the world by the tail by now. Instead this is the happiness they pursued: they stockpiled weapons. They smuggled arms. They trained their children to hate Jews enough to want to kill ANY of them, ANY OF THEM AT ALL at random, sight unseen, in any way that they could. They trained them to be able to walk right up to a grandmother and a toddler eating an ice cream cone and kill them. They trained them to walk right into a home and shoot a mother, her teenage son protecting her, her terrified crying 5 year old, and another child, dead. They trained them to point a gun at a baby cradled in its father arms, and shoot it in the head. That's no easy task for a human to accomplish. Most of humanity simply would not be capable of killing unarmed children at random like that. The Palestinians must have worked very hard to train their young to hate enough in order to do it. And more. They perverted sexual and ego acclamation desires, brain-washing their young to yearn for suicide, just so they would mass murder Jews in the process. So for eight years they had complete freedom to pursue their hopes, and only one hope emerged: the hope of killing Jews and destroying Israel. With single-minded determination, they have spent all their resources on it, trained their young for it, and their mothers are now maniacally, smilingly, sending their children off to commit sui-cide for it. Yet oddly, whenever statehood was offered they turned it down: 1937, 1947, 1993, 2000.

These people are suffering from nothing having their own state would cure. What they ARE suffering from is a virulent case of Hatred Against Jews. Force-fed the notion that the "Zionist entity" has stolen "their" country, given their own state they will inevitably continue the misguided task of "liberating ALL their lands". Giving Palestinians "hope" has never reversed that; it has exacerbated it.

American Cleric Kenneth W. Rawson says that, in fact, this very "hope" is the root cause of the bloodshed: "The Palestinian rewrite of history kills. The West Bank and Gaza are NOT occupied territories. Palestinians do not live under foreign occupa-tion. This Arab oil financed revisionism must be refuted. Land revisionism is the cause of terrorism. So-called freedom fighters are raised on these lies of hate." Jews are the indigenous people of the Holy Land with a 3,600 year history there, he notes, citing Arab historian Khaldun's findings. "It is established fact that Arabs only began immi-grating to the region after the Jews had created the opportunity for a better life there. Bartley Crum, a U.S. observer noted in 1946 that tens of thousands of Arabs were enter-ing Palestine "because of this better life - and they were still coming." Some writers claim that over 75% of today's Arab population are either immigrants or descendants of immigrants into the Holy Land after 1882." Rawson states that the West Bank and Gaza belong to Israel, and that it was wholly Israel's choice to cede large areas for Arab autonomy became bases of relentless terrorism.

"Peace falsely premised on historic Palestinian rights to the West Bank and Gaza will inevitably lead to a future war. Why? If so-called Palestinians have a historic right to the West Bank and Gaza, they also have that right to Israel proper. Beware of this long-pursued, two-stage strategy. All Palestinian maps of the Middle East have the name 'Palestine' instead of 'Israel' covering the area that is now Israel."

He further states that "worldwide anti-Semitism is being inflamed by the false concept that Palestinians are being denied basic historic land rights. Until this revisionism is demolished, Middle East peace is doomed to failure and world Jewry is doomed to increased anti-Semitism."

If there is ever to be peace in the Middle East and for Jews the world over it must be made clear to all that Israel has every historical, legal, and moral right to settle its lands as it sees fit. These are not 'occupied territories' just because Arabs and their supporters wish they were. Or because they have terrorists.

As long as the Arabs long to overwhelm Israel by demographics, terrorism, or war, giving them "hope" will predictably NOT bring peace to the Middle East, only more of the same cesspool of lawless violence, subterfuge, and deception we have been witnessing, and helping them cover up, since the first time they refused statehood in 1937.

Analysis: Palestinian Schoolbooks Fan The Flames Of Hatred

Amos Harel
Ha'Aretz
June 29, 2002

In the first years after the Oslo Accords, discussions about Palestinian incitement against Israel were deemed as borderline annoying, and the press did not take much interest in the subject. Bearing in mind Shimon Peres' propecy of "a new Middle East," picking through Palestinian schoolbooks and listening to declarations made by senior Palestinian officials seemed an exhausting act, if not completely irrelevant.

However, the wave of violence seen in the last two years apparently proves otherwise. The suicide bomber does not reach Netanya and Hadera just because of the occupation and desperation. Social ambiance, some of it directed by the Palestinain Authority itself and some of it by Islamic organizations, also dictates his actions.

With this in mind, it might be worthwhile to re-examine the contents of Palestinian schoolbooks. According to an investigative report conducted recently by the IDF's West Bank and Gaza Strip Liaison Office, it appears that the main theme in the textbooks is a militant and nationalistic one, far from recognizing the state of Israel - that same partner for "peace of the brave," as stated in the Oslo Accords by Palestinian Authority Chairman Yasser Arafat

The PA curriculum in the West Bank is based on Jordanian schoolbooks, while in the Gaza Strip schoolbooks from Egypt are used. The Jordanian ones, which include many anti-Semitic and inciting expressions, were actually written by Palestinians for sole use in the West Bank education system. Since the start of the 2000 school year, the Palestinian Education Ministry has handed out its own books for the first and second grades, in addition to fifth and sixth grades.

The investigation, led by Noah Meridor, from the liaison office, examined 23 such books. It revealed "systematic education to delegitimize the existence of the State of Israel, fanning the flames of hatred and violent revenge to destroy the country." The books express a lack of recognition of Israel, not even according to the 1967 borders, alongside adamant claims to Palestinian rule of all the land between the Jordan River and the Mediterranean Sea.

The Palestinians, the books claim, have first rights to the country. The "Arab Canaanites" were here before the Jews, therefore the Zionistic claim of rights to the land by virtue of forefathers are a lie. Zionism is described as a movement of which the seizing of land is foremost among its tenets. The act of populating Israel, including inside the Green Line, is considered "settlement."

The adoption of the term "settlement" in this context, the liaison investigators state, means a total de-legitimization of Jewish cities in Israel, expounded by the fact that the Palestinian public opinion enthusiastically supports harming all settlers.

Israel is described as an evil country, which exploits and degrades, where soldiers shoot merciful nurses, and Jews build gallows. The exploition and degradation of the Arabs are also achieved by changing the names of Arab villages and cities, and by defacing and stealing Arab manuscripts.

The name "Israel" is missing from many maps of the region, which is termed entirely "Palestine" by the books. Cities such as Haifa, Afula and Jaffa are described as belonging to Palestine, while statistics regarding the size of Palestine use those relevant to Israel.

The solution to the Palestinians' situation is revealed through the exultation of two goals: the Right of Return for refugees, and Jihad (holy war). The Right of Return is the solution for Palestinian refugees, and this is endorsed through songs, drawings, stories and history lessons. The vision of returning to Israeli lands is promoted as a legitimate national goal.

A drawing dedicated to the Palestinian independence day in a second grade book depicts a school, called "the Return," with a banner reading, "Our vacation is on the day of our return." In the second grade book, "Our beautiful language," a "trip across the homeland" is described: "The families of Kareem and Lilly leave for a trip in the city of Jaffa," the caption states, with an overhead picture of Jaffa.

Jihad is also considered a legitimate and esteemed course of action. Valorous fighting and dying in battle - as a "shaheed" (suicide bomber) - are considered worthy values. The words to the "Song of the Shaheed" are in a seventh grade book: "It is better to die without my stolen right and homeland, the flow of blood is music to my ears." The textbook goes on to explain: An honorable death is one in Allah's name, defending the homeland.

Even though the segments brought forth here from the investigation are all too true, sometimes the Israeli investigators have their own twist to the point of view.

Several additional drawings are depicted as incitement against Israel, including those showing IDF soldiers preventing families from visiting Palestinian prisoners, and bulldozers uprooting olive trees. Even if these pictures also make no effort to portray who is good and who is bad (the soldier with the mean face standing opposite the innocent child), they are familiar occurrences in the life of nearly every Palestinian child, as any voyage along West Bank and Gaza roads will show.

Apparently, the painter is aware of his surroundings: the soldiers in the picture are reservists. One of them even has sunglasses and a beard.

The Israeli-Palestinian Confrontation: Toward A Divorce

Ehud Ya'ari
Jerusalem Center For Public Affairs And
The Institute Of Contemporary Affairs
June 30, 2002

Arafat exercised a willing suspension of control at the start of the intifada, allowing irregular forces to attack while formal security forces remained on the sidelines.

One of the major concepts of Oslo was that in the end there would be a strong, centralized Palestinian authority/ government. This concept is gone.

We are heading toward a system in the territories of at least two but probably up to four or more undeclared principalities, each controlled, as is the situation now, by a different local coalition.

The Saudi peace plan and the ideas presented by President Mubarak indicate that independent decision-making by the Palestinians is now at least questioned by these states.

Arafat was not interested in a Palestinian state within the 1967 borders at peace with Israel. It was never Arafat's intention to end his political career as the president of a mini-Palestinian state, which he sees as a sovereign cage.

Arafat has a strategy dedicated to the Palestinian cause, not the Palestinian people, and Palestinians know it.

Arafat never saw Hamas as an adversary. For Arafat, Hamas is a partner.

No Palestinian believes that there will be meaningful reform as long as Arafat is in charge.

This war is about only one issue. It is not about settlements. It was never about occupation. It is about whether the Palestinian state is going to be born in peace - and for peace.

Arafat Issued the Orders

The chaotic situation today was consciously, deliberately, and intentionally introduced by Chairman Arafat, though it has extended beyond the time frame he originally conceived. I describe his actions as a willing suspension of control, first exercised on the night of September 28, 2000, when he issued the orders and instructions to his political leadership and the different commanders of the security agencies to embark upon this endeavor. The order for the formal security forces was to stick to the sidelines and allow the irregulars -- what later came to be known as the national and Islamic forces, an alliance of Tanzim, Hamas, Jihad, and the Fronts -- to do the job.

This policy is still being pursued to a great extent by whatever remains now of the Palestinian Authority. However, this chaotic situation at the outset was intended to create the false impression that this quasi-intifada was some sort of replay of the first intifada -- an eruption of popular resentment -- and not a direct challenge to Israel by the PA led by Chairman Arafat.

The United Palestinian Emirates

I call the situation "intifouda," "fouda" in Arabic meaning anarchy, and many Palestinians agree with this description. The situation has turned the areas under Palestinian control into something more resembling the United Palestinian Emirates.

One of the major concepts of Oslo was that at the end of the road there would be a strong, centralized Palestinian authority/government. Somebody very strong was supposed to be controlling the Palestinian areas and making sure there was no terrorism. This concept is gone and will not be returning for a long time. What we have now is the diversion of authority and power from the central government into the different districts. Therefore, from now on, we will have coalitions forming on the ground, and they are already forming very rapidly, with a leadership that will at one point replace Arafat.

We are heading towards a system in the territories which will have at least two, but probably up to four or more, undeclared principalities, each controlled, as they are now, by a different local coalition, each cooperating in different degrees with the coalitions in the other areas. A central government is going to shape up, once we hopefully reach the exit to this intifada, and it is going to look much different from what was originally conceived in Oslo.

Independent Palestinian Decision-Making?

Another concept which was destroyed by the intifada is what is called in Arabic "Istiqlaliyat al-Qarar al-Falastini," which means the complete and total independence of Palestinian decision-making on issues relating to Palestine. A companion Palestinian slogan was "no Arab wisayah," which means "no Arab patronage, sponsorship, interference, intervention." Arafat began his political career in 1958 by running on these slogans and denouncing the Arab world for betraying the Palestinians back in 1948. This is the essence of the Fatah movement, which in the late 1960s took control of the PLO.

From a historical perspective, we have reached a point very similar to one reached after the intifada of 1936-39, called by the Palestinians "The Great Arab Revolt." At that time, the neighboring Arab states returned to the scene and made decisions on behalf of the Palestinians, whether they liked it or not. Today, the Saudi peace plan and, more importantly, the ideas presented recently by President Mubarak, and many other signals, indicate that this ethos of independent Palestinian decision-making is now being questioned. I compare the situation to 1939, at the end of that intifada, when the British killed 5,000 Palestinians, and the Grand Mufti of Jerusalem was exiled. The Arab states were then called in to pick up from there.

No Mini-State at Peace with Israel

A basic tenet of the Oslo accord was the assumption that the Palestinian partner, Arafat, was/is interested in a Palestinian state within the 1967 borders, at peace with Israel. It was never Arafat's intention to end his political career as the president of a mini-Palestinian state, which he sees as a sovereign cage. This existed only in the fairy tales that Israelis and others were telling themselves. I don't know anyone from Arafat's closest entourage who believes in this.

The main fault in the Oslo Agreement was not the concept of seeing Israel's strategic interest, as I do, in the creation of a Palestinian state. The main fault of Oslo was in assuming it was indispensable, as they thought at the time, to start the process by bringing in seven brigades of the Fatah and the PA Liberation Army and having Arafat on the scene right from the start.

Three scenes sum up the problem. The first is during the summer of 1993 when Rabin sends his own men to Oslo. Joel Singer, the attorney, tells Abu Ala that Arafat is to get Gaza and Jericho, a crucial foothold in the West Bank. Abu Ala calls Arafat in Tunis and Arafat says to a few people around him, "We have a deal."

Twenty years earlier, Arafat had entered Lebanon according to the Cairo agreement with the Lebanese chief of staff, General Bustani, which allowed the PLO to have some armed personnel in the refugee camps and on the slopes of Mt. Hermon -- a very limited agreement. Arafat said, "We entered Lebanon through that crack in the wall, the Cairo agreement, and I ended up as Governor-General of Beirut." Arafat continued: "We are entering Palestine through this crack in the wall, Gaza-Jericho, and we will see where it leads."

The second scene is of Arafat arriving in peace and euphoria for the start of the implementation of Oslo. He comes to Rafah terminal in Gaza, and a young Israeli soldier turns to another and says: "Gee, I didn't know Arafat was so tall." Arafat arrived in a Mercedes and his kaffiyah was scraping the ceiling of the car. You have to be an NBA player for that to happen. It turned out that Arafat was sitting on somebody whom he was smuggling in -- Jihad Amarin -- and Mamduh Nofal, the former military commander of the Democratic Front, was hiding in the trunk. They also had a few kalashnikov rifles and night-vision equipment in the car.

The third scene is more recent. A senior European, who is very close to Arafat and regarded by the Palestinians as a friend, visited the chairman and said to him: "You have had hundreds of casualties by now. If you allow this to go on, there will be many more. Isn't it a shame?" Arafat replied: "They are all martyrs." In other words, "We can take it."

This sequence tells a story that is much more powerful than any expectations we might have had. Politically, I grew up in the Labor Party, but I did not believe for a fleeting moment that there was a chance that Arafat would perceive Oslo in the sense that it was perceived by many Israelis.

Arafat has a strategy dedicated to the Palestinian cause, not to the Palestinian people, and Palestinians know it. He is locked onto the objective; everything that serves that objective is fine. Agreement with Israel? Twice a day, no problem, as long as he does not have to become the undertaker of what he sees as basic, legitimate Palestinian rights. A deal with Israel, yes. An end to conflict, never.

Relations with Hamas

Arafat does not see Hamas as a rival or as an adversary. He never did. For Arafat, Hamas is a partner, which he keeps as a junior partner. Arafat's legacy is the com-

246

bined structure that he allowed to emerge during the intifada, an informal alliance, and now formal, among his own Fatah faction, Hamas, and the rest.

Arafat's most recent speeches reflect how deeply versed he is in Islamic tradition. Arafat grew up in the Moslem Brotherhood. He was expelled from Egypt by President Nasser in 1957 as a Moslem Brotherhood activist, together with the late Abu Jihad. It is this combination of his brand of nationalism and Islamic nationalism that he allowed to become the political culture of the PA during the intifada. Therefore, on the face of it, tensions between the different segments of society have been reduced.

I believe that once we move toward an exit from the intifada, we will see a dramatic reduction in the popularity of Hamas, in their room to maneuver, in the way they conduct themselves. I do not see a situation where Hamas will opt for a clash, for a confrontation with the Palestinian Authority, whoever is on top. They will challenge policies and try to force their agenda, of course, but they will not try to topple the Palestinian Authority itself.

Failures of the Quasi-Intifada

I would describe what happened after Arafat issued his instructions on the night of September 28, 2000, as a "quasi-intifada" because in many ways it lacks a popular dimension. It remains the effort of certain mobilized groups and has not become a popular uprising. For example, the Palestinian countryside, with 300 villages in the West Bank, is suffering badly but has not really become a part of it. Had they done so in the same way they did in the first intifada a decade ago, the situation of Israeli settlers and movement on the roads in the West Bank would be entirely different than it is today.

The Jerusalem region, with 300,000 Arabs, has not offered one good day of intifada since September 2000. Almost all of the incidents in the city came from either Ramallah or Bethlehem.

The student body, tens of thousands of Palestinians in colleges and universities, has largely stayed out of the current intifada, except for those in the chemical laboratory of Najah University trying to produce explosives. Akram Haniyye, an important Arafat advisor, wrote an article in despair entitled, "Where are the students?" in a variant of Arafat's popular mobilization slogan "Where are the millions?"

Arafat had also hoped to ignite the situation and create some sort of bloodbath in the territories that would spill over into the Arab world. There is bitterness in Arafat's circle about how the Egyptians, the Jordanians, and even the Syrians have conducted themselves. President Mubarak appeared on the popular television show "Good Morning Egypt" to say that "no one -- read Arafat -- will be allowed to fight to the last Egyptian soldier."

Thus, without a popular component, to quote a very important Palestinian friend of mine, "The intifada has committed suicide through suicide bombings."

Prospects for Reform

The nomination of Gen. Yahya to the position of interior minister is not going to bring a change. Arafat is in a position to hijack any reform efforts made in response to the widespread call for reform from within Palestinian society. Arafat still controls the game, and no coalition is powerful enough to establish itself in his courtyard.

Therefore, no Palestinian believes there will be any meaningful reform as long as Arafat is in charge. But Arafat will not become the Queen Mother or become like Israel's president, with his picture hanging from every wall but no one asking him for instructions or money.

Arafat and Succession

I believe in the absolute necessity of the "Muftization" of Arafat, referring to the Grand Mufti of Jerusalem. The concerns about the repercussions and tumultuous reaction there will be to the deportation of Arafat and a few others with him are much exaggerated. I think we missed an opportunity with the Karine A incident to deport Arafat. In many ways Arafat's finger is on our trigger, and whatever the cabinet did not want to approve yesterday, they will have to approve the day after.

I envision a short period after his expulsion when Arafat will be running around wherever he can go, but I think the focus of attention will switch here. Arafat's prestige has hit bottom and I don't think it can recover.
Arafat does not have a successor -- he has many successors. He and Barghouti, for example share a basically similar approach. But it is my impression that most of the people we are talking about are much more pragmatic, are willing to adjust to limitations, to the balance of forces, to pressure from outside. I see more Arab intervention coming, which can provide a basis for different day-to-day policies pursued by the new coalitions.

Today, the single most important Palestinian decision-making body is not the Palestinian legislative council, but rather the central committee of Fatah, which is not part of the PA. This is why Dahlan and Tanzim want elections in Fatah. Among the 15 remaining Fatah central committee members, for quite a while Arafat has often been in a minority with two others on major political issues.

The Central Issue

The Palestinian "right of return" is the central issue. A mini-state is not the central issue and it never was. You will not find a Palestinian leadership that will be willing to accept any of the formulas currently being discussed as a solution to this problem. The Palestinian national movement is about the right of return; it is not about the West Bank and Gaza. Israel will have to be more flexible, not in the sense of allowing more refugees, but in the sense of arriving at a more vague and creative formula that allows for a long period of time to deal with this issue.

Recommendations

This is the moment that an Israeli government should add some political offer to whatever is being done militarily. A good formula would be to say that Israel is willing to go back to the "gates of Camp David," knowing and emphasizing that we have a different narrative about what has happened and that there are consequences to the developments of the two years that have passed since our delegations left Camp David.

At the end of the day, it is crucial to explain to both the Israeli and Palestinian publics, and sooner rather than later, that we are talking about a two-state concept. But what does a two-state solution mean? According to my reading, it means two governments in the same country. We are mixed together with each other; hence, the importance of very close cooperation.

This war is only about one issue. It is not about settlements. It was never about occupation. It is about whether the Palestinian state is going to be born in peace and for peace, or whether it will be some sort of runaway state that is allowed to come into being without resolving the conflict with Israel, in order to maintain a state of fluctuating hostility.

Fact Sheet #5: Settlements

Mitchell Bard
Jewish Virtual Library
June 2002

Israel sought peace with its Arab neighbors for two decades before the first Jewish community was established in the West Bank and yet no Arab leader was willing to end the conflict.

Jews should have a right to live anywhere. If someone said that Jews would not be permitted to live in your hometown, you'd say that was anti-Semitism, discrimination, bigotry, and yet the Palestinians are allowed to go on TV day after day and say that Jews have no right to live in the West Bank. That's anti-Semitism, discrimination, and bigotry.

Jews have been living in Judea and Samaria, the area commonly called the West Bank, for centuries, far longer than Palestinians have lived in the area. The only time Jews have been prohibited from living in the territories in recent decades was during Jordan's rule from 1948 to 1967.

The right of Jews to live in the West Bank is clear. The issue of whether they should live there is entirely separate. Israelis debate this among themselves.

The question of the future status of settlements is the subject of final status negotiations with the Palestinians. The fact that Israel agreed to discuss the matter illustrates a willingness to compromise on this issue.

Neither the Declaration of Principles of September 13, 1993, nor the Interim Agreement contain any provisions prohibiting or restricting the establishment or expansion of Jewish communities in the West Bank or Gaza Strip.

Some people argue that settlements are an "obstacle to peace." Consider these facts:

From 1948 to 1967, Jordan occupied the West Bank. Israel did not control an inch of the territory and no Jews lived there and yet no Arab state would even negotiate with Israel.

Israel did not begin to build large numbers of settlements until after 1977. That is also when Egypt negotiated peace. Israel froze settlement building afterward in the hope that other Arab states would follow Egypt's example, none did.

Israel built more settlements in the 1980's and 1990's; nevertheless, King Hussein made peace with Israel, and settlements were not an issue.

In the Oslo agreements, Israel did not agree to dismantle any settlements or freeze construction and yet the Palestinians signed them.

In negotiations with Bill Clinton and Yasser Arafat in 2000, Prime Minister Barak offered to dismantle settlements in the West Bank, but Arafat refused to make peace.

At the end of negotiations, Israel wants to incorporate as many settlements as possible within its borders while the Palestinians want to expel all Jews from the territory they control.

An estimated 80 percent of the settlers live in what are in effect suburbs of major Israeli cities such as Jerusalem and Tel Aviv. Virtually the entire Jewish population believes Israel must retain these areas to ensure its security, and that they could be brought within Israel's borders with minor modifications of the 1967 border.

Strategic concerns have led both Labor and Likud governments to establish settlements. The objective is to secure a Jewish majority in key strategic regions of the West Bank, such as the Tel Aviv-Jerusalem corridor, the scene of heavy fighting in several Arab-Israeli wars.

Settlements do not violate the Fourth Geneva Convention, which prohibits the forcible transfer of people of one state to the territory of another state that it has occupied as a result of a war. The intention was to insure that local populations who came under occupation would not be forced to move. Jews are not being forced to go to the West Bank and Gaza Strip; on the contrary, they are voluntarily moving back to places where they, or their ancestors, once lived before being expelled by others. In addition, those territories never legally belonged to either Jordan or Egypt, and certainly not to the Palestinians, who were never the sovereign authority in any part of the land.

Fact Sheet #6: The '67 Border

Dr. Mitchell Bard
Jewish Virtual Library
July 2002

Israel had sought peace for nearly two decades before being forced to defend itself against Arab aggression in 1967. After defeating the Arab armies in just six days, Israelis thought the Arab leaders would realize they could not defeat Israel militarily and would instead choose the path of peace. Instead, after the war the Arab League declared: "no peace with Israel, no recognition of Israel, no negotiations with it...."

Israel would not have captured the West Bank or reunified Jerusalem if King Hussein had heeded the warning of Prime Minister Eshkol to stay out of the war. Instead Jordan attacked, and, in the course of defending itself, Israel found itself in control of these territories.

The Arab states lobbied the UN to require that Israel withdraw from "all the" territories it captured. This is the demand made by the Arab League in the plan recently put forward by Saudi Crown Prince Abdullah. The UN rejected this formulation when it adopted Resolution 242 because the Security Council understood the '67 border was not secure or defensible.

Since the war, Israel has consistently said that in the context of a peace agreement it was prepared to withdraw to the 1967 border "with modifications"; that is, to a new border that meets Resolution 242's requirement of being secure.

After the 1967 War, President Lyndon Johnson also rejected the idea that Israel should withdraw to the pre-war frontier: "There are some who have urged, as a single, simple solution, an immediate return to the situation as it was on June 4....this is not a prescription for peace but for renewed hostilities."

The Joint Chiefs of Staff concluded in 1967: "From a strictly military point of view, Israel would require the retention of some captured territory in order to provide militarily defensible borders." More than three decades later, Lieutenant General (Ret.) Thomas Kelly, director of operations for the Joint Chiefs of Staff during the Gulf War, reiterated Israel's strategic concern: "It is impossible to defend Jerusalem unless you hold the high ground....An aircraft that takes off from an airport in Amman is going to be over Jerusalem in two-and-a-half minutes, so it's utterly impossible for me to defend the whole country unless I hold that land."

More recently, President Bush put the border issue in perspective: "For a Texan, a first visit to Israel is an eye-opener. At the narrowest point, it's only 8 miles from the Mediterranean to the old Armistice line: That's less than from the top to the bottom of Dallas-Ft. Worth Airport. The whole of pre-1967 Israel is only about six times the size of the King Ranch near Corpus Christi."

A withdrawal to the 1967 border would not satisfy the radical Islamists. Hamas and Islamic Jihad have made clear that they will not end their terrorist campaign against Israel if it withdraws to the prewar frontier. These and other Muslim extremists have

252

said they will not accept the existence of a Jewish state in the Islamic world.

When Egypt's Anwar Sadat declared he was prepared to make peace, and matched his words with deeds, Israel withdrew completely from the Sinai, dismantled Jewish settlements, and gave up its oil fields. When King Hussein agreed to make peace, Israel agreed to return the small swath of Jordanian territory it held.

To date, Israel has withdrawn from approximately 93 percent of the territories it captured. In return for peace with Syria and an end to Palestinian terror, it is prepared to withdraw from most of the remaining 7% in dispute.

Israel remains committed to trading land for peace, and never annexed the West Bank or Gaza Strip because it expected to return part of these territories in negotiations. When the Palestinians finally declared that they would recognize Israel and renounce terrorism, Israel agreed to begin to withdraw. Since 1993, Israel has turned over approximately 80% of the Gaza Strip and more than 40% of the West Bank to the Palestinian Authority. Plans to withdraw from additional territory were scuttled by Palestinian terrorism and their violation of the Oslo agreements.

For peace, Israeli Prime Minister Barak offered to withdraw from 100% of the Gaza Strip and 95-97% of the West Bank, that is, to the 1967 border with minor modifications. He also agreed to dismantle settlements, and allow the Palestinians to establish a state with east Jerusalem as its capital if they would end the conflict. Arafat rejected the offer and did not even offer a counterproposal.

Israel offered to negotiate a return of the Golan Heights to Syria, and a succession of Prime Ministers declared a readiness to concede this strategic high ground in exchange for peace. Neither Syrian President Hafez Assad nor his son, who succeeded him, have been prepared to follow Sadat and Hussein's example and offer peace in return.

Food For Thought

Hirsh Goodman
The Jerusalem Report
July 2002

The motive driving suicide volunteers is revenge. They have stopped fighting to liberate Palestine. They have suspended the dream of a state. They now dream of killing as many Jews as possible, of revenge, of making life in Israel impossible -- and they truly believe they can do it.

Let me, as accurately as I can, describe a conversation I had with a Palestinian peace activist over dinner in a European capital one Friday night in mid-June. We have known each other for quite a few years and I have always had deep respect for his views, hence the importance I attach to what he said that night, despite the three glasses of wine that went down with his meal.

The Zionist experiment, he told me, is over. The Palestinians have discovered a strategic weapon: suicide bombers. Once anathema, they are now considered heroes. The shahids (martyrs), once seen as religious fanatics, are now nationalist freedom fighters. Moreover, he continued, they are growing in legitimacy all the time. The Arab world understands them and even some Europeans seem to. The Israelis have F-16s, the Palestinians, suicide bombers. The equivalency is obvious to all.

Now, he continued, there are thousands out there waiting in line to kill as many Israelis as they can, to make your lives hell on earth. They belong to no organization, but want revenge and are prepared to die for it. You think you are going to stop them by punishing their parents. You are wrong. You won't even know who they are or where they came from. Nothing will be left of them.

We are going to hit you everywhere we can: gas stations, theaters, parks, wedding halls. You will know no happiness. It will be one funeral after the next.

And then, while you are reeling, the 1.5 million Palestinian allies, the Israeli Palestinians, our brothers and your enemy, will rise up as well. They are just waiting for a sign from us. They know you better than you know yourselves. They speak your language and know every street in every one of your cities. They are familiar with every nook and every cranny. And they will join at the right time. Make no mistake about it.

And then what does Israel do? Transfer? Can you imagine CNN and the BBC reporting live as the Jews transfer truckload after truckload of Palestinians over the border? Your country will lose all legitimacy. The Arab world will go to war against it. You will be a pariah, worse than South Africa under apartheid. Your generals will be tried for war crimes. The world will impose sanctions. Your F-16s will run dry of fuel.

Your people will leave in droves, especially professionals.

The Zionist experiment is over.

That, in essence, was what was said. Was he entirely serious? Who knows? Was he trying to ruin my meal? Perhaps. But there are several harsh truths there and, in tune with the old adage that when wine goes in, secrets come out, I took note of the following: Advertisements in the Palestinian press against suicide bombings signed by several hundred Palestinian intellectuals notwithstanding, suicide bombings have the full support of the Palestinian people, including some intellectuals. It has become almost politically correct. Soldiers die in battle. The suicide bombers are soldiers, their deaths are legitimate and the killing of civilians is legitimate, they say. Israelis do it with tanks all the time.

The motive driving suicide volunteers is revenge. They have stopped fighting to liberate Palestine. They have suspended the dream of a state. They now dream of killing as many Jews as possible, of revenge, of making life in Israel impossible -- and they truly believe they can do it.

The strategy is to push Israel into responding in a way that would turn it into another South Africa, a pariah state. The goal is no longer to draw international intervention, which the Palestinians have been trying to do since the outbreak of the current conflict, but to achieve Israel's international isolation -- to strangle the country diplomatically, economically and morally while managing, with great dexterity and skill, to maintain the image of the Palestinians as victims.

If this thinking has indeed penetrated serious Palestinian circles, we are in for a long and hard period. But it will not follow the scenario my dinner partner outlined. Israel will build a fence, increase its vigilance, take security measures, exile the families of suicide bombers, maintain a constant presence in Palestinian-controlled territories if suspected terrorists are there, maintain the stranglehold it has over the cities and the roadblocks that makes it impossible to move from point to point. There are a million steps between suicide bombers and transfer and yes, there will be casualties. But Palestinian suicide bombers are not going to defeat the State of Israel. And, incidentally, there are gas stations on both sides.

Our Enemies, The Saudis

Victor Davis Hanson
www.commentary.org
July 2002

Even if we were not attempting to prosecute a war against terror, the time would have long since arrived to reconsider our relations with Saudi Arabia. That the Saudis, of all people, should now be regarded as a virtual ally in this conflict only underscores the need at last to settle matters between us. Although the catalog of disagreements on our agenda is long, and many of the items are by now familiar, it is helpful to review the list.

By any modern standard of civilization, the kingdom of Saudi Arabia is a bizarre place. In an age of spreading consensual government, the House of Saud resembles an Ottoman sultanate staffed by some 7,000 privileged royal cousins. The more favored are ensconced in plush multi-million dollar palaces and maintain luxury estates abroad in Paris, Geneva, Marbella, and Aspen. All 7,000 haggle over the key military and political offices of the kingdom-normally distributed not on the appeal of proven merit but more often through a mixture of blood ties, intrigue, and bribes.

Polygamy is legal, and practiced, among the Saudi elite. Everywhere in the kingdom, women are veiled, secluded, and subject to the harsh protocols of a sexual apartheid. A few female Saudi professionals who in 1991 drove cars as a sign of protest mostly ended up arrested and jailed. Women who have traveled to the West remain under the constant surveillance of the Committee for the Advancement of Virtue and Elimination of Sin, a Taliban-like government watchdog group of clerics and whip-bearing fanatics.

There is no religious tolerance in Saudi Arabia for creeds other than Islam; in our State Department's own muted nomenclature, "Freedom of religion does not exist" there. The Wahhabi strain of fundamentalist Islam-over 30,000 mosques and growing-is prone to occasionally violent spasms. The Saudi constitution is defined officially by governmental decree as the Qur'an, and the legal system is the domain of clerics who adjudicate by an array of medieval codes and punishments. Presently the UN Committee Against Torture is asking the Saudis to curtail flogging and amputations; so far, they have answered that such punishments have been an integral part of Islamic law "for 1,400 years" and so simply "cannot be changed."

Although Westernized Saudis in suits and ties, often personable, with impeccable English and an array of American friends, are ubiquitous on our air waves, they are mere darting phantoms of a free press. Dozens of state-run papers and private but publicly subsidized media vent the most virulent anti-Semitic hatred in the Arab world-fundamentalist screeds or "poetry" equating Jews with monkeys and calling for their extermination. Editors are free only in the sense that they can draw on their own creativity in expressing real dislike for the United States and Israel, perhaps to be rebuked on the rare occasions when such venom is made known to the very deferential American media elite who interview the royals on our evening television shows. The Saudi Press Agency is as careful in monitoring news accounts as informers are in observing classrooms or as clerics in scrutinizing cultural events for the presence of women.

Criticism of the royal family, Saudi government, and religious leaders is legally forbidden and strictly monitored. The few dissident writers in the kingdom are jailed, blacklisted, and sometimes have their books banned and driven off the Arab-language market. The names of the censoring ministries-Supreme Information Council, Press Information Council, Ministry of Information, Directorate of Publications-come right out of Orwell's 1984.

After September 11, the world is slowly learning how the Saudi princes have pulled off their grafting of a high-tech cultivar onto medieval roots. It has been accomplished through bribes to clerics, cash to terrorists, welfare to the commons, and largesse to prominent Americans: money in some form to any and all who find the House of Saud either too modern or too backward. Such inducements have been indispensable because the vast wealth that Western petroleum companies developed for the royal family, plus the tourist treasures of Mecca and Medina, brought neither a stable economy nor general prosperity. The kingdom's accidental boon was not invested broadly in viable industries, secular education, or political reform, but instead lavished on ill-conceived projects and a royal elite who consumed too much of it on luxury cars, houses, clothes, jewels, gambling, and trips abroad-sins against both Islam and Western laws of economic development.

But now the Saudis are $200 billion in debt. The population is soaring. The imams are worried more about unrest than about their stipends. Thirty percent of Saudis remain unschooled, and nearly as many are barely literate, their resentment against a coddled elite mitigated only by carefully measured doses of anti-Western Wahhabism and the satisfaction that at least the millions of guest Asian and Arab helots, imported for much of the society's wage labor, are more unfree than they. Efforts at creating viable irrigated agriculture and petrochemical industries have had but mixed success-and then only thanks to massive infusions of oil-dollar subsidies.

It is not just human capital that is bought from abroad. Almost every item deemed important to the modernization of the kingdom-from drilling bits and heavy machinery to the phone system and power grid-is shipped in. The expertise to use, repair, and improve such critical appurtenances rests either with foreigners or with the few thousand Saudis trained abroad.

The Saudi royals are thus these days an increasingly troubled bunch. They are quite understandably exasperated that they have failed to earn needed capital by developing nonpetroleum industries, and that their citizenry lacks either the practical skills to create thriving commercial enterprises or the individual drive and initiative to build businesses from the ground up. They are even more irked that their imported gadgets have brought with them hostile ideas, critical lectures, and unwelcome advice, as if air-conditioners and neurosurgeons should come without consequences and as freely as oil out of the desert. And they are still more dyspeptic that some people persist in thinking there is something unhealthy in the fact that fifteen of the nineteen hijackers on September 11 were Saudi nationals.

It is common to hear that Osama bin Laden, anaturalized Saudi Arabian whose family still has close ties to the inner circles of the monarchy, deliberately chose Saudi nationals for the September 11 murders in order to poison the otherwise amicable relations between the kingdom and the United States.

Maybe so-but the gambit, if that is what it was, was certainly made easier by the thousands of Saudis who willingly traveled to Afghanistan over the last few years to train in bin Laden's terrorist camps. Royal denials notwithstanding, Saudi government money has for years been funneled into madrassas to encourage radical anti-

Americanism as well as to fund the al Qaeda terrorists. Allegedly the purpose has been as much to provide insurance against subversive activity directed at the kingdom itself as to subsidize attacks on the United States. And there may be, after all, a sick genius in a system that can shift the hatreds of an illiterate Saudi youth away from the jet-setting sheiks who have diverted his nation's treasure and onto the anonymous Americans who created that wealth, who ship the kingdom its consumer goods, and who defend it from the neighborhood's carnivores.

But that anomaly raises the key question: why have close relations with the Saudis been a cornerstone of American foreign policy for decades, as brought to our attention most recently in a series of slick Saudi-financed ads showing American Presidents from Franklin Roosevelt to George W. Bush in warm embraces with a variety of sheiks? The answer is banal: oil, and nothing more. Otherwise, Saudi Arabia's small population of 22 million would earn it less clout than Egypt. Otherwise, the kingdom is no more strategically located than nearby Yemen. Otherwise, its sponsorship of terrorism would ensure it a place on the State Department's list of rogue states like Syria and Iran. In fact, a more sinister status: Saudi terrorists have killed more Americans than all those murdered by Iranians, Syrians, Libyans, and Iraqis put together.

The actual Saudi percentage of the world's crude oil and gas reserves is a matter of dispute. On the one hand, there are still unexplored vastnesses in the kingdom itself; on the other, there is an indeterminable amount of oil lying beneath Russia, West Africa, the Arctic, and the seas. But it is reasonable to suppose that Saudi Arabia holds 25 percent or more of the remaining petroleum now known to exist. Thus, for at least the next two decades, the kingdom's oil is thought to be critical to the world economy and in particular to the prosperity of Japan, Europe, and the United States.

In the past, our devil's bargain with the kingdom was as utilitarian as it was unapologetic. They kept pumping the oil-either to us directly or as untraceable currents into the huge world pool-and we promised to ignore both the primeval nature of their domestic society and their virulent hatred of Israel. In the cold war the geopolitics of containing an expansionist Soviet Union made this mutually beneficial concordat easier to stomach. There was also a certain familiarity bred by the growing multitude of Americans who traveled to Saudi Arabia to construct the civilized veneer of the kingdom and of Saudis who came here to obtain the expertise that would presumably ensure some kind of future autonomy. Perhaps the idealistic among us once thought that their intimate and sustained exposure to Americans might eventually lead to liberalization.

Even after the cold war, however, "stability," rather than autonomy or liberalization, was the operative word when it came to our interest in Saudi Arabia. In theory, we did not press the royal family for democratic reform on their assurances that something far worse and far more radical-à la Algeria or Iran-might come to power in the chaos of elections. This seemed fair enough; who wanted another Khomeini or Mullah Omar atop a quarter of the world's oil supply? Or, worse, a Hitler-like thug who would hold one election and one alone? So we both shrugged as the Saudis permitted our troops to defend them, our experts to train them, and our merchants to profit from their oil while they, for their part, managed to hold their noses at our liberated women, prominent Jews, and crass dissemination of videos, fast food, raucous music, and general cultural wantonness.

Marshall Wyllie, a former chargé at the embassy in Saudi Arabia, once summed up the American policy best: "We need their oil, and they need our protection." Armed to the teeth with American weaponry that for the most part they are unable to maintain or operate competently,* bolstered by a frontline tripwire of uniformed American soldiers, and static in their resistance to change, the Saudis preened that they were the reliable deliverymen of inexpensive and plentiful oil in a way that the lunocracies in Iraq, Iran, or Libya were not. And admittedly there was something to that claim, at least enough to enable us to think that our policy toward them was neither illogical nor even inherently amoral.

Saudi princes did tend to choose predetermined successors when the ruling sheik of the day passed on, without the gunplay typically seen in succession fights elsewhere in the Arab world. Unlike the Iraqis, they never torched the oil fields; unlike the Iranians, they never stormed our embassy for hostages; unlike the Libyans, they never bombed our airliners. But as if in imitation of their own perspective on reality, our approach to them has also been static and equally blinkered, and in particular has taken no account of the huge alterations in the post-cold-war world.

These changes were already in play well before September 11. The international oil matrix is far more complex than during the Gulf war even a decade ago. Russia is now rapidly becoming the world's most important producer, and the demise of the Soviet bloc has meant that the entire world is now under active exploration. Whereas most other nations are no longer overly worried about the politics of oil exportation, and are positively indifferent to the old Marxist rhetoric about Western capitalist exploitation, the petroleum policy of Saudi Arabia-which has threatened or implemented at least three embargoes in past decades-remains both entirely self-interested and never far from the radical interests in the Middle East.

The sheiks, however, are being led by events that are rapidly careering out of their control. If Saudi Arabia pumps less oil, there will be shocks and disruptions, but eager new producing countries will soon fill the void; if the Saudis export more, then the price may well collapse altogether. And because new, nonpetroleum-based technologies are on the horizon, both to produce electricity and to power transportation, not to mention the increased efficiency promised in the near future by hybrid engines, most exporting countries now worry about getting what oil they have out of the ground rather than watch it sit untapped and decline in value in the latter half of the century.

In sum, a Saudi Arabia with a sizable debt and no real nonpetroleum economy needs consumers as much as, or more than, buyers need Middle Eastern producers. Saudi Arabia is ever so slowly losing its vaunted place as the world's price-fixer, and its past history and present machinations reveal it to be no more or less a friend of the United States than any other Islamic exporting country. If the Saudis declared another embargo, it might fare about as well as Saddam Hussein's recent ban of exports to the United States-and cause a surge in pumping and exploration from Russia and South America.

There is, then, no real need for us to be frightened by the loss of the kingdom's oil friendship. But we should be concerned by the evidence of its strategic enmity. It may be true that the Saudis are neither Iraqis nor Iranians nor Libyans; but it is quite dangerous enough that they are Saudis.

The PLO archives made public by the Israeli army in the wake of its recent operations on the West Bank have confirmed that the kingdom actively gives cash to a variety of terrorist organizations and showers with money (or free trips to Mecca) the families of suicide bombers. This bounty can no longer be seen as mere postmortem charity, but rather as premeditated financial incentives for murder. What that means is that the kingdom's suicide-killers of September 11 who butchered our civilians were not so at odds with basic Saudi approaches to conflict after all.

The much-vaunted Saudi "peace plan" for the Middle East does not alter this troubling picture. What was striking (stunning, really) about the proposals was not the grudging willingness after a half-century to recognize the existence of the state of Israel but the complete absence in them of any gesture-planned state visits to Tel Aviv, direct talks with Jerusalem, cessation of state propaganda, curtailment of terrorist subsidies-that might suggest more than a public-relations ploy to deflect growing American furor after September 11. Current Saudi peace-feelers are mostly explicable as salve for wounds the Saudis themselves have inflicted, and which they are suddenly worried have become infected in a very aggrieved host.

Then there is radical Islam. Despite suicide bombings in Lebanon, the first World Trade Center attack, the 1996 assaults against the Khobar Towers complex in Saudi Arabia, the 1998 bombings at the embassies in Kenya and Tanzania, and the hole blasted in the USS Cole, distracted Americans used to believe that such vicious wasps deserved little more than an occasional swat. But after the murder of 3,000 Americans, and the various anthrax, dirty-bomb, and suicide-attack scares, Americans are finally seeing militant Islam not merely as a different religion, or even as a radical Jim-Jones-like cult, but as a threat to our very existence.

Saudi Arabia is the placenta of this frightening phenomenon. Its money has financed it; its native terrorists promote it; and its own unhappy citizenry is either amused by or indifferent to its effects upon the world. Surely it has occurred to more than a few Americans that, without a petroleum-rich Wahhabism, the support for such international killers and the considerable degree of ongoing aid to those who would destroy the West would radically diminish.

Finally, Saudi Arabia has shown an increasingly disturbing tendency to interfere in the domestic affairs of the United States, both in religious and political matters. Whereas our female soldiers, who are in the Arabian desert to preserve the power of the sheiks, cannot walk about unveiled, their hosts show no such cultural inhibitions when here in America. Right after September 11, the FBI was asked by the monarchy to help whisk away members of the bin Laden family from the Boston area to find sanctuary back home. Any government that can request-and promptly receive-federal help for the family of a terrorist, whose operatives, 75 percent of them Saudis, had hours earlier vaporized 3,000 American civilians, has too much confidence in its clout with the United States government.

Saudi television commercials seeking to influence American public opinion are now nightly fare. Thousands of Saudi students are politically active on American campuses. Local imams reflect the extreme and often anti-American views of senior Muslim clerics who channel the biggest subsidies from the Middle East. Saudi Arabia's cash infusions to Muslim communities in America ensure that Wahhabi fundamentalism takes hold among Arab guests living in the United States. As Daniel Pipes has tirelessly documented in these pages, the danger to us now is not just without but within, and its ultimate address is, more often than not, Riyadh.

To recapitualte, all the old reasons that prevented us from breaking away from Saudi Arabia are no longer compelling. More and more, the royals' oil policy is neither pro-Western nor so crucial as it once was in determining world pricing. The present government has been an active abettor of terror, and perhaps the most virulent anti-Israeli Arab country in the region. Al Qaeda and other terrorists have received bribe money from the Saudis, without which they could not operate so effectively. That the monarchy has not been forthcoming in tracking those with ties to the September 11 murderers reflects its real worry about where such investigations might lead. And Saudi cash has been a force for radicalism right here in the United States, casting into doubt the legitimacy and purpose of almost every Islamic charity now operating within our borders. Nor should we forget that no country in the world is more hostile to the American idea of religious tolerance, free speech, constitutional government, and sexual equality.

Can the U.S., then, revamp its policy toward Saudi Arabia, perhaps to conform with our stance toward similarly belligerent regimes like Libya or Syria? The beginning of wisdom is to acknowledge that such an about-face would hardly be easy-if for no other reason than that many of the royal family are close friends of powerful Americans in the oil and defense industries, on university campuses, and within government. Their pedigree stretches back to the likes of Clark Clifford, Spiro Agnew, and Richard Helms in the days when ARAMCO used to lobby to prevent American networks from broadcasting such delicacies as the 1979 film Death of a Princess (a surreal chronicle of the public execution of a royal Saudi princess and the beheading of her lover on charges of fornication).

Moreover, most elite Saudis here in America are longtime residents, generous hosts, and superficially friendly. They tend to be adept at American-style public relations, whether emerging in coats and ties for interviews, receptions, and political galas or time-traveling back to the ancient netherworld of flowing robes and headdress when negotiations toughen. The few American journalists who bring up the sordid side of Saudi behavior usually appear gratuitously rude to guests who come across as sensitive, hurt, and in full denial.

But the point in any attempt to change our relationship is not so much to punish the Saudis for past hostility and duplicity as to create a landscape for real revolution in the Middle East-a reordering that might in its turn prevent a future clash of civilizations. Such an attempt must be made with no illusions that we have any real control over distant events, and with full recognition of the impracticability of growing democracy in a culture without the soil of tolerance or a middle class. Are there Saudi dissidents who are committed to democracy and can stand up to Wahhabi madness? Our task is to find them, or help to create them, and then to aid them all.

This will sound like a mission impossible, but consider: American businessmen may find the royal family hospitable (over $300 billion in arms sales since the 1991 Gulf war), but most foreign workers in the kingdom mistrust their employers; most Arabs elsewhere resent the abject corruption and conspicuous consumption of the House of Saud; and most Saudis themselves would be happy to see the pampered princes go-some, admittedly, in exchange for Islamist clerics, but others for any consensual government that could end the present kleptocracy. Besides, while we were pursuing this long-term goal, there are steps that could and should be taken in the meantime.

One of them is to recalibrate our oil policy, encouraging-with loans, joint pipeline ventures, and long-term contracts-exploration in Russia and elsewhere in the former Soviet Union. Not only would such suppliers increase the pool of the world's oil and gas, and thereby lessen Saudi influence, but at least in the case of Russia we would be buying from a struggling democracy rather than from a small elite already as rich as many of its own silenced people are poor. And, speaking of energy, there are things to be done on the home front as well: conservatives might withhold their opposition to government-mandated efficiency standards for new cars and trucks, liberals their opposition to Arctic oil drilling.

Another interim but absolutely crucial step is the seemingly peripheral matter of dealing with Iraq. In a world where our enemies are perfectly prepared to blow up our buildings and murder our civilians at work, we can no longer tolerate the continuance of a mad regime with access to poison gas and potential nukes. Iraq is significant, moreover, not just for the evil that it is today but for the good that it might represent tomorrow. Once freed from Saddam Hussein, its rather prosperous and secular people could help change the moral balance of the Middle East, immediately posing a challenge to Saudi Arabia, Kuwait, and the other Gulf states. Not only would a liberated Iraq become a friendly oil producer, but its very existence would raise a host of fruitfully embarrassing questions about such matters as why there need be American troops in Saudi Arabia at all, and against whom those troops are defending the sheiks if not their own people.

What the United States should strive for in the Middle East is not tired normality-the sclerosis that led to September 11, the Palestinian quagmire, and an Iraq full of weapons of mass destruction. Insisting on adherence to the same old relationship is akin to supporting a tottering Soviet Gorbachev instead of an emerging Russian Yeltsin, or lamenting the bold new world ushered in by the fall of the Berlin Wall-a radical upheaval that critics once said was too abrupt and perilous given the decades of dehumanizing Soviet tyranny, the inexperience of East European dissidents, and the absence of a Westernized middle class. Wiser observers have long argued that where governments hate us most, the people tend to like us more, sensing that we at least oppose those who bring them misery.

Only by seeking to spark disequilibrium, if not outright chaos, do we stand a chance of ridding the world of the likes of bin Laden, Arafat, and Saddam Hussein. Just as a reconstituted Afghanistan eliminated the satanic Taliban and turned the region's worst regime into a government with real potential, so too a new Iraq might start the fall of dominoes in the Gulf that could wipe away the entire foul nest behind September 11.

Even should fundamental changes go wrong in Saudi Arabia, the worst that could happen would not be much worse than what we have now-thousands of our citizens dead, a crater in New York, millions put out of work, Israelis blown up weekly, and a half-billion people in the Arab world unfree, hungry, illiterate, and informed by the perpetrators of evil that America and Israel are at fault. As a student said to me shortly after September 11, "What are we afraid of? Are they going to blow up the World Trade Center with thousands in it?"

Saudi weapons are impressive, since 40 percent of the country's income is devoted to buying imported arms. But their pilots, their high command, and their men in the field have no record of distinction in modern modes of warfare. In the past, most of their expensive AWACS surveillance planes had to be either manned by mercenaries or stay grounded. The billions of dollars' worth of ultra-sophisticated jets, helicopters, and bombers simply lack qualified pilots to fly them, much less adequate mechanics to fix them. Those who do fight are hardly inspiring: had Saddam Hussein kept his tanks moving through Kuwait in the summer of 1991, he could have swallowed the kingdom in a few days well before we arrived to save it.

The Lessons Of Lebanon:
Iran And Syria Sponsor An Ominous Arms Build-Up
On Israel's Northern Border

Michael Rubin
Weekly Standard
July 1, 2002

THE ISRAEL-LEBANON BORDER

Yellow Hezbollah FLAGS fly over the rubble of the Tourmus agricultural station on the Israel-Lebanon border. Following Israel's May 2000 withdrawal from southern Lebanon, Hezbollah guerrillas dynamited the cattle pens and vaccination clinics where Lebanese farmers once brought their livestock for immunization. "It's a shame. Disease doesn't know the border, and everyone will suffer because of this," one local farmer said. Hezbollah does not care. Emboldened by the Israeli withdrawal and United Nations moral equivalency, Hezbollah is determined to further the conflict. Sadly, Israel's muddled anti-terrorism policy, like that of the Bush administration, encourages such terror.

More than two years after Israel's unilateral withdrawal, peace is increasingly distant. Syria and Iran saw Israel's retreat not as a gesture of peace, but as a sign of weakness. Rather than enjoy peace, Israeli border towns prepare for renewed terror. Residents of Manara, for example, live behind high fences, barbed wire, and watchtowers. The UNIFIL post ten meters away across the border in Lebanon provides little comfort, especially after the October 2000 incident in which UNIFIL troops concealed evidence of a Hezbollah kidnapping across the U.N.-certified border.

Hezbollah does not operate in isolation. "Syria is the brains and Iran is the heart," one counterterrorism expert explained. Twice a week, Iran Air cargo planes touch down at the Damascus airport, supplying increasingly sophisticated arms to terrorist camps across the border in Syrian-occupied Lebanon. In recent weeks, Hezbollah has deployed thousands of missiles capable of striking targets as deep inside Israel as Haifa. Intelligence reports indicate that Iranian Revolutionary Guard brigadier general Ali Reza Tamizr has begun training Hezbollah, the Popular Front for the Liberation of Palestine (PFLP), Hamas, and Arafat's Fatah on missiles capable of downing civilian aircraft.

The lessons of Israel's withdrawal from Lebanon are clear. Adversaries who do not desire peace will further conflict. The day after the completion of Israel's withdrawal, Hezbollah secretary general Hasan Nasrallah declared, "The road to Palestine and freedom is the road of the resistance and intifada! It should be neither the intifada that is framed by Oslo, nor that which is negotiated by the compromising negotiator in Stockholm. All you need is to follow the way of the martyred people of the past who shook and frightened the entity of this raping Zionist community."

Palestinian chairman Yasser Arafat concurred. Two months after Israel's pullback, Arafat turned down Israel's offer of a Palestinian state with its capital in Jerusalem, on 97 percent of the West Bank and Gaza and 3 percent of Israel proper. Instead, Arafat

263

launched a war designed to strike not only in disputed territories, but also in Israel.

The second Palestinian intifada is not a grass-roots uprising, but rather a terror campaign perpetrated largely by Arafat's overlapping Fatah, Tanzim, Al Aksa Martyrs Brigade, and Force 17, with overt Syrian, Iranian, Saudi, and Iraqi assistance. With the State Department floating trial balloons of new peace plans predicated upon further Israeli concessions, and self-righteous European Union and U.N. officials demanding a cessation of Israeli self-defense, state sponsors of terrorism smell blood and sense victory.

On June 5, four days after Syria assumed the Security Council presidency, terrorists detonated a car bomb next to a public bus near Megiddo, killing 17. Islamic Jihad claimed responsibility from its headquarters in Damascus. Three days later, the Iranian government rewarded the group by upping its budget 70 percent. When a suicide bomber killed 15 at a pool hall in a Tel Aviv suburb, Syria's state-controlled radio declared, "The wonderful and special suicide attacks [are] a practical declaration before the whole world of the way to liberate Arab Palestinian land." Clearly, Damascus is flaunting its support for terrorism.

The growth of anti-Israel terror is directly proportional to the decline of Israeli deterrence. When the Damascus-based PFLP assassinated Israel's tourism minister last October, Israel failed to retaliate against the group's headquarters. Sensing Israel's reluctance to hold him accountable for his proxy groups, Syrian president Bashar al-Assad grows increasingly bold.

On April 26, 2002, Israeli security forces intercepted an explosives-laden car bomb that the PFLP planned to detonate under the Azrieli Towers, Tel Aviv's equivalent of the World Trade Center. Ten thousand deaths would have resulted from the buildings' collapse. Less than a month later, terrorists attempted to blow up the Pi Glilot gas storage facility. Had they been successful, the entire population of Ramat Aviv Gimel--more than 20,000--would have perished in the fireball.

The tragedy of the situation is that Israel could end Syria's terror sponsorship within one month. After all, four years ago, Turkey forced Syria to do the same. Damascus once played host to Kurdistan Workers party (PKK) leader Abduallah Ocalan, a man responsible for tens of thousands of deaths in Turkey. In September 1998, Ankara decided it had had enough. President Suleyman Demiral declared, "We are losing our patience and we retain the right to retaliate against Syria." Prime Minister Mesut Yilmaz warned that the Turkish army was "awaiting orders" to attack. Turkey staged military exercises along the Syrian border. The result? Syria caved, expelled Ocalan, and closed down PKK offices. For Damascus, terrorism is a worthwhile policy tool only so long as the regime need not pay a military price.

As scholars such as Daniel Pipes, Efraim Inbar, and Ely Karmon have shown, Turkey's success provides lessons to both Washington and Jerusalem. First, terrorism can be stopped, but those fighting terror must be willing to go to war to eradicate it. Second, terrorism is black and white. Unfortunately, it's a lesson many in the Bush administration do not understand.

Prior to joining the State Department's policy planning staff, Brookings scholar Meghan O'Sullivan argued that the United States should seek a "more nuanced" approach to terrorism, whereby "lesser penalties would apply to lesser levels of state sponsorship." Such nuance is dead wrong, since it implies some terror to be permissible.

Washington (and Jerusalem) should not exculpate state sponsors for the actions of their proxy groups. Just as the key to constraining al Qaeda was toppling the Taliban, the key to constraining groups such as Hezbollah, the PFLP, and the Al Aksa Martyrs Brigade is a willingness to make their hosts pay the ultimate price.

Terror sponsorship cannot be subject to negotiation. When I taught in Iraq last year, my Baghdad University-trained translators consistently failed to comprehend three words: tolerance, compromise, and debate. Such concepts simply do not exist in Saddam Hussein's Iraq, nor do they in Syria and Iran. When urging dialogue and restraint, Secretary of State Colin Powell must understand that willingness to meet any terrorist demand, no matter how small, only rewards violence and indicates U.S. weakness. Terrorism is not the result of a cycle of violence. Rather, it is a result of too little retaliation.

The Prerequisite To Peace

Jeff Jacoby
Philadelphia Jewish Exponent
July 1, 2002

There are times, George Orwell is reputed to have said, when the first duty of an intelligent man is to restate the obvious. President Bush did his duty this week when he cut through the murk of the past nine years -- the years of the Middle East "peace process" -- to assert some obvious truths.

"Today, Palestinian authorities are encouraging, not opposing terrorism," he said. "Today, the elected Palestinian legislature has no authority, and power is concentrated in the hands of an unaccountable few. . . . Today, the Palestinian people live in economic stagnation, made worse by official corruption." All of this is true, all of it is plainly visible, and all of it has been persistently denied or ignored for years by most of the world's governments -- including, until very recently, those of Israel and the United States.

Having acknowledged obvious facts, Bush drew an obvious conclusion. Peace between Israel and the Palestinians will not be possible until there is "a new and different Palestinian leadership," one "not compromised by terror," nor until Palestinian society becomes "a practicing democracy based on tolerance and liberty." Only when that transformation takes place can a lasting peace between Israelis and Palestinians be fashioned. And only then will it make sense to talk of a Palestinian state.

Unfortunately, there is no chance that the Palestinians will willingly undertake such a transformation. For one thing, the current Palestinian rulers will not agree to go. That includes not only Yasser Arafat, but his thuggish lieutenants -- the likes of Jibril Rajoub, Mohammed Dahlan, Mahmoud Abbas, Ahmed Qurei, and Marwan Barghouti, all of whom are "compromised by terror." For his part, Arafat wasted no time in brushing off Bush's call for new Palestinian leaders, telling reporters the next day that the president was "definitely not" referring to him.

But it is not only Arafat and his aides who are compromised by terror. The Palestinian people themselves are openly wedded to it and deeply opposed to co-existence with Israel. Bush fudged when he said, "The hatred of a few holds the hopes of many hostage." The dismal truth is that among the Palestinians, it is the many who nurse hatred and who support the slaughter of civilians.

Just this month, a poll by the Jerusalem Media and Communication Center (a Palestinian institute) found that 68 percent of Palestinians approve of suicide bombings and 51 percent favor the liquidation of Israel. Palestinian TV extols the terror attacks that have been turning Israeli pizza shops and commuter buses into horrific scenes of massacre. Palestinian muftis preaching in the mosques of Gaza exhort the faithful to kill Jews "wherever you meet them." Summer camps indoctrinate Palestinian kids in jihad; schoolbooks teach them that Israel must be destroyed.

The nearly nine years of Arafat's misrule have severely poisoned Palestinian society, and in such toxic soil peace cannot take root. Palestinians have been steeped in hatred and bloodlust; great numbers of them are convinced that it is only a matter of time until the Jews are expelled and all of "Palestine" is theirs. It is folly to think that they could abruptly change course, and extend to Israel the hand of neighborly goodwill.

As a prerequisite to peace, Palestinian culture must be drastically reformed. The venom of the Arafat era must be drained. Persons implicated in terrorism must be punished and ostracized; democratic norms must be instilled; the virtue of tolerance must be learned. There is only one way to effect such wholesale changes: The Palestinian Authority must be dealt a devastating military defeat, one that will crush Arafat and his junta and shatter forever the Palestinian fantasy of "liberating" Israel and driving the Jews into the sea.

Then the Palestinian territories must be reoccupied, the terror chieftains executed, and the putrescence of Arafat and Hamas flushed away. That will make it possible to rebuild the structures of civil society -- the legislature, the courts, the police, the media, and above all, the schools -- from the ground up. The Palestinian polity can become a true liberal democracy, one committed to pluralism, civil rights, competitive elections, and the marketplace of ideas. When that happens, peace with Israel will be a given, and no one will fear the creation of a Palestinian state.

A fanciful pipe dream? Not at all. There is a historical model for just this sort of transformation: the US occupation of Japan.

In 1945, the United States dealt the brutal Japanese empire an annihilating defeat. The atom bomb broke Japan's will to fight and forced upon it the shame of occupation and unconditional surrender. General Douglas MacArthur was Japan's supreme ruler for the next seven years -- years he used to forcibly remake Japanese society. A new constitution was imposed, new laws were written, a new educational system was mandated. The values of democracy were explained and popularized. By the time the occupation ended in 1952, a frenzied warmonger had been transformed into a peaceable democracy, one that remains to this day a trusted ally of the West. The postwar treatment of Germany was much the same.

There are differences, of course -- no one proposes to drop an A-bomb on Gaza -- but what was done to Japan and to Germany can be done to the Palestinians. Pulverizing defeat, followed by occupation and transformation. It would be a blessing to all the peoples of the Middle East -- to the Palestinians above all.

"Pro-Israel Lobby" Is Not Why America Supports Israel

Dennis Prager
"By permission of Dennis Prager and Creator's Syndicate, Inc."
July 3, 2002

All those who disagree with American support of Israel -- the Arab world and its supporters in America such as the Council on American-Islamic Relations (CAIR), the left and the State Department (privately, if not publicly) -- explain American support of Israel by attributing it to the "pro-Israel lobby" and its alleged power over Congress.

This is a thought-through charge that has both explicit and implicit meanings.

Explicitly, it means that were it not for the power of a special interest group, the "pro-Israel lobby," America would not support Israel. Therefore, this lobby -- and by implication the pro-Israel position itself -- does not serve America's interests and may therefore even be somewhat disloyal.

Implicitly, "pro-Israel lobby" means "American Jews," thereby suggesting that this small percentage of Americans is responsible for America's support of Israel.

Given the grave implications of this charge -- that pro-Israel policy is against America's interests and that Jews and their money are the reasons for American support of Israel -- it is very important to clarify why the charge is untrue.

The first reason is that it ignores Christians, specifically evangelical Christians. These Americans have supplanted Jewish Americans as the most powerful support group for Israel. They believe the Bible when it says, in Genesis, that the Creator will bless those who bless the Jews and curse those who curse the Jews. They are, incidentally, quite right: America and the Arab world today are examples of that biblical promise. They also believe that the return of the Jews to Israel was prophesied thousands of years ago in the Bible.

This, more than any other single factor, explains the powerful support given to Israel by President George W. Bush. The president is a Bible-believing Christian (and therefore considerably more supportive of Israel than his father, whose Christianity was more "mainstream Protestant"). If the "pro-Israel lobby" were the reason for American support of Israel, and if it were synonymous with Jews, President Bush would hardly be susceptible to its influence. President Bush received few Jews' votes and few Jews' money.

The second error is to suppose that pro-Israel support is a function of politics and money. Opponents of Israel and the Jews do not want to acknowledge that most congressmen support Israel because their values impel them to do so. Most Americans have a strong preference for free societies over tyrannies and understand that the real underdog in the Middle East is the tiny state of Israel struggling to survive in a sea of medieval hate.

Has Vice President Dick Cheney always supported Israel because of the "pro-Israel lobby's" efforts? Was the former Wyoming congressman beholden to Wyoming's

268

Jewish electorate? Or does he support Israel because of his values?

What about Secretary of Defense Donald Rumsfeld? To what lobby is he (an appointed, not elected, official) beholden?

And what about Condoleezza Rice? What influence does any lobby have with her?

The third error in attributing support for Israel to the "pro-Israel lobby" and to using that term as a euphemism for American Jews is that many American Jews do not support Israel. Many Jews are leftists -- that is their identity as well the source of their values, not Judaism. Anti-Israel rhetoric from Jews is so common that letters to the editor about the Middle East signed with a Jewish surname are now almost as likely to be anti-Israel as pro-Israel.

American support for Israel emanates from the deepest of America's core values -- support for societies that reflect American values and opposition to those that threaten such societies. Of course, there are Jews and Christians and atheists and Democrats and Republicans who lobby Congress on Israel's behalf, and they have clout. But in the final analysis, it is a libel of America, its president and its Congress to assert that they have all sold their souls for a pot of gold, when in fact their pro-Israel policies and votes reflect America at its best.

Become A Muslim Warrior

Daniel Pipes
Jerusalem Post
July 3, 2002

"Become a Muslim warrior during the crusades or during an ancient jihad." Thus read the instructions for seventh graders in Islam: A Simulation of Islamic History and Culture, 610-1100, a three-week curriculum produced by Interaction Publishers, Inc. In classrooms across the United States, students who follow its directions find themselves fighting mock battles of jihad against "Christian crusaders" and other assorted "infidels." Upon gaining victory, our mock-Muslim warriors "Praise Allah."

Is this a legal activity in American public schools? Interaction says it merely urges students to "respect Islamic culture" through identification with Islam. But the Thomas More Law Center, a public-interest law firm based in Michigan, disagrees and last week filed a federal lawsuit to prohibit one school district, in Byron, California, from further using the Interaction materials on Islam.

The Interaction unit contains many other controversial elements. It has students adopt a Muslim name ("Abdallah," "Karima," etc.). It has them wear Islamic clothing: For girls this means a long-sleeved dress and the head covered by a scarf. Students unwilling to wear Islamic clothes must sit mutely in the back of the class, seemingly punished for remaining Westerners. Interaction calls for many Islamic activities: taking off shoes, washing hands, sitting on prayer rugs, and practicing Arabic calligraphy.

Students study the Koran, recite from it, design a title page for it, and write verses of it on a banner. They act out Islam's Five Pillars of Faith, including giving zakat (Islamic alms) and going on the pilgrimage to Mecca. They also build a replica of the "sacred Kaaba" in Mecca or another holy building.

It goes on. Seventh graders adopt the speech of pious believers, greeting each other with "assalam aleikoom, fellow Muslims" and using phrases such as "God willing" and "Allah has power over all things."

They pronounce the militant Islamic war-cry, Allahu akbar ("God is great.") They must even adopt Muslim mannerisms: "Try a typical Muslim gesture where the right hand moves solemnly... across the heart to express sincerity."

In the same pious spirit, the curriculum presents matters of Islamic faith as historical fact. The Kaaba, "originally built by Adam," it announces, "was later rebuilt by Abraham and his son Ismail." Really? That is Islamic belief, not verifiable history. In the year 610, Interaction goes on, "while Prophet Muhammad meditated in a cave ... the angel Gabriel visited him" and revealed to him God's Message" (yes, that's Message with a capital "M.") The curriculum sometimes lapses into referring to "we" Muslims and even prompts students to ask if they should "worship Prophet Muhammad, God, or both."

The Thomas More Law Center is absolutely correct: This simulation blatantly contradicts Supreme Court rulings which permit public schools to teach about religion on condition that they do not promote it. Interaction openly promotes the Islamic faith, contrary to what a public school should do. As Richard Thompson of the center notes, the Byron school district "crossed way over the constitutional line when it coerced impressionable 12-year-olds to engage in particular religious rituals and worship, simulated or not."

Islam: A Simulation serves as a recruitment tool for Islam, for children adopting a Muslim persona during several weeks amounts to an invitation to them to convert to Islam. (One can't but wonder did John Walker Lindh take this course?) The educational establishment permits this infraction due to an impulse to privilege non-Western cultures over Western ones. It never, for example, would permit Christianity to be promoted in like fashion ("Become a Christian warrior during the crusades," for example.)

Militant Islamic lobbying groups want Islam taught as the true religion, not as an academic subject. They take advantage of this indulgence, exerting pressure on school systems and on textbook writers. Not surprisingly, Interaction Publishers thanks two militant Islamic organizations by name (the Islamic Education and Information Center and the Council of Islamic Education) for their "many suggestions."

Americans and other Westerners face a choice: They can insist that Islam, like other religions, be taught in schools objectively. Or, as is increasingly the case, they can permit true believers to design instruction materials about Islam that serve as a mechanism for proselytizing. The answer will substantially affect the future course of militant Islam in the West.

Solving The "Arab Problem"

Jack Kemp
Copley News Service
July 12, 2002

In a startling U.N. report, Arab Human Development Report 2002, a team of Arab scholars, led by Jordan's former Deputy Prime Minister Rima Khalaf Hunaidi, examined the following question: "Why is Arab culture, why are Arab countries lagging behind?"

The report confirmed that during the past 20 years, per capita income growth in Arab countries, which averaged a stagnant 0.5 percent a year, was the lowest in the world with the exception of sub-Saharan Africa. Labor productivity declined 0.2 percent while unemployment averaged 15 percent, three times the world average.

The report concluded that a paucity of resources is not the problem: The Arab world is "richer than it is developed. Arab countries have the resources to eradicate absolute poverty in less than a generation." Instead, the Arab report identified "three deficits" that pose "serious obstacles to human development: freedom, empowerment of women and knowledge."

Democracy, the report found, "has barely reached the Arab states," and a third of the adult population is illiterate -- half of all Arab women cannot read or write. "This freedom deficit undermines human development." Ranking countries on a widely used freedom index that encompasses civil liberties, political rights, freedom of the press and government accountability, the Arab world finished dead last. Women, in particular, are oppressed, denied freedom to move about, attain an education, engage in commerce or even receive adequate medical care.

While the report was a remarkably courageous exercise in self-examination by Arab scholars, there was one conspicuous omission. It neglected to recognize a fourth deficit of no less importance to the equation of social progress: a tolerance deficit.

Tolerance and liberty are the interlocking pillars of a free society. Liberty means having the freedom to think and advocate anything you desire and to live your life any way you want, so long as doing so does not encroach on other people's freedom do the same.

Tolerance means granting that same freedom to others, and the tolerance deficit in the Arab countries is glaring. It can be measured by their abysmal record on religious tolerance. According to a global survey of religious freedom by Freedom House in December 2000, "The religious areas with the largest current restrictions on religious freedom are countries with an Islamic background." Not a single Arab country protects religious rights, and most discriminate against non-Muslims. Some, such as Saudi Arabia, prohibit the worship of any religion other than Islam and execute converts.

Religious freedom is of particular importance because by maintaining that the Creator's will is a matter of personal faith, it ensures a society's ability to curb the power of those who seek to impose their "truth." It is no coincidence that in Arab countries where Islam is officially the only path to God, oppression and violence are so often perpetuated in the name of religion. It is in the name of religion that women are subjugated. It is also in the name of religion that political violence is fomented. Some Arab governments have developed sinister apparatuses of indoctrination that use national educational, media and religious institutions to brainwash Arabs, young and old, to hate and kill in the name of Islam -- that is, their "official" version of Islam. Two would-be "moderate" regimes, Egypt and Saudi Arabia, stand out for stoking the flames of intolerance.

As the intellectual and religious centers of the Islamic world, their religious leaders have a great influence on the attitudes of the region. Government-appointed leaders such as the new Mufti of Egypt, Sheikh Dr. Ahmad Al-Tayyeb, have endorsed suicide-killings against Israeli civilians as a religious duty: "The Islamic countries, peoples and rulers alike, must support these martyrdom attacks," he declared in April.

The Egyptian Christian Copt minority is persecuted by the government, and hundreds have been massacred by Islamist groups since 1998. Saudi Television broadcasts weekly sermons from Mecca and Medina that praise jihadist terrorists around the world, call Muslims to rule over the "infidels" and preach the annihilation of Jews."

In his recent speech on the Middle East, President George W. Bush recognized how this infrastructure of intolerance within the Arab world feeds terrorism: "Every leader actually committed to peace will end incitement to violence in official media and publicly denounce homicide bombings." Western democracies and Israel have laws against hate speech and public incitement of violence. It is time that the Arab countries did the same.

Islamic civilization's greatest contributions to science, medicine, architecture and the arts occurred when it showed the most tolerance toward religious minorities. The 21st century can usher in an Arab Renaissance. By erasing the tolerance deficit and showing respect for other religions, Arab democracy can bloom, freedom can flourish and the full potential of the Arab people can be unleashed to close the development gap with the rest of the world.

Palestinian Democracy: Relevant And Realistic

Natan Sharansky
Ha'Aretz
July 22, 2002

Three weeks ago, U.S. President George W. Bush articulated a vision, which is based on a clear understanding that only a democratized Palestinian society can establish a state that will not endanger Israel's security.

One would have expected that the Israeli left, which has long championed the idea of two states living side by side, and which ostensibly supports the advancement of democratic principles, would have celebrated a speech that promoted both. But its reaction was one of profound disappointment.

Apparently, this disappointment stems from a ubiquitous belief that by linking American diplomacy to internal Palestinian reforms, President Bush has made the prospects of peace even more remote. Those who accept this view generally believe that while promoting democracy may be a worthy endeavor, it has little to do with the exigencies of peacemaking. Moreover, even those who accept the notion that Palestinian democracy and Israeli security are interconnected, are nevertheless skeptical about whether democracy can emerge in the Arab world. Put simply, it is widely assumed that the push for Palestinian democratization is either irrelevant, unrealistic or both.

The idea that democracy among our Palestinian neighbors is irrelevant is not new. In fact, one of the central premises behind Oslo was that the non-democratic nature of Arafat's regime - without a Supreme Court, without B'Tselem and without all kinds of bleeding heart liberals - would allow him to combat terror effectively.

From the beginning, I believed that the notion that strong dictators can make a strong peace was a dangerous illusion. In 1993, soon after the Oslo Accords were signed, I argued that by giving PA Chairman Yasser Arafat absolute control over Palestinian lives, we were endangering Israel's security. My concerns did not hinge on my assessment of whether Arafat himself remained an unreformed terrorist, but rather were based on experiences in the Soviet Union that had taught me that there is an inextricable connection between internal repression and external aggression. I believed then that a Palestinian dictatorship, regardless of who was at the helm, would inevitably endanger Israel's security.

In linking American diplomacy to the liberalization of Palestinian society, the Bush administration has clearly shown that promoting democracy is enormously relevant to Middle East peacemaking.

But many on the Israeli left have largely been unmoved by Bush's bold vision. Skeptical that the Palestinians will ever be able to build a free society, they see an American policy that is linked to Palestinian democratization as hopelessly naive. After all, they argue, the Arabs have no democratic tradition that might inspire confidence.

The idea that there are certain peoples whose values are incompatible with democracy has a long pedigree; it resurfaces each time the West is faced by the choice of whether to support a friendly dictator or to interfere in his internal affairs and bring about changes in his regime. It was said of certain Latin America peoples. It was said of the Germans. It was said of the Japanese. It was said of the peoples in the Far East. And of course - of the Russians. Now this is being said of the Arabs - both by the United States in its attitude toward the Saudis, and the Israelis - in their approach to the Palestinians. And, like the other peoples whose values did not prove inimical to democracy, I have no doubt that the Arabs will also prove the skeptics wrong.

The source of my faith is a belief that the essence of democracy has universal appeal. For me, that essence is the right to express one's view and opinions without the fear of imprisonment. While each culture is unique and may have its own ordering of values, I do not believe that any people wants to live in a society where the fear of imprisonment is omnipresent.

Today, the Palestinians live with this fear and do not yet have the opportunity to speak their minds. The institutions of democracy - from a free press to independent courts, from genuine opposition parties to human rights organizations - that enable people to fearlessly express their views are all absent.

Holding elections today in the PA will not change the situation at all. For the Palestinians to have an opportunity to express their opinions freely, it is imperative, first and foremost, to establish and develop stable institutions of democracy. The reforms that are necessary will not create a liberal democracy overnight. But given a genuine chance to build a free society, I have no doubt that the Palestinians will seize it.

Any attempt to leap over the "democratic obstacle" that President Bush has erected reminds me of the attempt to establish a "New Middle East" by bolstering a friendly dictator. Now, as then, the only results that are to be expected are a protracted conflict and brutal terror.

Instead of again making last-ditch efforts to strengthen a dictatorial regime - either under the leadership of Arafat or someone else - the Israeli left should instead join the efforts of aiding the Palestinians in building a free society, thereby helping the two peoples create a stable peace in the region.

What Occupation?

Efraim Karsh
www.frontpagemagazine.com
July 24, 2002

No term has dominated the discourse of the Palestinian-Israeli conflict more than "occupation." For decades now, hardly a day has passed without some mention in the international media of Israel's supposedly illegitimate presence on Palestinian lands. This presence is invoked to explain the origins and persistence of the conflict between the parties, to show Israel's allegedly brutal and repressive nature, and to justify the worst anti-Israel terrorist atrocities. The occupation, in short, has become a catchphrase, and like many catchphrases it means different things to different people.

For most Western observers, the term "occupation" describes Israel's control of the Gaza Strip and the West Bank, areas that it conquered during the Six-Day war of June 1967. But for many Palestinians and Arabs, the Israeli presence in these territories represents only the latest chapter in an uninterrupted story of "occupations" dating back to the very creation of Israel on "stolen" land. If you go looking for a book about Israel in the foremost Arab bookstore on London's Charing Cross Road, you will find it in the section labeled "Occupied Palestine." That this is the prevailing view not only among Arab residents of the West Bank and Gaza but among Palestinians living within Israel itself as well as elsewhere around the world is shown by the routine insistence on a Palestinian "right of return" that is meant to reverse the effects of the "1948 occupation"-i.e., the establishment of the state of Israel itself.

Palestinian intellectuals routinely blur any distinction between Israel's actions before and after 1967. Writing recently in the Israeli daily Ha'aretz, the prominent Palestinian cultural figure Jacques Persiqian told his Jewish readers that today's terrorist attacks were "what you have brought upon yourselves after 54 years of systematic oppression of another people"-a historical accounting that, going back to 1948, calls into question not Israel's presence in the West Bank and Gaza but its very legitimacy as a state.

Hanan Ashrawi, the most articulate exponent of the Palestinian cause, has been even more forthright in erasing the line between post-1967 and pre-1967 "occupations." "I come to you today with a heavy heart," she told the now-infamous World Conference Against Racism in Durban last summer, "leaving behind a nation in captivity held hostage to an ongoing naqba [catastrophe]":

In 1948, we became subject to a grave historical injustice manifested in a dual victimization: on the one hand, the injustice of dispossession, dispersion, and exile forcibly enacted on the population .... On the other hand, those who remained were subjected to the systematic oppression and brutality of an inhuman occupation that robbed them of all their rights and liberties.

This original "occupation"-that is, again, the creation and existence of the state of Israel-was later extended, in Ashrawi's narrative, as a result of the Six-Day war:

Those of us who came under Israeli occupation in 1967 have languished in the West Bank, Jerusalem, and the Gaza Strip under a unique combination of military occupation, settler colonization, and systematic oppression. Rarely has the human mind devised such varied, diverse, and comprehensive means of wholesale brutalization and persecution.

Taken together, the charges against Israel's various "occupations" represent-and are plainly intended to be-a damning indictment of the entire Zionist enterprise. In almost every particular, they are also grossly false.

In 1948, no Palestinian state was invaded or destroyed to make way for the establishment of Israel. From biblical times, when this territory was the state of the Jews, to its occupation by the British army at the end of World War I, Palestine had never existed as a distinct political entity but was rather part of one empire after another, from the Romans, to the Arabs, to the Ottomans. When the British arrived in 1917, the imme-diate loyalties of the area's inhabitants were parochial-to clan, tribe, village, town, or religious sect-and coexisted with their fealty to the Ottoman sultan-caliph as the reli-gious and temporal head of the world Muslim community.

Under a League of Nations mandate explicitly meant to pave the way for the creation of a Jewish national home, the British established the notion of an independ-ent Palestine for the first time and delineated its boundaries. In 1947, confronted with a determined Jewish struggle for independence, Britain returned the mandate to the League's successor, the United Nations, which in turn decided on November 29, 1947, to partition mandatory Palestine into two states: one Jewish, the other Arab.

The state of Israel was thus created by an internationally recognized act of national self-determination-an act, moreover, undertaken by an ancient people in its own homeland. In accordance with common democratic practice, the Arab population in the new state's midst was immediately recognized as a legitimate ethnic and religious minor-ity. As for the prospective Arab state, its designated territory was slated to include, among other areas, the two regions under contest today-namely, Gaza and the West Bank (with the exception of Jerusalem, which was to be placed under international control).

As is well known, the implementation of the UN's partition plan was aborted by the effort of the Palestinians and of the surrounding Arab states to destroy the Jewish state at birth. What is less well known is that even if the Jews had lost the war, their ter-ritory would not have been handed over to the Palestinians. Rather, it would have been divided among the invading Arab forces, for the simple reason that none of the region's Arab regimes viewed the Palestinians as a distinct nation. As the eminent Arab-American historian Philip Hitti described the common Arab view to an Anglo-American commis-sion of inquiry in 1946, "There is no such thing as Palestine in history, absolutely not."

This fact was keenly recognized by the British authorities on the eve of their depar-ture. As one official observed in mid-December 1947, "it does not appear that Arab Palestine will be an entity, but rather that the Arab countries will each claim a portion in return for their assistance [in the war against Israel], unless [Transjordan's] King Abdallah takes rapid and firm action as soon as the British withdrawal is completed." A couple of months later, the British high commissioner for Palestine, General Sir Alan Cunningham, informed the colonial secretary, Arthur Creech Jones, that "the most likely arrangement seems to be Eastern Galilee to Syria, Samaria and Hebron to Abdallah, and the south to Egypt."

The British proved to be prescient. Neither Egypt nor Jordan ever allowed

Palestinian self-determination in Gaza and the West Bank-- which were, respectively, the parts of Palestine conquered by them during the 1948-49 war. Indeed, even UN Security Council Resolution 242, which after the Six-Day war of 1967 established the principle of "land for peace" as the cornerstone of future Arab-Israeli peace negotiations, did not envisage the creation of a Palestinian state. To the contrary: since the Palestinians were still not viewed as a distinct nation, it was assumed that any territories evacuated by Israel, would be returned to their pre-1967 Arab occupiers-Gaza to Egypt, and the West Bank to Jordan. The resolution did not even mention the Palestinians by name, affirming instead the necessity "for achieving a just settlement of the refugee problem"-a clause that applied not just to the Palestinians but to the hundreds of thousands of Jews expelled from the Arab states following the 1948 war.

At this time-we are speaking of the late 1960's-- Palestinian nationhood was rejected by the entire international community, including the Western democracies, the Soviet Union (the foremost supporter of radical Arabism), and the Arab world itself. "Moderate" Arab rulers like the Hashemites in Jordan viewed an independent Palestinian state as a mortal threat to their own kingdom, while the Saudis saw it as a potential source of extremism and instability. Pan-Arab nationalists were no less adamantly opposed, having their own purposes in mind for the region. As late as 1974, Syrian President Hafez alAssad openly referred to Palestine as "not only a part of the Arab homeland but a basic part of southern Syria"; there is no reason to think he had changed his mind by the time of his death in 2000.

Nor, for that matter, did the populace of the West Bank and Gaza regard itself as a distinct nation. The collapse and dispersion of Palestinian society following the 1948 defeat had shattered an always fragile communal fabric, and the subsequent physical separation of the various parts of the Palestinian diaspora prevented the crystallization of a national identity. Host Arab regimes actively colluded in discouraging any such sense from arising. Upon occupying the West Bank during the 1948 war, King Abdallah had moved quickly to erase all traces of corporate Palestinian identity. On April 4, 1950, the territory was formally annexed to Jordan, its residents became Jordanian citizens, and they were increasingly integrated into the kingdom's economic, political, and social structures.

For its part, the Egyptian government showed no desire to annex the Gaza Strip but had instead ruled the newly acquired area as an occupied military zone. This did not imply support of Palestinian nationalism, however, or of any sort of collective political awareness among the Palestinians. The local population was kept under tight control, was denied Egyptian citizenship, and was subjected to severe restrictions on travel.

What, then, of the period after 1967, when these territories passed into the hands of Israel? Is it the case that Palestinians in the West Bank and Gaza have been the victims of the most "varied, diverse, and comprehensive means of wholesale brutalization and persecution" ever devised by the human mind?

At the very least, such a characterization would require a rather drastic downgrading of certain other well-documented 20th-century phenomena, from the slaughter of Armenians during World War I and onward through a grisly chronicle of tens upon tens of millions murdered, driven out, crushed under the heels of despots. By stark contrast, during the three decades of Israel's control, far fewer Palestinians were killed at Jewish hands than by King Hussein of Jordan in the single month of September 1970 when, fighting off an attempt by Yasir Arafat's PLO to destroy his monarchy, he dispatched (according to the Palestinian scholar Yezid Sayigh) between 3,000 and 5,000 Palestinians, among them anywhere from 1,500 to 3,500 civilians. Similarly, the number of innocent Palestinians killed by their Kuwaiti hosts in the winter of 1991, in revenge for the PLO's support for Saddam Hussein's brutal occupation of Kuwait, far exceeds the number of Palestinian rioters and terrorists who lost their lives in the first intifada against Israel during the late 1980's.

Such crude comparisons aside, to present the Israeli occupation of the West Bank and Gaza as "systematic oppression" is itself the inverse of the truth. It should be recalled, first of all, that this occupation did not come about as a consequence of some grand expansionist design, but rather was incidental to Israel's success against a pan-Arab attempt to destroy it. Upon the outbreak of IsraeliEgyptian hostilities on June 5, 1967, the Israeli government secretly pleaded with King Hussein of Jordan, the de-facto ruler of the West Bank, to forgo any military action; the plea was rebuffed by the Jordanian monarch, who was loathe to lose the anticipated spoils of what was to be the Arabs' "final round" with Israel.

Thus it happened that, at the end of the conflict, Israel unexpectedly found itself in control of some one million Palestinians, with no definite idea about their future status and lacking any concrete policy for their administration. In the wake of the war, the only objective adopted by then-Minister of Defense Moshe Dayan was to preserve normalcy in the territories through a mixture of economic inducements and a minimum of Israeli intervention. The idea was that the local populace would be given the freedom to administer itself as it wished, and would be able to maintain regular contact with the Arab world via the Jordan River bridges. In sharp contrast with, for example, the U.S. occupation of postwar Japan, which saw a general censorship of all Japanese media and a comprehensive revision of school curricula, Israel made no attempt to reshape Palestinian culture. It limited its oversight of the Arabic press in the territories to military and security matters, and allowed the continued use in local schools of Jordanian textbooks filled with vile anti-Semitic and anti-Israel propaganda.

Israel's restraint in this sphere-which turned out to be desperately misguided-is only part of the story. The larger part, still untold in all its detail, is of the astounding social and economic progress made by the Palestinian Arabs under Israeli "oppression." At the inception of the occupation, conditions in the territories were quite dire. Life expectancy was low; malnutrition, infectious diseases, and child mortality were rife; and the level of education was very poor. Prior to the 1967 war, fewer than 60 percent of all male adults had been employed, with unemployment among refugees running as high as 83 percent. Within a brief period after the war, Israeli occupation had led to dramatic improvements in general well-being, placing the population of the territories ahead of most of their Arab neighbors.

In the economic sphere, most of this progress was the result of access to the far larger and more advanced Israeli economy: the number of Palestinians working in Israel rose from zero in 1967 to 66,000 in 1975 and 109,000 by 1986, accounting for 35 percent of the employed population of the West Bank and 45 percent in Gaza. Close to 2,000 industrial plants, employing almost half of the work force, were established in the territories under Israeli rule.

During the 1970's, the West Bank and Gaza constituted the fourth fastest-growing economy in the world-ahead of such "wonders" as Singapore, Hong Kong, and Korea, and substantially ahead of Israel itself. Although GNP per capita grew somewhat more slowly, the rate was still high by international standards, with per-capita GNP expanding tenfold between 1968 and 1991 from $165 to $1,715 (compared with Jordan's $1,050, Egypt's $600, Turkey's $1,630, and Tunisia's $1,440). By 1999, Palestinian per-capita income was nearly double Syria's, more than four times Yemen's, and 10 percent higher than Jordan's (one of the betteroff Arab states). Only the oil-rich Gulf states and Lebanon were more affluent.

Under Israeli rule, the Palestinians also made vast progress in social welfare. Perhaps most significantly, mortality rates in the West Bank and Gaza fell by more than two-thirds between 1970 and 1990, while life expectancy rose from 48 years in 1967 to 72 in 2000 (compared with an average of 68 years for all the countries of the Middle East and North Africa). Israeli medical programs reduced the infant-mortality rate of 60 per 1,000 live births in 1968 to 15 per 1,000 in 2000 (in Iraq the rate is 64, in Egypt 40, in Jordan 23, in Syria 22). And under a systematic program of inoculation, childhood diseases like polio, whooping cough, tetanus, and measles were eradicated.

No less remarkable were advances in the Palestinians' standard of living. By 1986, 92.8 percent of the population in the West Bank and Gaza had electricity around the clock, as compared to 20.5 percent in 1967; 85 percent had running water in dwellings, as compared to 16 percent in 1967; 83.5 percent had electric or gas ranges for cooking, as compared to 4 percent in 1967; and so on for refrigerators, televisions, and cars.

Finally, and perhaps most strikingly, during the two decades preceding the intifada of the late 1980's, the number of schoolchildren in the territories grew by 102 percent, and the number of classes by 99 percent, though the population itself had grown by only 28 percent. Even more dramatic was the progress in higher education. At the time of the Israeli occupation of Gaza and the West Bank, not a single university existed in these territories. By the early 1990's, there were seven such institutions, boasting some 16,500 students. Illiteracy rates dropped to 14 percent of adults over age 15, compared with 69 percent in Morocco, 61 percent in Egypt, 45 percent in Tunisia, and 44 percent in Syria.

All this, as I have noted, took place against the backdrop of Israel's hands-off policy in the political and administrative spheres. Indeed, even as the PLO (until 1982 headquartered in Lebanon and thereafter in Tunisia) proclaimed its ongoing commitment to the destruction of the Jewish state, the Israelis did surprisingly little to limit its political influence in the territories. The publication of proPLO editorials was permitted in the local press, and anti-Israel activities by PLO supporters were tolerated so long as they did not involve overt incitements to violence. Israel also allowed the free flow of PLO-controlled funds, a policy justified by Minister of Defense Ezer Weizmann in 1978 in these (deluded) words: "It does not matter that they get money from the PLO, as long as they don't build arms factories with it." Nor, with very few exceptions, did Israel encourage the formation of Palestinian political institutions that might serve as a counterweight to the PLO. As a result, the PLO gradually established itself as the predominant force in the territories, relegating the pragmatic traditional leadership to the fringes of the political system.*

Given the extreme and even self-destructive leniency of Israel's administrative policies, what seems remarkable is that it took as long as it did for the PLO to entice the residents of the West Bank and Gaza into a popular struggle against the Jewish state. Here Israel's counterinsurgency measures must be given their due, as well as the low level of national consciousness among the Palestinians and the sheer rapidity and scope of the improvements in their standard of living. The fact remains, however, that during the twoand-a-half decades from the occupation of the territories to the onset of the Oslo peace process in 1993, there was very little "armed resistance," and most terrorist attacks emanated from outside-from Jordan in the late 1960's, then from Lebanon.

In an effort to cover up this embarrassing circumstance, Fatah, the PLO's largest constituent organization, adopted the slogan that "there is no difference between inside and outside." But there was a difference, and a rather fundamental one. By and large, the residents of the territories wished to get on with their lives and take advantage of the opportunities afforded by Israeli rule. Had the West Bank eventually been returned to Jordan, its residents, all of whom had been Jordanian citizens before 1967, might well have reverted to that status. Alternatively, had Israel prevented the spread of the PLO's influence in the territories, a local leadership, better attuned to the real interests and desires of the people and more amenable to peaceful coexistence with Israel, might have emerged.

But these things were not to be. By the mid1970's, the PLO had made itself into the "sole representative of the Palestinian people," and in short order Jordan and Egypt washed their hands of the West Bank and Gaza. Whatever the desires of the people living in the territories, the PLO had vowed from the moment of its founding in the mid1960's-well before the Six-Day war-to pursue its "revolution until victory," that is, until the destruction of the Jewish state. Once its position was secure, it proceeded to do precisely that.

By the mid-1990's, thanks to Oslo, the PLO had achieved a firm foothold in the West Bank and Gaza. Its announced purpose was to lay the groundwork for Palestinian statehood but its real purpose was to do what it knew best-namely, create an extensive terrorist infrastructure and use it against its Israeli "peace partner." At first it did this tacitly, giving a green light to other terrorist organizations like Hamas and Islamic Jihad; then it operated openly and directly.

But what did all this have to do with Israel's "occupation"? The declaration signed on the White House lawn in 1993 by the PLO and the Israeli government provided for Palestinian self-rule in the entire West Bank and the Gaza Strip for a transitional period not to exceed five years, during which Israel and the Palestinians would negotiate a permanent peace settlement. During this interim period the territories would be administered by a Palestinian Council, to be freely and democratically elected after the withdrawal of Israeli military forces both from the Gaza Strip and from the populated areas of the West Bank.

By May 1994, Israel had completed its withdrawal from the Gaza Strip (apart from a small stretch of territory containing Israeli settlements) and the Jericho area of the West Bank. On July 1, Yasir Arafat made his triumphant entry into Gaza. On September 28, 1995, despite Arafat's abysmal failure to clamp down on terrorist activities in the territories now under his control, the two parties signed an interim agreement, and by the end of the year Israeli forces had been withdrawn from the West Bank's populated areas with the exception of Hebron (where redeployment was completed in early 1997). On January 20, 1996, elections to the Palestinian Council were held, and shortly afterward both the Israeli civil administration and military government were dissolved.

The geographical scope of these Israeli withdrawals was relatively limited; the surrendered land amounted to some 30 percent of the West Bank's overall territory. But its impact on the Palestinian population was nothing short of revolutionary. At one fell swoop, Israel relinquished control over virtually all of the West Bank's 1.4 million residents. Since that time, nearly 60 percent of them-in the Jericho area and in the seven main cities of Jenin, Nablus, Tulkarm, Qalqilya, Ramallah, Bethlehem, and Hebron-have lived entirely under Palestinian jurisdiction. Another 40 percent live in towns, villages, refugee camps, and hamlets where the Palestinian Authority exercises civil authority but, in line with the Oslo accords, Israel has maintained "overriding responsibility for security." Some two percent of the West Bank's population-tens of thousands of Palestinians-continue to live in areas where Israel has complete control, but even there the Palestinian Authority maintains "functional jurisdiction."

In short, since the beginning of 1996, and certainly following the completion of the redeployment from Hebron in January 1997, 99 percent of the Palestinian population of the West Bank and the Gaza Strip have not lived under Israeli occupation. By no conceivable stretching of words can the anti-Israel violence emanating from the territories during these years be made to qualify as resistance to foreign occupation. In these years there has been no such occupation.

If the stubborn persistence of Palestinian terrorism is not attributable to the continuing occupation, many of the worst outrages against Israeli civilians likewise occurred-contrary to the mantra of Palestinian spokesmen and their apologists-not at moments of breakdown in the Oslo "peace process" but at its high points, when the prospect of Israeli withdrawal appeared brightest and most imminent.

Suicide bombings, for example, were introduced in the atmosphere of euphoria only a few months after the historic Rabin-Arafat handshake on the White House lawn: eight people were murdered in April 1994 while riding a bus in the town of Afula. Six months later, 21 Israelis were murdered on a bus in Tel Aviv. In the following year, five bombings took the lives of a further 38 Israelis. During the short-lived government of the dovish Shimon Peres (November 1995-May 1996), after the assassination of Yitzhak Rabin, 58 Israelis were murdered within the span of one week in three suicide bombings in Jerusalem and Tel Aviv.

Further disproving the standard view is the fact that terrorism was largely curtailed following Benjamin Netanyahu's election in May 1996 and the consequent slowdown in the Oslo process. During Netanyahu's three years in power, some 50 Israelis were murdered in terrorist attacks-a third of the casualty rate during the Rabin government and a sixth of the casualty rate during Peres's term.

There was a material side to this downturn in terrorism as well. Between 1994 and 1996, the Rabin and Peres governments had imposed repeated closures on the territories in order to stem the tidal wave of terrorism in the wake of the Oslo accords. This had led to a steep drop in the Palestinian economy. With workers unable to get into Israel, unemployment rose sharply, reaching as high as 50 percent in Gaza. The movement of goods between Israel and the territories, as well as between the West Bank and Gaza, was seriously disrupted, slowing exports and discouraging potential private investment.

The economic situation in the territories began to improve during the term of the Netanyahu government, as the steep fall in terrorist attacks led to a corresponding decrease in closures. Real GNP per capita grew by 3.5 percent in 1997, 7.7 percent in 1998, and 3.5 percent in 1999, while unemployment was more than halved. By the beginning of 1999, according to the World Bank, the West Bank and Gaza had fully recovered from the economic decline of the previous years.

Then, in still another turnabout, came Ehud Barak, who in the course of a dizzying six months in late 2000 and early 2001 offered Yasir Arafat a complete end to the Israeli presence, ceding virtually the entire West Bank and the Gaza Strip to the nascent Palestinian state together with some Israeli territory, and making breathtaking concessions over Israel's capital city of Jerusalem. To this, however, Arafat's response was war. Since its launch, the Palestinian campaign has inflicted thousands of brutal attacks on Israeli civilians-suicide bombings, drive-by shootings, stabbings, lynching, stonings-murdering more than 500 and wounding some 4,000.

In the entire two decades of Israeli occupation preceding the Oslo accords, some 400 Israelis were murdered; since the conclusion of that "peace" agreement, twice as many have lost their lives in terrorist attacks. If the occupation was the cause of terrorism, why was terrorism sparse during the years of actual occupation, why did it increase dramatically with the prospect of the end of the occupation, and why did it escalate into open war upon Israel's most far-reaching concessions ever? To the contrary, one might argue with far greater plausibility that the absence of occupation-that is, the withdrawal of close Israeli surveillance-is precisely what facilitated the launching of the terrorist war in the first place.

There are limits to Israel's ability to transform a virulent enemy into a peace partner, and those limits have long since been reached. To borrow from Baruch Spinoza, peace is not the absence of war but rather a state of mind: a disposition to benevolence, confidence, and justice. From the birth of the Zionist movement until today, that disposition has remained conspicuously absent from the mind of the Palestinian leadership.

It is not the 1967 occupation that led to the Palestinians' rejection of peaceful coexistence and their pursuit of violence. Palestinian terrorism started well before 1967, and continued-and intensified-after the occupation ended in all but name. Rather, what is at fault is the perduring Arab view that the creation of the Jewish state was itself an original act of "inhuman occupation" with which compromise of any final kind is beyond the realm of the possible. Until that disposition changes, which is to say until a different leadership arises, the idea of peace in the context of the Arab Middle East will continue to mean little more than the continuation of war by other means.

Think Again: Yasir Arafat

By Dennis B. Ross
Foreign Policy Magazine
July/August 2002

In 1974, Yasir Arafat, chairman of the Palestine Liberation Organization (PLO), declared before the United Nations that he came "bearing an olive branch and a freedom-fighter's gun." Nearly 20 years later, the world still does not know if Arafat is a statesman dedicated to peaceful coexistence with Israel or a resistance leader dedicated to armed struggle. As the Israeli-Palestinian conflict enters a tenuous new phase of peace negotiations, understanding Arafat's true motives will be essential to fostering a lasting agreement.

"Arafat's Goal Is a Lasting Peace With the State of Israel"

I doubt it. Throughout the Oslo peace process, everyone involved—Palestinians, Israelis, Americans, Egyptians, Saudis, and other Arab leaders—shared the belief that Arafat wanted peace with Israel. It seemed logical. After all, Arafat had crossed the threshold and recognized Israel, incurring the wrath of secular and religious rejectionists. And he had authorized five limited or interim agreements with the Israelis. Although Arafat held out until the last possible minute and strived for the best deal, he eventually made the compromises necessary to reach those interim agreements.

Unfortunately, such short-term progress masked some disquieting signals about the Palestinian leader's intentions. Every agreement he made was limited and contained nothing he regarded as irrevocable. He was not, in his eyes, required to surrender any claims. Worse, notwithstanding his commitment to renounce violence, he has never relinquished the terror card. Moreover, he is always quick to exaggerate his achievements, even while maintaining an ongoing sense of grievance. During the Oslo peace process, he never prepared his public for compromise. Instead, he led the Palestinians to believe the peace process would produce everything they ever wanted—and he implicitly suggested a return to armed struggle if negotiations fell short of those unattainable goals. Even in good times, Arafat spoke to Palestinian groups about how the struggle, the jihad, would lead them to Jerusalem. Too often his partners in the peace process dismissed this behavior as Arafat being caught up in rhetorical flourishes in front of his "party" faithful. I myself pressed him when his language went too far or provoked an angry Israeli response, but his stock answer was that he was just talking about the importance of struggling for rights through the negotiation process.

But from the start of the Oslo negotiations in 1993, Arafat focused only on what he was going to receive, not what he had to give. He found it difficult to live without a cause, a struggle, a grievance, and a conflict to define him. Arafat never faced up to what he would have to do—even though we tried repeatedly to condition him. As a result, when he was finally put to the test with former President Bill Clinton's proposal in December 2000, Arafat failed miserably.

Is there any sign that Arafat has changed and is ready to make historic decisions for peace? I see no indication of it. Even his sudden readiness to seize the mantle of reform is the result of intense pressure from Palestinians and the international community. He is maneuvering now to avoid real reform, not to implement it. And on peace, he does not

284

appear ready to acknowledge the opportunity that existed with Clinton's plan, nor does he seem willing to confront the myths of the Palestinian movement.

"Arafat Missed a Historic Opportunity When He Turned Down the Clinton Proposal"

Yes. It is true that Arafat did not "reject" the ideas the Clinton administration offered in December 2000. Instead, he pulled a classic Arafat: He did not say yes or no. He wanted it both ways. He wanted to keep talking as if the Clinton proposal was the opening gambit in a negotiation, but he knew otherwise. Arafat knew Clinton's plan represented the culmination of the American effort. He also knew these ideas were offered as the best judgment of what each side could live with and that the proposal would be withdrawn if not accepted.

To this day, Arafat has never honestly admitted what was offered to the Palestinians—a deal that would have resulted in a Palestinian state, with territory in over 97 percent of the West Bank, Gaza, and Jerusalem; with Arab East Jerusalem as the capital of that state (including the holy place of the Haram al-Sharif, the Noble Sanctuary); with an international presence in place of the Israeli Defense Force in the Jordan Valley; and with the unlimited right of return for Palestinian refugees to their state but not to Israel. Nonetheless, Arafat continues to hide behind the canard that he was offered Bantustans—a reference to the geographically isolated black homelands created by the apartheid-era South African government. Yet with 97 percent of the territory in Palestinian hands, there would have been no cantons. Palestinian areas would not have been isolated or surrounded. There would have been territorial integrity and contiguity in both the West Bank and Gaza, and there would have been independent borders with Egypt and Jordan.

"The offer was never written" is a refrain uttered time and again by apologists for Chairman Arafat as a way of suggesting that no real offer existed and that therefore Arafat did not miss a historic opportunity. Nothing could be more ridiculous or misleading. President Clinton himself presented both sides with his proposal word by word. I stayed behind to be certain both sides had recorded each word accurately. Given Arafat's negotiating style, Clinton was not about to formalize the proposal, making it easier for Arafat to use the final offer as just a jumping-off point for more ceaseless bargaining in the future.

However, it is worth pondering how Palestinians would have reacted to a public presentation of Clinton's plan. Had Palestinians honestly known what Arafat was unwilling to accept, would they have supported violence against the Israelis, particularly given the suffering imposed on them? Would Arafat have remained the "only Palestinian" capable of making peace? Perhaps such domestic pressure would have convinced Arafat, the quintessential survivor, that the political costs of intransigence would be higher than the costs of making difficult concessions to Israel.

"Arab Leaders Stand Behind Arafat"

Reluctantly. I have never met an Arab leader who trusts Arafat or has anything good to say about him in private. Almost all Arab leaders have stories about how he has misled or betrayed them. Most simply wave their hands dismissively when examples of his betrayal of commitments are cited—almost as if they are saying, "We know, we know." The Saudis, in particular, saw his alignment with Iraqi President Saddam Hussein in 1991 as proof of his perfidy.

But no Arab leader is prepared to challenge him. All acknowledge him as the symbol of the Palestinian movement, and no one sees an alternative to him. But no one is prepared to go out on a limb for him, either.

Many suggest that in the absence of broad Arab support, Clinton's proposal was too hard for Arafat to accept. Furthermore, some argue, since the United States failed to secure the support Arafat needed, it bears some responsibility for his inability to say yes. That argument is more myth than reality. First, if Clinton's offer was so hard to accept, why has Arafat never honestly portrayed it? Why not say he was offered 97 percent, instead of Bantustans or cantons? Why not admit he would have had Arab East Jerusalem as the capital of the state, instead of denying that?

Second, we did line up the support of five key Arab leaders for Clinton's plan. On December 23, 2000, the same day that President Clinton presented his ideas to Israeli and Palestinian negotiators, he called Egyptian President Hosni Mubarak, Saudi Crown Prince Abdullah, and Jordanian King Abdullah ii to convey the comprehensive proposal he had just presented to the parties. Shortly thereafter, he also transmitted the ideas to King Mohammed IV of Morocco and President Zine al-Abidine Ben Ali of Tunisia. All these Arab leaders made clear they thought Clinton's ideas were historic, and they pledged to press Arafat to accept the plan. However, when Arafat told Arab leaders he had questions, they backed off and assumed the position they had adopted throughout the Oslo peace process. They would support whatever Chairman Arafat accepted. They were not about to put themselves in a position in which Arafat might claim that President Mubarak or Crown Prince Abdullah or King Abdullah was trying to pressure him to surrender Palestinian rights.

There is a lesson here for today: Getting Arab leaders to fulfill their responsibilities—to be participants and not just observers—is essential. On existential questions in which concessions on the Palestinian side are required, Arab leaders will likely restrict their pressure to private entreaties. But that is not where real leverage is to be found. Pressure in public would be pressure as Arafat defines it. Arafat's great achievement for the Palestinians has been putting them on the map, producing recognition, giving them standing on the world stage. He embodies the cause, and that is why Arab leaders find it so hard to criticize him in public. Yet he cannot afford the imagery that he and the Palestinian cause are separate. If Arab leaders would say that his being only a symbol and not a leader threatens Palestinian interests, then Arafat's very identity would be called into question. That would move him.

"The World Must Deal With Arafat Since He Is the Palestinians' Elected Leader"

Not necessarily. The United States, Russia, the European Union, and the United Nations have adopted this position. An election in the territories in 1996 made Arafat the chairman of the Palestinian Authority. But the international community does the Palestinians no favor when it emphasizes Arafat's popular election as justification for dealing with him. It is important to remember that anger on Palestinian streets before the eruption of the Al-Aqsa Intifada was directed against Israel and also against the corruption and ineptitude of the Palestinian Authority. Now that the dust is settling after Israeli military operations and massive reconstruction is needed in the West Bank, Palestinians are demanding reform. They are demanding elections, rule of law, an independent judiciary, transparency, accountability, streamlined security services governed by standards (not by Arafat's whims), and an end to corruption.

Palestinians are not looking to oust Chairman Arafat. They simply want to limit his arbitrary use of power. Given the pressure he is under (from within, from among Arabs to stop manipulating violence and to assume responsibility, and from the international community), it is not hard to see why Arafat is trying to seize the mantle of reform. Yet he cannot be permitted to speak of reform and at the same time avoid its consequences. Otherwise, the momentum will be lost. True reform is an essential part of any political process designed to promote peace. The more serious the reform, the more the Israeli public will see that Palestinian behavior is changing—and the more likely Israel will accept the possibility of partnership again. If Arafat is allowed to escape pressure for genuine reform, the Israeli government will be under no pressure to resume political negotiations.

One could argue that the world must deal with Arafat because he is the symbol of the Palestinian movement, because he is the only address available, and because he is the only one who can be held responsible for Palestinian behavior. That would be a more honest explanation than saying he is the popularly elected leader of the Palestinians. However, Arafat's role as a symbol is not the reason the U.S. government recognized him in the first place. The United States made the decision to deal directly with Arafat in September 1993 when, as part of the Oslo documents, he formally agreed to renounce terror, to discipline and punish any Palestinian violators of that pledge, and to settle all disputes peacefully. Suffice to say, Arafat has not abided by those commitments.

No one but the Palestinians can choose the Palestinian leader. But the rest of the world can choose not to deal with a leader who fails to fulfill obligations. Governments can tell the Palestinian public they recognize it has legitimate aspirations that must be addressed and that those aspirations can only be addressed politically, not militarily. But those aspirations will not be satisfied until Palestinians have a leadership—whether it is Arafat, a successor, or a collective body that limits the chairman's power—that will fulfill its responsibilities on security and declare that suicide bombers are enemies of the Palestinian cause. When a Palestinian leadership lives up to those commitments, the Palestinians and the Arab world will have an American partner determined to help ensure that Palestinian needs are met.

"Arafat Can't Control the Militants in the Palestinian Authority"

He can, but he won't. Arafat has demonstrated in the past that he can prevent violence—most notably in the spring of 1996 when he cracked down on Hamas and also in the first year of former Prime Minister Ehud Barak's administration, when Israel, for the only time in its history, had a year in which it did not suffer a single fatality from terror.

Yet from the beginning of the peace process, Arafat made clear he prefers to co-opt, not confront, extremist groups. This approach reflects his leadership style: He never closes doors. He never forecloses options. He never knows when he might want to have a particular group, no matter what its ideology or purpose, on his side. This strategy has certainly been true of his dealings with Hamas and Islamic Jihad. In 1996, he suppressed extremists because they were threatening his power, not because they carried out four suicide bombings in Israel in nine days. Even then, the crackdown, while real, was limited. Arafat did not completely shut the door on either group.

In the past, whenever Arafat cracked down or threatened to do so, the militants backed down. But that stopped in September 2000 with the eruption of the Al-Aqsa Intifada. Those who say Arafat cannot carry out his security responsibilities because Israeli military incursions have devastated his capabilities fail to recognize that Arafat didn't act even before Israelis destroyed his infrastructure. In the 20 months leading up to May 2002, he never gave unequivocal orders to arrest, much less stop, those who were planning, organizing, recruiting, financing, or implementing terror attacks against Israelis. Whether one thinks—as the Israelis believe recently captured documents demonstrate—Arafat directs the violence or that he simply acquiesces to it, the unmistakable fact is that he has made no serious or sustained effort to stop the violence.

If nothing else, it is time for Arafat to use his moral authority to make clear that armed struggle only threatens the Palestinian cause—that those who persist in the violence are not martyrs but enemies of Palestinian interests and needs. Let him make such declarations consistently, rather than repeating the pattern of the past as when he called for a cease-fire on December 16, 2001, only to call for a million martyrs to march on Jerusalem shortly thereafter. Pressing Arafat to speak out consistently does not relieve him of the need to act. Nor does it relieve the Israelis of finding a way to meet their legitimate security needs without making the Palestinians suffer. Ultimately, keeping the territories under siege is self-defeating. This approach only fosters anger and a desire to make Israelis feel comparable pain. The Israeli military has succeeded in creating a necessary respite from terrorist attacks. Now Israel should seek a political path that builds on that respite and gives Palestinians an interest in making it more enduring.

"The Time Has Come to Impose a Peace Deal on Arafat and Sharon"

Absolutely not. Nearly two years of conflict, the spiraling violence, the deepening sense of gloom, and the seeming inability of the two sides to do anything on their own give credence to the argument that now is the time to impose a solution. If an imposed solution were possible and would hold, I would be prepared to support it. But an imposed solution is an illusion.

No Israeli government (not Ariel Sharon's, not Ehud Barak's, not Benjamin Netanyahu's, not Shimon Peres's) has accepted or will accept an imposed outcome. It goes against the Israeli ethos that a partner for peace must prove its commitment by directly negotiating an agreement. Paradoxically, the very terms Israeli governments might find difficult to accept if imposed would probably be acceptable if Israelis believed they had a real partner for peace. Those who argue for an imposed solution claim no Israeli leader can make the hard decisions, such as giving up settlements, most of the West Bank and Gaza, and the Arab part of East Jerusalem. Yet Barak was prepared to do so; and before the Al-Aqsa Intifada, the Israeli public was ready to support him. In a recent trip to Israel, I found a far-reaching consensus—encompassing the left and the right in Israel—for acceptance of a Clinton-like solution, provided the Palestinians are truly prepared to forsake terror, violence, and the right of return to Israel.

Trying to impose a solution that the Israeli government will not accept—and the Sharon government will surely not accept Clintonesque ideas in the current environment—will only result in strong resistance. Even if the United States could pressure the Israelis to reluctantly accept an imposed outcome, would it endure? I doubt it.

Arafat would certainly go along with an imposed outcome. He has always preferred such an option. It would relieve him of the responsibility to make a decision. He can outwardly acquiesce, saying he has no choice. But inevitably, Palestinians will oppose at least part of an imposed outcome. Will new issues—what we might call Palestinian "Sheba farms"—suddenly emerge? Recall that Israel withdrew from Lebanon in accordance with U.N. Security Council Resolution 425 and that the U.N. secretary-general certified this withdrawal. Yet Hezbollah now claims that the Sheba farms area of the Golan Heights is Lebanese and that lasting "Israeli occupation" justifies continued armed resistance, including Katyusha rocket attacks. Will there not be a Palestinian equivalent of this situation after an imposed solution? And given Arafat's poor track record, how can anyone expect he would defend the existing peace agreement against such newly discovered grievances?

If one overriding lesson from the past persists, it is that the Palestinians must make decisions and bear the responsibility of those decisions. No enduring peace can be reached until the Palestinian leadership levels with its public, resists the temptation to blame every ill on the Israelis or the outside world, assumes responsibility for controversial decisions, and stands by its decision in the face of opposition.

An imposed solution will only delay the day when all sides, but especially the Palestinians, have to assume real responsibilities. Consequently, an imposed solution would be no solution at all.

Fact Sheet #8: Jerusalem

Mitchell Bard
Jewish Virtual Library
July 2002

In its quest for peace, Israel has offered dramatic and risky compromises to satisfy Palestinian interests in Jerusalem. Prime Minister Ehud Barak offered to withdraw from 95% of the West Bank and to create a Palestinian state with its capital in East Jerusalem, but Yasser Arafat rejected the deal.

During the 2000 Camp David Summit, Yasser Arafat said that no Jewish Temple ever existed on the Temple Mount. The Jewish connection to the Temple Mount dates back more than 3,000 years and is rooted in tradition and history. When Abraham bound his son Isaac upon an altar as a sacrifice to God, he is believed to have done so atop Mount Moriah, today's Temple Mount. The First Temple's Holy of Holies contained the original Ark of the Covenant, and both the First and Second Temples were the centers of Jewish religious and social life until the Second Temple's destruction by the Romans.

Ever since King David made Jerusalem the capital of Israel more than 3,000 years ago, the city has played a central role in Jewish existence. The Western Wall in the Old City "the last remaining wall of the ancient Jewish Temple, the holiest site in Judaism" is the object of Jewish veneration and the focus of Jewish prayer. Three times a day, for thousands of years, Jews have prayed "To Jerusalem, thy city, shall we return with joy," and have repeated the Psalmist's oath: "If I forget thee, O Jerusalem, let my right hand forget her cunning."

Jews have been living in Jerusalem continuously for nearly two millennia. They have constituted the largest single group of inhabitants there since the 1840's.

Jerusalem was never the capital of any Arab entity. Jerusalem never served as a provincial capital under Muslim rule nor was it ever a Muslim cultural center. For Jews, the entire city is sacred, but Muslims revere a site "the Dome of the Rock" not the city.

In 1947, the Jewish Agency agreed to accept the UN plan to internationalize Jerusalem in the hope that in the short-run it would protect the city from bloodshed and the new state from conflict. Since the partition resolution called for a referendum on the city's status after 10 years, and Jews comprised a substantial majority, the expectation was that the city would later be incorporated into Israel. The Arab states were as bitterly opposed to the internationalization of Jerusalem as they were to the rest of the partition plan.

In May 1948, Jordan invaded and occupied East Jerusalem, dividing the city for the first time in its history, and driving thousands of Jews "whose families had lived in the city for centuries" into exile.

Jordan denied Israelis access to the Western Wall and to the cemetery on the Mount of Olives. The gravestones, honoring the memory of rabbis and sages, were used as pavement and latrines in army camps. The ancient Jewish Quarter of the Old City was ravaged, 58 Jerusalem synagogues "some centuries old" were destroyed or ruined.

Under Jordanian rule, only limited numbers of Israeli Christians were permitted to briefly visit the Old City and Bethlehem at Christmas and Easter. Jordan placed restrictions on Christian schools and required that the Koran be taught. Christians emigrated from Jerusalem in droves, their numbers declining from 25,000 in 1949 to less than 13,000 in June 1967.

In 1967, Jordan ignored Israeli pleas to stay out of the Six-Day War and attacked the western part of the city. The Jordanians were routed by Israeli forces and driven out of East Jerusalem, allowing the city's unity to be restored.

After the 1967 war, Israel abolished all the discriminatory laws promulgated by Jordan and guaranteed freedom of access to the holy places of all faiths. Israel also entrusted administration of the holy places to their respective religious authorities.

Muslim rights on the Temple Mount have not been infringed. Although it is the holiest site in Judaism, Israel has left the Temple Mount under the control of Muslim religious authorities (the Waqf). The Waqf has subsequently prevented Israeli inspectors from overseeing work done on the Mount that is believed to be causing irreparable damage to archaeological remains from the First and Second Temple periods.

Since 1967, hundreds of thousands of Muslims and Christians "many from Arab countries that remain in a state of war with Israel" have come to Jerusalem to see their holy places. Arab leaders are free to visit Jerusalem to pray if they wish to, just as Egyptian President Anwar Sadat did at the al-Aksa mosque.

The only times Israel has prevented any Muslims from going to the Temple Mount were during periods of high tension when the threat of violence necessitated restrictions on the entrance into the area. These measures were taken to protect worshipers of all faiths and the shrines in the Old City. They usually have lasted only for a day or two and other mosques remain accessible.

Along with religious freedom, Palestinian Arabs in Jerusalem have unprecedented political rights. Arab residents were given the choice of whether to become Israeli citizens. Most chose to retain their Jordanian citizenship. Moreover, regardless of whether they are citizens, Jerusalem Arabs are permitted to vote in municipal elections and play a role in the administration of the city.

The only time that the eastern part of Jerusalem was exclusively Arab was between 1949 and1967, and that was because Jordan occupied the area and forcibly expelled all the Jews. This area of the city also contains many sites of importance to the Jewish religion, including the City of David, the Temple Mount and the Western Wall. In addition, major institutions like Hebrew University and the original Hadassah hospital are on Mount Scopus in eastern Jerusalem.

The Jerusalem Embassy Act of 1995 declared that Jerusalem should be recognized as the undivided, eternal capital of Israel and required that the U.S. embassy in Israel be established in Jerusalem no later than May 1999. The law also included a waiver that allowed the President to essentially ignore the legislation if he deemed doing so to be in the best interest of the United States.

During the 2000 presidential campaign George W. Bush promised that as President he would immediately "begin the process of moving the United States ambassador to the city Israel has chosen as its capital." In June 2001, however, Bush followed Clinton's precedent and used the presidential waiver to prevent the embassy from being moved.

While critics of Congressional efforts to force the administration to recognize Jerusalem as Israel's capital insist that such a move would harm the peace process, supporters of the legislation argue the opposite is true. By making clear the United States position that Jerusalem should remain unified under Israeli sovereignty, they say, unrealistic Palestinian expectations regarding the city can be moderated and thereby enhance the prospects for a final agreement.

The Oslo agreements leave open the status of Jerusalem. The agreement also says that the final status will be based on UN Security Council Resolutions 242 and 338, neither of which mentions Jerusalem.

Arabs Ignore Palestinians' Plight
The Suffering of Refugees is Not the Fault of Israel Alone

Marc Ginsberg
Reprinted from The Wall Street Journal (c)
August 11, 2002, Dow Jones Company, Inc. All Rights Reserved.

The latest flare-up in the Middle East is once again drawing attention to the plight of millions of destitute Palestinian living in squalid refugee camps. Arabs claim to be outraged by the Palestinians' plight, but in reality they have contributed little to the welfare of the Palestinian people.

The humanitarian tragedy of the Palestinian refugees in countries like Lebanon, Syria and Jordan, and the unrealistic hope that their "right of return" to Israel will be realized, is one of the most vexing problems in the Arab-Israeli conflict. United Nations General Assembly Resolution 194, which offers displaced Palestinians the choice of returning to their homes or being compensated, helped to torpedo the 2000 Camp David summit, due to Yasser Arafat's adamancy that it must be preserved.

But the "right of return," if implemented, would irrevocably alter the nature of Israel as a Jewish state. This is one of the reasons why Arafat warrants such suspicion and mistrust from Israelis.

During Israel's war for independence in 1948, 750,000 Palestinians (representing three-quarters of the native population of Palestine) either fled or were forced out of their homes in what is now Israel. At the same time, hundreds of thousands of Jews living in Arab countries were also compelled to leave, likewise without compensation or any right of return. Another 300,000 Palestinians fled the West Bank and Gaza during the 1967 Arab-Israeli war. Since then, their number has ballooned to 3.7 million, of whom more than 1.2 million remain jammed into 59 squalid refugee camps located in Lebanon(12), Syria (10), Jordan (10), the West Bank (19) and Gaza (eight). The rest live throughout the West Bank and Gaza--most not better off than their brethren in the camps. Except for Jordan, no Arab state has granted them citizenship.

They remain stateless dependents of the U.N. who rely upon humanitarian programs administered principally by the U.N. Relief and Works Agency, which was created in 1949 to care for these Palestinians. (Several other U.N. agencies provide additional assistance.) The cost for caring and feeding the refugees, in other words, is borne largely by the international community. UNRWA faces a major funding crisis. Its general funding per refugee will drop to $60 per year by 2003--almost 40% lower than a decade earlier.

The economic crisis facing the Palestinian refugees comes at a time of sharp economic downturn in the Middle East. Yet it is still significant that, of UNRWA's $340 million annual operating budget, the Arab states combined donate less than $5 million (or just under 2%), compared to nearly $90 million from the U.S.--well over 30% of UNRWA's budget. Egypt, the largest recipient of U.S. foreign aid, gives only $10,000 per year, and the wealthy Persian Gulf states of Saudi Arabia, Kuwait and the United Arab Emirates collectively donate a paltry $4.5 million.

It would have been a nice gesture if the hundreds of millions of dollars donated to

Saudi Arabia's "Martyr's Telethon" had been given to UNRWA to help Palestinian refugees. Instead, we are all left to wonder if that money is going into the hands of the corrupt Palestinian Authority and the families of suicide bombers. To those who genuinely care about the fate of the Palestinian people it is surely a disgrace that the U.N. has played into the hands of Arab governments and the Palestinian Authority. Insisting that the refugee camps remain temporary shelters ensures that Arafat's demands for the right of return are not undermined. It has been an exercise of the most cynical sort--using those whose cause is championed as political pawns.

Any reasonable attempts to develop long-range rehabilitation programs or to improve the conditions of these camps have been consistently thwarted by the Arab League and the Palestinian Authority. It is not by accident that the infamous Jenin refugee camp--the site of so much recent controversy-gave birth to at least 28 suicide bombers. The inhumanness of these camps and the endless, hopeless exile create fertile recruiting grounds for extremist groups.

When President Bush called on Arab states to assume more of the burden of peacemaking in the Middle East, he surely had the Palestinian refugees in mind. So far the Arab states have not risen to the challenge, failing even to match America's annual contribution to UNRWA. They can afford to do much more. It makes one wonder if they really want to get rid of the conditions that breed extremism in the region.

Palestinian Lies & Western Complicity
A continuing story

Daniel Doron
National Review Online
August 14, 2002

Recent Palestinian allegations about a massacre in the Jenin "refugee camp" (in reality, a fortified terrorist base) were spread like bushfire by the Western media, despite no corroborating evidence. So was Yasser Arafat's poisonous charge, upon emerging from isolation in his compound, that Israel was setting fire to the Church of the Nativity — a transparent effort to incite Christian rage against the Jews (maybe Arafat knew about Hitler's success in setting fire to the Reichstag).

The ease with which Western media gave currency to such dubious "news" illustrated once again how Western complicity helps the Arabs to spread disinformation damaging to Israel's — and the West's — war against terrorism.

The Arabs have successfully pilloried Israel in the court of public opinion through the deft propagation of two big lies. Relying on the sketchy historical knowledge of most people, and on the propensity of oft-repeated lies to become accepted wisdom, Arab officials have fabricated a historical narrative that has gained wide acceptance. It justifies Arab aggression, even terror, as an understandable response to cruel Israeli "occupation" and to the "stealing of Palestinian lands." The charges often stick, even though they are based on falsehoods.

JUST THE FACTS
What are the facts, then?

Since the second stage of Oslo was implemented in 1995, and most Palestinian towns and villages were ceded to the control of Arafat's Palestinian Authority, over 95 percent of the Palestinian Arab population of the West Bank and Gaza have not been under physical Israeli occupation. Yet amazingly, Arab spokesmen keep talking about their need to fight Israeli occupation, and officials and the media seldom challenge them. It seems like everyone forgot that in signing the 1992 Oslo accords, Israel recognized Arafat's PLO as the official representative of the Palestinian people. Arafat was brought back, with his henchmen, from exile in Tunisia and given control of territories that Israel occupied in the defensive 1967 war — areas that never belonged to any Palestinian entity.

In return for self-government, the Palestinians undertook to revoke parts of their national covenant that called for Israel's destruction, and never again to resort to violence. These pledges were constantly violated the moment the Israeli occupation was removed.

Still, Israel, exhausted by incessant Arab attacks, and eager for peace, continued implementing the Oslo agreements — including the ceding of territory and relinquishing control over their population. Since Oslo 2, the Palestinians have enjoyed self-rule of sorts. We say "of sorts," not because of the repeated incursions Israel had to make to thwart suicide bombing attacks, but because rule by Arafat's Palestinian Authority was not really "self-determination." The election by which Arafat was elected with an over 90 percent majority, Bolshevik style, was rather questionable and was never repeated again.

In fact, the "Authority" Arafat has established is even more repressive than many of the 21 dictatorships governing all other Arab states. His Tunisian henchmen did what they knew best. They immediately established a rule of terror, brooking no opposition, and wrested control from the local leadership. They systematically violated the Palestinians' most rudimentary human rights, engaging in extortion, kidnap, torture, and summary execution. They robbed the inhabitants of their livelihood, creating such mayhem that the Palestinian standard of living was cut by half and unemployment rose to over 60 percent. Every resource was exploited to wage a war against Israel, including considerable funds earmarked by the EU and U.S. as aid for the refugees.

Arafat's war disrupted trade with Israel and the employment there of most Palestinian labor — both sources of increasing Palestinian wealth. A nascent Palestinian civil society was destroyed, enabling the PLO to radicalize an increasingly impoverished population, and to transform their misery into pathological hatred for Israel.

Yes, the Palestinians are right in feeling under occupation and oppressed. But they are mistaken to think it is by Israel.

The audacious lie about the occupation is based, of course, on a bigger, more basic falsehood: namely, that Israel stole "Palestinian Arab lands" and that the PLO is fighting for the restitution of these illegally "occupied lands," especially those ostensibly usurped for Israeli "settlements" (which occupy, in fact, less than three percent of the West Bank's area, and were built on empty government-owned land).

Palestinian propagandists insist that contemporary Jews are not descended from Biblical Jews, and have usurped "Palestinian Arab lands" in three stages. They first allegedly penetrated Palestine in the late 19th century, settling it by stealth under imperial colonialist protection. Then in 1948, after the U.N. partition, they took more land by force, displacing an indigenous Palestinian Arab population fighting for self-determination; and finally, in the 1967 Six-Day War, Israel aggressively expanded, occupying the "West Bank" and the Gaza Strip and holding its Palestinian inhabitants in bondage, as they have ever since.

NOTHING NEW
Historical fact, however, belies this enticingly simplistic narrative.

The disputed territories, together with the territories that are now Israel and Jordan, were originally (in Biblical and post-Biblical times) Jewish kingdoms, and for most of the last seven centuries part of the Ottoman Empire. After the defeat and disintegration of the Ottoman Empire in the wake of the First World War, the League of Nations divided most of its former possessions in the 1922 peace conference. The Arabs were granted rights to most of the formerly Turkish-controlled lands, to an area that was 500 times larger in size than the small area reserved for a Jewish homeland in Palestine. The British received an international mandate over Palestine because they undertook to establish a Jewish national home there, which the League considered as an act of "restoration" of ancient Jewish rights to the land — rights that outweighed any Arab claims based on later conquest and residence.

At first, the Arab representatives to the Versailles conference gladly accepted this division. It gave them control over vast areas lost centuries ago, without requiring them to sacrifice hundreds of thousands of soldiers, as the Allies had, to liberate these lands from Turkish dominion. They did not then consider the tiny sliver of South Syrian wasteland, known to Jews as Judea and Samaria and to the Europeans as the Holy Land, of any significance, politically or religiously, and were happy to give it up in exchange for what they so surprisingly gained. The Emir Faisal, who represented the Arabs, signed a draft agreement with the Zionist movement, welcoming the Jews back to their homeland and pledging cooperation.

So the disputed territories of the West Bank and the Gaza strip were never "Palestinian lands" — neither as national patrimony nor as private property. In fact, until the institution of the British mandate, the Holy Land never had a separate political identity or a distinct people inhabiting it. It was a neglected province of South Syria, whose few and destitute Arab inhabitants considered themselves South Syrians. As Bernard Lewis notes, "From the end of the Jewish state in antiquity to the beginning of British rule, the area now designated by the name Palestine was not a country and had no frontiers, only administrative boundaries... within a larger entity" of Syria.

Indeed, to date, 93 percent of the land in what was the British Mandate — including the lands of the West Bank — are still government-owned. They were so despoiled, malaria-infected, and sparsely populated that no private owners evinced any interest in owning them, so they were kept by the sultan and then inherited by the British mandate in safekeeping for the Jews.

On a visit to the Ottoman-controlled Holy Land in 1860, Mark Twain described it as "the prince of desolation." "The hills are barren... the valleys unsightly deserts... peopled by swarms of beggars struck with ghastly sores and malformations... Palestine sits in sackcloth and ashes... only the music of angels could charm its shrubs and flowers again into life." Other writers and artists visiting the Holy Land (chiefly from Britain and Germany) — as well as geographers, archeologists, and cartographers — were equally stunned by its utter desolation.

It was only toward the end of the 19th century, when a growing stream of Jewish immigrants rehabilitated the land — draining swamps, reclaiming deserts, and controlling the diseases (chiefly malaria) — that a decimated Arab population began increasing. The resuscitation of the land by the Jews and the economic opportunity they created brought an influx of Arab immigrants from dirt-poor neighboring Arab states to swell the number of Arabs in Palestine, so that by the turn of the century there were about 250,000 Arab Muslims and 150,00 Jews living there. 100,000 Christians and others

It was in fact British colonial machinations that turned initial Arab acceptance of a Jewish homeland in British-protected Palestine into unmitigated and disastrous hostility. British behavior in the Middle East in general, and in Palestine in particular, was common colonial practice: divide and rule. In India, it enabled the British to subdue the subcontinent with few troops by pitting hostile segments of the indigenous population against each other. They employed this strategy in Palestine too.

From the very first days of the mandate, a group of very influential British officials in the Colonial and the War Offices, who wanted to maintain control over the land and to prevent the establishment of an independent Jewish national home, started undermining their government's efforts to fulfill its obligation toward the Jews. These British officials, many of them avowed anti-Semites, fanned Arab resentment over broken British promises to make the Arabian chieftain, Faisal, king of Damascus and Syria, and redirected it against Jewish aspirations in Palestine.

Indeed, their naming the mandate over the Holy Land "Palestine," rather than the land of Israel, was a deliberate effort to obliterate the Jewish connection to the land by calling it by its Roman name. They also, in 1923, unilaterally removed from the original mandatory area all the land east of the Jordan River-75 percent of the territory promised to the Jews — and gave it to the Emir Abdullah of Arabia, Faisal's brother, in compensation to the Hashemite family for other broken promises. They did so despite objections from the League of Nations. The small area that had been designated as a home for the Jews was thus reduced to a mere sliver.

A distinct Palestinian Arab nationalism evolved only after the dream of an Arab Syrian kingdom — the brainchild of T. E. Lawrence — was shattered when the French evicted his protégé, the Emir Faisal, from Damascus in 1920. Only then did the South Syrian Arabs living under Britain's Palestine mandate separate themselves from Syria and start defining themselves as Palestinians. The process was accelerated by their growing negative reaction to the League of Nations' designation of Palestine as a Jewish national home.

The British helped make hostility to Zionism the defining issue of local Arab politics, and assisted in its exploitation as a lethal weapon in bloody Arab inter-clan struggles for dominance. Muslim clerics and Arab effendis exploited hostility against the Jews, always convenient scapegoats, to deflect the rage of their destitute, exploited people.

The British appointed an extremely radical upstart politician, Hajj Amin al-Hussieni, with a record of violence and incitement, as chief mufti of Jerusalem. They gave him the authority of a spiritual leader to the Arabs, and control of the considerable funds and properties managed by Muslim religious trusts. The mufti promptly proceeded to exploit these resources for his nefarious campaign against the Jews and against his Arab opponents — much as Arafat does today.

The mufti was, in fact, the originator of the murderous religious incitement used so effectively today by Arafat. Since the beginning of the British mandate in 1920, he used mosques, schools, and charitable associations to mount a racist campaign against the Jews, accusing them of betraying the Prophet Mohammed and of trying to defile and destroy Islamic holy places. The incitement resulted in periodic outbreaks of violence which culminated in several massacres and the eviction of Jews from Arab-dominated areas — notably in Hebron, where the Jews, who had lived there for centuries, were butchered by their Arab neighbors after the mufti spread a rumor through the preachers in the mosques that the Jews were conquering and defiling the El-Aksa Mosque.

The British not only failed to stop the carnage, but also arrested any Jew who bore arms in defense. British colonial officials then exploited Arab rage as an excuse to put more and more restrictions on Jewish immigration to Palestine and land purchase. They reneged, in fact, on their obligation to establish a Jewish national home. They even illegally blocked the entrance of Jews who were desperately trying to escape Europe. They did so even when the danger to Jewish life became obvious, helping Hitler to trap and kill many Jews.

The mufti accompanied his 1936-39 war against the Jews with a campaign of terror against his Arab opponents (again, just like Arafat). His henchmen assassinated not only every political rival that contemplated some sort of accommodation, but also practically anyone who could even potentially become a political rival. Hundreds of Arabs were liquidated, a large part of the Palestinian elites. Many more were forced to flee.

It was a tragedy from which the Palestinians, who were developing by then a hateful, xenophobic nationalism, never recovered. It explains why to date, the Palestinian, many of whom are talented, hard-working people, have been unable to build a civil society with legitimate political institutions. It was the loss and demoralization of their leadership that prevented the Palestinian Arabs from establishing a state in 1948. That in turn facilitated the takeover of their political life by the radical and criminal elements that have brought on them repeated catastrophes.

The British officials who have encouraged and exploited radical Arab elements are to a large extent responsible for the continued tragedy of Arab politics and for the repeated disasters the Arabs suffered. Most of the Arab states established by the colonialists remain artificial entities barely able to contain the hostile ethnic groups that were arbitrarily incorporated into them. Lacking a unifying principle and legitimacy, they remain politically, socially, and economically extremely unstable, held together by the military dictatorships the colonial powers left behind.

In 1948, the British gave up the mandate and the U.N. partitioned Palestine, offering the Jews only a sliver of the area originally designated as a Jewish national home. Partition arbitrarily deprived the Jews of their internationally sanctioned legal rights to all of Palestine, including what is now the kingdom of Jordan. Nevertheless, Israel accepted it.

The Palestinians, and the Arab states supporting them, refused to accept partition and launched a war of annihilation against Israel. The British left on May 15, 1948, doing everything they could to render the Jews defenseless before the onslaught of six Arab armies — including an Arab legion led by British officers which put siege to Jerusalem and almost starved its population. Against all odds, and at great cost (every ninth Israeli was a casualty of the war), Israel repulsed the Arab attacks and established itself within the 1949 armistice lines. Jordan unilaterally annexed the remaining heartland territories designated for a Palestinian state, and Egypt took control of the Gaza Strip. The Palestinians never protested — perhaps because they considered Jordan their own, since the majority of its inhabitants were Palestinians.

Before Israel ejected Jordan from the "West Bank" and Egypt from the Gaza Strip, in 1967, Palestinians lived for almost two decades under a very repressive Jordanian occupation and under brutal Egyptian military rule in the Gaza Strip — in utter destitution and with no rights at all. Gaza was, in effect, a large Egyptian prison camp. Yet they did not protest. Their anger was skillfully directed against Israel, so that they wished it destroyed even though it did not then occupy "their land" or hold them captive. Nor did any of their friends who today pretend to defend their right for self-determination raise then even a squeak.

The true intentions of the Authority's leadership under Arafat were made apparent when Israel's prime minister, Ehud Barak, offered to cede 96 percent of the disputed territories to the Palestinian Authority and even compensate it for the remaining 4 percent. As is well known, Arafat rejected the offer and launched his war of terror against Israel, hoping to force it to accept the "return" of Arab refugees, and to undermine Israel from within by swamping it with "returning" refugees.

Barak made these far-reaching concessions despite the fact that there were conflicting legal claims to the disputed territories, and that the settlements, built on empty government land, have not displaced any Palestinians or taken any of their private property (except in rare cases for security or public works purposes).

GETTING NOWHERE

Still, the two big lies about continued Israeli "occupation" and "stolen Arab lands" continue to be used by the Arabs and have scored great successes, especially in Europe.

Since the Second World War, their alleged friends in the European Union — especially the French — systematically supported and sustained Arab dictatorships. The oppression generated by these dictators, and the poverty they perpetuated, helped create the backlash of radical Islamist fundamentalism. America's unqualified support for the repressive and corrupt regimes of Saudi Arabia and Egypt has also contributed its share to a continued Middle East catastrophe. Defense of the arch-terrorist Arafat, whose PLO the Saudis and the Egyptians created, fund, and support, is the logical conclusion of this dangerous policy.

The Europeans have at least good, if cynical, realpolitik reasons for supporting dictatorships in the Arab world. They sell them billions in armaments, helping to offset some of the cost of Middle East oil. They profit from "special" trade terms acquired from these corrupt regimes through the extensive use of bribery (a great competitive advantage over U.S. firms, which are forbidden by law from engaging in such practices). Israel's security is only another sop they willingly throw to these dictators in the furtherance of their interests.

They cannot, of course, openly admit such cynical behavior, since it might not sit well with their "liberal" constituencies and leftist supporters. So they cover up their cynicism with the pretence of seeking justice for the Palestinians — a pretence that plays well among their pro-third world, anti-American supporters.

The European elites are thus willing accomplices in the propagation of Arab lies that demonize Israel. Demonizing Israel makes it possible for them to support, with a clear conscience, the most horribly repressive Arab dictatorships and even the destruction of the only democracy in the Middle East. Barely 60 years after the Holocaust, Arab calumnies help the European salve their conscience so successfully that they are even ready to help Muslim rogue states acquire weapons of mass destruction, and to protect these rogue states against preventative action by the U.S.

It takes democracies a long time to absorb even the most recent and most costly lessons of history. A Europe that fell easy prey to the Big Lies Goebbels spread to keep it disarmed was to pay heavily for its complacency towards Nazi aggression. Last September 11, Americans paid heavily for their own failure to identify in time a danger from a radical and deadly challenge to their basic values and institutions — a challenge that before long may be mounted with weapons of mass destruction.

The West will continue to be exposed to grave danger until it finally wakes up and realizes how Arab lies have managed to lull it to the danger from implacable Muslim fundamentalism, a danger Israel has already been facing for so many years.

The Territorial Truth

Jack Kemp
www.jewishworldreview.com
August 16, 2002

As we are learning in Afghanistan, ending the war is just the beginning of securing the peace. The same will be true of the Arab/Israeli conflict, which is why I have written extensively about the need for a Marshall Plan for Palestine and the Middle East. It will be necessary for the West to remain engaged in the Middle East in order to ensure democracy and freedom for all the Christians, Jews and Muslims living in the region.

George Orwell said that the first duty of intelligent men is to restate the obvious, and that is precisely what Secretary of Defense Donald Rumsfeld did last week with respect to the territorial dispute between Jews and Arabs, Israelis and Palestinians. Speaking at a briefing last Wednesday, he gave a quick history lesson on the Middle-East that in one sentence summarized the essence of the problem: "If you have a country that's a sliver and you can see three sides of it from a high hotel building, you've got to be careful what you give away and to whom you give it."

When Israeli diplomats refer to Israel's "security," they are not just talking about defending its people -- Jewish and Arab -- from terrorist attacks; they are talking about enabling Israel to defend itself from those who seek to destroy it. It is not the case that Israel refuses to grant the Palestinians self-rule, and we should never forget that under Menachem Begin's Likud government Israel gave the Siani back to Egypt.

There have been two formal attempts by the international community since Jordan achieved independence to create Palestinian self-rule in the territories that roughly encompass Gaza and the West Bank, once in 1947 and again in 2000, which the Arab world rejected in 1947 and then Yasser Arafat rejected in 2000. After the Arabs rejected the 1947 effort under the U.N. partition plan and Israel was created the following year, Azzam Pasha, secretary-general of the Arab League, declared, "This will be a war of extermination." True to his word, the armies of Egypt, Jordan, Lebanon, Syria and Iraq attacked Israel. During this war, Jordan illegally occupied the West Bank territories and Egypt illegally occupied Gaza.

Efforts to destroy Israel continued unabated during the next 19 years, and in 1967 war broke out again. This time, it was Egypt's President Gamel Nasser who said, "Our basic objective will be the destruction of Israel." During the ensuing Six Day War, Jordan lost the West Bank and Egypt lost Gaza to Israel.

This is the history to which Rumsfeld had reference when he said: "My feeling about the so-called occupied territories is that there was a war, Israel urged neighboring countries not to get involved in it once it started, they all jumped in, and they lost a lot of real estate to Israel because Israel prevailed in that conflict. In the intervening period, they've made some settlements in various parts of the so-called occupied area, which was the result of a war, which they won."

Between 1948 and 1967, when the West Bank and Gaza were under Arab control, no attempt was ever made to create a separate Palestinian state there. Instead,

Jordan annexed the West Bank and gave its residents full Jordanian citizenship. The question overwho should control what parts of the so-called occupied territories remains a legitimate dispute today. Those lands, including the cities of Hebron, Schechem and Bethlehem, have ancient biblical roots. Jews always lived there until they were pushed out in the 1920s. The land also included the Western Wall of Jerusalem, and people tend to forget that until the 1967 war, Jews could not pray at that, their most holy of sites. Hence it is not correct to describe Israeli communities that grew up on this disputed territory as "settlements" on "occupied territory." The problem with those who claim that the conflict would be over if the Israelis simply ended the occupation is that they assume Palestinians are the legal, sovereign owners of these territories and what their borders should be. As Rumsfeld pointed out, those are precisely the questions that still need to be resolved.

Rumsfeld deserves commendation for his truth-telling and his clarity. As we all work and pray for a peaceful solution to the crises in the Middle East, we will do well to keep his reservations in mind. History can repeat itself, so who could fault a sliver of a democracy for insisting that there be a functioning Palestinian democracy before it gives back precious land it won in a defensive war?

Ultimately, there will have to be compromise on both sides, and the United States will have to support economic aid and free trade for the region. We already have a free-trade agreement with Jordan, which could be extended to other Arab nations willing to make peace with Israel and guarantee Israel's security from terrorist assault.

303

Index to Authors

Bard, Mitchell. "Fact Sheet #2 - The Right of Return."
Jewish Virtual Library. June 6, 2002..192-193

Bard, Mitchell. "Fact Sheet #5 - Settlements."
Jewish Virtual Library. June 2002...250-251

Bard, Mitchell. "Fact Sheet#6 - The '67 Border.'"
Jewish Virtual Library. July 2002..252-253

Bard, Mitchell. "Fact Sheet#8 - Jerusalem."
Jewish Virtual Library. July 2002..290-292

Bennett, William J. and Jack Kemp. "Standing Up For Israel Is
Standing Up for Our Principles." *Empower America.*
October 19, 2001..82-83

Bennett, William J. "Why I stand With Israel." *Jerusalem Post*
May 7, 2002...165-167

Bennett, William J. with Jack Kemp and Jeanne Kirkpatrick.
"Twenty Facts About Israel and the Middle East."
Empower America. May 21, 2002..172-174

Bin-Nun, Yehezkel. "The Myth Of The Palestinian People." *Israeli Insider.*
January 7, 2002..98-100

Brook, Yaron and Peter Schwartz. "Israel Has a Moral Right to its Life."
Israeli Insider. June 23, 2002.. 215-217

Brooks, David. "How Suicide Bombing Became Not Just a
Means to an End." *Atlantic Online.* June 1, 2002...180-183

Bush, George W. "Replacing Arafat Is First Step To Statehood."
Remarks at Rose Garden. June 24, 2002... 218-221

Doron, Daniel "Palestinian Lies & Western Complicity:
A continuing story." *National Review Online.* August 14, 2002.....295-300

Friedman, Thomas L. "Suicidal Lies." *New York Times.* March 31, 2002.............115-116

Friedman, Thomas L. "Nine Wars Too Many." *New York Times.*
May 15, 2002..170-171

Ginsberg, Marc "Arabs Ignore Palestinians' Plight:
The Suffering of Refugees is Not the Fault of Israel Alone."
The Wall Street Journal. August 11, 2002.................................... 293-294

Glazov, Jamie. "Ten Tips on How to Be an Arafat Apologist."
Frontpage Magazine. April 11, 2002...127-135

Gniwisch, Mayer. "A Crash Course In The Real Facts."
www.netanyahu.com. April 2, 2001...56-57

Gold, Dore. "Untenable Linkages: Tying A Cessation of Palestinian
Violence To an Israeli Settlement Freeze." *Jerusalem Center for
Public Affairs.* May 15, 2001..58-65

Gold, Dore. "Occupied Territories or Disputed Territories?"
  Jerusalem Center For Public Affairs. September 2, 2001..........................75-76

Gold, Dore, "One Year of Yasser Arafat's Intifada: How it Started and
  How it Might End." *Jerusalem Center for Public
  Affairs*. October 1, 2001..79-81

Gold, Dore. "How Arafat's Palestinian Authority Became an
  Entity Supporting Terrorism.'" *Jerusalem Center for
  Public Affairs*. December 9, 2001..84-86

Gold, Dore. "Washington Misled: Saudi Arabia's Financial Backing of
  Terrorism." *Jerusalem Center For Public Affairs*. May 6, 2002.................162-164

Gold, Dore. "Jerusalem in International Diplomacy."
  Jerusalem Center for Public Affairs. June 2001........................... 66-70

Hirsh Goodman. "Food For Thought."
  The Jerusalem Report. July 2002...254-255

Goodenough, Patrick. "Radical Islam: The Enemy in Our Midst."
  www.floridajewish.com. October 18, 2000.......................................51-53

Gorfinkel, Jordan B. "Everything's Relative," *gorf@jewishcartoon.com*..............303-304

Halevi, Yossi Klein. "How Despair Is Transforming Israel."
  National Review Online. June 26, 2002..228-232

Hanson, Victor Davis. "From Defeat to Reconciliation to Peace."
  National Review Online. April 30, 2002...149-151

Hanson, Victor Davis. "Our Enemies, The Saudis." *www.commentary.org*.
  June 26, 2002 256-262

Harel, Amos. "Analysis: Palestinian Schoolbooks Fan The Flames Of
  Hatred." *Ha'Aretz*. June 29, 2002...242-243

Hoffer, Eric, "Israel's Peculiar Position." *Los Angeles Times.*, May 5, 1968.............36

Horowitz, David. "Know The Enemy (And What He Believes)."
  Front Page Magazine. June 25, 2002...224-227

Huntley, Steve. "Israel's Debate Is A Sign Of Strength."
  Chicago Sun Times. February 25, 2002...105

Inhofe, James M. "Peace in the Middle East." U.S. Senate. March 4, 2002........108-115

Israeli, Raphael. "Poison: The Use of Blood Libel in the War
  Against Israel." *Jerusalem Center For Public Affairs*. April 15, 2002......136-140

Jacoby, Jeff. "The Canary in Europe's Mine." *Boston Globe*. April 28, 2002........147-148

Jacoby, Jeff. "The Prerequisite To Peace." *Philadelphia Jewish Exponent*.
  July 1, 2002...266-267

Johnson, Paul. "Israel On the Edge." *Jerusalem Post*. June 12, 2002...................197-198

Karsh, Efraim. "What Occupation?" *www.frontpagemagazine.com*.
  July 24, 2002...276-283

Pipes, Daniel. "First Accept Israel." *Israeli Insider*. September 10, 2001................77-78

Pipes, Daniel. "The Only Solution Is Military." *Israeli Insider*.
February 26, 2002..106-107

Pipes, Daniel. "A New Round of Anger and Humiliation:
Islam After 9/11." *Stanford: Hoover
Institution Press*. 2002 pp. 41-61 . January 1, 2002.....................87-97

Pipes, Daniel. "Israel's Moment Of Truth." *Commentary Magazine*.
February 1, 2000..37-44

Pipes, Daniel. "6 Days Of War." *New York Post*. June 4, 2002..................186-187

Pipes, Daniel. "Become A Muslim Warrior." *Jerusalem Post*. July 3, 2002............268-269

Prager, Dennis. "Why Does The Left Support The Palestinians?"
Creator's Syndicate. June 25, 2002.......................................222-223

Prager, Dennis. "'Pro-Israel' Lobby Is Not Why America Supports Israel."
Creator's Syndicate. July 3, 2002..270-271

Ragen, Naomi. "Why Our Enemies Are Winning." *www.naomiragen.com*.
June 18, 2002...206-207

Ross, Dennis B. "Think Again: Yasir Arafat." *Foreign Policy*. July/Aug 2002.......282-287

Rubin, Michael. "The Lessons of Lebanon." *Daily Standard*. July 1, 2002..........261-263

Safire, William. "Calling Arabs' Bluff." *New York Times*. May 23, 2002................168-169

Schwartz, Peter and Yaron Brook. "Israel Has a Moral Right to its Life."
Israeli Insider. June 23, 2002...215-217

Sharansky, Natan. "Afraid of the Truth." *www.floridajewish.com*.
October 12, 2000..49-50

Sharansky, Natan. "Palestinian Democracy: Relevant And Realistic."
Ha'Aretz. July 22, 2002...272-273

Stanislavski, George M. "Wanted: Aggressive Israeli Hasbara."
Israeli National News. Washington. D.C. June 19, 2002...........................208-210

Stephens, Bret. "What's Wrong With Israel's Hasbara?" *Jerusalem Post*.
June 6, 2002..188-191

Tell, David. "The U.N.'s Israel Obsession: A Primer." *Weekly Standard*.
April 30, 2002..152-154

Tell, David. "The Baby Face of Hate: MEMRI Releases an Astonishing
Example of the 'True Muslim' Faith." *Daily Standard*.
June 12, 2002...199-201

Thomas, Cal. "Two States of Mind." *Jewish World Review*. June 13, 2002............202-203

Thornton, Bruce S. "Why America Must Support Israel."
Frontpage Magazine. June 14, 2002...204-205

Tobin, Jonathan. "June 1967 Revisited." *Philadelphia Jewish Exponent*.
June 11, 2002...194-196

West, Charlotte. "On 'Hope'." *Israel National News.* June 28, 2002.......................239-241

West, Diana. "The Killing Mantra." *Washington Times.* June 21, 2002.................213-214

Wiesel, Elie. "We Affirm Our Solidarity with Israel." *www.floridajewish.com.*
    October 12, 2000..47-48

Will, George F. "Anti-Semitism Abides." *Sacramento Bee.* May 2, 2002................156-157

Will, George F. "Dispensing With Arafat." *Washington Post.*
    June 26, 2002...235-236

Ya'ari, Ehud. "The Israeli-Palestinian Confrontation: Toward A
    Divorce." *Jerusalem Center For Public Affairs.* June 30, 2002....................244-249

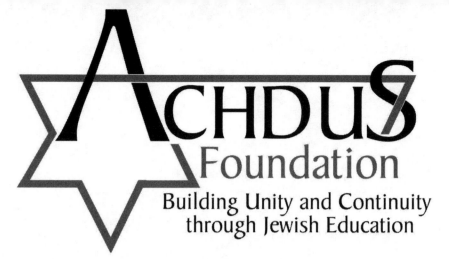

Achdus Foundation
Building Unity and Continuity through Jewish Education

The Jewish people are not a monolith nor a stereotype. The Jewish community is a diverse group of individuals who share a rich heritage and a common history. The Jewish people have made significant contributions to civilization from time immemorial. This story must be told and not be forgotten.

Jewish education begins with our children. The Jewish community must mobilize adequate financial resources to insure all Jewish children, irrespective of affiliation or their familiesí finances, are able to receive a high quality, affordable intensive Jewish education. Jewish education for our children will guaranty the continuity of the Jewish people. It is not a luxury; it is a necessity.

The mission of the Achdus Foundation and each of its affiliates is to build unity and continuity through Jewish education. We are focused and dedicated to insuring that this necessity is an everlasting reality.

Affiliates of the Achdus Foundation:
The Jewish Education Leadership Institute of Loyola University;
Operation Jewish Education/The 5% Mandate;
The Jewish Broadcasting Network;
The Jewish Basketball League;
The Yad LíYad Vocational Training Institute;
The Achdus Education Trust Fund and
Zionist Advocacy Program (ZAP)

Achdus Foundation
333 West Wacker Dr.-Suite 2750-Chicago, IL 60606
Ph: 312-332-4172- Fx: 312-332-2119

NOTES

NOTES

NOTES

NOTES

NOTES

NOTES